Teaching and Researching Language Learning Strategies

APPLIED LINGUISTICS IN ACTION

General Editors:

Christopher N. Candlin and David R. Hall

Books published and forthcoming in this series include:

Teaching and Researching
Language Learning Strategies

Rebecca L. Oxford

Longman
is an imprint of

Harlow, England • London • New York • Boston • San Francisco • Toronto
Sydney • Tokyo • Singapore • Hong Kong • Seoul • Taipei • New Delhi
Cape Town • Madrid • Mexico City • Amsterdam • Munich • Paris • Milan

Pearson Education Limited

Edinburgh Gate
Harlow CM20 2JE
United Kingdom
Tel: +44 (0)1279 623623
Fax: +44 (0)1279 431059
Website: www.pearsoned.co.uk

First published in Great Britain in 2011

Pearson Education is not responsible for the content of third party internet sites.

ISBN: 978-0-582-38129-2

British Library Cataloguing in Publication Data
A CIP catalogue record for this book can be obtained from the Library of Congress

Library of Congress Cataloging in Publication Data
Oxford, Rebecca L.
  Teaching and researching language learning strategies / Rebecca L. Oxford.
    p. cm. — (Applied linguistics in action)
  ISBN 978-0-582-38129-2 (pbk.)
  1. Language and languages—Study and teaching.   2. Second language acquisition.
I. Title.
  P53.O94 2010
  418.0071—dc22

                                                             2010034352\

10 9 8 7 6 5 4 3 2 1
14 13 12 11 10

Typeset in 10.5/12pt Janson by Graphicraft Limited, Hong Kong
Printed in Malaysia, CTP-KHL

I believe that we owe it to our learners to get the theory right. I see too many failing young people in UK language classrooms to risk getting the theory wrong. So, yes, we do need to define more precisely what a strategy is. Yes, we do need to sort out the relationship between strategy use and success by finding out why people use strategies differently. Yes, we do need to relate strategies to specific tasks and then see how learners feel about those tasks (self-efficacy). And yes, we do need to get our strategy instruction programmes right and show, consistently, that they work.

Ernesto Macaro, 2007

Contents

Section IV   Resources

General Editors' Preface

Applied Linguistics *in Action*, as its name suggests, is a Series which focuses on the issues and challenge to teachers and researchers in a range of fields in Applied Linguistics and provides readers and users with the tools they need to carry out their own practice-related research.

The books in the Series provide the reader with clear, up-to-date, accessible and authoritative accounts of their chosen field within Applied Linguistics. Starting from a map of the landscape of the field, each book provides information on its main ideas and concepts, competing issues and unsolved questions. From there, readers can explore a range of practical applications of research into those issues and questions, and then take up the challenge of undertaking their own research, guided by the detailed and explicit research guides provided. Finally, each book has a section that provides a rich array of resources, information sources and further reading, as well as a key to the principal concepts of the field.

Questions the books in this innovative Series ask are those familiar to all teachers and researchers, whether very experienced, or new to the fields of Applied Linguistics.

- What does research tell us, what doesn't it tell us and what should it tell us about the field? How is the field mapped and landscaped? What is its geography?
- How has research been applied and what interesting research possibilities does practice raise? What are the issues we need to explore and explain?
- What are the key researchable topics that practitioners can undertake? How can the research be turned into practical action?
- Where are the important resources that teachers and researchers need? Who has the information? How can it be accessed?

Each book in the Series has been carefully designed to be as accessible as possible, with built-in features to enable readers to find what they want quickly and to home in on the key issues and themes that concern them. The structure is to move from practice to theory and back to practice in a cycle of development of understanding of the field in question.

Each of the authors of books in the Series is an acknowledged authority, able to bring broad knowledge and experience to engage teachers and researchers in following up their own ideas, working with them to build further on *their* own experience.

The first editions of books in this series have attracted widespread praise for their authorship, their design, and their content, and have been widely used to support practice and research. The success of the series, and the realization that it needs to stay relevant in a world where new research is being conducted and published at a rapid rate, have prompted the commissioning of this second edition. This new edition has been thoroughly updated, with accounts of research that has appeared since the first edition and with the addition of other relevant additional material. We trust that students, teachers and researchers will continue to discover inspiration in these pages to underpin their own investigations.

Chris Candlin and David Hall
General Editors

Acknowledgements

During the long gestation period of this book, I received the support of many people. I wish to thank first and foremost the series editors, Christopher Candlin and David Hall. Their patience, brilliance, and dedication helped to foster this book at every stage. The great staff at Pearson Longman, especially Kate Ahl, Josie O'Donoghue, and Liz Johnson, deserve my greatest thanks as well. My thanks also go to Kathy Auger of Graphicraft.

My colleagues in the strategy field, such as Ernesto Macaro, Pamela Gunning, Roberta Lavine, Anna Uhl Chamot, Peter Gu, Joan Rubin, Vee Harris, Kyoung Rang Lee, Karen Schramm, Carol Griffiths, Ma Xiaomei, Meng Yaru, and others, offered me many materials and ideas along the way. I particularly thank Andrew D. Cohen, my dear friend and colleague, for having faith in me when I truly needed it.

I am grateful to my students, especially Ma Rui and Lin Chien-Yu, for all those Saturdays spent reading and commenting on this book's chapters over hot chocolate or tea. I thank Yesim Yilmazel-Sahin, Yoni Siegel, Tasha Parrish, and Rebecca Boggs for their suggestions.

My greatest gratitude is owed to my husband Clifford Stocking and to dear Sophia. They uncomplainingly and graciously dealt with my obsession with this book, and their support was beyond measure.

Rebecca L. Oxford
December 2010

Publisher's Acknowledgements

We are grateful to the following for permission to reproduce copyright material:

Figures

Figures 6.3 and 6.4 from Pamela Gunning. Reproduced by authorization of Lidec, Inc. © Lidec, Inc.

Photos

The publisher would like to thank the following for their kind permission to reproduce their photographs:

Pearson Education Ltd: Figure 1.3, p. 18, (top) Ellen Massey, (bottom) POD/Photodisc. C Squared Studios, Tony Gable; Figure 6.2, p. 192, POD/ Digital Vision.

Text

Concept 7.9 adapted from Creswell, J. (2008) *Research Design: Qualitative, Quantitative, and Mixed Methods Approaches.* Third edition. Thousand Oaks, CA: Sage.

Every effort has been made to trace the copyright holders and we apologise in advance for any unintentional omissions. We would be pleased to insert the appropriate acknowledgement in any subsequent edition of this publication.

Introduction to This Book

Section I encompasses Chapters 1–4. It outlines the conceptual foundation for language learning strategies and for the rest of the book. Chapter 1 presents the *Strategic Self-Regulation (S²R) Model* of language learning by offering definitions, terminology, key features, the role of the learner, the differences between strategies and metastrategies, the nature of "metaknowledge," flexible use of strategies for different purposes, and task-phases in the model. Chapter 1 also explains the role of mediated learning, the value of deep processing strategies, the double utility of strategies for ordinary learning and for severe problems, the role of tactics, the relationship between learning styles and learning strategies, and nine ways in which the S²R Model differs from other models of learning strategies.

Chapter 2 focuses on the model's cognitive dimension, which includes cognitive strategies for remembering and processing language and metacognitive strategies for enabling such processing to occur. Chapter 2 explores a larger range of highly relevant theories than found in most books on learning strategies: schema theory, cognitive information-processing theory, activity theory, cognitive load theory, and theories of the relationship of neurobiology to cognition. In practical, understandable terms, the chapter shows how these theories shed light on learning strategies and why they are important.

Chapter 3 concerns the second dimension, the affective realm, which includes emotions, beliefs, attitudes, and motivation. This dimension has been largely ignored by many learning strategy specialists, although it has a tremendous influence on language learning and on strategy use. The chapter introduces the concept of linking affective strategies with meta-affective strategies. The relationships among strategies, emotions, beliefs, and attitudes are a key component of this chapter. A special feature is the explanation of how strategies are linked to multiple facets of motivation (motivational orientation and intensity, volition, and willingness

1

to communicate). The subject of goals is an important factor in motivation and is at the heart of strategies. The final topic in this chapter is the close association among neurobiology, affect, and strategies.

Chapter 4 presents novel and innovative arguments for language learning strategy research in the third dimension, sociocultural-interactive (SI), which involves strategies for contexts, communication, and culture. The chapter explains SI strategies and the meta-SI strategies that guide their use. This chapter demonstrates how learning strategies relate to communication. Extending beyond most strategy research and theory, the chapter reveals how strategies align with discourse, contexts, cultural models, identity, and power relations, as well as discussing the crucial theme of investment. Moving still further into the sociocultural realm, the chapter then explores how learners tie their learning strategies to counter-stories, resistance, non–participation, opposition, and accommodation, hitherto unexamined in detail by strategy researchers.

Section II, including Chapters 5 and 6, focuses on very practical applications of the S^2R Model. Chapter 5 opens with the purposes of strategy assessment and then immediately discusses key issues, such as self-report versus other report, degree of task authenticity, cultural appropriateness, and degree of quantification. The range of strategy assessment possibilities in this chapter is immense, from simple, live observations to computerized trace measures, from verbal reports to task-strategy colour coding, from portfolios to interviews, and from questionnaires to learner narratives. The chapter provides a highly practical discussion of measurement validity and reliability for qualitative assessment tools and an explanation of quality criteria for qualitative measurement instruments. Advantages and disadvantages of each tool are explained.

Chapter 6 explains strategy assistance in an understandable and useful fashion. The chapter contends that direct strategy instruction by the teacher, while very important, is just one of many modes for assisting learners in developing optimal strategies. Regarding direct strategy instruction, the chapter explores features that can make it successful, learner variables to consider, practical classroom models and guidebooks for strategy instruction, and the use of portfolios and metascripts. All of these tools are managed by the teacher in direct strategy instruction. However, beyond direct strategy instruction by the teacher, the chapter offers ways to integrate strategy instruction into textbooks, course materials, learner counselling/consultation, and distance learning. Benefits and limitations of these strategy assistance techniques are important.

Section III, consisting of Chapters 7 and 8, concerns research on language learning strategies. Chapter 7 introduces and discusses strategy research tools, methodologies, and ideas. It focuses on quantitative research methods, including experimental, quasi-experimental, and non-experimental (survey) research. The chapter then explains how the following qualitative approaches can be useful for strategy research: phenomenology, grounded theory, case study, ethnography, and narrative research. Mixed methods approaches, which combine quantitative and qualitative perspectives and tools, are also presented here for strategy research applications. The chapter offers abundant illustrations of strategy studies to portray different research modes. Validity of studies and research ethics are significant themes in Chapter 7. For new researchers interested in strategies, as well as experienced researchers, this chapter provides rich, detailed assistance in research methodology and ideas.

Chapter 8 synthesizes existing research results on learning strategies with the aim of uncovering what we currently know and what we still need to know. The chapter presents strategy research on reading, writing, listening, speaking, vocabulary, and grammar and then compares the status of strategy research across these areas. It also offers findings across studies that encompass multiple areas simultaneously. Included are discussions of linearity or curvilinearity, causality, factors in strategy use, distance learning strategies, and effectiveness of strategy instruction.

Section IV, which includes Chapter 9, concludes the book by situating learning strategies within the various disciplines and offering advice and resources for further reading and exploration. Chapter 9 is an "intellectual geography" that reviews the landmarks of the S^2R Model and explores the terrain of self-regulated learning strategies in applied linguistics, educational psychology, and educational research. This chapter presents information on professional associations, conferences, journals, online bibliographies, and databases for further strategy exploration. The main point made in Chapter 9 is that this book is a beginning, not an ending, to discovering more about language learning strategies and fostering excellent learning for language students.

I The Strategic Self-Regulation (S^2R) Model of Language Learning

Introducing the *S*trategic *S*elf-*R*egulation (S²R) Model of language learning

You can't cross the sea merely by standing and staring at the water.

Rabindranath Tagore

Preview questions

1. What are the dimensions in the Strategic Self-Regulation (S²R) Model of language learning?
2. How do "metastrategies" and other strategies contribute differently to strategic self-regulation?
3. What are the six types of metaknowledge, and why are they important for learning languages?
4. Why are tactics necessary in self-regulated learning?
5. In what ways do models of self-regulated learning differ?

Self-regulation is one of the most exciting developments in second or foreign language (L2) learning. Models of learner self-regulation applied to L2 learning have been called by many names, such as "learner-self-management" (Rubin, 2001), "learner self-direction" (Dickinson, 1987), "self-regulated or autonomous L2 learning" (Oxford, 1999a), and "mediated learning" (Scarcella and Oxford, 1992, based on Vygotsky, 1978). This book presents the *S*trategic *S*elf-*R*egulation (S²R) Model of language learning. In this model, learners actively and constructively use strategies to manage their own learning.

Self-regulated L2 learning strategies are important throughout the world. The *Common European Framework of Reference for Languages* (Council of

Europe, 2001) promotes "learning how to learn" and the use of learning strategies (Little, 2006; Mariani, 2004). Key research handbooks (e.g., Alexander and Winne, 2006; Flippo and Caverly, 2008; Hinkel, 2005; see also Chapter 9) discuss the significance of strategies in learners' self-regulation in many fields, including L2 learning. In the last few years publishers have offered several important, edited volumes (e.g., Cohen and Macaro, 2007; Griffiths, 2008) focused wholly or largely on L2 learning strategies. Every year journals around the globe publish articles on topics such as learning strategies, metacognitive strategies, and strategies for various L2 areas (reading, writing, speaking, listening, pragmatics, grammar, and vocabulary). Many teachers attend conference sessions on how to help their students become more strategic, self-regulated, and successful. As important contributors to self-regulated learning, L2 learning strategies deserve attention. Table 1.1 provides a preview of this chapter.

1.1   Overview of this book

Figure 1.1 presents an overview of this book. *Section I*, consisting of the first four chapters, is devoted to the S²R Model of language learning and the factors and theories underlying the model. Chapter 1 introduces the model in terms of factors and integrated theories. Chapter 2 presents strategies

Table 1.1   **Overview of this chapter**

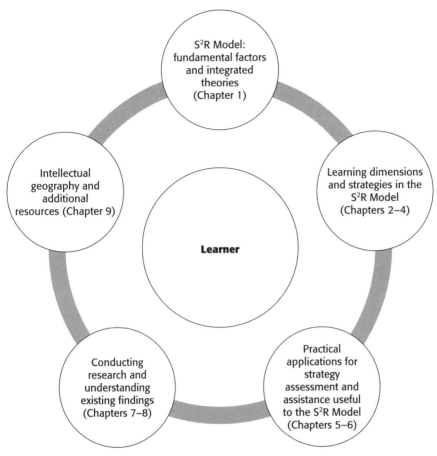

Figure 1.1   **Preview of the chapters in this book**

and theories in the cognitive dimension for remembering and processing language. Chapters 3 and 4 offer strategies and theories in relation to two dimensions that have received inadequate attention from many strategy researchers: the affective dimension for emotion, beliefs, attitudes, and motivation and the sociocultural-interactive dimension for contexts, communication, and culture. *Section II* includes important practical applications within the S²R Model: strategy assessment (Chapter 5) and strategy assistance (Chapter 6). The two chapters in *Section III* deal with strategy research. Chapter 7 explores an array of research approaches that readers can use for investigating strategies for self-regulated L2 learning. Chapter 8 synthesizes existing L2 strategy research findings by language area, e.g., reading or vocabulary learning. *Section IV* contains Chapter 9, which reviews the landmarks of the S²R Model, maps self-regulated L2 learning strategies in relation to various disciplines, and offers further resources for exploration.

1.2   Why this book is needed now

In an advance review of this book, Gu (2010) summarized the state of the art in language learning strategies and explained why this book is needed now. See Concept 1.1.

Concept 1.1   **State of the art in language learning strategies and why this book is needed now** (Review comments by Dr. Yongqi Gu, 2010)

• **State of the Art**

After 30 years, language learning strategy (LLS) researchers have accumulated a critical mass of knowledge. It is now timely and critical to identify and reflect upon the various issues that have emerged across decades. We need systematic and coherent efforts to chart the field and map out the issues.

Unfortunately, the intensity of interest in language learning strategies in the 1980s and the 1990s and the high expectations from theorists, researchers, teachers and learners have left many people frustrated, especially because of the conceptual fuzziness and elusiveness of the LLS construct. Classroom teachers are rightly concerned that LLS researchers have not provided enough applications for classroom teaching and learning. As those most concerned about strategic learning, learners and teachers cannot and should not have to wait. We do not need the same old research questions asked time and again; we need new, innovative research paths that lead to help for learners and teachers.

• **Why This Book Is Needed Now**

At this time, we urgently need this book's conceptual cross-fertilization and its concerted effort in theory-building so that more useful research avenues can be explored and more practical findings can be made available to the language classroom. This book opens the way to more research on the self-regulated learner's active involvement and the way strategies influence learning ability, proficiency, and the learner's identity as a self-initiating, reflective, responsible social agent.

This book is therefore definitely coming out at the right time. In fact, few would be more suitable than Rebecca Oxford, who has inspired so many in the field, to write a book on teaching and researching language learning strategies at this point in time. This book is the best attempt in recent years to face the existing challenges and issues. For researchers and teachers alike, the book provides a feast of theoretical perspectives, smoothly integrated and clearly addressed, as well as practical suggestions. It also discusses criticisms, queries, and misconceptions of language learning strategies.

To me, the book points to a renewed agenda for LLS as a worthwhile line of research. This agenda involves: (a) closer integration of LLS research into the mainstream of applied linguistics and educational psychology in terms of theorizing and empirical research; (b) closer integration of LLS into the teacher's metapedagogical awareness, reflection, and classroom instruction; and (c) closer examination of individual strategies and tactics for learning effectiveness. With this book, Rebecca Oxford has redesigned the LLS garden, redrawn the LLS landscape. I call for a re-injection of research energy and labour. Let a hundred strategy flowers bloom for the cultivation of a theoretically colourful and practically useful garden, nourished by diverse ideas.

Note: Dr. Gu is co-editor of *The Asian Journal of English Language Teaching* and a strategy research expert.

1.3   The S²R Model

This section highlights key aspects of the S²R Model. It begins with definition, terminology, and concepts, followed by key features of strategies in the model and a description of strategically self-regulated learners. It presents strategies, metastrategies, and the metaknowledge that underlies metastrategies; details the flexible use of strategies; and explains strategies in relation to three task-phases. Next it portrays mediated learning, deep processing strategies, double utility of strategies, and strategy orchestration. Finally, this section explains strategies and tactics and shows linkages among strategies, tactics, and learning styles.

1.3.1   Definitions, terminology, and concepts in the S²R Model

The quotation below defines self-regulation as applied to learning.

Quote 1.1 Self-regulation in learning

Self-regulation comprises such processes as setting goals for learning, attending to and concentrating on instruction, using effective strategies to organize, code, and rehearse information to be remembered, establishing a productive work environment, using resources effectively, monitoring performance, managing time effectively, seeking assistance when needed, holding positive beliefs about one's capabilities, the value of learning, the factors influencing learning, and the anticipated outcomes of actions, and experiencing pride and satisfaction with one's efforts.

Dale H. Schunk and Peggy A. Ertmer (2000, p. 631)

Concept 1.2 presents a definition of *self-regulated L2 learning strategies* in the S²R Model. These strategies help learners regulate or control their own learning, thus making it easier and more effective. Self-regulation, according to its Latin roots, involves not only self-management but also "self-righting," i.e., self-adjustment or self-adaptation if something goes off track or needs improvement. See Concept 1.2 for an important distinction between skills and self-regulated L2 learning strategies, and look to Chapter 2 for information on how skills develop.

Concept 1.2 Definition of self-regulated L2 learning strategies

- In the S²R Model, *self-regulated L2 learning strategies* are defined as deliberate, goal-directed attempts to manage and control efforts to learn the L2 (based on Afflerbach, Pearson, and Paris, 2008). These strategies are broad, teachable actions that learners choose from among alternatives and employ for L2 learning purposes (e.g., constructing, internalizing, storing, retrieving, and using information; completing short-term tasks; and/or developing L2 proficiency and self-efficacy in the long term).

  Examples: Planning, Evaluating, Obtaining and Using Resources, Reasoning, Going Beyond the Immediate Data, Generating and Maintaining Motivation, and Overcoming Knowledge Gaps in Communicating.

- *Learning strategies* are sometimes confused with *skills*. Skills are automatic and out of awareness, whereas strategies are intentional and deliberate.

- It is impossible to tell whether an action is a strategy or a skill without finding out whether it is under the learner's automatic or deliberate control.

Strategic, self-regulated language learning is crucial, as explained below.

Quote 1.2 **The importance of strategic, self-regulated learning and of strategy instruction**

Strategic, self-regulated learning lies at the heart of second/foreign language acquisition. Over the decades, we have seen applied linguists suggesting the right amount of comprehensible input, opportunities for output, corrective feedback, task-based presentation, and contextual scaffolding in the classroom. But after all this, the only thing teachers can do is to wait and hope that learners will notice the patterns or automatically activate their implicit learning mechanisms. While this might happen, the central thesis behind language learning strategy research is that learners, supported by teachers and curricula, can play a much more active role in managing and controlling the learning process, thereby maximising the outcomes of learning. Instruction in strategic learning can result in better learners.

Yongqi Gu (2010, p. 1)

Gu (2010) defined strategic, self-regulated learning as "ways of tackling the learning task at hand and managing the self in overseeing the learning process . . . under the constraints of the learning situation and learning context for the purpose of learning success" (p. 2). In other words, the learner must not only effectively do the task and manage himself or herself but must also deal with (and make the most of) the learning environment.

When learning strategies became well known in the 1980s and 1990s, some people might have believed that strategies would remove all the hard work from language learning and teaching. However, "Strategies are not a 'super-drug'" (Gu, 2010, p. 2). "A simplistic, static, and gimmick-oriented expectation," as if strategies "could offer quick fixes . . . , is unrealistic" (Gu, 2010, p. 1). Though learning strategies do make learning easier in some senses, their purpose is much more significant: strategies make learning deeper, more productive, and more lasting (Cohen and Macaro, 2007; Holschuh and Altman, 2008; Winne and Perry, 2000).

Quote 1.3 Strategically self-regulated learners

"Strategic" describes the way in which these [self-regulated] learners approach challenging tasks and problems by choosing from a repertoire of tactics those they believe best suited to the situation, and applying those tactics appropriately. . . . The labels of tactic and strategy also reflect differences in grain size, the latter being larger . . .

Philip H. Winne and Nancy E. Perry (2000, pp. 533–534, 557)

This book uses the term *learning strategies* rather than the term *learner strategies* (see Wenden and Rubin, 1987; Cohen and Macaro, 2007) for two key reasons. First, the focus here is on strategies for learning, although communication often occurs at the same time. People often learn as they communicate and vice versa. Second, learning-focused researchers in virtually all other fields employ the term *learning strategies*. For discussions about the terminology of strategies, see Cohen (2007) and Oxford and Cohen (1992).

1.3.2   Key features of strategies in the S²R Model

Concept 1.3 describes the features of strategies in the S²R Model. In a nutshell, these strategies involve various types of consciousness, facilitate learning, involve the whole learner rather than just the cognitive side, and are used flexibly.

Concept 1.3   **Features of self-regulated L2 learning strategies**

- Self-regulated L2 learning strategies . . .
  - are employed consciously, involving four elements of consciousness (awareness, attention, intention, and effort, Schmidt, 1995);
  - make learning easier, faster, more enjoyable, and more effective;
  - are manifested through specific tactics in different contexts and for different purposes;
  - reflect the whole, multidimensional learner, not just the learner's cognitive or metacognitive aspects;
  - are often combined into *strategy chains*, i.e., groups of strategies working together (see later in this chapter); and
  - are applied in a given situation but can be transferred to other situations when relevant.
- Some strategies, such as Planning or Monitoring, are deployed for learning many subjects and for problem-solving in general throughout one's life.
- Other strategies, such as Overcoming Knowledge Gaps in Communicating (e.g., through making up new words or switching back to the home language briefly), are often tied to language learning.

1.3.3   The learner in the S^{2}R Model

The S^{2}R Model draws upon research on strategically self-regulated learners (see Concept 1.4). The research is strikingly consistent on these learners' active control of learning through the effective use of learning strategies. A key for such learners is choosing appropriate strategies for the purpose and situation and evaluating the success of these strategies. Learners can use strategies to regulate many aspects of their learning: their internal mental states, beliefs, observable behaviours, and the learning environment.

1.3.4   Strategies and metastrategies in the S^{2}R Model

The S^{2}R Model includes strategies for three major, mutually influential dimensions of L2 learning: cognitive, affective, and sociocultural-interactive. *Cognitive strategies* help the learner construct, transform, and apply L2 knowledge. An example of a cognitive strategy is Activating Knowledge (when needed for a language task). *Affective strategies* help the learner create positive emotions and attitudes and stay motivated. An example of an affective strategy is Generating and Maintaining Motivation. *Sociocultural-interactive (SI) strategies* help the learner with communication, sociocultural contexts, and identity. An example of an SI strategy is Interacting to Learn

---

Concept 1.4   **What we know about strategically self-regulated learners**

Strategically self-regulated learners . . .

- actively participate in their own learning (Griffiths, 2008; Malpass, O'Neil, and Hocevar, 1999, 2006).

- achieve learning goals by controlling various aspects of their learning (Malpass, O'Neil, and Hocevar, 1999; Oxford, 1990).

- regulate their cognitive and affective states (*covert self-regulation*), their observable performance (*behavioural self-regulation*), and the environmental conditions for learning (*environmental self-regulation*) (Zimmerman, 2000).

- use strategies to control their own beliefs about learning and themselves (Schunk and Zimmerman, 1998).

- cognitively move from declarative (conscious) knowledge to procedural (automatic) knowledge with the use of strategies (Anderson, 1976, 1985; O'Malley and Chamot, 1990).

- choose appropriate strategies for different conditions, purposes, situations, and settings (Ehrman, Leaver, and Oxford, 2003). An *appropriate strategy* is one that (a) addresses the learner's goal or need, (b) fits the learning circumstances and the sociocultural context, (c) works well with the student's learning styles, i.e., general learning preferences, or in some cases helps bring greater flexibility to those preferences; and (d) positively influences learning.

- understand that no strategy is necessarily appropriate under every circumstance or for every purpose (Hsiao and Oxford, 2002; Cohen and Macaro, 2007). For instance, a strategy that a learner uses effectively to read a airport timetable in Russian does necessarily not work when he or she is reading an editorial in the Russian newspaper *Izvestiya*.

- show awareness of the relationship between strategy use and learning outcomes; i.e., these learners consider whether a given strategy is associated with successful performance (Malpass, O'Neil, and Hocevar, 1999).

---

and Communicate. Crucial mental processes or tools, called *metastrategies* (such as Planning, Organizing, Monitoring, and Evaluating), help the learner control and manage the use of strategies in each dimension: cognitive, affective, and sociocultural-interactive. Concept 1.5 lists the strategies and metastrategies in the S²R Model. Metastrategies are shown first, because they powerfully influence the three dimensions and are part of each dimension.

As shown in Concept 1.5, three types of metastrategies exist. *Metacognitive strategies* (the best known type of metastrategies, as described by O'Malley and Chamot, 1990 and Oxford, 1990) help the learner control cognitive strategy use, while *meta-affective strategies* facilitate learner control of affective strategy use, and *meta-SI strategies* enable the learner to

---

Concept 1.5   **Metastrategies and strategies in the Strategic Self-Regulation (S^2R) Model of L2 learning**

Metastrategies and strategies	Purpose
8 metastrategies (metacognitive, meta-affective, and metasociocultural-interactive):	
Paying Attention Planning Obtaining and Using Resources Organizing Implementing Plans Orchestrating Strategy Use Monitoring Evaluating	Managing and controlling L2 learning in a general sense, with a focus on understanding one's own needs and using and adjusting the other strategies to meet those needs
6 strategies in the cognitive dimension:	
Using the Senses to Understand and Remember Activating Knowledge Reasoning Conceptualizing with Details Conceptualizing Broadly Going Beyond the Immediate Data	Remembering and processing the L2 (constructing, transforming, and applying L2 knowledge)
2 strategies in the affective dimension:	
Activating Supportive Emotions, Beliefs, and Attitudes Generating and Maintaining Motivation	Handling emotions, beliefs, attitudes, and motivation in L2 learning
3 strategies in the sociocultural-interactive dimension:	
Interacting to Learn and Communicate Overcoming Knowledge Gaps in Communicating Dealing with Sociocultural Contexts and Identities	Dealing with issues of contexts, communication, and culture in L2 learning

control SI strategy use. Why is it helpful to talk about metastrategies, a broader category, as opposed to only metacognitive strategies? Why should we think about meta-affective and meta-SI strategies in addition to meta-cognitive strategies? Here are the reasons. *Metacognitive* simply means "beyond the cognitive" and includes strategies that provide general management (control) of cognitive strategies. Unfortunately, prior taxonomies of strategies had no term to describe control of two other key dimensions of L2 learning strategies: (a) the affective dimension and (b) the social dimension. Hence, until now the term *metacognitive* was (confusingly, in my view) applied to the control of strategies in the affective and social realms, not just to the control of cognitive strategies. The S²R Model fills this major gap by including meta-affective strategies and meta-SI strategies, respectively. The importance of filling this gap is revealed especially in Chapters 3 and 4, which explore these strategies in detail. Many effective L2 learners have used such strategies for years, though there was no official name for them.

The concept of metastrategies – more than just that of metacognitive strategies alone – reflects the multidimensional reality of the L2 learner. Support for more than just one category of metastrategy comes from Alexander, Graham, and Harris (1998), who stated that self-regulation pertains not just to the learner's management of cognition but also to regulation of affective states and the social environment, in which communication occurs. Additional support comes from Wolters (2003), who highlighted the need for strategies to manage affect (emotions, motivation, etc.) at the "meta" or general level.

Figure 1.2 shows cognitive, affective, and sociocultural-interactive strategies as interlocking cogs and depicts metastrategies as the arrows that surround

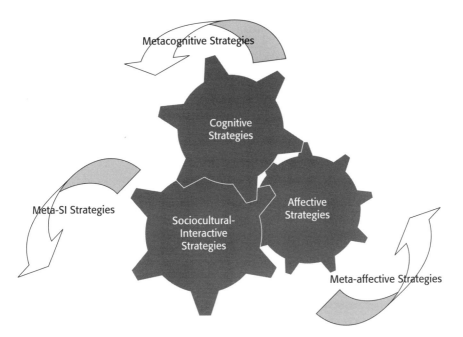

Figure 1.2   Dynamic interaction of strategies and metastrategies for L2 learning (cogs and arrows metaphor) in the S²R Model
Note 1: Metastrategies include metacognitive, meta-affective, and metasocial strategies.
Note 2: Certain strategies are more important than others in various situations. The size of a strategy type in this figure does not indicate importance in all situations.

the cogs. Of course, actual L2 learning is not as mechanistic as cogs in a wheel, but Figure 1.2 is a useful metaphor of (a) multiple, interrelated aspects of learning and (b) the way metastrategies (metacognitive, meta-affective, and meta-SI) control the use of cognitive, affective, and SI strategies. Figure 1.3 shows the same idea in a different way. The metastrategies (metacognitive, meta-affective, and meta-SI) serve as the orchestra conductor, and various sections of the orchestra (wind, string, and percussion instruments) are cognitive, affective, and SI strategies, guided by the conductor.

Metastrategies, by virtue of their executive-control and management function, help the learner know whether and how to deploy a given strategy and aid in determining whether the strategy is working or has worked as intended. Strategies and metastrategies in the model are highly

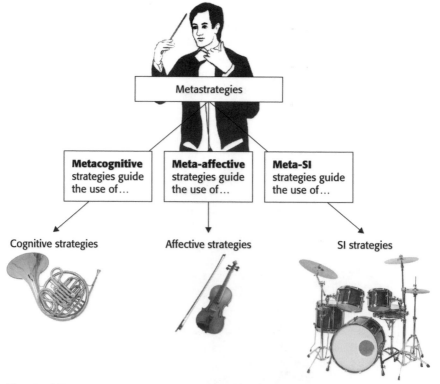

Figure 1.3   Metastrategies guide the use of cognitive, affective, and sociocultural-interactive (SI) strategies (orchestra–conductor metaphor) in the S²R Model

Note: In the past, *metacognitive strategies* were viewed as guiding the use of all other strategies. However, in a more articulated and more precise manner, *metastrategies (metacognitive, meta-affective, and meta-SI strategies)* guide the use of cognitive, affective, and sociocultural-interactive strategies, respectively.

Source: (top) Ellen Massey, (bottom) POD/Photodisc. C Squared Studios, Tony Gable.

dynamic, because they respond to changing needs of the learner for varying purposes in different sociocultural contexts. *Metastrategic regulation* is the learner's use of metastrategies of any kind (metacognitive, meta-affective, and/or meta-SI) with the purpose of self-regulated learning. This is an expansion of Flavell's (1978, 1979) term *metacognitive regulation*, which identified the use of metacognitive strategies in Flavell's system.

1.3.5   Metaknowledge underlying metastrategies in the S²R Model

Underlying the use of metastrategies in the S²R Model are six types of *metaknowledge*, defined in Concept 1.6: *person knowledge*, which is contrasted with broader knowledge of cultural or group norms (*group/culture knowledge*); *task knowledge*, which is contrasted with broader, *whole-process* knowledge; *strategy knowledge*; and *conditional knowledge*, which draws on any of the other types of knowledge. In an earlier theory, Wenden (1991), building on Flavell (1978, 1979), mentioned only three types of metaknowledge (person, task, and strategy knowledge) and called all three *metacognitive knowledge*.

Concept 1.6   **Six types of metaknowledge**

- *Person knowledge* concerns learning styles, goals, strengths, and weaknesses of the learner (or someone else). Focus is on the individual.

- *Group or culture knowledge* deals with norms and expectations in the group/ culture – either the home group/culture or the "target" group/culture to which the learner wants to gain entry. Focus is on the collective group, not on a single individual.

- *Task knowledge* relates largely to the characteristics and requirements of the immediate L2 learning task.

- In contrast, *whole-process knowledge* goes beyond task knowledge to embrace the characteristics and requirements of the long-term process of learning the language. Whole-process knowledge is often necessary for learners who seek to develop high proficiency and who have a "future orientation" to learning (Simons, Vansteenkiste, Lens, and Lacante, 2004).

- *Strategy knowledge* is knowledge of available learning strategies and metastrategies and how they work. Strategy knowledge can be examined in terms of strategies for "doing" and metastrategies for executive control and management.

- *Conditional knowledge* of when, why, and where to use a given learning strategy. Conditional knowledge can draw on any or all of the other five types of metaknowledge.
  - For example, knowing when and why to use a given strategy is facilitated by being aware of: (a) person knowledge about oneself, e.g., one's learning style, goals, strengths, and weaknesses; (b) group or culture

knowledge, e.g., norms, values, and expectations of the group or culture;
(c) task knowledge, e.g., demands and characteristics of the immediate
task; (d) whole-process knowledge, e.g., probable requirements and
features of long-term L2 learning; and (e) strategy knowledge, e.g.,
available strategies and metastrategies and how they work.

○ Pintrich (2002) classified conditional knowledge as being only part of
"task knowledge," but this is too limited, because some learners can
apply conditional knowledge well beyond single tasks.

○ Learners with a future time orientation often apply conditional knowledge over longer periods containing multiple tasks.

I argue that *metacognitive knowledge*, as applied by prior researchers to
encompass person, task, and strategy knowledge, is far too restricted a term.
The term *metacognitive knowledge* literally points only to knowledge helpful for controlling the cognitive dimension of learning, but in actuality the
learner's *metaknowledge* must include but go beyond the cognitive arena.
Such knowledge must also address the affective and sociocultural-interactive
dimensions of L2 learning. Therefore, it is more accurate to speak of metaknowledge rather than just metacognitive knowledge when considering the
knowledge types that underlie metastrategies in general.

Wenden's and Flavell's knowledge types – person, task, and strategy
knowledge – are necessary but not sufficient for explaining the learner's
control and management of L2 learning. For instance, person knowledge
does not imply knowledge of expectations of the group or culture in which
the learner is located or which the learner wishes to enter, though such
knowledge is needed for self-regulated L2 learning. Task knowledge refers
to understanding the demands and features of the immediate task but
does not imply long-term, whole-process knowledge, which is especially
valuable for learners who hope to reach distinguished levels of proficiency
and/or whose self-regulation involves taking a "long view" or future-time
perspective. Knowledge of strategies does not necessarily indicate that the
learner knows how, when, or why to use a particular strategy to fulfill a
specific purpose in the flux and complexity of a given sociocultural setting
(conditional knowledge). Therefore it was necessary for me to create
names for two heretofore missing types of metaknowledge, *group/culture
knowledge* and *whole-process knowledge*, and to include *conditional knowledge*
(Pintrich, 2002) as the sixth type of metaknowledge. See Figure 1.4.

Concept 1.7 on pages 22–23 shows how each type of metaknowledge
(person knowledge, group/culture knowledge, task knowledge, whole-
process knowledge, strategy knowledge, and conditional knowledge) is
applied in more concrete detail to cognitive, affective, and sociocultural-
interactive dimensions.

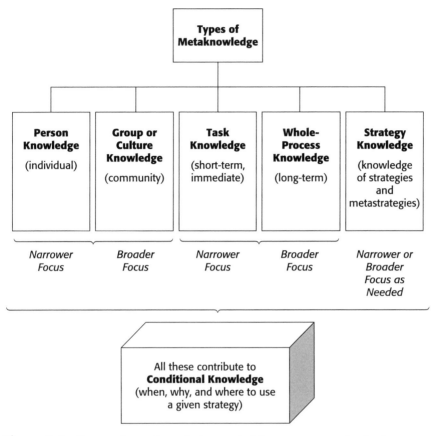

Figure 1.4 Types of metaknowledge underlying metastrategies in the S²R Model

Figure 1.5 on page 24 outlines in brief the structure of the S²R Model, emphasizing strategies and metastrategies. These elements interact to improve L2 learning and move students to higher levels of proficiency.

1.3.6 Flexible use of strategies in the S²R Model

Not every learner needs to use every type of strategy at all times. For instance, if a learner, Brian, is demotivated, stressed, or feeling overly challenged, he might need affective strategies, but at other times, when he feels motivated, calm, and sufficiently but not overly challenged, such strategies might be unnecessary. Highly advanced L2 learners who have reached distinguished levels of proficiency tend not to need affective strategies any longer, according to Leaver (2003a), though this might depend somewhat on the learner's personality or general (non-L2) level of anxiety.

Concept 1.7 Types of metaknowledge as applied to cognitive, affective, and sociocultural-interactive dimensions of L2 learning

Dimensions of L2 learning in which metaknowledge operates	Types of metaknowledge					
	TYPE 1: **Person knowledge** (can refer to knowledge of self or of another person) (Narrower)	TYPE 2: **Group or culture knowledge** (Broader)	TYPE 3: **Task knowledge** (immediate L2 learning task) (Narrower)	TYPE 4: **Whole-process knowledge** (longer-term, future-time orientation) (Broader)	TYPE 5: **Strategy knowledge – Knowledge of strategies and metastrategies** (cognitive, affective, and SI strategies and metacognitive, meta-affective, and meta-SI strategies)	TYPE 6: **Conditional knowledge** of when, where, and why to use a given strategy, drawing on the other types of metaknowledge
Cognitive dimension	Knowledge of one's own or another's cognitive level, cognitive learning style, goals, and related strengths and weaknesses	Knowledge of group/cultural norms and expectations in relation to cognitive elements of L2 learning	Knowledge of the cognitive demands of the immediate L2 learning task	Knowledge of longer-term cognitive demands of learning the L2	Knowledge of cognitive strategies	Knowledge of meta-cognitive strategies	Knowledge of when, where, and why to use a cognitive strategy or a metacognitive strategy for a given purpose in a specific setting

Affective dimension	Knowledge of one's own or another's emotions, motivations, and related strengths and weaknesses	Knowledge of group/cultural norms and expectations in relation to affective elements of L2 learning	Knowledge of affective (emotional or motivational) demands of the immediate L2 learning task	Knowledge of longer-term affective demands of learning the L2	Knowledge of affective Strategies	Knowledge of meta-affective strategies	Knowledge of when, where, and why to use an affective strategy or a meta-affective strategy for a given purpose in a specific setting
Sociocultural-interactive dimension	Knowledge of one's own or another's social interaction patterns, social learning style, related strengths and weaknesses, and the sociocultural setting	Knowledge of group/cultural norms and expectations in relation to interaction and sociocultural elements of L2 learning	Knowledge of sociocultural-interactive demands of the immediate L2 learning task	Knowledge of longer-term sociocultural-interactive demands of learning the L2	Knowledge of sociocultural-interactive (SI) strategies	Knowledge of meta-SI strategies	Knowledge of when, where, and why to use a sociocultural-interactive strategy or a meta-SI strategy for a given purpose in a specific setting

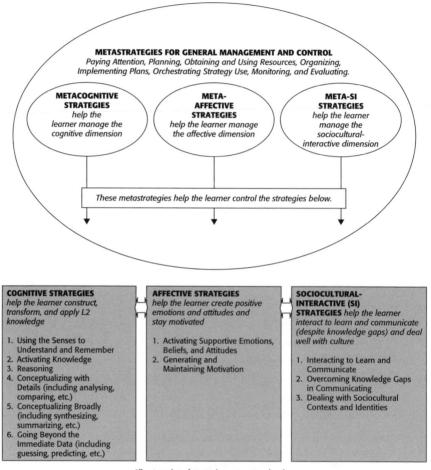

Figure 1.5   One view of the S²R Model, emphasising metastrategies and strategies

Learners are not likely to "grow out of" their need for metacognitive strategies and sociocultural-interactive strategies. No matter what the level of L2 proficiency, if a learner is losing concentration, he or she might need to employ the metacognitive strategy of Paying Attention, or if the learner wants to build a significant, long-term relationship with someone in the L2, he or she might need to employ a sociocultural-interactive strategy, such as Dealing with Sociocultural Contexts and Identities.

Certain cognitive strategies, such as Conceptualizing with Details and Reasoning, are valuable for multiple purposes at all proficiency levels, but these strategies must be applied in ways that fit the situation. If a native

English speaker is listening to a lecture in Romanian and trying to pick out the key content points, it would not help him or her to analyse the structure of every sentence and all the word endings.

1.3.7   Task-phases in the S²R Model

The S²R Model includes a sequence of phases for doing a task or solving a problem (Figure 1.6). The sequence is as follows:

- Task-phase 1 is *strategic forethought*. In Task-phase 1, the learner pays attention to the demands of the task, sets goals, plans how to address them, and activates existing knowledge.

- Task-phase 2 is *strategic performance* (sometimes called *strategic implementation, monitoring, and control*). In this task-phase, the learner (a) implements the plan, (b) monitors how well the plan is working, and (c) decides whether to continue the task as it is going, stop entirely, or make changes in the approach to the task. The aspect labelled (c) in the prior sentence is the "control" or "regulation" part of Task-phase 2. Some theorists of self-regulated learning have tried to split this phase into distinct phases of monitoring and control, yet the same theorists have stated, "empirical work on monitoring . . . and control/regulation . . . does not find much separation of these processes in terms of people's experiences" (Wolters, Pintrich, and Karabenick, 2003, p. 6).

- Task-phase 3 is *strategic reflection and evaluation* and includes making judgments of value about outcomes, effectiveness of strategies, and self (e.g., self-efficacy, which is the learner's belief he or she can meet a given goal).

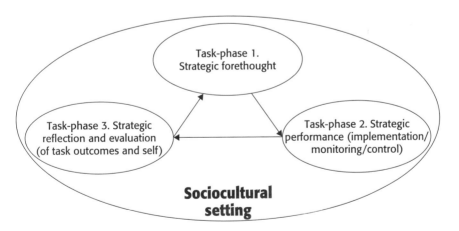

Figure 1.6   **Task-phases in the S²R Model**
Note: Learners do not always follow this linear order.
Source: Adapted from Zimmerman, Bonner, and Kovach (1996).

In social-cognitive research on self-regulated learning, Zimmerman *et al.* (1996) showed that learners used a cycle similar to the one in Figure 1.6 for comprehending and summarizing texts, taking classroom notes, planning and managing time, and preparing for tests, resulting in increases in learning and self-efficacy. Other names are sometimes used for the task-phases (Bandura, 1997; Eisenberg and Berkowitz, 1988; Winne and Hadwin, 1998).

The S²R Model employs these task-phases because they suggest *approximately* when certain learning strategies or metastrategies are likely to be useful. For example, the strategies of Planning and of Activating Knowledge occur primarily in Task-phase 1, strategic forethought. The metastrategy of Monitoring naturally occurs in Task-phase 2, strategic performance (strategic implementation, monitoring, and control). Task-phase 2 is the natural home for strategies such as Conceptualizing Broadly, Conceptualizing with Details, Going Beyond the Immediate Data, and Overcoming Knowledge Gaps in Communicating. The metastrategy of Evaluating emerges mostly in Task-phase 3, strategic reflection and evaluation.

However, the task-phases are not always neatly linear; some learners use the phases in a different order. For example, although one learner, Mark, uses the Task-phase 1 – 2 – 3 order as shown, a different learner, Alexander, jumps directly into task performance (Task-phase 2) without any planning and then, when he feels lost, he goes back and plans (ordinarily Task-phase 1, but not for him). In addition, the phases are not always strategically distinct, because some strategies can appear in multiple phases. For instance, the strategy of Activating Knowledge logically occurs as part of strategic forethought (Task-phase 1), but knowledge can be reactivated in Task-phase 2. The metastrategy of Planning is obviously necessary for Task-phase 1, but the learner can re-plan during Task-phase 2 if the original plan goes awry. In fact, this type of strategic adjustment is exactly what self-regulation is all about. The metastrategy of Evaluating can occur at any time during learning, even though it is most predominant in Task-phase 3, strategic reflection and evaluation.

Quote 1.4 Not always linear

… [T]here is no strong assumption that the phases are hierarchically or linearly structured such that earlier phases must always occur before later phases.

Christopher Wolters, Paul Pintrich, and Stuart A. Karabenick (2003, p. 6)

Although task-phases have heuristic value for considering how and when strategies are used, L2 tasks offer just one way of looking at strategic learning. Another viewpoint on strategies, as mentioned earlier, is the future-time perspective, which considers the longer-term strategic process of learning a language. For instance, the learner might ask, "What does it take to reach professional proficiency in Chinese? What strategies do I want to use to achieve that goal? Is strategy X still helping me, as it did before, or does it get in my way now? Should I drop this strategy as I move up the proficiency scale?"

1.3.8   Mediated learning in the S²R Model

Two strong assumptions of the S²R Model are: (a) Almost everyone can learn an additional language effectively by employing appropriate strategies, assuming some basic interest in learning the language and sufficient time. (b) Strategies can be learned through mediation or assistance. Not every student has strategic expertise at the outset. Expertise in employing language learning strategies "is not present in every learner; it . . . needs to be developed" (Gu, 2010, p. 1) with help or mediation from others.

The mediated ability of people to learn even very difficult things is the foundation of Reuven Feuerstein's Instrumental Enrichment (IE) Program, which has been successfully used with learners of English as a foreign language, disadvantaged students, and many others (Burden and Williams, 1998; Garb and Kozulin, 1998; International Center for Enhancement of Learning Potential, 2007). The IE Program was designed to help modify mental structures (schemata) and teach operations (i.e., strategies) through mediation by a skilled teacher (Feuerstein, Falik, Rand, and Feuerstein, 2006; Feuerstein, Rand, Hoffman, and Miller, 1997). The IE Program's mediated learning experiences help learners draw out general rules and principles (the "abstraction" process) from tasks and then bridge to other tasks and applications. One of the most fascinating aspects of IE's mediated learning is the use of *dynamic assessment*, which is a "test-teach-test" mode involving a dialogue between the learner and a more competent person, who first tests the learner's performance, then teaches operations or strategies for improving performance, and finally retests the strategy-enhanced performance (Feuerstein, Rand, and Hoffman, 1979; Kozulin and Garb, 2001). Tested performance is consistently better after students have had the opportunity to learn and use strategies.

In Vygotsky's sociocultural model, as well as in the S²R Model, all learning is assumed to be assisted (mediated) performance. Vygotsky stated that the "more capable other" leads the actively engaged student, by means of mediation (various kinds of assistance and scaffolding), through that student's "zone of proximal development," or ZPD (the area of learning that a particular student can optimally traverse with assistance). The teacher or other person helps the learner by modelling "higher mental functions," such as Conceptualizing with Details or Conceptualizing Broadly, which the S²R Model calls strategies. Even if the student is learning outside of a classroom, learning is always mediated by interaction with cultural tools, such as books, media, technology, and language itself. See Concept 1.8 for Vygotsky's model of self-regulated learning.

Concept 1.8   **Vygotsky's model of dialogic, self-regulated learning**

- Vygotsky's model of self-regulated learning states that learning is mediated through language and especially through dialogues with a more capable person (or through books, technology, or other means).

- The learner appropriates (actively internalizes and transforms) essential features of the dialogues by means of three stages: social speech (other-regulation), egocentric speech (the learner subvocalizes but does not fully self-regulate), and inner speech (self-regulation).

- To facilitate internalization of the dialogues and help the learner traverse the zone of proximal development, the more knowledgeable individual offers scaffolding (assistance), such as modelling or providing materials and explanations. Scaffolding is withdrawn when no longer needed.

- Building on Oxford (1999a), it is possible to identify the following self-regulated learning strategies in Vygotsky's work: Planning, Conceptualizing with Details (especially analysing), Conceptualizing Broadly (especially synthesizing), Monitoring, and Evaluating, all of which Vygotsky (1981) called *higher-order psychological functions*.

- In the dialogic relationship between the learner and the more capable person, the strategy of Interacting to Learn and Communicate is also evident.

- Inner speech can be used for metastrategic, self-management purposes.

- Cognition is *distributed*. This means that learning, knowledge, and even intelligence are distributed across people and across social practices and cultural tools (symbols, technologies, artifacts, and language) used by communities (Gee, 2007; Vygotsky, 1978).

Source: Summarized from Vygotsky (1978, 1979, 1981) and Oxford (1999a). For related but not identical view of learning strategies in Vygotsky's model, see McCaslin and Hickey (2001).

Related to the idea of mediation in the S²R Model is the concept of *situated cognition* or *situated learning*. Sociocultural theories suggest that all learning is embedded or situated in particular sociocultural settings (Brown, Collins, and Duguid, 1989; Greeno, 1998), which offer properties (called *affordances*) that either encourage or constrain learning (Van Lier, 1997). In situated cognition, learners are viewed as active agents, whose choice of strategies is influenced but not determined by the sociocultural context (Oxford, 2003).

The S²R Model agrees with several sociocultural models, which state that learners are part of *communities of practice*. A community of practice is an authentic, meaningful group centred on specific practices, goals, beliefs, and areas of learning within an environment, which can be local or electronically networked (Fine, 1987; Lave and Wenger, 1991; Wenger, McDermott, and Snyder, 2002). Newcomers or apprentices at first "participate peripherally" in the community and observe strategies used by those who have been in the group longer, especially central people known as "old-timers" or experts (Lave and Wenger, 1991; Levine, Reves, and Leaver, 1996). Gradually newcomers move closer to the centre of the community of practice if the circumstances are welcoming.

In a community of practice, a learner ideally participates in what is called *cognitive apprenticeship*, i.e., a strategic, practical learning-based relationship with a more capable other (Collins, 1988). Cognitive apprenticeship helps students to acquire, develop, and use learning strategies in authentic activities via interaction, social construction of knowledge, scaffolding, modelling, goal-setting, peer sharing, and learner reflection (Brown, Collins, and Duguid, 1989). Learners' strategy use can be similar for cognitive apprenticeships in literacy in the native language (L1) and the L2 (Lee, 2007) if the languages are relatively similar, but their strategy use can differ dramatically across the L1 and the L2 if one is an alphabetic language and the other language involves characters. An example of cognitive apprenticeship is the Reciprocal Teaching Approach to reading (Palincsar and Brown, 1984). In this approach, the teacher first models and scaffolds expert reading strategies, such as summarizing (part of Conceptualizing Broadly in the S²R Model) or inferring and predicting (both are aspects of Going Beyond the Immediate Data in the S²R Model), and then "fades" the scaffolding gradually when it is no longer needed. Students share their summaries, inferences, and predictions and receive feedback from other students in groups within the classroom. Graham and Harris' (1996) model, Self-Regulation Strategy Development (SRSD), involves both group and individual writing strategies. Research shows that strategically self-regulated learning in classroom communities of practice is useful for all students, from the most expert learners to those who have serious linguistic or cognitive disabilities (Harris and Graham, 2005).

Learners need to know and use strategies to get the most out of mediated learning, whether in the classroom, in informal learning, or at a distance (Kozulin, Gindis, Ageyev, and Miller, 2003; White, 1995). Metastrategies such as Planning or Paying Attention, affective strategies such as Generating and Maintaining Motivation, and sociocultural-interactive strategies such as Interacting to Learn and Communicate can all enable learners to expand the fruitful interactions with teachers or other mediators.

1.3.9   Deep processing strategies in the S²R Model

The cognitive and metacognitive strategies in the S²R Model are *deep processing strategies*, which facilitate understanding, increase meaningful mental associations, and are the most useful strategies for long-term retention of information. For example, cognitive strategies of Reasoning, Conceptualizing with Details, and Conceptualizing Broadly and metacognitive strategies of Planning, Monitoring, and Evaluating can contribute to deep processing. The students who regularly use deep processing strategies are often intrinsically motivated for learning or personal growth, and they show task persistence, good performance, and ability to regulate their own learning (Vansteenkiste, Simons, Lens, Sheldon, and Deci, 2004; Alexander, 1997).

Quote 1.5   Why a deep approach is necessary

... [S]tudents who adopt deep approaches to learning tend to personalize academic tasks and integrate information so that they can see relationships among ideas.... Deep approaches... allow the learner to build on previous knowledge in a meaningful way that facilitates long-term learning.... Students who use deep approaches have been shown to be more successful at both selecting strategies and monitoring when comprehension breaks down...

Jodi Patrick Holschuh and Lori Price Aultman (2008, p. 123)

In contrast, *surface* strategies help learners memorize material in order to repeat it when necessary, but without a goal of learning. Students who adopt surface strategies, such as rote memorization, as their *only* strategies are typically poor in test grades, task persistence, and long-term retention of information (Schmeck, 1988; Vansteenkiste *et al.*, 2004). "... [S]tudents who adopt surface approaches begin a task with the sole purpose of task completion rather than learning, which leads to verbatim recall or the use of rote memorization strategies" (Holschuh and Aultman, 2008, p. 123). Vansteenkiste *et al.* (2004, p. 246) argued that the use of surface strategies is related to having unstable self-esteem, making "excessive social comparisons," or being in a situation that discourages self-regulation. This does not mean that rote memorization strategies are a total waste of effort; Chapter 2 explores the potential value of rote strategies. However, if such strategies are the only ones a learner uses for L2 learning, the results can be negative. Too much use of surface strategies "can impair students' ability to inter-relate concepts ... [and cause learners to] reach a point where they are unable to grasp new material" (Holschuh and Aultman, 2008, p. 123).

Alexander's research (1997) shows that at the acclimation or novice stage of learning in a given domain (field), the learner has low knowledge, is situationally interested rather than personally engaged with the material, and uses only surface strategies. However, other studies (Ehrman, Romanova, Braun, and Wei, 2004; Oxford, Lavine, Felkins, Hollaway, and Saleh, 1996) show that even when learning an additional language for the very first time, some talented, creative learners develop or apply deep processing strategies rather than surface strategies right away and are personally, intrinsically interested from the outset. Teachers can help other learners to employ deep processing strategies at a relatively early stage if the learners believe these strategies can help them (Lee and Oxford, 2008). Thus, the fact that a learner has only a very limited amount of L2 knowledge does not prevent the use of deep processing strategies for gaining more L2 knowledge. Quote 1.5 from Holschuh and Aultman (2008) explains why a deep approach is essential.

1.3.10   Inclusion of tactics in the S²R Model

The S²R Model includes tactics as well as strategies. Tactics are the specific manifestations of a strategy or metastrategy by a particular learner in a given setting for a certain purpose. Stated another way, tactics are the highly specific, "ground-level" applications of strategies or metastrategies in real-life situations for specific purposes and needs. In comparison, strategies are broad and general, and many possible tactics can relate to a given strategy (Winne and Perry, 2000). Inclusion of tactics is a very important feature of the S²R Model. The conceptual distinction between strategies and tactics helps reduce the imprecision that has dogged prior strategy models (see Stevick, 1989, and Oxford and Cohen, 1992, for comments). Concept 1.9 contrasts strategies and tactics in a theoretical sense, while Table 1.2 on page 33 gives practical examples of strategies and tactics. Later chapters provide many more examples of strategies and associated tactics.

Concept 1.9   **About strategies and tactics**

- The term *strategy* comes from the Greek *stratēgía*, meaning the command of a general in an attempt to win a war. Aside from military parlance, the term *strategy* has come to mean a general plan of action used to meet a goal. *Tactics*, also based on ancient Greek usage, are ways to win battles, but the term *tactics* has also evolved to denote the specific, applied way or ways in which a strategy is being used to meet a goal in a particular situation and instance (Oxford, 1990).
- Schmeck (1988) and Wade, Trathen, and Schraw (1990) suggested that a learning strategy is "composed" of a set of learning tactics. However, in my view, *self-regulated L2 learning tactics* are specific, goal-directed actions that a given learner employs in a particular sociocultural setting for particular learning-related purposes and needs. Tactics are the way or ways the learner applies the strategy at a specific level in a given situation to meet immediate requirements.
- Winne and Perry (2000) included knowledge of tactics and strategies as one of several "cognitive conditions" for learning.

- *Example* of a metastrategy and possible tactics: A learner who is applying the metastrategy of Paying Attention might use the tactic of listening for specific information in a conversation, e.g., who, what, when, and where. Many other tactics are possible for the metastrategy of Paying Attention, depending on the learner, the language being learned, the dimension of learning (cognitive, affective, or sociocultural-interactive), the physical and social environment, the purpose, and the needs. Some tactics reflecting the metastrategy of Paying Attention might be focusing on the prefixes of Russian verbs of motion, identifying in detail the emotions and attitudes of the main characters while reading a French short story, listening closely to understand the lyrics of the Hungarian folk song, or noticing one's own social anxieties about having to give a presentation in German.

- Strategies and metastrategies for L2 learning occur in the mind and are hence unobservable. ". . . [M]any facets of SRL [self-regulated learning] are not directly observable" (Winne and Perry, 2000, pp. 533–534).

- Macaro (2006) raised the question about where strategies are "located" and answered the question by stating that strategies occur only in working memory, but his statement is somewhat incomplete; strategies involve multiple aspects of memory and brain functioning, not just working memory.

- Though strategies are internal, we can frequently observe tactics in particular sociocultural settings (e.g., a learner, Michael, asks his older Chinese mentor for pronunciation help, reflecting the strategy of Interacting to Learn and Communicate), while other tactics are unobservable (e.g., a learner, Misha, thinks about what he has already learned so far in reading the *Aeneid* and predicts what Aeneus will do next, reflecting the strategy of Going Beyond the Immediate Data).

- The number of L2 learning tactics is theoretically infinite, because situations and needs differ for various learners at different times and for different purposes.

- In this book, learning strategies and metastrategies are distinguished by **initial capital letters**, as in Evaluating, because they are the central core of the S²R Model. Tactics are written as ordinary words or phrases without capitalization, because there are countless tactics, tied to specific situations and needs. This distinction is used in all cases except when describing the research of others, who did not typically make this differentiation.

The number of tactics employed for a given strategy depends on the learner, the need, and the circumstances. For instance, many tactics (e.g., setting goals, determining the study schedule, deciding on steps to take, and so on) can reflect the strategy of Planning, and different learners use varied numbers of Planning-related tactics. Milli, a very deliberate, systematic learner, uses all the Planning-related tactics just listed when preparing for the task of writing a short L2 article for the class newspaper, while Becca, a more spontaneous learner, only sets a vague goal for writing a newspaper article in the L2 and uses no other tactics for the Planning strategy. Milli

Table 1.2   Examples of strategies, metastrategies, and tactics

STRATEGY OR METASTRATEGY	**TACTIC** REPRESENTING THE STRATEGY OR METASTRATEGY IN ACTION FOR A GIVEN LEARNER IN A GIVEN SITUATION
Going Beyond the Immediate Data	Quang guesses English meanings from the context of the reading. Specifically, he uses headings, familiar vocabulary, and topic sentences to guess the meaning from the context. (Each of these – using headings, familiar vocabulary, and topic sentences – can be considered a tactic.)
Obtaining and Using Resources	If Quang still does not understand a given structure that is essential for understanding the reading, he goes to the online dictionary or the pocket dictionary for help.
	Seven-year-old Sunitha practises her English using CALLA's (Cognitive Academic Language Learning Approach, Chamot and O'Malley, 1986) strategic stuffed animals, like Planning Panda, Monitoring Monkey, Checking Chick, and Researching Racoon.
Planning	To help her rebuild schools in the war zone, Betty Lou plans to review her knowledge of Arabic dialects and grammar at night so she can know exactly what to say and how to say it.
	Mark plans his schedule carefully so he has time for distance university French lessons, despite his hectic job and raising two children.
	Ileana decides to review her new Slovak vocabulary in carefully spaced intervals.
Conceptualizing Broadly	Ashraf draws "semantic maps" with lines and arrows pictorially showing the linkages between words or concepts while learning Portuguese.
Conceptualizing with Details	Yoshinori learns Albanian words by breaking them down into their components.
Paying Attention	Amy pays close attention to the Korean language's politeness features so she can appropriately address Koreans of different ages.
	Vicky listens attentively to the speech of Bantu speakers so that she can use the correct expressions in ceremonial situations.
Interacting to Learn and Communicate	Omneya and Maia study German together, particularly before a major test.
Activating Supportive Emotions, Beliefs, and Attitudes	Charles gives himself encouragement through positive self-talk while preparing to give a presentation in Swahili about Tanzanian education.
Reasoning	Marco makes deductions about English based on grammar rules he already knows.
Activating Knowledge	Jing and Irina brainstorm the technical English vocabulary and the examples they need when making a presentation on international conflict resolution.
Overcoming Knowledge Gaps in Communicating	While Irina presents what she is supposed to say, she cannot remember the term *bilateral negotiation*, so she "talks around" it, saying, "Both sides come together to talk about what they want," and thus she continues gaining speaking practice instead of stopping.

also checks her work extensively, using a variety of tactics associated with the metastrategies of Monitoring and Evaluating, while Becca does not take the time. Becca's written work is not as polished as Milli's because of the limited Planning-, Monitoring-, and Evaluating-related tactics she uses but, on the other hand, her pervasive spontaneity is sometimes helpful for L2 speaking.

Self-regulated L2 learners frequently use a *strategy-tactic chain*, which is a set of organized, sequential or interlocking strategies (Oxford, 1990, 2001), manifested in a given situation by specific tactics. Table 1.3 contains detailed examples of four different L2 learning strategy-tactic chains for different learners.

Chamot *et al.* (1996) presented a generic L2 learning strategy chain called the Problem-Solving Process Model: (a) Planning, (b) Monitoring, (c) Solving Problems (i.e., finding solutions to problems just identified), and (d) Evaluating. Rubin's (2001) Interactive Model of [L2] Learner Self-Management included the following strategy chain: Planning, Monitoring, Evaluating, Problem-Identification/Problem-Solution, and Implementation of Problem-Solution. This model integrates expert learners' knowledge base with strategies needed to manage and control learning. Weak L2 learners do not use effective learning strategy chains and often do not select appropriate strategies in the first place (Reiss, 1981, 1983; Vann and Abraham, 1989, 1990). Well-known strategy chains outside of the L2 field are found in Schoenfield's (1985) problem-solving process (Analyze, Explore, i.e., consider equivalent problems and break the problem into subgoals, and Verify) and DeCorte, Verschaffel, and Op'T Eynde's (2000) cognitive-metacognitive performance framework (Orient, Organize, Execute, and Verify).

1.3.11   Double utility of strategies in the S²R Model

The S²R Model asserts that learning strategies are useful for "ordinary" and "severe" L2 learning problems (*double utility of strategies*). Ordinary and severe problems are not dichotomous but are instead on a continuum. Relatively straightforward, expected, ordinary L2-learning problems are generally not fraught with emotional difficulties, but more complex, unexpected, severe L2-learning problems often involve or generate anxiety and have multiple cognitive issues that must be addressed. While both types of problems benefit from using multiple strategies, the second type often requires more strategies and more concerted effort. Let us consider examples involving two learners: José and Mari. José has a rather ordinary learning problem, while Mari has a more severe one.

José's L2 assigned learning task is to prepare for a discussion in English, his L2, and carry out that discussion with another learner. He does not feel overly stressed, because his problem is straightforward: how to prepare, how to maintain motivation, and how to speak and listen as effectively as

Table 1.3 Strategy-tactic chains showing tactics and associated strategies or metastrategies

COLUMN A WHOSE CHAIN	COLUMN B WHAT THE LEARNER DOES (TACTICS) IN THE PARTICULAR SITUATION AND FOR A SPECIFIC GOAL	COLUMN C STRATEGY OR METASTRATEGY ASSOCIATED WITH THE TACTIC
1. Luis' Chain	To improve his English speaking, Luis seeks out a native English speaker, Tom, to be a conversation partner after class.	Obtaining and Using Resources
	He practises his English with Tom several times a week.	Interacting to Learn and Communicate
	While in a conversation with Tom, Luis monitors his understanding of what Tom is saying.	Monitoring
	After a month, Luis evaluates whether he is now more comfortable than before when speaking English.	Evaluating
2. Madeline's Chain	Madeline sets the goal of reading a new geopolitics book in Russian.	Planning
	First she plans to get familiar with the book before going into the book deeply.	Planning
	In familiarizing herself with the book, she skims the table of contents and the index to find the main ideas contained in the book.	Conceptualizing Broadly
	She also uses the skimming to help her evaluate what she already knows in terms of content and vocabulary.	Evaluating
	She uses this information to decide how much time to allow for studying the content as she reads the book.	Planning
3. Aurelia's Chain	Aurelia's task is to read a lengthy news article in English, her second language, and to write a summary of it in English. She starts with thinking about the steps she must take.	Planning
	She skims the article for the main idea.	Conceptualizing Broadly
	She scans the article for specific examples or evaluative words.	Conceptualizing with Details
	She takes notes verbatim for a little while.	Conceptualizing with Details
	She considers whether taking notes verbatim is helping. Actually, it seems to be taking too long and does not appear to be a good way to proceed right now.	Monitoring

Table 1.3 Strategy-tactic chains showing tactics and associated strategies or metastrategies (continued)

COLUMN A WHOSE CHAIN	COLUMN B WHAT THE LEARNER DOES (TACTICS) IN THE PARTICULAR SITUATION AND FOR A SPECIFIC GOAL	COLUMN C STRATEGY OR METASTRATEGY ASSOCIATED WITH THE TACTIC
3. Aurelia's Chain (Continued)	In an instant, she plans a better way: prioritizing the most important things to focus on as she takes notes.	Planning
	In her new note-taking, she focuses on (a) who, what, when, and why and (b) the topic sentence in each paragraph.	Conceptualizing with Details
	She then summarizes what she has learned in the prior steps and puts it into the best summary form she knows.	Conceptualizing Broadly
	She evaluates the summary against expected standards.	Evaluating
4. Helmut's Chain	Helmut has a writing task that involves looking up new words in an L1–L2 dictionary. He first evaluates prior strategies he used in doing this, considering which of these strategies worked and which caused problems.	Evaluating
	He considers any problems he might have this time and plans how to handle them.	Planning
	He thinks about the parts of speech and recognizes the one he needs to seek when looking up a particular word.	Conceptualizing with Details
	He compares all the definitions given for that particular word.	Conceptualizing with Details
	He compares collocations (words that generally go along with the target word) in the L1 and the L2.	Conceptualizing with Details
	He predicts the definition that might be the most useful and the collocations he might need.	Going Beyond the Immediate Data
	As he copies the word, he checks to make sure he is doing it correctly.	Monitoring
	He checks his predictions (see above) during the task.	Monitoring
	He checks to make sure that the word makes sense in the sentence generated.	Monitoring
	At the end of the writing task, he evaluates how well he has done.	Evaluating

Note: Macaro termed the actions in Example 4, Column B *strategies*, but in the current system they are highly specific *tactics* reflecting strategies or metastrategies (Column C).

possible. He employs the metacognitive strategy of Planning, using this tactic: "I plan to review relevant vocabulary one hour before and then 15 minutes before the discussion." He also uses the metacognitive strategy of Paying Attention by means of the tactic: "I pay very close attention to my discussion partner's main points, so I can understand and respond well." He deploys the affective strategy of Generating and Maintaining Motivation by using the tactic: "I pretend I am having a chat with my best friend."

In Mari's case, the task is more difficult, and the problem is experienced as much more severe. Mari, a native English speaker, is studying advanced German and political science in a German university. To prepare a very important paper in German on the topic of immigration reform in the European Union, her task is to synthesize information from many different, conflicting sources written in German. She feels cognitively overwhelmed and confused, as well as fearful. She thinks she cannot do the work and is thinking of giving up on the paper, although that would be a disastrous step academically. She is in a crisis mode, but she believes that she can help herself by means of strategies and tactics. Mari first turns the situation around with the strategy of Activating Supportive Emotions, Beliefs, and Attitudes, specifically with this tactic: "I act as though the contradictions are my favourite part of the research, and I decide to highlight them in the paper." After this, she is able to employ the metacognitive strategy of Paying Attention, applying it by means of the tactic: "I pay close attention to the conflicting information in order to find the main contrasting viewpoints." Keeping in mind the cognitive strategy of Going Beyond the Immediate Data, she uses the tactic: "I speculate on the possible reasons why the various experts have reached widely different conclusions." She also asks for help by means of the tactic, "I ask Horst, my German boyfriend, to verify my speculations and to help me express my ideas more clearly," which reflects the SI strategy of Interacting to Learn and Communicate. By using these tools, Mari regulates her own learning. She learns much more, experiences far greater control over the research and writing process, and regains confidence. Because of these steps, she performs excellently on the paper. Thus, strategies and tactics can help with very serious learning situations, such as Mari's, as well as with less difficult ones, such as José's.

1.3.12 Relationship of styles and strategies in the S²R Model

Learning styles are the learner's general, preferred, or habitual approach to learning. A learning style is often expressed by an adjective (e.g., visual style or extroverted style), while a learning strategy is an action and should always be expressed using some form of a verb, e.g., Planning, and a tactic is a specific action in a highly particular situation for a given need and (at least in this book) is expressed by a longer description (see Concept 1.10). The learner can become conscious of his or her own present

Concept 1.10 Common learning style domains, aspects, definitions/comments, and examples of relevant tactics and strategies

Style domains	Style aspects in each domain	Definitions and comments	Examples of a relevant tactic and an associated strategy	
			A tactic related to the style aspect	Strategy that corresponds to the tactic
Sensory-style domain	Visual style	Prefers to take in (perceive) information through sight. "I see what you mean."	I remember the Arabic words about diplomacy by creating mental pictures to represent them.	Using the Senses to Understand and Remember
	Auditory style	Prefers to take in information through sound. "I hear what you're saying."	I use tapes to compare my pronunciation of the Federico García Lorca poem to that of a native Spanish speaker.	Using the Senses to Understand and Remember
	Hands-on (kinesthetic-tactile) style	Prefers to take in information through touch or movement. "I grasp it," "I get it," "This moves me" or even (humorously) "This tickles me."	I practise my Russian vocabulary for Unit 9 while working out on the treadmill.	Using the Senses to Understand and Remember
Social-style domain	Extroverted style	Prefers to gain energy from people and activities; likes to work with others.	I meet with Laura and Roberto to study German this Tuesday.	Interacting to Learn and Communicate
	Introverted style	Gets energy from inner thoughts and feelings; likes to work alone or with one other person.	I work alone to study the seven Khmer infixes, because being alone allows me to think more deeply and reason things out.	Reasoning

Processing-style domain			
Analytic style	Systematically breaks information down into parts to understand or show relationship among the parts.	I analyse the essay by Montaigne to determine the main argument and the evidence he gives.	Conceptualizing with Details
Combinatory (synthesis-oriented) style	Systematically brings parts together in a combination or synthesis to understand or reveal the big picture.	I skim the Czech story very quickly to get the main idea before reading it more carefully.	Conceptualizing Broadly
Concrete-sequential style	Prefers concrete facts, other-directed, step-by-step; does not want too many choices; likes to have an authority figure.	I closely follow the steps in the Japanese assignment and the specific grading criteria the teacher provides.	Paying Attention
Abstract-intuitive style	Prefers abstract theories and multiple possibilities; often nonsequential; prefers to make own rules; does not want authority figures.	Based on many examples of a given structure that I encounter, I figure out the grammar rule in Hungarian. It's not as interesting when someone else tells me the rules.	Reasoning
Closure-oriented style	Needs quick decisions; prefers to work toward specific deadlines; more serious than playful.	I set clear goals for studying Dari during this week, April 4–10, and check how well I fulfill them.	(a) Planning and (b) Evaluating
Open style	Prefers to keep decisions open and continue taking in information; dislikes deadlines; more playful than serious.	I care more about enjoying the Hebrew lesson with my pal Andrew than about meeting any artificial deadlines.	Interacting to Learn and Communicate

Notes: An immature version of the analytic style is the *hyperfocused* style, which likes small pieces of information, is hyperfocused on details but not relationships between details, and avoids systematic analysis, while an immature version of the combinatory style is the *overly fuzzy* style, which prefers no analysis and few details, accepts only highly general information, and ignores any need for accuracy (Oxford, Massey, and Anand, 2005).

Source: Expanded from Oxford (2003a).

cluster of learning styles by means of general self-reflection or by taking a learning style survey. Some aspects of a given learner's styles – especially introverted/extroverted, concrete-sequential/abstract-intuitive, and closure-oriented/open – can be influenced by the sociocultural context, the subject area, and the learner's level of expertise and are therefore not fixed throughout the lifespan. A welcoming sociocultural context might cause a learner to prefer lots of interaction, while a rejecting or indifferent sociocultural context might influence the same learner to prefer to work alone and be silent (Norton, 2010). A learner might prefer deadlines in courses in international relations but, in another field, like learning French, want to keep taking in information for much longer. In other words, although the learner might have some strong style tendencies, they are not set in stone and are influenced by the sociocultural context.

1.4   Nine ways the S²R Model is different

In this chapter we have discussed many aspects of the S²R Model of L2 learning, and subsequent chapters offer still more aspects. In comparison to other strategy-related models of L2 learning, this model opens up new doors in nine ways. The S²R Model systematically integrates three major traditions of learning theory and research: psychological, social-cognitive, and sociocultural. The psychological tradition of strategies is very diverse, including strategies as related to schema (mental structure) development, comprehension, cognitive information-processing, metacognition, motivation, emotion, and beliefs (this chapter and Chapters 2 and 3). The social-cognitive strand deals with strategies as associated with task-phases, self-efficacy, and social comparisons (this chapter). The sociocultural tradition involves strategies (often called "higher mental functions" or "operations") as linked with mediated learning, instrumental enrichment, the ZPD, communities of practice, and cognitive apprenticeship (this chapter and Chapter 4).

Second, the S²R Model provides a better balance of dimensions than many prior learning strategy models. This model overtly recognizes that L2 learning is not just a cognitive/metacognitive process but is also influenced by a complex web of beliefs, emotional associations, attitudes, motivations, sociocultural relationships, personal interactions, and power dynamics. Therefore, sufficient attention must be paid to affective strategies and meta-affective strategies (Chapter 3) and socio-interactive strategies and meta-SI strategies (Chapter 4), as well as cognitive and metacognitive strategies, which often garner the most attention (Chapter 2).

Third, the S²R Model introduces not just metacognitive but also meta-affective and meta-SI strategies as part of a new and important concept, metastrategies, discussed earlier in this chapter. The use of metastrategies, which include but are not limited to metacognitive strategies, makes good sense semantically, logically, and theoretically.

Fourth, the S²R Model states that metastrategies, such as Planning, Organizing, Monitoring, and Evaluating, are naturally usable at either the task level or the whole-process level. Several social-cognitive models of self-regulated learning view these as only related to a particular task-phase (e.g., strategies used before, during, and after the task), but the current chapter says otherwise.

Fifth, the S²R Model underscores the importance of deep processing strategies, as opposed to surface strategies, as noted in this chapter. Other models do not necessarily discuss the difference between deep processing strategies and surface strategies.

Sixth, the S²R Model mentions "double utility" of strategies and metastrategies. Double utility means that they can be used in situations involving ordinary learning problems or circumstances marked by severe or crisis-like learning problems.

Seventh, the S²R Model includes the fewest strategies and metastrategies (a total of 19) needed for self-regulated L2 learning; therefore, the model can be viewed as scientifically elegant. At the same time, the model's inclusion of tactics allows for tremendous flexibility and adaptability. As explained in this chapter, tactics are the very particular applications of strategies or metastrategies in real-life situations for specific purposes and needs. Tactics can often be "chained" or smoothly interlocked for best effect, building on my concept of strategy chains (Oxford, 1990). The way tactics fit into activity theory is portrayed in Chapter 2.

Eighth, the S²R Model pays close attention to the neurological elements of L2 learning and to cognitive load, which most L2 strategy models do not adequately discuss. Chapters 2 and 3 show why these elements are important and how they relate to strategies.

Finally, the S²R Model embraces a large number of valuable techniques for assessing L2 learning strategies and assisting learners in expanding their strategy repertoire. Some of these techniques have not been included in prior published discussions of L2 learning strategies. All of these aspects make the S²R Model different from other strategy models and an enhancement to the field of L2 learning strategies.

1.5   Conclusion

This chapter has focused on the Strategic Self-Regulation (S²R) Model of L2 learning. This model, with its rich interdisciplinarity, echoes Bakhtin's (1998) concept of *heteroglossia*, which is defined as a multiplicity of voices, dialects, styles, vocabularies, and idioms shared among people. The model is intentionally heteroglossic, echoing the voices and vocabularies of different viewpoints, such as psychological, social-cognitive, and sociocultural. At the same time it is a unified, logically coherent system. I have used and tested the evolving S²R Model in my teaching of international graduate students for the last six years.

The S²R Model deserves further empirical testing in sociocultural contexts around the world, although most of its component theories and aspects have been widely researched and accepted within educational psychology, as shown in Chapters 2 through 4. Each of those chapters examines one dimension of L2 learning and of self-regulated L2 learning strategies, reveals many examples of relevant strategies and tactics in action, and presents supporting theories and research. All the strategies and tactics included in this book come from actual learners.

Further reading

Boekaerts, M., Pintrich, P.R., and Zeidner, M. (2000) *Handbook of Self-Regulation*. San Diego, CA: Academic Press. This book reveals and dissects the close ties between strategies and self-regulation in education, psychology, and other areas, with strategies mentioned or emphasized in almost all learning-related chapters. See especially chapters by Zimmerman; Pintrich; and Weinstein, Husman, and Dierking.

Cohen, A. and Macaro, E. (eds) (2007) *Language Learner Strategies: Thirty Years of Research and Practice*. Oxford: Oxford University Press. This landmark book explores the field of L2 learning strategies over the last three decades of research and practice. Some of the chapters push strategy theory into the sociocultural arena and explore critiques of L2 learning strategy research and theory.

Griffiths, C. (ed.) (2008) *Lessons from Good Language Learners*. Cambridge: Cambridge University Press. This book explores strategies along with motivation, aptitude, and other learner factors and presents updates on research on all the major language skill areas. The skill-related chapters can be read in parallel with those in Cohen and Macaro (2007).

Kozulin, A., Gindis, B., Ageyev, V.S. and Miller, S.M. (2003) *Vygotsky's Educational Theory in Cultural Context*. Cambridge: Cambridge University Press. Vygotsky's higher-order mental functions, which are very similar to learning strategies (McCaslin and Hickey, 2001), are well portrayed here, as are other key concepts in Vygotskyian theory.

Oxford, R.L. (1990) *Language Learning Strategies: What Every Teacher Should Know*. Boston, MA.: Heinle and Heinle/Cengage. This is a highly practical work on L2 learning strategies. It spurred much strategy research around the world and encouraged teachers to understand and foster learners' use of learning strategies.

Zimmerman, B.J. and Schunk, D. (eds) (2001) *Self-Regulated Learning and Academic Achievement*. Second edition. Mahwah, NJ: Erlbaum. This book presents a variety of theoretical and practical perspectives on self-regulated learning in academic settings and is essential reading.

Chapter 2

Dimension 1 (cognitive): Strategies for remembering and processing language

Learning without thought is labour lost.

Confucius

Preview questions

1. What is the relationship between metacognitive knowledge and metacognitive strategies?
2. How do metacognitive strategies help L2 learners manage their own learning?
3. Why are schemata important to L2 learning, and how do strategies affect schemata?
4. What is cognitive load, and what is its relationship to strategies?
5. How does neurobiology relate to metacognitive and cognitive learning strategies?

This chapter continues and deepens the S²R Model by presenting strategies in the cognitive dimension of L2 learning. Two types of strategies assist this learning dimension: metacognitive and cognitive strategies. Both types of strategies in this dimension are essential to learning at all levels of proficiency, even at the distinguished level (Anderson, 2008; Leaver, 2003a, 2003b; Leaver and Shekhtman, 2004). These strategies never lose their value for successful learners, who rely on the coordinated operation of metacognitive and cognitive strategies.

Table 2.1 shows how this chapter is organized. It starts with metaphors, moves into strategies, and then leads to relevant theories and concepts.

Table 2.1   Overview of this chapter

2.1   Linked metaphors for metacognitive and cognitive strategies: construction manager and construction workers

In the S²R Model, metacognitive strategies are, figuratively speaking, the "construction manager" whose job is to focus, plan, obtain resources, organize, coordinate, monitor, and evaluate the construction of L2 knowledge. Metacognitive strategies, if operating effectively, are the mind's masters that set guidelines and manage the creation of the L2 edifice. Metacognitive strategies include, among others, Planning for Cognition, Obtaining and Using Resources for Cognition, and Evaluating Cognition. These strategies are infused with metacognitive knowledge of various kinds: person, group or culture, task, whole-process, strategy, and conditional knowledge.

Cognitive strategies in the S²R Model include actions such as Using the Senses to Understand and Remember, Reasoning, and Going Beyond the Immediate Data. Such strategies might be called the "construction workers," who build internal mental frameworks (schemata) into increasingly elaborate, integrated, and automatic structures. Cognitive strategies thus directly facilitate the construction of the mental edifice of L2 language and culture. Optimally, cognitive strategies follow metacognitive guidance. Sometimes unmanaged cognitive strategies – the builders operating without supervision – can cause significant problems, like a ceiling falling in or a door being off its hinges (e.g., major academic or communication failures), and this can result in the need for significant repairs.

2.2 Metacognitive knowledge, metacognitive strategies, and metacognition

Chapter 1 explained six types of metaknowledge in the S²R Model: person, group or culture, task, whole-process, strategy, and conditional metaknowledge. As applied in the cognitive dimension, these six types can be collectively called *metacognitive knowledge*.

Metacognitive strategies, which manage cognitive aspects of L2 learning, are used by highly successful L2 learners around the world at all levels of proficiency. Even distinguished L2 learners continue to plan, organize, monitor, and evaluate their own learning (Leaver, 2003a). Metacognitive strategies are crucial for independent learners (Jacobsen, Maouri, Mishra, and Kolar, 1995; Rubin, 2001; White, 1995) and for classroom-based learners (Chamot, 2004; Oxford, 1990).

The eight metacognitive strategies include the following:

- *Paying Attention to Cognition*
- *Planning for Cognition*
- *Obtaining and Using Resources for Cognition*
- *Organizing for Cognition*
- *Implementing Plans for Cognition*
- *Orchestrating Cognitive Strategy Use*
- *Monitoring Cognition*
- *Evaluating Cognition.*

Some tactics associated with metacognitive strategies are as follows: (a) "I decide to focus my attention primarily on the prefixes of Russian verbs in the next week so that I can learn them efficiently," manifesting the strategy of Paying Attention to Cognition; (b) "If I focus only on strategies for *accuracy* in Turkish, I can hardly communicate because I try to be perfect; so I readjust my strategy use to balance fluency and accuracy," reflecting the strategy of Orchestrating Cognitive Strategy Use; and (c) "I look for and correct my mistakes while writing the three-page essay in French," revealing the strategy of Monitoring Cognition. The tactics are expressed in students' own words, not pared down to fit into an academic box. Each tactic addresses a particular student's situation and need.

One of the most widely researched metacognitive strategies is Monitoring Cognition. Forms of Monitoring Cognition include checking for one's own errors; making judgements about how easy the learning was, whether one has learned, and how confident one is about the learning; and assessing feelings of knowing (Nelson and Narens, 1994). Monitoring and other metacognitive strategies, along with a vast range of tactics, are found in Appendix I.A, found at the end of Section I.

Metacognition consists of *metacognitive knowledge* and *metacognitive regulation* (Flavell, 1979), as seen in Figure 2.1. When knowledge and strategies cooperate effectively, metacognition is at its finest.

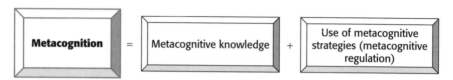

Figure 2.1   Metacognition and its components

Quote 2.1 Metacognition

Metacognition is often considered to be the highest level of mental activity, involving knowledge, awareness, and control of one's lower level cognitive skills, operations and strategies. . . .

Alex Kozulin (2005, p. 2)

2.3   Cognitive strategies

As construction workers, cognitive strategies aid the learner in putting together, consolidating, elaborating, and transforming knowledge of the language and culture. *Cognition* refers to the mental process or faculty of knowing, including aspects such as awareness, perception, reasoning, and certain kinds of judgements. The S²R Model contains six cognitive strategies:

- *Using the Senses to Understand and Remember*
- *Activating Knowledge*
- *Reasoning*
- *Conceptualizing with Details*
- *Conceptualizing Broadly*
- *Going Beyond the Immediate Data.*

Some tactics associated with cognitive strategies include: (a) "I understand better when I look at the visible structure of the Spanish story," reflecting the strategy of Using the Senses to Understand and Remember;

(b) "I distinguish between more important and less important information that I read in Hungarian," echoing the strategy of Conceptualizing
with Details; and (c) "I use what I know about the topic – the upcoming
election in Andhra Pradesh – to predict what my Telegu-speaking friend
might say next," manifesting the strategy of Going Beyond the Immediate
Data. Appendix I.B, found at the end of Section I, shows a large range of
cognitive strategies and examples of related tactics.

2.4 Relevant theories and concepts

Below I present theories and concepts in which cognitive strategies and
metacognitive strategies (and associated tactics) play a role: (a) schema
theory, (b) cognitive information-processing theory, (c) activity theory,
(d) cognitive load theory, and (e) neurobiological aspects of cognition. The
S²R Model honours these seemingly diverse perspectives. In actuality, each
perspective offers something important that the other perspectives do not
address, so these views are not contradictory but complementary.

2.4.1 Schema theory

The first theory, schema theory, helps us understand learning strategies and
concept development. Concept 2.1 on page 48 explains how strategies are
related to schema theory.

   The strategies of Paying Attention and Organizing are highly useful
in initially developing schemata. The first of these helps learners focus,
and the second helps learners link new information with what they already
know.

2.4.2 Cognitive information-processing theory

The second perspective, cognitive information-processing theory as
applied to L2 learning (O'Malley and Chamot, 1990), coordinates with
schema theory, because schemata are built in the first and second stages
of cognitive information-processing and fully automatized in the third
stage. The strategies named above for schema theory are directly relevant
to stages one and two of cognitive information-processing. A key goal of
cognitive information-processing theory is to transform (conscious, effortful)
declarative knowledge to (unconscious, automatic) procedural knowledge
(Anderson, 1985, 1990, 1993). Concept 2.2 on page 49 depicts the stages in
the cognitive information-processing model with clearer terminology than
in John Anderson's original model from the Adaptive Control of Thought
(ACT) theory. Anderson's technical terms for the first and third stages are

Concept 2.1   **Schema theory and strategies**

- A *schema* (plural = *schemata*) is a mental structure by which the learner organizes information. A schema contains the learner's knowledge on a certain topic and the organized interrelationships among components of that knowledge (Chi, Glaser, and Rees, 1982).
- Schema theory suggests that the very act of organizing information makes the material more memorable (Mandler, 2001).
- Movement of information from short-term memory (STM) to long-term memory (LTM) involves building schemata, elaborating them and making them more flexible, and calling on these schemata often for practice and authentic use.
- It is helpful to organize information in *categories*, with larger categories containing more detailed information (Mandler, 2001).
  - This effort unites the learning strategies of (a) Organizing and (b) Conceptualizing Broadly, resulting in higher-level chunks of information that are simpler to remember.
  - If the learner labels a chunk (category) of information meaningfully ("all the words about weather" or "Japanese expressions for interaction with older, respected people"), this helps strengthen the retrieval cues for remembering the category in general and the more detailed information inside it.
  - "Chunking" reduces cognitive load (Paas, Renkl, and Sweller, 2004; see later), thus freeing working memory for other uses.
  - It can be helpful to place the most relevant information into one mental chunk and the less important information into a different one (using the strategies such as Paying Attention and Conceptualizing with Details), and then focus only on the first chunk, at least at the current time.
- Organizing information in memorable *sequences* or *strings* (Mandler, 2001) can also be valuable. This is useful for terms and sayings that always go in the same order. It also applies to the words and sentences in a dialogue that must be memorized. Sequences or strings can be learned via Using the Senses to Understand and Remember (e.g., through sounds and images or through other strategic means).
- Of course, information can also be learned in nonsequential ways by making associations via any of a host of strategies: Conceptualizing with Details, Conceptualizing Broadly, Reasoning, and Using the Senses to Understand and Remember.
- To use L2 information, it must be pulled from STM or LTM into working memory (Leaver *et al.*, 2005).
  - Repeated use of L2 information is essential for learning (Leaver *et al.*, 2005).
  - Use of the information elaborates schemata through richer associations and can eventually make them automatic.

Concept 2.2   Stages in cognitive information-processing: New L2 knowledge, moving from declarative to procedural, and the relationship to strategies and tactics at each stage

Stage	Characteristics of this stage	Nature of strategies and tactics in this stage
1. Declarative knowledge stage	Learner encounters new L2 information. Knowledge of the new L2 information is *static, conscious, effortful, halting, nonhabitual, and expressible in words.*	Learner uses strategies and tactics to aid in noticing, taking in, integrating (into schemata, i.e., mental frameworks) the information, which is called declarative knowledge.
2. Associative stage	*Practice* of the new L2 information occurs. Learner practises the new L2 information, combines it in new ways, and thereby *strengthens and expands the schemata.* The new L2 information becomes increasingly familiar and much easier to use. It is becoming partly proceduralized.	Learner uses strategies and tactics to practise the new L2 information and associate it more strongly with what is already in memory.
3. Procedural knowledge stage	Knowledge of the new L2 information *is dynamic, unconscious, effortless, automatic, habitual, and tacit (difficult or impossible to express in words).* It is now second nature to the learner, part of himself or herself. It is fully proceduralized. (Note: In a fully functioning system, new declarative L2 knowledge on other topics or in other areas is probably being encountered and integrated at this time.)	Strategies and tactics are *no longer needed* for this L2 information, which has become automatic and habitual. The information is now called procedural knowledge.

A very basic example: How *il y a* is learned

Tactic: I place French [L2] sounds in a sentence with the English [L1] meaning: "There is Ilya" to remember the French phrase *il y a*, which means "there is." At first this takes effort and thought (declarative knowledge), but it soon becomes automatic through practice.

confusing. He uses the term *cognitive* to label the first stage, although this term also refers to the entire cognitive information-processing model. He employs the term *autonomous* to refer to the automaticity of the third stage, although in education and philosophy that term has many different meanings unrelated to Anderson's usage. Therefore, I have clarified the terminology while adopting the general structure.

In this discussion, I do not go into Anderson's more recent version, Adaptive Control of Thought-Rational (ACT-R), which asserts that a comprehensive "architecture" or framework for all cognition can be revealed neurologically (Anderson, Bothell, Byrne, Douglass, Lebiere, and Qin, 2004), although later in this chapter I mention how learning strategies and neurobiology fit together.

Stage 1: Gaining declarative knowledge

The first stage involves gaining *declarative knowledge*, which always involves effort. Declarative knowledge is "declarable" (speakable, identifiable) and is hence not automatic or outside of consciousness. It consists of *semantic knowledge* (facts, concepts, names, dates, rules) and *episodic knowledge* (based on memory of an event). A learning strategy can be a form of declarative knowledge if the learner can readily talk about it. Learners mentally organize and represent declarative knowledge as schemata. Such knowledge is easily lost if not practised and used. Consider an analogy: knowing about starting a car, backing up, and then driving off. At the first stage of cognition, this knowledge consists of declarative facts about the key, the ignition, the brake pedal, the gear shift, the accelerator, and so on. At this stage, the knowledge can be discussed by the learner as a set of details that are in conscious awareness, not mentally automatic.

Stage 2: Making deeper and stronger associations and correcting misinterpretations

At the second stage, learners build up ever richer, more complex, and more elaborate mental frameworks or schemata. Also during this stage, mistakes and misinterpretations learned in the first stage are detected and eliminated, and associations are strengthened through practice (Anderson, 1985). At this stage, that which is being learned – whether L2 information or a new learning strategy – becomes more integral to the learner, but it has not become automatic. In the driving analogy, the learner is now practising turning the key, starting the ignition, putting the car into reverse, backing up, and driving off, and these steps are better coordinated. This process is not yet automatic or habitual, but it is becoming a sequence of linked actions and is no longer merely a set of discussable facts or abstract concepts about how to drive.

Stage 3: Making knowledge automatic (procedural)

At the third stage, knowledge that was once conscious and effortful has become unconscious, instantaneous, and habitual. Such knowledge now consists of effortless "if-then productions" that are completely out of awareness (i.e., "if X occurs, then do Y," O'Malley and Chamot, 1990). The third stage involves expertise and fluidity, not conscious thought. In the driving example, by this stage the person can jump into the car, turn the key, back up the car, and drive off, all done in the twinkling of an eye and without conscious thought. In the L2, use of procedural knowledge might occur in a routine, smooth, effortless conversation or the use of well rehearsed, fully learned phrases in an essay.

Possibilities. For a given learner, some areas of L2 knowledge might have progressed from the first stage to the second stage and then to the third stage. However, new L2 input keeps entering the system as declarative knowledge. The learner might be in the third stage for certain earlier information and the first stage for new information. The cycle continues as long as the learner actively accepts new knowledge and keeps on processing it. Thus, different aspects of the L2 "intake" can be at different stages of processing simultaneously. In a sociocultural analogy based on Vygotsky's (1978) theory, some of the information might be fully internalized while other information might be only partly internalized, with new information still coming in from the outside. Thus, the process is very dynamic.

Learning new L2 learning strategies or tactics. When a student learns a new learning strategy or tactic, the same declarative-to-procedural process occurs. For example, if the metacognitive strategy of Monitoring Cognition is used with great frequency, it can become a habit and is automatic (procedural knowledge). IMPORTANT: *When the strategy has become automatic through extensive practice, it is no longer a strategy but has instead been transformed into something else, which could be called an unconscious habit.* Some experts outside of the L2 field call this automatized action a *skill.* However, in the L2 field the term *skill* can too easily be confused with the general "skill area" of reading or speaking, so the term *skill* is replaced here by the term *habit*, referring to an action that was formerly effortful but has become unconscious, automatic, and habitual. See Concept 2.3 for two examples.

Strategic awareness as related to proceduralization and proficiency level. Interestingly, in some groups, advanced learners are less strategically aware than intermediate learners, because advanced learners have made strategies automatic and unconscious (Green and Oxford, 1995). This creates a curvilinear pattern of strategy use, with low use for low-proficiency learners, higher use for intermediate learners, and low use for advanced learners. (Linear correlations between strategy use and proficiency would miss this pattern.) However, Leaver (2003a) found that distinguished L2 learners, who had

Concept 2.3   New knowledge of *strategies and tactics,* moving from declarative to procedural knowledge, and the nature of strategies and tactics at each stage

Stage	Characteristics	Nature of strategies and tactics
1. Declarative knowledge stage	Knowledge of the *strategy or tactic* is static, conscious, effortful, halting, nonhabitual, and expressible in words.	Learner encounters a new strategy or tactic. To help with L2 learning, the strategy or tactic itself needs to be learned.
2. Associative stage	Practice of the *strategy or tactic* occurs. It becomes more familiar and increasingly easy to use.	Learner practises the new strategy or tactic on one or more tasks.
3. Procedural knowledge stage	Knowledge of the *strategy or tactic* is dynamic, unconscious, effortless, automatic, habitual, and tacit (difficult or impossible to express in words).	The strategy or tactic has become automatic and is *therefore no longer a strategy or tactic.* A (former) strategy or tactic that is habitual is called a *habit* in the S^2R Model.

Example 1:

"In my Spanish language textbook I saw the strategy of Monitoring. It made sense, of course, to monitor and correct my own work very carefully rather than waiting for the teacher to do it. I started using the tactic of daily monitoring my written Spanish homework for errors or misunderstandings after the intensive Spanish class. At first I had to think about it, but as I used the tactic more, it became easier and took less thought. Now I do it without even realizing I'm doing it."

Example 2:

"When I was at much lower levels of Ukrainian proficiency, I used to write down Ukrainian synonyms and collocations (words that normally go together in phrases for native speakers). It took a lot of work, but I came up with a great, detailed collection of synonyms and collocations. I intentionally practised these in speaking. Now I automatically collect synonyms and collocations and plug them into my memory somewhere, without even thinking about what I am doing. These important words and phrases are always ready to roll out for use when I speak. I can describe this process now because you specifically asked me about vocabulary learning, but most of the time it is a really helpful but unconscious thing."

been taught to optimize their strategies since the very beginning, continued consciously using metacognitive and cognitive strategies even at their high proficiency level. They were constantly aware of their strategies and used them well for strategic improvement of proficiency.

Bringing a former strategy (now a habit) back into action as a strategy. Sometimes it is possible for certain strategies that have become automatic (procedural knowledge) to move back to the stage of declarative knowledge (see Macaro, 2006). This can occur through personal reflection, spurred by any awareness-raising technique: class discussions, strategy questionnaire completion, think-aloud procedures, diaries or journals, and other types of activities that jog learners' memories about their habits of learning. Sometimes the question "How did you learn that?" can stimulate learners to examine an automatic, unconscious behaviour and bring it back into consciousness. It can occasionally be helpful to bring back to consciousness some former strategies when needed, as in the example of Joseph, to be discussed shortly.

2.4.3   Activity theory in relation to cognitive information-processing

The third perspective is Leontiev's (1981) activity theory, which helps us to understand certain cognitive and affective aspects of L2 learning and is related to cognitive information-processing. For Leontiev (1981), the unit of analysis is the *activity as a whole*.

> **Quote 2.2** Activity
>
> Activity . . . is the who, what, when, where, and why, the small recurrent dramas of everyday life, played on the stage of home, school, community, and workplace.
>
> Richard T. Donato and Dawn E. McCormick (1994, p. 455)

An activity serves to satisfy a human *need*, is thus based on a *motive*, and exists as action and action chains (Leontiev, 1974). (See Concept 2.4.) An activity contains the following elements (Leontiev, 1978):

- a *subject* or person;
- an *object* or goal;
- the *actions*, i.e., strategies employed to move toward the goal (Donato and McCormick, 1994);
- the *conditions* of the situation, task, person, and sociocultural context; and
- *operations*, or specific ways by which the actions are carried out, manifested, or implemented, depending on the conditions in given situations.

Concept 2.4   **How activity theory provides a useful context for terms in the S²R Model: An overview**

	Column A Terms used in activity theory	**Column B** Terms used in the S²R Model
	Subject (person)	Learner
A C T I V I T Y	Object (goal, aim)	Goal(s) [Also any problems or difficulties in the way of meeting those goals]
	Action or action chain to fulfill the object	Strategy or strategy chain (to meet the goals/solve the problems)
	Conditions (immediate situation or context), which can change	Conditions (immediate situation or context), which can change
	Operations (specific ways in which the action or action chain is carried out or manifested under the present conditions)	Tactics (specific ways in which the strategy or strategy chain is carried out or manifested under the present conditions)

Source: Column A is summarized from Leontiev (1974). Column B is original.

Operations are the same as *tactics* in the S²R Model. Just as actions (strategies) address goals, operations (or tactics) address conditions. In other words, choice of a specific tactic relates to the particular situation, task, or context.

The learner (*subject*) can choose among different possible goals (*objects*). An object or goal for any given learner "could range from full participation in a new culture to receiving a passing grade required for graduation" (Donato and McCormick, 1994, p. 455). An object or goal could be successfully reading a magazine article or a book chapter in the L2, writing an L2 essay for a scholarship or job application, or something more personal, such as making a new friend who speaks the L2 natively. Changing conditions cause changes in how an action (strategy) is implemented; these conditions can "realign" (Donato and McCormick, p. 455) the way the strategy is manifested in operations (tactics). Concept 2.5 and Figure 2.2 show how changing conditions alter what a learner named Joseph does to learn to read Spanish newspapers, and they also reveal the linkage between activity theory and cognitive information-processing (especially movement from declarative to procedural knowledge). In the example shown, the changing conditions are largely external or situational. However, changing conditions could also include internal learner factors, such as interest, degree of motivation, or energy level.

Concept 2.5 Components of Leontiev's activity theory with a focus on learning strategies and tactics over time

Background: *Joseph, the subject, has a need to become skilled in Spanish for his career. His strongest motive is to learn to read Spanish effectively. His current, immediate object (aim, goal) is to learn to read the Spanish newspaper with understanding. He performs an action (learning strategy = Going Beyond the Immediate Data, specifically guessing from the context) to move toward the object. The action is carried out under certain conditions, which governs the operations (the way he implements or manifests the action/strategy) at a given time. When conditions change, operations change. Column A influences Column B.*

Column A Condition under which the action occurs at a given time	Column B Operation (way the action is enacted, given the condition)
Time 1 (Monday): Reading an article. Joseph encounters words he does not know. He is not yet adept at guessing from context.	Joseph expends effort and consciousness to guess from context. The tactic is therefore a form of *declarative knowledge*.
Time 2 (Tuesday): Same thing happens with two more articles.	
Time 3 (Wednesday): Articles are at about the same level as Times 1 and 2, but Joseph is becoming more comfortable with guessing contextually as he reads two more articles on Wednesday.	He does not have to expend quite as much effort or thought as he continues to guess contextually. This tactic is still mostly in awareness (*declarative knowledge*), but it is becoming less conscious (*partly procedural knowledge*).
Times 4, 5, and 6 (Thursday, Friday, and Saturday): Articles are at about the same level as before. He is fully adept at guessing contextually while reading six more articles during these three days.	He guesses from the context automatically. This is now a habit or skill, i.e., *procedural knowledge*.
Time 7 (Sunday): *Condition changes!* A new article is much more difficult and has many long, complex words. He cannot merely guess without effort.	He remembers that he used to guess from the context. Now he does it again, with consciousness and effort. It is again – temporarily – *declarative knowledge*.
Time 8 and beyond (after Sunday): *Condition changes!* Articles are not so difficult. He is fully adept at guessing contextually.	He guesses new words automatically. It is again *procedural knowledge*.

Note: The relationship between learning strategies and activity theory comes from Oxford and Schramm (2007). Thanks to Donato and McCormick (1994) for their ideas about conceptual guessing in light of activity theory.
Note: In this table, I link activity theory (subject, action, object, condition, operation) with cognitive information-processing (declarative and procedural knowledge). For pictorial details, see Figure 2.2.

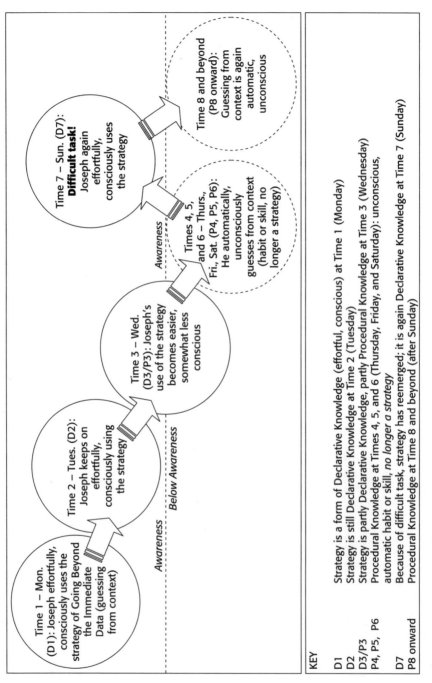

Figure 2.2 Joseph's changing patterns of strategy use (explained by activity theory, declarative knowledge, and procedural knowledge)

2.4.4   Cognitive load theory

Cognitive load theory (Chandler and Sweller, 1992; Sweller, 2005) suggests that several types of *cognitive load* exist. Cognitive load can be either positive or negative (see Concept 2.6). *Intrinsic cognitive load* refers to the number of information elements and their interconnectedness; it is related to the innate complexity of the information to be learned. *Non-intrinsic cognitive load* consists of two forms, *germane cognitive load* and *extraneous cognitive load*, the former of which is helpful and the latter of which is deleterious (Clark, Nguyen, and Sweller, 2005). Concept 2.6 not only defines the types of cognitive load but also indicates how L2 learning strategies and tactics (metacognitive and cognitive) can help the learner with them.

2.4.5   Neurobiology, metacognitive strategies, and cognitive strategies

Many brain areas, as well as learning strategies, are involved in different aspects of L2 learning and processing. Brain areas for perception and attention, both essential for L2 learning, are linked to the cognitive strategy of Using the Senses to Understand and Remember and the metacognitive strategy of Paying Attention. The parietal, temporal, and occipital lobes of the brain control perception. (See Figure 2.3.) In a visual processing task, paying attention to key information was linked to activation of relevant, right frontal-parietal regions but the deactivation of irrelevant, left temporal-limbic areas, and those who did not pay attention or

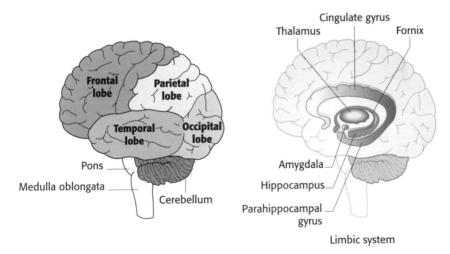

Figure 2.3   Simplified anatomy of the brain, exterior and interior

Concept 2.6 Types of cognitive load and how L2 learning strategies relate to them

Type of cognitive load	How L2 learning strategies and tactics relate to these types
Intrinsic – load imposed by the number of information elements and their interactivity (interconnectedness). Intrinsic cognitive load is often known as "complexity" or "difficulty" of what is to be learned.	The learner cannot change intrinsic cognitive load but can handle it effectively. **Examples of tactics:** Soraya figures out that the task of writing the essay can be broken down into a series of parts, such as brainstorming ideas, outlining, writing, checking, revising, and so on. These tactics come from the following strategies: Planning for Cognition; Conceptualizing with Details. After implementing her plan, she evaluates her use of strategies for reducing the load and also checks the quality of her writing. These tactics come from the strategy of Evaluating Cognition.
Non-intrinsic Germane – positive load imposed by tasks or materials that help with the learner's schema development and automation.	Germane cognitive load can be increased by combining the senses to process the information (cf. Cooper, 1998). **Example of tactic:** Czech-learner Myron watches a Czech film drama with the help of closed-captioning. He receives help in understanding Czech through sounds and two kinds of visual input, screen images and print. This tactic manifests the strategy of Using the Senses to Understand and Remember.
Extraneous – negative load imposed by tasks or materials that do not help with the learner's schema development and automation. A key element of extraneous cognitive load is split attention, which occurs when the tasks or materials are poorly designed, forcing learners to pay attention to irrelevant information.	Extraneous cognitive load can be managed by means of strategies and tactics. **Example of tactic:** The Italian language-learning computer program Graeme is using is ill-designed because of too many graphics and animations, splitting his attention. Graeme sets aside information irrelevant to what he is learning, especially ignoring the animations. This tactic reflects the strategy of Paying Attention to Cognition.

Source: Based on theories by Paas, Renkl, and Sweller (2004).

activate/deactivate appropriately performed more poorly on the task (Lawrence, Ross, Hoffman, Garavan, and Stein, 2003). Lawrence *et al.* hypothesized that "two independent [neurological] circuits" for activation and deactivation might be involved.

Tucked deep in the limbic system, the hippocampus helps convert information from STM to LTM, passes information to other parts of the limbic system and elsewhere in the brain, and helps create mental coherence among perceptual, spatial, and cognitive representations (McClelland, McNaughton, and O'Reilly, 1995). Cognitive and metacognitive strategies to help convert L2 information from STM to LTM, such as Using the Senses to Understand and Remember, Conceptualizing Broadly, and Paying Attention, were mentioned earlier.

Declarative language input activates the frontal cortex and the temporal cortex and is strengthened through a trace-transfer-consolidation process below the cortex (subcortical), after which declarative memories loop back to the cortical areas. Procedural memory, or memory of "how to" without conscious declarative knowledge, also occurs in cortical and subcortical areas but in a different route. See cognitive information-processing earlier. Memories are stored in specific locations and connected through networks. In recall – when the learner needs to call up the learned information for actual use later – the information is reconstructed, though not necessarily through the same processes as were initially used for putting the information into long-term memory.

Higher cognition, such as abstract thought, operates in the prefrontal cortex (frontal lobe) but has linkages elsewhere in the brain. Some relevant cognitive strategies are Reasoning, including inductive and deductive; Conceptualizing with Details, including analysing and comparing; and Conceptualizing Broadly, including synthesizing and summarizing. General management or executive control processes (e.g., metacognitive strategies like Evaluating and Planning) operate in the frontal lobe (prefrontal cortex) of the brain but with linkages to deeper, motivation-related components, such as the amygdala, located within the temporal lobes. The quotation below indicates the neurobiological aspect of metacognition, but be aware that metacognition can also be intentionally developed.

Quote 2.3 Neurobiology of metacognition

The general assumption is that impaired metacognitive processes are related to frontal lobe damage...

Asher Koriat (2002, p. 266)

2.4.6   Synthesis of theories and concepts

The theories and concepts in this section are different ways of looking at L2 phenomena and are linked in multiple ways. For instance, uniting related schemata into smaller numbers of categories can reduce cognitive load while making the schemata stronger and more elaborate and eventually automatic (procedural knowledge). The cognitive information-processing paradigm is a step-by-step description of this process, starting with declarative knowledge and moving to procedural knowledge. Changing conditions can cause alteration in the choice of tactics to use at a given moment, according to activity theory. Neurobiological theories reveal the activation of different brain components for various L2 learning purposes and involving different strategies. Thus, this chapter has contained a web of interlocking theories, all of which are relevant to the S²R Model.

2.5   Conclusion

This chapter portrayed metacognitive strategies as the construction manager of L2 learning. Such strategies help the learner concentrate attention, plan, gather resources, organize, monitor, and evaluate, using metacognitive knowledge as a basis. Cognitive strategies, the construction workers, directly build up and elaborate schemata and aid in making them automatic and effortless. Metacognitive and cognitive strategies are essential for L2 learning at multiple levels of proficiency and are a necessary part of the S²R Model.

Further reading

Macaro, E. (2006) Strategies for language learning and for language use: revising the theoretical framework. *Modern Language Journal*, 90(3): 320–337. This is a highly cognitive approach to L2 learning strategies. It is an interesting and important attempt at theory-building, though it could have given more attention to the socio-cultural context.

O'Malley, J.M. and Chamot, A.U. (1990) *Learning Strategies in Second Language Acquisition.* Cambridge: Cambridge University Press. This book helped establish cognitive information-processing as an important theoretical framework for L2 learning strategies but paid less attention to affective and social aspects of L2 learning.

Wenden, A.L. (1998) Metacognitive knowledge and language learning. *Applied Linguistics*, 19(4): 515–537. This is a valuable update and expansion of Wenden's earlier work on metacognitive knowledge. It emphasizes three types of metacognitive knowledge, whereas the current book identifies six.

Chapter 3

Dimension 2 (affective): Strategies linked with emotions, beliefs, attitudes, and motivation

When it is obvious that the goals cannot be reached, don't adjust the goals, adjust the action steps.

Confucius

Preview questions

1. What are meta-affective strategies, and what forms of meta-affective knowledge support them?
2. What is the difference in purpose of meta-affective strategies and affective strategies in the S²R Model?
3. What problems exist regarding emotions, beliefs, and attitudes in L2 learning?
4. What are major motivational issues in L2 learning?
5. How can learners deal strategically with emotions, beliefs, attitudes, and motivation in L2 learning?

Affect plays a key role in L2 learning in the S²R Model. Affect, which consists of emotions, beliefs, attitudes, and motivation, is integral to all learning (Damasio, 1994; LeDoux, 1996; Wolters, 2003). Affect interacts closely with cognition at many learning stages, and this is particularly true in L2 learning, which is an adventure of the whole person rather than merely a cognitive exercise (Oxford and Burry-Stock, 1995).

Eight *meta-affective strategies* allow L2 learners to be aware of and manage their affect in general terms, while two *affective strategies* help L2 learners directly promote positive emotions, beliefs, and attitudes and initiate and maintain motivation. Wolters (2003) called for considering a possible "meta" level that controls affective strategies. To my knowledge, Wen Quifang (1996, 2003) was the first to actually use the term *meta-affective strategies*, but only in Chinese. I view meta-affective strategies as very important. Just as cognitive strategies have metacognitive strategies to provide control (Chapter 2), affective strategies need meta-affective strategies to bring control. This chapter explains affective factors in L2 learning and the meta-affective and affective strategies that can help the learner deal with them.

Table 3.1 shows the organization of the rest of the chapter. It starts with metaphors, shifts to strategies, and presents theories and concepts related to strategies and affect.

Table 3.1 **Overview of this chapter**

3.1 Linked metaphors for meta-affective and affective strategies: electricity manager and electricity workers

3.2 Meta-affective knowledge, meta-affective strategies, and meta-affect

3.3 Affective strategies

3.4 Relevant theories and concepts
    3.4.1 Importance of affect in L2 learning
    3.4.2 Emotions, beliefs, and attitudes in relation to strategies
    3.4.3 Strategies in association with motivation, volition, and willingness to communicate
    3.4.4 Goals and strategies
    3.4.5 Neurobiology in relation to affect and strategies
    3.4.6 Synthesis of theories and concepts

3.5 Conclusion
    Further reading

3.1 Linked metaphors for meta-affective and affective strategies: electricity manager and electricity workers

In the S²R Model, *meta-affective strategies* can be viewed metaphorically as the "electricity manager," responsible for managing the electricity of L2 learning – the affective spark of emotions, feelings, attitudes, beliefs, and motivation that keep the L2 learner moving. The spark can go out, become dim, or be clouded over by difficulties. When this happens, the manager provides attention, planning, resources, organizational strength, orchestration, monitoring, and evaluation – whatever the situation requires.

Affective strategies can be seen as the "electricity workers" in the S²R Model. They operate optimally with the guidance of the manager. When the manager pinpoints an affective problem or need, the workers are alerted and can then take action. The main functions of the affective strategies are to create optimistic emotions, beliefs, and attitudes and to spur and maintain motivation. Through monitoring and evaluation, the manager checks whether workers have successfully done their job.

3.2   Meta-affective knowledge, meta-affective strategies, and meta-affect

As shown earlier, six types of metaknowledge (see Chapter 1) exist in the S²R Model: person, group or culture, task, whole-process, strategy, and conditional knowledge. When applied to the affective dimension, these forms of knowledge are called *meta-affective knowledge.*

Meta-affective strategies are needed because L2 learners are not just cognitive information-processing machines; instead, they are human beings with emotions, beliefs, attitudes, and motivations. Without meta-affective strategies, learners might be less likely to reflect on their affective needs and hence might not take the affective control that is often necessary for L2 learning, particularly in the early stages.

The eight meta-affective strategies include the following:

- *Paying Attention to Affect*
- *Planning for Affect*
- *Obtaining and Using Resources for Affect*
- *Organizing for Affect*
- *Implementing Plans for Affect*
- *Orchestrating Affective Strategy Use*
- *Monitoring Affect*
- *Evaluating Affect.*

Examples of tactics associated with meta-affective strategies are: (a) "I set the goal of finding ways to stay engaged and interested in my Czech learning when it gets difficult," associated with the strategy of Planning for Affect; (b) "I look for blogs and websites to learn more about reducing my anxiety in language learning," reflecting the strategy of Obtaining and Using Resources for Affect; and (c) "I needed to stay motivated and on task in French, so I told myself why I wanted to learn French (a positive approach) and what would happen if I didn't try hard enough (a negative or 'scare' approach)," which, altogether, reflects the strategy of Orchestrating Affective Strategy Use. Appendix I.C, found at the end of Section I, contains a detailed list of meta-affective strategies and associated tactics.

Meta-affect comprises *meta-affective knowledge* and *meta-affective regulation*, as Figure 3.1 indicates. Neither meta-affective knowledge nor meta-affective strategies can operate independently. They are synergistic.

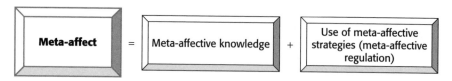

Figure 3.1   **Meta-affect and its components**

3.3   Affective strategies

The affective dimension is fundamental to living in general (Rogers, 1983) and to L2 learning (Horwitz, 2007). No one can learn a language without motivation, positive attitudes and beliefs, and supportive emotions. Affective strategies help learners directly optimize their emotions, beliefs, attitudes, and motivation for the purpose of L2 learning (O'Neil and Spielberger, 1979; Oxford, 1990). Affective strategies are particularly crucial for distance L2 learners, who do not have in-person support from a teacher or class (White, 1995), even if they have a mentor at a distance. These strategies are also important to L2 learners at lower levels, those with certain learning styles (particularly a style that emphasizes feelings and emotions), those dealing with generalized anxiety or depression, or those in any phase of culture shock.

There are two affective strategies in the S²R Model:

- *Activating Supportive Emotions, Beliefs and Attitudes*
- *Generating and Maintaining Motivation*

Tactics associated with affective strategies include, among others, the following: (a) "I remind myself that it helps my motivation to meditate fifteen minutes before starting to study Farsi each day," related to the strategy of Generating and Maintaining Motivation; (b) "When I am feeling negative about my ability in Italian, I think about the time I was at the Plaza d'Espana and talked for hours over wine and Italian ices," manifesting the strategy of Activating Supportive Emotions, Beliefs, and Attitudes; and (c) "When I compare my Danish pronunciation to the native pronunciation on the tape, I keep myself motivated (and not feeling deficient) by remembering that my pronunciation is usually comprehensible to Danish people," related to both of the affective strategies. See Appendix I.D, found at the end of this Section I, for a detailed list of affective strategies and related tactics.

Interestingly, a few tactics associated with affective strategies show "reverse psychology," in which negative thinking is used, like a blunt weapon, to force a positive affective result. An example is: "I make the Korean task much harder than it has to be by adding extra steps or more details. That way, if I bomb the task, I will have a very good excuse, but if I do well, I will feel great about myself and what I achieved." This is a form of *self-handicapping*. Some learners consider both protection from guilt (over bad performance) and a sense of pride (over good performance) to be positive, so they self-handicap as part of L2 learning.

3.4   Relevant theories and concepts

This section presents: (a) the importance of affect in L2 learning; (b) emotions, beliefs, and attitudes in relation to affective strategies; (c) strategies in association with motivation, volition, investment, and willingness to communicate; (d) goals and strategies; and (e) neurobiology in relation to affect and strategies. The first four are very strongly related to the S²R Model. The fifth is largely related, but the neurobiological theory of "mental foraging" needs futher exploration for its practical relevance link to the S²R Model.

Quote 3.1 Components of language learning

...[T]he affective component contributes at least as much [as] and often more...than the cognitive skills.

H.H. Stern (1983, p. 386)

3.4.1   Importance of affect in L2 learning

Learning a new language can be highly stressful and can challenge learners' views of themselves, especially in settings in which L2 communication is not just possible but necessary (Arnold, 1998; Stevick, 1989). Emotions "pervade all of our activities" (MacIntyre, 2002, p. 61) in L2 learning, and they can sometimes be troubling. The learner's emotions, beliefs, and attitudes have a strong influence on L2 learning motivation, which is also shaped by a host of contextual factors (Gardner and Lambert, 1972; Gardner, Tremblay, and Masgoret, 1997; Oxford and Shearin, 1994). All this makes the affective side of L2 learning a complex, challenging phenomenon that must be understood and worked with, rather than ignored. Meta-affective and affective strategies have an important role in helping learners deal with these complicated aspects of L2 learning. In a study of L2 learning crises, the learners who successfully emerged from the crises used meta-affective strategies, such as Monitoring Affect, in order to take control (Oxford, Meng, Zhou, Sung, and Jain, 2007). They also exhibited affective strategies, i.e., Generating and Maintaining Motivation or Activating Supportive Emotions, Beliefs and Attitudes, to lift themselves out of negative states, such as low L2 motivation, poor attitudes, language anxiety, anger, and frustration. Even in non-crisis situations, many L2 learners need these strategies (Oxford, 1990).

> **Quote 3.2** An unsettling psychological proposition
>
> The task of learning a new language is a profoundly unsettling psychological proposition.
>
> Alexander Guiora (1983, p. 8)

The misfortune of downplaying affect

However, not everyone believes that the affective dimension is very important to L2 learning or to learning in general. Diminution of the role of affect reflects longstanding philosophical arguments. Socrates and the Stoics argued that reason alone, without affect, is necessary for virtue (Homiak, 2007). Much later, Kant in 1788 virtually ignored affect, while hailing practical reason as crucial for selected men; he considered all women and many men incapable of reason (Kant, 1788/1997; Sullivan, 1989).

Jacobson and Faltis (1990, p. 24) mentioned a "significant problem" soon after L2 learning strategies emerged as a field: the serious neglect of affective strategies for L2 learning. This situation has not changed dramatically since that time, despite my urging (Oxford, 1990, 1996c, 2001). Few L2 strategy researchers have explored affective strategies in sufficient depth. Macaro (2006), despite his many excellent contributions to the L2 strategy field, downplayed the importance of affective strategies by suggesting that they are simply part of metacognition. I seriously tested Macaro's suggestion by trying to place affective and meta-affective strategies in the category of metacognitive strategies (where they would have to be if they were part of metacognition), but this created a long, heterogeneous list that was theoretically unsupportable.

Giving affect its due

Like Plato and Aristotle, I contend that both reason (a form of cognition) and affect are essential to virtue (Homiak, 2007). Like Piaget, I argue that affect and cognition are inextricably linked in learning.

Quote 3.3   Affective factors that accompany cognition

... [S]tates of pleasure, disappointment, eagerness, as well as feelings of fatigue, effort, boredom, etc., come into play [along with cognition].... [F]eelings of success or failure may occur; and finally the student may experience aesthetic feelings stemming from the coherence [of what is learned] ... Intrinsic or extrinsic interest is always evident. Perceptual activity, too, involves affective factors.

Jean Piaget (1981, p. 3)

My theory and research in the field of L2 learning, including the S²R Model, have consistently highlighted the importance of the affective dimension, along with the cognitive dimension and the social dimension (called the sociocultural-interactive dimension in the S²R Model). This model specifically includes affective and meta-affective strategies. It is very surprising that so few prior L2 learning strategy models have included affective strategies as a strong component. Many learners need affective learning strategies to deal with anxiety, frustration, low motivation, and uncertain self-efficacy. It is also striking that our field has not, until the publication of this book, included meta-affective strategies as an element in L2 learning, much less an important and systematic element. Meta-affective strategies help these learners plan, monitor, and evaluate what is happening in the affective dimension and take greater control.

3.4.2   Emotions, beliefs, and attitudes in relation to strategies

Emotions, beliefs, and attitudes can influence L2 learning and can be modified by strategies. This fact is important in the S²R Model.

Emotions in L2 learning

The myth that emotions are only a minor part of learning is one of the most amazing confabulations of all time, but it has seemed to influence research in our field. Of all L2 learners' emotional self-descriptions (see Table 3.2), in my view only *anxious* or worried has been deeply enough studied by L2 researchers (see, e.g., Horwitz and Young, 1991 and Horwitz, 2007). The self-description *interested* has been explored to some degree through L2 motivation research (Oxford and Shearin, 1994), and the self-description *confident* has been investigated through research on the Socio-Educational Model of L2 motivation (Gardner, 1988), willingness to communicate (MacIntyre, Clément, Dörnyei, and Noels, 1998), and L2 self-efficacy (National Capital Area Resource Center, 2000a, 2000b). However, most of the emotional self-descriptions of L2 learners have not been adequately

Table 3.2 Emotional self-descriptions on continua showing intensity and positive/negative axis

NAME OF CONTINUUM	INTENSITY (−3 TO +3)						
	−3	−2	−1	+1	+2	+3	
Fear/Relaxation	terrified	anxious	mildly apprehensive	calm	somewhat relaxed	very relaxed	
Boredom/Interest	world-weary	bored	indifferent	interested	engaged	fascinated	
Anger/Happiness	furious	angry, upset	annoyed, dissatisfied	accepting, satisfied	happy, pleased	delighted	
Shame/Pride	mortified	humiliated, ashamed	embarrassed	self-accepting	confident	proud	
		more negative			more positive		

Note: Of the emotional self-descriptions above, only *anxious* and *interested* have been well studied in the L2 field. The emotional term *confident* has been investigated to some extent through research on L2 self-efficacy and willingness to communicate. Most of the descriptions have not been adequately addressed, meaning that the research field is wide open for investigation. Especially useful would be research on the relationships among emotional self-descriptions, strategy use, and proficiency levels.

addressed through research. A potentially rich field of L2-related emotions awaits scholars who would like to conduct research. Especially useful would be research on the relationships among emotional self-descriptions, strategy use, and proficiency levels in a range of sociocultural contexts.

L2 learning anxiety

L2 learning anxiety (called *language anxiety*) is a distinct form of anxiety in which the learner is afraid of socially performing in the L2, especially speaking. Language anxiety has many negative repercussions for learning. For instance, anxiety freezes the cognitive effort of L2 learners (MacIntyre, 2002). Language anxiety is associated with "deficits in listening comprehension, impaired vocabulary learning, reduced word production, low scores on standardized tests, low grades in language courses or a combination of these factors" (Gardner, Tremblay, and Masgoret, 1997, p. 345). Language anxiety is tied to reduced willingness to communicate in the L2 (MacIntyre, 2003) and linked to other forms of avoidance, such as skipping classes and forgetting assignments. Language anxiety leads to damaged self-concept, "reduced personality," lowered self-confidence, diminished belief in the possibility of attaining proficiency, and a lowered sense of agency or control (Horwitz, 2007; Oxford, 1998).

As a form of social anxiety, language anxiety often shows physical symptoms, such as tense muscles, sinking sensations, dry throat, trembling, palpitations, twitching, stammering, and blushing (Shepherd, 2006). Though Alpert and Haber (1960) argued that a mild level of anxiety (so-called "facilitative anxiety") aids cognitive effort, this is more accurately called *tension*, not anxiety (Oxford, 1998). In my view, anxiety can more readily be viewed as debilitative or negative than in any sense facilitative. Anticipatory anxiety, manifested as *hyper-intention*, "produces precisely that of which the [person] is afraid" (Frankl, 1997, p. 123).

White (1995) noted distance L2 learners' stress and anxiety in the absence of personal support from a teacher, and she identified these learners' need for affective strategies. In a study of distance L2 learners, Hauck and Hurd (2005) found two useful affective tactics, self-encouragement to take risks and positive self-talk, but found that many of these learners do not have strategies (or tactics) to deal with their language anxiety. In contrast with Hauck and Hurd (2005), Shepherd (2006) argued that distance learning can socially protect anxious learners because it does *not* require face-to-face interactions.

Beliefs about self: self-esteem, self-efficacy, and self-concept

Self-esteem is the emotional self-perception of competence or self-worth in a given area or more generally. Naturally most people want to feel good about themselves (have high self-esteem). However, high self-esteem is not always linked with positive performance or good outcomes (Cole, 2003). Some people can feel positive about themselves even when performing poorly, and others can feel bad about themselves even when performing well. Low self-esteem can be addressed by using the affective strategy of Activating Supportive Emotions, Beliefs, and Attitudes. This strategy is reflected in tactics such as using positive self-talk or, on the other hand, telling oneself that failing in a given area is not harmful because the area is not important anyway.

Self-efficacy is defined as the person's level of confidence that he or she can successfully complete a task or a series of tasks (Bandura, 1997; Zimmerman, 1989, 1990). Self-efficacy is related to *agency*, i.e., belief in one's control over outcomes or being the cause of an effect. Bandura (1997) noted four influences on self-efficacy: (a) past experience of success or failure; (b) modelling (vicarious experience), in which observing a peer's success increases the observer's self-efficacy and observing a peer's failure lowers the observer's self-efficacy; (c) social persuasion, such as encouragement or discouragement from others; and (d) the person's belief about his or her body, such as interpreting physical symptoms of anxiety as a sign of low ability. Self-efficacy is often strengthened when learners use L2 learning strategies (Chamot, Barnhardt, El-Dinary, and Robbins, 1996; Zimmerman and Martinez-Pons, 1990). Virtually *any* strategy that helps an individual have better learning performance can indirectly improve perceptions of self-efficacy and agency. In addition, the affective strategy of Activating Supportive Emotions, Beliefs, and Attitudes (reflected in tactics such as thinking about past successes rather than failures, paying attention to peers' successes rather than failures, and not overinterpreting anxiety symptoms) can directly help make perceptions of self-efficacy more positive.

Self-concept is the self-perception of competence in a given area or field, such as L2 learning or musical performance, or more generally in one's life. Self-concept is relative, depending at least partly on a social comparison with other people (Festinger, 1954; Marsh, 1984). Any strategies that facilitate good L2 learning can ultimately result in positive social comparisons and an improved self-concept. In addition, the strategy of Activating Supportive Emotions, Beliefs, and Attitudes can also enhance self-concept.

Beliefs about L2 learning

Language anxiety can be based on negative beliefs about L2 learning. A common (and often true) belief is that learners might make mistakes if they try to speak or write in the L2, and this belief can lead to language anxiety (Horwitz, 2007). Another common belief is that only two years of nonintensive coursework is enough to become fluent in a foreign language, and learners become anxious or upset when they find this belief to be a misconception (Horwitz, 2007).

Cultural and personal beliefs influence the selection and use of learning strategies (Bedell and Oxford, 1996; Horwitz, 1987, 1999; Law, Chan, and Sachs, 2008) and affect L2 learning in general (Cotterall, 1999). Learners try to use strategies they believe will be helpful, often based on cultural norms (Barcelos, 2000; Kajala and Barcelos, 2003). Among Chinese learners of English as a foreign language (EFL), Yin (2008) discovered that beliefs about the value of EFL learning and about learning strategies significantly affected the use of compensatory vocabulary-learning strategies. For Taiwanese EFL students, Yang (1992, 1999) found significant linkages among strategy use, self-efficacy, and beliefs about English learning. In Yang's research, students' use of all types of strategies, especially functional practise strategies, was strongly related to students' self-efficacy and beliefs about English learning, whereas the use of formal, oral-practise strategies was associated with beliefs about the value and nature of learning spoken English. Campbell, Shaw, Plageman, and Allen (1993) found that university students in beginning Spanish and French courses believed that learning grammar was more difficult than learning vocabulary and chose strategies accordingly; however, teachers can influence the accuracy of students' beliefs about L2 learning and their use of learning strategies.

Attitudes

L2 learners' attitudes can concern L2 learning, the teacher, the language (attitudes about its prestige, sound system, writing system, grammar, metaphors, communicative value, and so on), the culture, and native speakers of the language. Attitudes are generally viewed as either positive or negative and can strongly affect L2 learning. Influences on attitudes are learning contexts (Yashima and Zenuk-Nishide, 2008), experiences, and beliefs. Learners can change their attitudes by using tactics tied to the L2 learning strategy of Activating Supportive Emotions, Beliefs, and Attitudes. An example is, "I say that is fine for me not to understand everything I hear in Amharic. Accepting this makes me able to understand better".

3.4.3   Strategies in association with motivation, volition, and willingness to communicate

Three main psychological constructs concern the desire to engage in and learn the L2: motivation, volition, and willingness to communicate (WTC). An associated sociocultural construct, investment, is explained in Chapter 5. Each of these is related to L2 learning strategies in the S²R Model.

Motivation

Some experts have defined *motivation* as the first or initial spark that learners need to start the task, course, or programme of study. Other specialists view motivation as not only involving the initial spark but as also embracing the maintenance of desire over time (Dörnyei and Skehan, 2003; Dörnyei and Ushioda, 2010). Gardner (2001) defined L2 motivation as requiring (a) expenditure of consistent effort (persistence), (b) desire to achieve the goal; and (c) enjoyment of L2 learning. He also noted that motivated individuals set goals, make attributions for successes and failures, and experience satisfaction when they succeed and dissatisfaction when they do not. Dörnyei and Ushioda, (2010) offered the following principles for L2 motivation. First, L2 motivation requires positive conditions. Second, there must be not only initial motivation but continued motivation. Finally, motivation necessitates a positive self-evaluation.

Rather than being a stable trait, motivation is dynamic and changeable, depending on internal and external influences (Alexander, 2006a; Kaufman and Husman, 2004; Oxford and Shearin, 1994, 1996). In research using Gardner's Socio-Educational Model of L2 learning, motivation was shown to be a cause of both self-confidence and the use of L2 learning strategies (Dörnyei and Skehan, 2003). Use of affective learning strategies (regulation of affect, including motivation) requires effort, which in turn requires some degree of motivation (Wolters, 2003).

Some well known types of motivation in any area include:

- *intrinsic motivation* (desire to do something based on a combination of interest, enjoyment, and personal challenge, Ryan and Deci, 2000).
- *extrinsic motivation* (desire to do something based on a desire for external rewards, such as grades or salary, Ryan and Deci, 2000).

Quote 3.4 Intrinsic motivation

... [T]he optimal kind of motivation from within is identified as *intrinsic motivation* – that is, doing something as an end in itself, for its own self-sustaining pleasurable rewards of enjoyment, interest, challenge, or skill and knowledge development. ... [I]ntrinsically motivated learners are deeply concerned to learn things well, in a manner that is intrinsically satisfying and arouses a sense of optimal challenge ... [S]uch learners are likely to display much higher levels of involvement in learning, engage in more creative thinking processes, use a wider range of problem-solving strategies, and interact with and retain material more effectively ...

Ema Ushioda (2008, pp. 21–22)

Csíkszentmihályi (1990, 1996, 1998) stated that a person is most content when experiencing *flow*, the ultimate state of intrinsic motivation in which the individual is completely engaged, feels fulfilled, and simultaneously experiences both challenge and competence. The experience of flow is described further below. It is my view that because learning strategies can promote competence (Chapter 2) and stimulate motivation (this chapter), they contribute to flow.

Quote 3.5 Flow

Contrary to what we usually believe, ... the best moments in our lives ... are not passive, receptive, relaxing times – although such experiences can be enjoyable, if we have worked hard to attain them. The best moments usually occur when a person's body or mind is stretched to its limits in a voluntary effort to accomplish something difficult and worthwhile.

Mihály Csíkszentmihályi (1990, p. 3)

Two major "motivational orientations," which can be roughly under-stood as reasons for learning an L2, are (a) the instrumental orientation, or the desire to learn the L2 for practical reasons, such as a job; and (b) the integrative orientation, which reflects a genuine desire to come closer psychologically or socially to the other language community or identify with that community (Gardner, 2001). Additional motivational orienta-tions, include, among others, curiosity about the language structures and interest in the culture or language without a desire to integrate into the language community (Oxford, Park, Ito, and Sumrall, 1993a, 1993b).

Noels and her colleagues (Noels 2001; Noels *et al.*, 2000; McIntosh and Noels, 2004) developed a motivational orientation framework based on Deci and Ryan's (1985) Self-Determination Theory. McIntosh and Noels (2004, p. 2) reported a range of motivational orientations emerg-ing from learners in response to the question, "Why are you learning a second language?" The orientations were: (a) Intrinsic Motivation (IM) – Knowledge, "for the satisfied feeling I get in finding out new things;" (b) IM-Accomplishments, "for the enjoyment I experience when I grasp a difficult construct in the second language;" (c) IM-Stimulation, "for the 'high' that I experience while speaking the second language;" (d) Integrated Regulation, "because it is a part of my identity;" (e) Identified Regulation, "because I think it is important for my personal development" (a personal goal); (f) Introjected Regulation, "because I would feel guilty if I didn't know a second language" (self-imposed pressure); and (g) External Regulation, "in order to get a more prestigious job later on." These researchers included amotivation (". . . I don't understand what I am doing studying a second language") as a motivational orientation, but I do not view amotivation as being in the same class as the other orientations, all of which give an actual reason for learning the language. Strategies can be fruitfully used to support a number of these motivational orientations, but not amotivation.

Volition

The term *volition* is sometimes used to mean persistence after initial motivation is over (Deimann and Keller, 2006; DeWitte and Lens, 1999). Corno (2001, 2004, similar to Elstad, 2008) claimed that volition is a form of self-regulation that governs all stages of learning. Volition is inversely related to learned helplessness (Kuhl, 1984). However, to William James (1910/1987), volition was the "hot" merger of personal desire, excitement, will, and tension to create a higher level of energy. In a related vein, Pintrich, Marx, and Boyle (1993) mentioned learners' "hot" conceptual change, which is related to affect and to the sociocultural context.

Willingness to communicate

WTC is the probability that an individual will choose to initiate communication, more specifically talk, when free to do so (MacIntyre, 2003). WTC in the L1 and the L2 was found to be positively correlated with self-perceived oral communication competence and negatively correlated with anxiety about communication (communication apprehension) (Barraclough, Christophel, and McCroskey, 1988; MacIntyre, 2003). Participating in L2 communication experiences increases one's willingness to do so further (MacIntyre, 2003). The sociocultural role and vitality of the L2 influence WTC (Clément, Baker, and MacIntyre, 2003). MacIntyre, Clément, Dörnyei and Noels (1998) proposed a "pyramid model" involving L2 WTC. The top level of the pyramid is actual communication in the L2. The next level down is behavioural intention, which is embodied in WTC and supports L2 use. The third layer down is a combination of two situational factors: (a) desire to communicate with a specific person in the L2 and (b) current ("state") situational self-confidence about communicating. The fourth layer down contains three motivational tendencies: (a) interpersonal motivation, (b) intergroup motivation, and (c) L2 self-confidence in general. The fifth layer down is the affective-cognitive context: (a) intergroup attitudes, (b) the social situation, and (c) communicative competence. The bottom layer, the base of the pyramid, comprises the social and individual context, i.e., (a) intergroup climate and (b) personality.

Strategies (tactics) for motivation, volition, and WTC

Affective strategies, often for motivation, were among the most frequently used in a Canadian ESL children's study (Gunning, Oxford, and Gatbonton, forthcoming). Such strategies also had the strongest relationship with proficiency among all strategy categories in a Taiwanese EFL children's study by Lan and Oxford (2003). Oxford and Nyikos (see below) used a spiral image to explain that strategy use is related to motivation and self-esteem as well as to proficiency.

Quote 3.6 Spiraling

We would expect that use of appropriate strategies leads to enhanced actual and perceived proficiency, which in turn creates higher self-esteem, which leads to stronger motivation, spiraling into still more use of strategies, greater actual and perceived proficiency, higher self-esteem, improved motivation, and so on.

Rebecca Oxford and Martha Nyikos (1989, p. 295)

Motivation, volition, and WTC can all be enhanced by tactics that reflect the strategy of Generating and Maintaining Motivation. Such tactics include: (a) self-efficacy tactics, such as positive self-talk; (b) planning for self-reward or self-punishment, depending on anticipated outcomes (self-consequating); (c) listening to music, exercising, and relaxing (stress management); (d) reminding oneself of the value of the goals and remembering positive incentives (commitment control); (e) eliminating boredom by adding humour or a new twist (satiation control); (f) structuring the environment to decrease off-task behaviour or create social pressure; (g) blaming failures on external factors, not ability (controlling attributions); (h) highlighting unpreparedness or inability in order to pressure oneself to try harder (defensive pessimism); (i) reminding oneself of negative consequences (negative incentives) of failing; (j) blocking negative thoughts or feelings that undermine motivation; and (k) making the task more difficult (self-handicapping). Notice that some of these tactics related to motivation also involve adjusting emotional and attitudinal states (see the strategy of Activating Supportive Emotions, Attitudes, and Beliefs). This is because motivation cannot operate independently of feelings and attitudes.

Another way to increase motivation, volition, and WTC is to have positive experiences of L2 learning that lead to greater self-efficacy and stronger communicative competence. As we have seen, a sense of competence, along with low anxiety, increases WTC. Therefore, almost any strategies that improve learners' experiences and sense of competence can have a positive feedback effect, making learners more eager to engage in and learn the L2 later on. Hence, a host of strategies in the cognitive, affective, and sociocultural-interactive dimensions can spur further desire to learn and participate.

Viewing volition as persistence after initial motivation has gone, DeWitte and Lens (1999) argued that anxious learners need volitional strategies but that calm students do not. Assuming that volition drives all learning, Corno (2001, 2004) promoted the use of volitional strategies for all learners. Mixing motivation and volition, Wolters (2003) discussed volitional strategies for removing motivational obstacles (Concept 3.1). Shepherd (2006) described her "volitional model" as including motivational strategies. The area of volitional strategies shows differences in theory and terminology (see Pintrich, 1999). I hope researchers will eventually iron out their differences about volitional strategies, because this is an important area.

3.4.4   Goals and strategies

Goal-setting is part of the metastrategy of Planning and is hence an important part of the S²R Model. Goals can improve motivation, evaluation of progress, beliefs in one's capabilities, mobilization of learning strategies, and ability to alter strategies if needed (Schunk, 2002). Perceived discrepancies between one's present performance and the goal may stimulate greater effort if the goal is realistic. Self-set goals are more motivating than those set by others for the individual (Locke, 1996). Meeting goals in learning involves overcoming problems. Some learning problems are mild, while others are serious; some are well-defined, while others are ill-defined (Alexander, 2003a, 2003b).

Mastery goals and performance goals

Mastery goals are achievement goals oriented to developing competence, while *performance goals* are achievement goals aimed at demonstrating competence in comparison to other people (social comparison) and avoiding the relative appearance of incompetence. Much early research had a *mastery goal perspective*. That perspective showed that students with mastery goals, compared with students who had performance goals, chose more cognitively challenging tasks, persisted longer, were more strategically self-regulated, and had better outcomes. Such research also revealed that students aiming for mastery, compared with those oriented merely toward performance, had more positive attitudes, stronger motivation, and greater emotional stability (Forgas, Williams, and Laham, 2004; Harris, Yuill, and Luckin, 2008; Linnenbrink, 2005).

However, other researchers found that performance goals can sometimes be motivating and lead to good outcomes. Performance-approach goals

Concept 3.1 **Wolters' eight strategies for motivation and volition**

Strategy	Nature or aim
Self-consequating	Providing oneself a reward or praise for good progress or achievement; or threatening to remove from oneself a desired activity for not doing well or reaching the goal.
Using goal-oriented self-talk	Using positive self-talk about reasons for achieving the goals.
Enhancing interest	Making learning a game, adding creative drawings, etc. to make the learning process less boring or repetitive.
Structuring the environment	Type 1: Decreasing the possibility of off-task behaviour by reducing distractions or intensity of distractions. Type 2: Altering the environment to create readiness or the proper mood: eating or drinking to increase attention; listening to music.
Self-handicapping	Manufacturing obstructions before or during a task to make performing the task more difficult (e.g., putting off work to the last minute, avoiding studying, staying up late before an exam). Can give an excuse for poor performance on a test, or alternatively can force students to relax and focus without worrying about appearing inadequate. However, might be a maladaptive strategy, even when linked with decreased anxiety and increased enjoyment, because it is linked with less time spent practising.
Controlling attributions	Purposefully selecting causal attributions to maintain or increase motivations; avoiding blaming academic setbacks on uncontrollable internal factors (ability) because this leads to helplessness; instead purposefully using attributions that reflect controllable internal factors (effort, strategy use).
Managing efficacy	Three ways: Setting proximal (shorter-term) goals; using defensive pessimism (highlighting one's unpreparedness, lack of ability, etc. to convince oneself that it is impossible to do well, and this can sometimes spur motivation to work harder); using efficacy self-talk (positive self-talk about one's own ability to reach the goal).
Regulating emotions	Counting up to ten, controlling breathing, controlling excitement, using inner speech to control anxiety ("Don't worry"), self-affirming to counter negative emotions; can include masking emotions. Young children have special physical means of soothing themselves and also use avoidance.

Source: Summarized from Wolters (2003) with additional comments from Rebecca Oxford.

(desire to outperform others) can be motivating in situations of certainty, i.e., when answers are clear, but performance-approach goals are not motivating in situations of uncertainty (Damon, Harackiewicz, Butera, Mugny, and Quiamzade, 2007). Performance-avoidance goals (desire to avoid performing more poorly than others) have consistently poor effects (Damon *et al.*, 2007). Results of such research have caused some investigators to argue for a *multiple goals perspective*, in which both mastery goals and performance goals can be viewed as positive (in terms of affect, strategies, and outcomes) under the right conditions, especially when these two types of goals are combined (Barron and Harackiewicz, 2001; Linnenbrink, 2005). See Concept 3.2.

Concept 3.2   **Positive effects of combinations of mastery and performance-approach goals, with linkages to the Planning strategy**

Type of effect	Explanation	Relationship to strategies *During the implementation of the Planning strategy . . .*
Additive effects	Each goal is independently beneficial for a single outcome.	The learner might consider the benefits of each goal separately.
Interactive effects	Having both mastery goals and performance-approach goals simultaneously is more useful than either goal alone for a single outcome.	The learner might think about how mastery goals and performance-approach goals can interact. The joint effect is greater than the sum of the parts.
Specialized effects of each goal across multiple outcomes	Mastery goals might be helpful for outcomes like interest or emotional well-being, and performance-approach goals might be helpful for outcomes such as achievement.	The learner might consider which type of goal relates to outcomes like interest and emotional well-being and which type of goal relates to achievement outcomes.
Selective effects	Effect of the student's own goals depends on the match with the "goal context" of the classroom.	The learner should probably set goals that overlap (at least somewhat) with the "goal context" of the classroom.

Source: First two columns summarized from Barron and Harackiewicz (2001). Third column original.

Tactics for setting goals

Because of the utility of different types of goals under different circumstances, L2 learners benefit from knowing more about how to set goals. Learners need this information in order to be strategic planners of their own learning. To be most effective for self-regulated learning, goals must have certain characteristics: *specificity* (not just "try hard"), *proximity* (long-term goals to boost performance, divided into short-term, proximal goals for motivation purposes), and *difficulty* (neither too hard nor too easy) (Schunk, 2002). A student-friendly formula for goals is: *s*pecific, *m*easurable, *a*ttainable, *r*ealistic, and *t*imely (SMART) (Norquest, 2007). In addition, goals must also be sustainable (Locke, 1996). Brodscholl, Kober, and Higgins (2006) discuss self-regulation in goal attainment and goal maintenance.

L2 learners who have a *future time perspective* (Husman, McCann, and Crowson, 2000; Simons, Vansteenkiste, Lens, and Lacante, 2004) are particularly concerned about setting appropriate long-term goals via the Planning strategy. Some possible long-term goals might be to reach a specific proficiency level, gain self-confidence in using the L2 to communicate, strengthen metacognitive self-management, develop linguistic accuracy, become fluent in the L2, and use appropriate vocabulary, structures, and body language in different sociocultural settings and circumstances. L2 learners who do not have a future time perspective can also use tactics associated with the Planning strategy, but their tactics might help them set short-term goals for linguistic knowledge at lower levels of proficiency (Leaver and Shekhtman, 2004) and for passing an L2 course or doing well on immediate L2 tasks.

3.4.5 Neurobiology in relation to affect and strategies

Neurobiology shows that emotion is directly tied to learning in multiple ways. For instance, the stronger the emotional connections and the more meaningful the information and linkages, the stronger the memory trace will be (Haberlandt, 1998). However, sometimes anxiety clouds the picture so much that the learner remembers in great detail the learning situation that caused the anxiety but forgets (or never learns) the L2 information from that situation.

The frontal lobe of the brain (see Figure 2.3 in the prior chapter) works with deeper brain structures to control emotion and motivation. For instance, the ability to override immediate gratification in favor of future goals is centered in the frontal lobe. Electroencephalograph (EEG) evidence suggests that there are two unipolar affective systems, one creating positive feelings about possible reward (left frontal lobe) and the other generating feelings of anxiety over possible punishment (right frontal lobe) (Carver and Scheier, 2000; Sobotka, Davidson, and Senulis, 1992).

The *hypothalamus*, also in the limbic system, is an organizer and co-ordinator: it organizes basic nonverbal responses associated with emotions, coordinates survival behaviour, and helps control the autonomic nervous system and the endocrine system. The *amygdala*, deep in the temporal lobes of the brain and part of the primitive limbic system, produces and responds to nonverbal signs of anger, avoidance, defensiveness, and fear, as well as being the center of the appraisal system mentioned by Schumann (2001a, 2001b), discussed below. The amygdala might provide the nonverbal, deeply emotional connection to the less emotional, highly verbal thoughts about and considerations of strategies that occur in the frontal cortex. The *hippocampus* has a memory conversion function, but it also appears to be involved in the "downregulation" (reduction of intensity) of difficult or negative emotions (Kuhl, 2000), such as anxiety, frustration, and anger. Tactics related to the affective strategy of Activating Supportive Emotions, Beliefs, and Attitudes can affect the working of these structures. For instance, deep breathing is a tactic that learners can employ in fear-inducing circumstances in order to help the hippocampus reduce the intensity of anxiety.

An additional neurobiological theory might be relevant to the S^2R Model, although this tie has not yet been explored. Schumann (2001a, 2001b) viewed sustained, deep learning as *mental foraging*, involving a stimulus *appraisal system* heavily weighted toward affect. In Schumann's theory, motivation for sustained, deep L2 learning involves multiple neurobiological structures: the amygdala, the orbitofrontal cortex (above the orbits of the eyes), and major body systems, such as the autonomic nervous system (part of the peripheral nervous system), the endocrine system, and the musculoskeletal system. The appraisal system learns to recognize environmental cues predicting rewards for the learner. The learner rapidly evaluates these cues with five criteria: relevance (significance) to needs/goals, coping potential, pleasantness, novelty, and compatibility to self and social image. The appraisal creates a bodily state (somatic marker), communicated to the brain as a feeling, on which the learner makes learning decisions, including strategy use decisions. Thus, emotion, motivation, and cognition are directly linked. After frequent associations between bodily states and stimulus appraisals, the bodily states become "centrally represented in the brain itself, obviating the need for processing in the peripheral nervous system" (Schumann, 2001b, p. 23). The neurobiological system is related to the actions described as learning strategies (Schumann, 2001b). Schumann described a learner named Barbara, who made repeated stimulus appraisals as she decided which languages to learn and which learning strategies to use in varied contexts over the years. Her strategies were more than merely "motivated behaviours," because they reflected the application of various types of metacognitive knowledge and self-regulation. Concept 3.3 summarizes Schumann's theory of sustained, deep learning as mental foraging and extends and applies it to L2 learning strategy use.

Concept 3.3 Schumann's theory of sustained, deep learning as mental foraging, extended and applied to L2 learning strategy use

Column A Themes in the theory	Column B Aspect	Column C Additions and applications to L2 learning strategy use
What mental foraging is, where it occurs, and what it notices	Mental foraging is sparked by a *stimulus appraisal system*. The appraisal system operates in the *amygdala* and the *orbitofrontal cortex*, as well as in the various body systems, such as the autonomic nervous system (part of the peripheral nervous system), the endocrine system, and the musculoskeletal system. This system learns to recognize environmental cues predicting reward: events, agents, and objects that facilitate learning.	The learner's authentic need for assistance (e.g., facing a difficult task) should logically also be noted by the appraisal system. It is a problem or need that sparks the use of a learning strategy. Strategies presented via strategy instruction might be among the environmental cues picked up by the appraisal. If the meaning of "environment" is expanded to include the learner's own *inner environment*, then already known strategies might also be among the cues.

Concept 3.3   Schumann's theory of sustained, deep learning as mental foraging, extended and applied to L2 learning strategy use (continued)

Column A Themes in the theory	Column B Aspect	Column C Additions and applications to L2 learning strategy use
What the learner evaluates and how	The learner evaluates the environmental cues by using five criteria: relevance to needs/goals, coping potential, pleasantness, novelty, and compatibility to self and social image. These are motivating to the learner.	With reference to strategies, the learner – often in a flash – appraises the situation and possible strategies to use in the situation, considering especially the following: • how relevant the strategies are to current goals and needs, • whether strategies might help in coping (managing the situational demands), • whether the strategy is compatible with self-image and social image, and • whether the strategy is pleasant and novel/interesting.
Physical state	The appraisal causes a bodily/physical state (somatic marker) which is communicated to the brain as a feeling. This serves as the basis for the learner to decide what to do.	The learner feels either positive or negative based on this appraisal and then decides (metacognitively) whether to use the strategy now and perhaps later.
Physical states becoming mentally represented	After frequent associations between physical states and stimulus appraisals, these states become mentally represented in the brain, without having to be processed each time in the peripheral nervous system.	After the associations are made repeatedly, the peripheral nervous system no longer has to send a message (feeling) to the brain about the strategy. Decision-making about whether to use the strategy for a given purpose has become automatic and unconscious. The strategy itself might become automatic (a habit).

3.4.6   Synthesis of theories and concepts

In the S²R Model, the affective dimension in L2 learning is extremely important and interacts with the cognitive dimension (Chapter 2). For instance,
L2 motivation is often lower if the teacher focuses purely on cognitive
aspects of L2 learning without paying attention to learners' affective needs
and issues. The affective dimension also interacts with the sociocultural-
interactive dimension (Chapter 4). For example, language anxiety is a fear
of social performance, typically in oral communication; and WTC occurs
in the sociocultural context.

My suggestions are these. First, more teachers, researchers, and learners
should recognize that practical learning strategies exist for reducing anxiety
and for transforming inaccurate beliefs, negative attitudes, low motivation,
unwillingness to communicate, and vague goals, all of which are related to
negative L2 learning outcomes. Second, those interested in expanding their
understanding should read more of the extensive research on emotions,
beliefs, attitudes, and motivation in learning outside of the L2 field. Third,
L2 researchers should extensively study L2-related emotions, beliefs, attitudes, motivation, and neurobiology in relation to strategy use.

3.5   Conclusion

This chapter has underscored the undeniable importance of affective factors
in learning in general, in L2 learning in specific, and in the S²R Model. The
role of affective and meta-affective strategies is crucial for many learners,
especially at lower levels of proficiency. It is surprising that few L2 learning
strategy theorists and researchers have explored this area in depth. This
chapter has aimed to alter the situation and has intended to open the door
to wisdom-hungry teachers who want to understand their students.

Further reading

Arnold, J. (1999) (ed.) *Affect in Language Learning*. Cambridge, UK: Cambridge
    University Press. This book is a useful research compendium concerning affective
    variables in L2 learning. It includes far-ranging perspectives, such as psychological
    styles and neurobiology.
Dörnyei, Z. (2005) *Psychology of the Language Learner*. Mahwah, NJ: Erlbaum. This book
    presents many important aspects regarding the psychology of L2 language learners.
    Motivation is especially well discussed.
Dörnyei, Z. and Ushioda, E. (2010) *Teaching and Researching Motivation*. 2nd ed. Harlow,
    Essex, UK: Pearson Longman. This volume offers the most in-depth, up-to-date
    perspective on motivation in the L2 field and is written by the two strongest experts
    on the topic.

Horwitz, E. and Young, D. (eds) (1991) *Language Anxiety: From Theory and Research to Classroom Implications*. Englewood Cliffs, NJ: Prentice Hall. *Also:* Young, D. (ed.) (1999) *Affect in Foreign Language and Second Language Learning: A Practical Guide to Creating a Low-Anxiety Classroom Atmosphere*. Boston, MA: McGraw-Hill. These two books are practical while at the same time based on sound theory about language anxiety and associated themes.

Husman, J., McCann, E.J., and Crowson, H.M. (2000) Volitional strategies and future time perspective: embracing the complexity of dynamic interactions. *International Journal of Educational Research*, 33: 777–799. Future time perspective, for me, clarifies the need for volitional strategies. See also Simons, Vansteenkiste, Lens, and Lacante (2004).

MacIntyre, P.D. (2002) Motivation, anxiety, and emotion in second language acquisition. In Robinson, P. (ed.), *Individual Differences and Instructed Language Learning*. Amsterdam: John Benjamins: 45–68. This chapter includes physiological as well as psychological mechanisms of emotion and challenges us to consider multiple motivations and emotions in L2 learning.

Stevick, E. (1989) *Success with Foreign Languages: Seven Who Achieved It and What Worked for Them*. Englewood Cliffs, NJ: Prentice Hall International. This inteview-based book describes the learning histories of seven highly talented language learners. It reveals how their strategies intertwine with emotions, attitudes, motivation, and the sociocultural setting.

Chapter 4

Dimension 3 (sociocultural-interactive): Strategies for contexts, communication, and culture

There is more than a verbal tie between the words common, community, and communication.

John Dewey

"Language expresses cultural reality" (Kramsch, 1998, p. 3). Three layers of culture are (a) the social (current, synchronic), (b) the historical (diachronic), and (c) the imaginative, consisting of the future-oriented imaginings, dreams, and hopes embedded in the culture, as in Martin Luther King's speech, "I have a dream . . ." (Kramsch, 1998, p. 8). Adapting ideas from Kramsch (1998), Gee (2005, 2007), and Hall (2010), the S²R Model views the *sociocultural context* as embodying all three cultural layers at once, funnelled into a given place and time. For instance, the sociocultural context as we experience it includes the social identities of communicators; shared assumptions, imaginings, hopes, and dreams; the communication setting; the communication activity; and the social, cultural, cognitive, material, and political effects of all of these (Gee, 2005). Learning is called "hot" partly because it is embedded in dynamic, lively and significant sociocultural contexts, as well as because it involves emotions and motivation (Pintrich, 2000a; Pintrich, Marx, and Boyle, 1993). This recalls, at least in part, William James' (1910/ 1987) description of "hot" volition mentioned in Chapter 3.

Quote 4.1   Culture and language

... [W]ithout rich sociocultural and sociolinguistic competence, students do not make it past the minimum level of professional proficiency – and ... in today's world, that is simply not good enough. ... We need foreign-language students who, whether or not they acculturate, understand the significance of [cultural] variations in behavioural norms, lexica that ... carry divergent cultural salience, paralinguistic communication, pragmatics, dialectical and idiolectal manners of expression ... For future generations to survive an unfortunately increasingly hostile, and at the same time, interdependent world, we need ... foreign-language graduates who exhibit greater sophistication of expression, comprehension, and analysis, ... and who are more cognizant of cultural differences, ... more culturally sensitive and accepting.

Betty Lou Leaver (2008, p. 11)

In the S²R Model, culture's three layers, social, historical, and imaginative, interact constantly. Sociocultural context is the immediate context (embodying all aspects of culture) in which communication occurs. This chapter describes two categories of strategies: *sociocultural-interactive (SI) strategies* and *meta-SI strategies*. Table 4.1 presents a chapter overview.

Table 4.1   **Overview of this chapter**

4.1   Linked metaphors for meta-SI strategies and SI strategies: community manager and community workers

4.2   Meta-SI knowledge, meta-SI strategies, and the "meta" level of sociocultural-interaction

4.3   SI strategies

4.4   Relevant theories and concepts
    4.4.1   Communication and learning
    4.4.2   Discourse and contexts
    4.4.3   Cultural models
    4.4.4   Identity, power relations, and investment
    4.4.5   Counter-stories
    4.4.6   Resistance and non-participation
    4.4.7   Opposition and accommodation
    4.4.8   Synthesis of theories and concepts

4.5   Conclusion
    Further reading

4.1   Linked metaphors for meta-SI strategies and SI strategies: community manager and community workers

Metaphorically speaking, we can view *meta-SI strategies* in the S^2R Model as the "community manager," i.e., overall manager of contexts, communication, and culture in L2 learning. For a community to function effectively, there is always a leader with managerial responsibility, such as paying attention, planning, gaining resources, organizing, orchestrating, monitoring, and evaluating. An example of a meta-SI strategy therefore is Paying Attention to Contexts, Communication, and Culture.

In the S^2R Model, the "community workers" are known as the sociocultural-interactive (SI) strategies, with an emphasis on the situated nature of learning. Community workers directly facilitate communicating and hence learning, even when knowledge barriers are present; and they aid in understanding immediate sociocultural contexts and one's roles in those contexts. An example of an SI strategy is Dealing with Sociocultural Contexts and Identities.

Section 4.2 provides further information on meta-SI strategies, while section 4.3 offers more depth regarding SI strategies. Section 4.4 presents theories and concepts related to these two categories.

4.2   Meta-SI knowledge, meta-SI strategies, and the "meta" level of sociocultural interaction

Meta-SI knowledge is the form of metaknowledge that is directed toward the cultural and communication dimension of L2 learning. This knowledge, like all metaknowledge, covers six areas: person knowledge, culture or group knowledge, task knowledge, whole-process knowledge, strategy knowledge, and conditional knowledge.

Metastrategies that are concerned with general management of the L2 sociocultural-interactive dimension are called *meta-SI strategies*. The eight meta-SI strategies include the following:

- *Paying Attention to Contexts, Communication, and Culture*
- *Planning for Contexts, Communication, and Culture*
- *Obtaining and Using Resources for Contexts, Communication, and Culture*
- *Organizing for Contexts, Communication, and Culture*
- *Implementing Plans for Contexts, Communication, and Culture*

- *Orchestrating Strategies for Contexts, Communication, and Culture*
- *Monitoring for Contexts, Communication, and Culture*
- *Evaluating for Contexts, Communication, and Culture.*

A few specific examples of tactics associated with meta-SI strategies are: (a) "I look for opportunities to practise my Italian with other people online," a tactic related to the strategy of Obtaining and Using Resources for Contexts, Communication, and Culture; (b) "I find a place where it is quiet enough to talk easily in Russian," a tactic associated with the strategy of Organizing for Contexts, Communication, and Culture; and (c) "I monitor my accuracy and cultural understanding during conversations in my Arabic class," a tactic linked to the strategy of Monitoring Contexts, Communication, and Culture. Appendix I.E, found at the end of this Section I, contains a large number of tactics associated with meta-SI strategies and will help readers understand these strategies.

The "meta" level of sociocultural-interaction is composed of *meta-SI knowledge* and *meta-SI regulation*, the latter of which refers to the use of meta-SI strategies. See Figure 4.1.

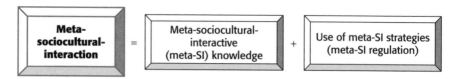

Figure 4.1 Meta-SI and its components

4.3   SI strategies

SI strategies – strategies for sociocultural contexts and communication – directly facilitate communication and deep understanding of the sociocultural context and one's roles in it. Three such strategies are included in the new S²R Model:

- *Interacting to Learn and Communicate*
- *Overcoming Knowledge Gaps in Communicating*
- *Dealing with Sociocultural Contexts and Identities.*

These strategies help learners interact and collaborate with others, seek help, continue social interaction even when knowledge gaps arise, and deal with sociocultural issues of identity and power. Examples of tactics that accompany sociocultural interaction strategies are as follows: (a) "I work with a mentor who is a native speaker of Hungarian and who has lots of patience with me," which reflects the strategy of Interacting to Learn and Communicate; (b) "I use a synonym or even an antonym ('it's not this,' 'the opposite of this') if I cannot think of the word I need," manifesting the strategy of Overcoming Knowledge Gaps in Communicating; and (c) "I especially focus on the amount of silence (waiting times or just peaceful silence) and the presence or absence of interruptions (by whom? between whom?) that are expected in conversations and try to figure out more about the culture based on this," revealing the strategy of Dealing with Sociocultural Contexts and Identities.

Appendix I.F, found at the end of Section I, presents detailed examples of SI strategies and accompanying tactics. The range of these strategies is very broad because of all the possible contexts in which interaction can occur.

4.4   Relevant theories and concepts

Strategies play a great role in the sociocultural-interactive dimension of the S²R Model. Here I explain (a) communication in relation to learning strategies; and (b) sociocultural concepts and learning strategies.

4.4.1   Communication and learning

Communication is a key to the S²R Model and to L2 learning in general. ". . . [L2] theorists and practitioners alike almost unanimously emphasize communication of one kind or another" (Kumaravadivelu, 1993, p. 12). Although communication is important, definitions of communication are diverse: exchanges of ideas and information among people, words or silences that have influential message value, and an overall system of relationships (see Johnson-Laird, 1990). Studies included by Ellis (1999) showed that interaction affects acquisition of L2 word meanings and grammatical knowledge. Communicative interaction is a key focus in many L2 classrooms (Anton and DiCamilla, 1999; Gass, 1997; Kowal and Swain, 1994) and in L2 simulation and games, both in classrooms and online (Crookall and Oxford, 1990). Vygotskyian approaches, mentioned earlier, explore how L2 learners communicate interactively (e.g., Brooks and Donato, 1994).

Communicative-interactive classrooms

Communicative-interactive classrooms focus largely on meaning, although form is important as well (Ellis, 2005). Meaning includes not just the semantic meaning of words but also the pragmatic meaning (contextual appropriateness) of communication acts. The development of true fluency requires opportunities to create pragmatic meaning (Ellis, 2005). The S²R

Model's meta-SI strategies (e.g., Planning for Contexts, Communication, and Culture; Monitoring Contexts, Communication, and Culture) and SI strategies (i.e., Interacting to Learn and Communicate; Overcoming Knowledge Gaps in Communicating; and Dealing with Sociocultural Contexts and Identities) help learners participate in authentic, communicative interaction that involves context-appropriate meanings. In addition, the two affective strategies, Generating and Maintaining Motivation and Activating and Sustaining Positive Emotions, Beliefs, and Attitudes, can help to facilitate the appropriate affective state to participate in L2 communication and thus learn the L2. See also Chapter 3 for Willingness to Communicate.

Learning while communicating

The S²R Model stresses that L2 learners at many levels encounter social communication situations in which they lack crucial knowledge of grammar points, vocabulary items, or fine shades of semantic or pragmatic meaning. By continuing to use the L2 despite knowledge gaps with the aid of paraphrasing, borrowing, and (sometimes) changing the topic, L2 learners can keep the door open to both communication and further learning. *Paraphrasing* includes approximating the message, coining a new word, or "talking around" the word. *Borrowing* entails translating literally, switching languages temporarily (code switching), asking for assistance, and miming/gesturing. *Avoidance* does not mean avoiding L2 communication and is therefore a somewhat unfortunate or confusing term; instead, it refers substituting an easier or more familiar topic for a more difficult or less familiar one. Paraphrasing, borrowing, and using avoidance are sometimes collectively called *communication strategies* because they allow continued communication despite gaps in knowledge. See Chapter 8.

Like Selinker (1972), Cohen included communication strategies in a category called *language use strategies*, on the assumption that such strategies are not mainly for the purpose of learning but instead "focus primarily on employing the language that learners have in their current interlanguage" (Cohen, 1996, p. 3). Other language use strategies, according to Cohen (1996, 2010), are retrieval strategies, rehearsal strategies, and cover strategies. *Retrieval strategies* are strategies for retrieving information when it is needed for communication, and these strategies include, among others, using mnemonics and visual images. *Rehearsal strategies* are strategies, such as form-focused practice, for rehearsing target language structures. *Cover strategies* are coping strategies learners use to create the false impression they have control over L2 material in the hope of not appearing unprepared, foolish, or stupid.

The S²R Model rejects any strong dichotomy between language learning strategies and language use strategies. "Learning takes place *through* communication" (Faerch and Kasper, 1983, p. xviii), and learners can "use the language to learn it" (Howatt, 1984, in Oxford, 1990). Therefore, "Communication, learning, and instruction interact and influence each other" (Candlin, 1983, p. x). See Concept 4.1 for research-based and practical reasons for rejecting a strong split between learning and use strategies.

Concept 4.1   **Why the S²R Model rejects a strong split between language learning and language use (as applied to strategies or tactics)**

- For research on learning, a strong distinction between language use and language learning contradicts long-established, research-based learning principles.
  - First, as John Dewey (1956/1990) theorized and supported with decades of research, learning occurs through experience, not in the absence of experience. In the L2 field, a research-based example of learning through experience or use is "talking to learn" (MacIntyre, Baker, Clément, and Donovan, 2003).
  - Second, learning does not need to be divorced or separated from the use of knowledge. In fact, research shows that *learning* relies crucially on *using* that which is being learned. Specifically, active use of information that is being learned helps strengthen schemata in long-term memory (Mandler, 2001), and this process is essential for learning (see Chapter 2).
  - Third, it is often the case that the learning, especially schema-building, that occurs during L2 communication is more important in the long run than the fleeting interaction.
  - Fourth, research indicates that unless information is used, it will be lost from long-term memory (Leaver et al., 2005).
  - Fifth, L2 learning involves awareness (e.g., noticing and understanding, Schmidt, 1995), which does not stop when the learner uses the L2. Learners frequently improve their accuracy, fluency, and pragmatic competence just by being aware of what happens while they communicate. Every opportunity for L2 use therefore offers chances for greater learning (Little, 2003) for any learner who is awake and aware.
  - Sixth, cognitive psychologists (e.g., O'Neil, 1978; Weinstein, Goetz, and Alexander, 1988) have consistently classified memory-related strategies for retrieval and rehearsal as learning strategies for the last three to four decades and have conducted important studies on these types of learning strategies.
  - Seventh, research shows that it is often impossible to tell whether a given action by the learner is for learning or for communication, and whatever the purpose, it often changes midstream (Bialystok and Sharwood Smith, 1985; Tarone, 1981, 1983).
  - For these research-supported reasons, any strategies or tactics promoting the use of and practice with the L2 should be viewed not merely aiding language use but also fostering language learning.

- A strong split between language use strategies and language learning strategies flies in the face of practicality in regard to learning.
  - In a practical sense, most language use strategies allow learners to stay in conversations much longer, have more sustained opportunities to practise, receive more feedback during communication, and thus learn more.
  - Even cover strategies, while mainly aimed at saving face during communication, can ease anxiety and sometimes keep the learner communicatively involved so that further learning is possible. Whether learning occurs with the use of cover strategies largely depends on how anxious the learner is. (See L2 anxiety in Chapter 3.)
- For these reasons, when conducting research on L2 learning strategies, it is unhelpful to accept a strong distinction between L2 learning strategies and L2 use strategies.
- However, *when conducting research on pragmatics rather than on L2 learning,* a focus on strategies for L2 use is valuable (Cohen, personal communication, April 7, 2010).

The following discussion delves into sociocultural concepts of great importance to L2 learning and hence to learning strategies. These concepts are discourse and contexts; cultural models; identity, power relations, and investment; counter-stories; resistance and non-participation; and opposition and accommodation.

4.4.2   Discourse and contexts

According to Gee (2005) discourse has both linguistic and sociocultural/ sociopolitical aspects, the latter of which is more critically attuned to the world at large. The linguistic aspect of discourse is oral or written language in use, as opposed to an abstract linguistic system, whereas in the sociocultural/sociopolitical perspective, discourse is always "situated" in a given place and time and involves particular people.

In the latter perspective, the *social* is also the *political*, referring to the situation in which social interests and social goods are at stake (Gee, 2005). Because discourse is a social practice, it is necessarily political. In this perspective, discourse is that which can be said or communicated about a given topic in a particular sociocultural context. See Concept 4.2 for multiple meanings of the term *context*.

Norton and Toohey (2001, p. 312) added that contexts are "complex and overlapping communities in which variously positioned participants learn specific, local, historically constructed, and changing practices." For Gee (2005), these contexts "repeat" and "accumulate" across time and space, creating the relative enduring shapes of history, institutions, and

---

Concept 4.2   **Meanings of context**

- The social identity of the speaker or writer in that particular moment and sociocultural setting,
- The social activity he or she is trying to accomplish (e.g., formally advising versus commenting as a friend),
- The setting where this is being done (e.g., a classroom or meeting, or in a certain institution, such as a family, community, academic discipline, university, school, business, media, government, or religion),
- Prior communication,
- Shared assumptions and knowledge, and
- The social, cultural, cognitive, material, and political effects of all of these.

Source: Adapted from Gee (2005)

---

society. Discourses that both reflect and shape repeated, accumulated social contexts (history, institutions, society) are called "Discourses" ("big D Discourses").

4.4.3   Cultural models

Gee (2007) described the meaning of words as linked to cultural models, i.e., unexamined, taken-for-granted theories or storylines about how things are. Cultural models belong to socioculturally defined groups of people. A given cultural model is not stored in just one person's mind but is distributed across different kinds of expertise and varied viewpoints in the group. The linkage between word meanings and cultural models is not surprising, because the symbolic power of language (Bourdieu, 1999) is often cultural (Swartz, 1998). Cultural models organize knowledge, thought, and situated meanings in various groups. Cultural models indicate what or who counts as normal, valuable, desirable, and hence powerful in particular sociocultural settings and what or who is understood to be deviant, less valuable, less desirable, and less powerful. Concept 4.3 presents strategy categories that can deal with cultural models and associated meanings.

Here is an example of two contrasting cultural models. Cultural Model A involves complex social networks, mutual support within one's group, high regard for the wisdom of older members of the group, reliance on tradition, maintenance of in-group knowledge, and implicit rather than explicit communication of meaning. In contrast, Cultural Model B stresses individualism, competition, little regard for the wisdom of older group members, an emphasis on innovation, less concern for in-group knowledge, and explicit (often to the point of blunt) communication. People learning another language and culture, and particularly those who wish to go beyond

Concept 4.3   **Strategy types needed to deal with cultural models and the situated meanings in those models**

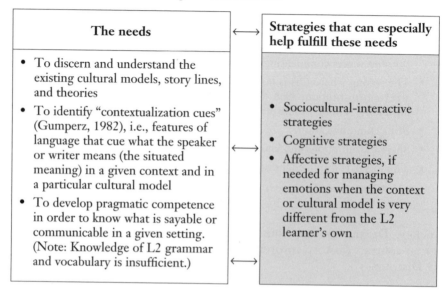

The needs	⟷	Strategies that can especially help fulfill these needs
• To discern and understand the existing cultural models, story lines, and theories • To identify "contextualization cues" (Gumperz, 1982), i.e., features of language that cue what the speaker or writer means (the situated meaning) in a given context and in a particular cultural model • To develop pragmatic competence in order to know what is sayable or communicable in a given setting. (Note: Knowledge of L2 grammar and vocabulary is insufficient.)	⟷ ⟷ ⟷	• Sociocultural-interactive strategies • Cognitive strategies • Affective strategies, if needed for managing emotions when the context or cultural model is very different from the L2 learner's own

the first few years of L2 study, need to understand cultural models in the native culture and the target culture. Therefore, the tactics manifesting the strategy of Dealing with Sociocultural Contexts and Identities can be very valuable. An understanding of cultural models is needed to identify "contextualization cues" (Gumperz, 1982), i.e., features of language that cue what the speaker or writer means (the situated meaning) in a given context and in a particular cultural model. Cultural models are also a backdrop for developing pragmatic competence, or the ability to communicate appropriately in given contexts.

4.4.4   Identity, power relations, and investment

The S²R Model acknowledges that in the sociocultural contexts of L2 learning, issues of identity are always present as a potential site of struggle. The L2 learner, especially in a situation in which the majority of people speak the language that the learner is trying to learn, has a complex, changing, and sometimes contradictory social identity (or rather, multiple social identities) understandable in relation to larger social structures. Another relevant term is *subjectivity*, defined as "the conscious and unconscious thoughts and emotions of the individual, her sense of herself and her ways of understanding her relation to the world" (Weedon, 1987, p. 32). When communicating with those who grew up speaking the language (target language speakers), L2 learners experience "unequal relations of power" between themselves and target language speakers (Norton and Toohey, 2001, p. 312). L2 learners "are not only exchanging information with target language speakers but they are [also] constantly organizing and reorganizing a sense of who they are and how they relate to the social world" (Norton Pierce, 1995, p. 18).

This brings up Bonny Norton's concept of *investment*, i.e., the "socially and historically constructed relationship of learners to the target language, and their often ambivalent desire to learn and practise it" (Norton, 2000/ 2010, p. 10). Norton emphasized that learners respond to and act upon relations of power. Learners' degree of investment in the L2 is related to their desires and their beliefs about themselves (see Chapter 3) and to the sociocultural power relations that either marginalize these learners or welcome them.

Quote 4.2   Investment in L2 learning

When learners invest in learning a new language, they do so with the under-standing that they will acquire a wider range of symbolic and material resources, which will enhance their cultural capital, their conception of them-selves, and their desires for the future. A person's investment in a language may be mediated by other investments that conflict with the desire to speak, such as fear of being marginalized . . . , or resistance when one's professional status or cultural background is not valued or when access to desired symbolic and material resources is denied.

Ema Ushioda (2008, p. 24)

The learner interacts with a specific sociocultural context and considers the nature of the opportunities to practise the L2 in the given context. We cannot label a learner, like Saliha in Norton's (2000/2010) book, as always introverted or extroverted, anxious or relaxed, unmotivated or motivated, silent or talkative. Instead of labelling the learner, we must consider the L2 learner's fluctuating social identity, which is related to how he or she perceives the power dynamics in the sociocultural context in which the L2 is being used (the target cultural context). When the context is welcoming, thus giving the learner a degree of social power, the learner experiences a stronger sense of belonging in the setting and greater confidence, L2 investment, and success in using the L2 for communication. On the other hand, when the context is exclusionary, thus exposing the learner to indif-ference or rejection by those with greater social power, the learner feels less identified with the context, less confident, less invested in the L2, and less successful. Even a potentially confident L2 learner can be laid low by native speakers who are indifferent or punitive, especially in a sociocultural context that sets up obvious barriers against the learner's participation. In some cultures, this happens more often than one would think.

Quote 4.3   Opportunities, investment, and identities

... [T]he opportunities these [learners of English] had to practise English were structured by unequal relations of power in the home and workplace.... [T]heir efforts must be understood with reference to their investment in English and their changing identities across historical time and social space.... [T]ruth is indeed stranger than fiction, life more intriguing than art.

Bonny Norton (2000, p. 2)

However, the sociocultural context itself is not always definitive; some learners respond to an exclusionary context by trying even harder to be accepted and by investing as fully as possible in the L2 as an instrument for breaking into the seemingly closed community. Their degree of success depends partly on whether those with power are ever willing to *recognize* them and allow them to enter. Recognition or lack of it is one of the keys to the learner's identity in situations of unequal power relations.

Quote 4.4   Recognition, misrecognition, and identity

Our identity is partly shaped by recognition [of or by others] or its absence, often by misrecognition of others, and so a person or group of people can suffer real damage, real distortion, if the people of society [e.g., native or fluent speakers of the target language] around them mirror back to them a confining or demeaning or contemptible picture of themselves.

Charles Taylor (1994, p. 25)

4.4.5   Counter-stories

Some L2 learners are imaginative and courageous enough and have sufficient resources to create *counter-stories* (counter-discourses, counter-images, new public identities) to oppose negative, prejudicial images that target language speakers have of them. Norton and Toohey (2001) described two immigrants, Eva and Julie, one an adult and the other a child, who fought against the images others had of them in their new country, Canada. Eva and Julie found that the new, self-created images made them more attractive and acceptable to the Canadians. These two learners found ways to evoke Canadians' recognition, in Charles Taylor's sense of the concept (earlier). Creating a specific, new counter-story to stimulate positive recognition by those with greater social power is a tactic reflecting the strategy of Dealing with Sociocultural Contexts and Identities. This sociocultural-interactive strategy can be supported by affective strategies, (a) Generating and Maintaining Motivation and (b) Activating and Sustaining Positive Emotions, Attitudes, and Beliefs, as well as by metastrategies such as Planning, Monitoring, and Evaluating.

4.4.6   Resistance and non-participation

Research shows that if minority L2 learners are not recognized and respected by members of the dominant culture and are denied positive inter-action with those members, some minority L2 learners resist the dominant culture and its language and forge their own identities apart from the mainstream. In the U.S., *resistance* is seen in some minority L2 learners, often native Spanish-speakers, who (a) join gangs, often violent ones, to receive acceptance and experience a "positive" identity in relation to other gang members; (b) refuse to invest in learning English well because, for them, it is a symbol of the social oppressor; and (c) drop out of high school in massive numbers. In short, they reject the society that fails to recognize them positively. Flores-Gonzalez (2002) discussed identity development among Latino students in the U.S., contrasting "school kids" and "street kids." Valdes (2001) traced the sociocultural roots of Latino students' decision to learn or not learn English. Norton (2001) and Kanno and Norton (2003) documented *non-participation* in imagined communities and illustrated the role of identity in non-participation.

4.4.7   Opposition and accommodation

Opposition is a different identity-management route. Unlike outright resist-ance, opposition allows some *accommodation* to the dominant culture when useful. Many students around the world learning English are caught between clashing desires, maintenance of their own cultural identity versus socio-economic needs (Canagarajah, 1993, p. 601), and therefore show ambivalent opposition rather than outright, radical resistance (Giroux, 1983). The choice of opposition instead of resistance reflects the learner's recognition of a "domination [that] reaches into the structure of personality itself" (Giroux, 1983, p. 106). The identity balance between opposition and accom-modation can be negotiated through tactics associated with the strategy of Dealing with Sociocultural Contexts and Identities. In addition, meta-SI strategies such as Planning and Evaluating help the learner decide just how far and how much to invest and accommodate without losing their sense of identity. Opposition can occur among minority L1 students as well as minority L2 learners. Canagarajah (1997) portrayed the L1 strategies of a group of African-American students entering a largely white university setting: at first scrupulously presenting favourable academic identities (p. 48), then revealing their opposition to cultural and racial domination through quoting oppositional scholars, expressing anger, and promoting racial solidarity ("STAY BLACK") on the computer discussion board. The students thus developed a temporary "safe house." Their tactics of intra-group interaction and social support helped them survive in a culturally threatening context.

Quote 4.5 Opposition and accommodation

Minority students may ... display a complex range of attitudes toward domination with a mixture of oppositional and accommodative tendencies. ... [C]omplexity of students' opposition ... has to be qualified by their belief in the benefits of English, resulting in examination-oriented motivation.

Suresh Canagarajah (1993, pp. 603, 624)

Even in somewhat more accepting sociocultural contexts, high beginning or intermediate L2 learners – particularly if they are in the minority – often feel their cultural identity being challenged by the beliefs and values of the target culture. Although Grenfell and Macaro (2007) were dubious about whether identity-management is relevant to L2 learning, my work on L2 learners in crisis (Oxford et al., 2007) implied that identity-management using the strategy of Dealing with Sociocultural Contexts and Identities, backed up by strategies such as Planning, Monitoring, and Evaluating, can be a strongly positive influence on L2 learning.

4.4.8   Synthesis of theories and concepts

This section has explored important theories and concepts related to social, cultural, and interactional aspects of L2 learning. Several of these theories and concepts are central to the S²R Model. First, communication involves semantic meaning and pragmatic meaning. Teachers should offer practice in both kinds of meanings and teach strategies for learning both. Second, overcoming knowledge barriers in communicating is not just a matter of language use but is an important part of L2 learning. Third, learning to communicate involves learning cultural models and negotiating one's own identity.

4.5 Conclusion

Analysis of L2 learning strategies in the sociocultural-interactive dimension has been sorely limited in the past. However, this chapter emphasizes two types of strategies in this dimension, meta-SI strategies and SI strategies, and thereby opens up a new area of information about these strategies. This is important to the S^2R Model.

The chapter, along with the S^2R Model, is also aimed at providing a counterweight to certain existing theories and systems in need of adjustment. For example, socially-related learning strategies in some prior strategy taxonomies were extremely limited, i.e., these strategies dealt almost solely with asking questions (e.g., for verification or clarification). Although asking questions is important, it only scratches the surface of the sociocultural-interactive dimension of L2 learning. A second example is the assertion that language *use* strategies – viewed largely as compensatory strategies but actually having potentially deeper functions in some cases – are somehow separate from and irrelevant to L2 *learning*. In reality, educational and cognitive psychologists have consistently demonstrated that actively using information (language information or any other type) is the only way to learn it and that not using information is the best way to lose it. Also, some strategies classified for language use, such as retrieval and rehearsal, have been known as learning strategies for decades outside of the L2 field. A third illustration of a needed adjustment is some theorists' questioning of the relevance of strategic identity-management to L2 learning. Evidence cited in this chapter suggests that identity has much to do with L2 learning and that identity-management strategies might be very important to learners who seek higher L2 proficiency and wish to be meaningfully recognized in the target culture.

Although strategies in the sociocultural-interactive dimension have often been a hidden stepchild in L2 learning, the S^2R Model gives them major attention. This model reveals the importance of meta-SI strategies, such as Planning for Contexts, Communication, and Culture, and SI strategies, such as Interacting to Learn and Communicate. The challenge to researchers is to start studying more intensively learners' use of these strategies, the factors relating to such strategy use, and outcomes (e.g., communicative L2 performance, cultural understanding, and changes in sociocultural identity). The challenge to teachers and other practitioners is to find multiple ways and opportunities to enable learners use appropriate meta-SI and SI strategies to enhance their learning. The S^2R Model is designed to help.

Further reading

Canagarajah, A.S. (1993) Critical ethnography of a Sri Lankan classroom: Ambiguities in opposition to reproduction through ESOL. *TESOL Quarterly*, 27(4): 601–626. *Also:* Canagarajah, A.S. (1997) Safe houses in the contact zone: coping strategies of African-American students in the academy. *College Composition and Communication*, 48(2): 173–196. These two critical articles reveal the importance of identity in the sociocultural context and the strategic use of opposition.

Cohen, A.D. (2010) *Strategies in Learning and Using a Second Language*. Second edition. Harlow, Essex, UK: Pearson Longman. This book presents Cohen's reasoning about why strategies for L2 learning and strategies for L2 use are not the same. However, Chapter 4 has just suggested the need for rethinking the theory of a major split between L2 learning and L2 use, given that learning can only be fully accomplished through use.

Gee, J.P. (2005) *An Introduction to Discourse Analysis: Theory and Method*. Second edition. London: Routledge. *Also:* Gee, J.P. (2007) *Social Linguistics and Literacies: Ideology in Action*. London: Taylor and Francis. These two books explain Gee's important socio-political perspective on discourse, cultural models, and ideology in literacy.

Hall, J.K. (2010) *Teaching and Researching Language and Culture*. Second edition. Harlow, Essex, UK: Pearson Longman. This book offers a thorough treatment of language and culture for teachers and researchers. It grapples with the complexities of language and culture in an approachable, useful way.

MacIntyre, P.D., Baker, S., Clément, R. & Donovan, L.A. (2003) Talking in order to learn: Willingness to communicate and intensive language programs. *Canadian Modern Language Review*, 59: 589–607. This article shows that using the language is the way to learn it (i.e., language use and language learning are not separate phenomena). It clearly presents the concept of willingness to communicate.

Norton, B. (2010) *Identity and Language Learning: Gender, Ethnicity and Educational Change*. Second edition. Harlow, Essex, UK: Longman/Pearson Education. This book is a key to understanding the language and identity in sociocultural contexts. Its poststructuralist viewpoint is influential and needed.

Section

Appendices

Appendix I.A   Metacognitive strategies and examples of related tactics (metaphor: "construction manager")

Metacognitive strategy names: *Paying Attention to Cognition, Planning for Cognition, Obtaining and Using Resources for Cognition, Organizing for Cognition, Implementing Plans for Cognition, Orchestrating Cognitive Strategy Use, Monitoring Cognition, and Evaluating Cognition*

STRATEGY	SOME BASIC FUNCTIONS	EXAMPLES OF RELATED TACTICS, AS REPORTED BY LEARNERS
Paying Attention to Cognition	Paying attention to cognition more broadly (floodlight, general attention)	I decide to pay close attention in class every day. When I tried to learn German before, I did not do this well enough.
		I pay attention to the explanation in every lesson, because it's important for doing the exercises.
		I state an intention to tune in to what the lecturer is saying in Spanish, rather than being just caught up in the music of the language.
		I know I have an "analysing style" preference, but many of the tasks in the textbook call for summarizing and synthesizing, so I have to use general attention as well.
	Paying attention to cognition more sharply (flashlight, focused attention)	I decide to focus my attention primarily on the prefixes of Russian verbs in the next week so that I can learn them efficiently.
		I am paying attention to the third part of tonight's German homework.
		I try to minimize disruptions and focus my attention while I do Italian listening tasks with Rosetta Stone. For instance, I turn the cell phone off and avoid all forms of IM [instant messaging].
		I focus my attention to the details when conjugating verbs.
Planning for Cognition	Setting cognitive goals	For a given task, I have to figure out my goals: whether I should emphasize communicative fluency or accuracy of using grammar and vocabulary. Sometimes my goal can be both at the same time.
		I think about the textbook's stated objectives for a lesson and then set my own goals. My goals are sometimes different from (or more than) the goals given in the textbook.

When I am reading, I sometimes have several goals: to understand the meaning, to learn about the topic, to learn to read more quickly, and to pick up new vocabulary words. Other times I just have one goal.

I reflect on my goals for the long term when I am learning Arabic. I know the proficiency level I want to reach, and I know how this will help me become a member of the foreign service.

The more I advance in Spanish, the clearer my long-range goals become. One of my goals is to develop my skills to the point that I can study in a Mexican medical school and understand the lectures fully.

I am working on English to improve my TOEFL score, and that will help me get accepted at an English-speaking university. My later goal is to use English for business. These goals help me study hard.

Planning ahead for cognition	When I am getting ready to do a task, I plan ahead. I think about the task's ease or difficulty, whether I have already done a task like this, and whether I need to break it into parts.

I plan to visit three or four travel-related sites to prepare myself for the class discussion about travel to South America.[1]

I plan my study time based on the complexity of the task and how energetic I am.

I think about whether the language task is important or not and how much time I want to spend on it. If it does not seem as important as other things, I won't spend much time on it.

Once I know whether I want to emphasize fluency or accuracy or both for a given task, then I can plan the strategies to use for the task.

In planning, I prioritize and schedule the tasks that I need to do for learning Somali.

I decide to use automatic computer reminders to help me remember my study schedule for the week.

At proficiency level 3+, I set up an individualized study plan (ISP) so that I can move ahead rapidly.

I figure out how much time and effort it will take to complete the course in Wolof, and I set a schedule to do it (including planning in time for disruptions).

I set realistic long-term goals for myself in learning Tagalog.

I plan to do all of the self-check rubrics in the book so that I can identify my French progress.[2]

[1] This is also related to Obtaining and Using Resources for Cognition.
[2] This is a combination of Planning and Evaluating.

Appendix I.A   Metacognitive strategies and examples of related tactics (continued)

STRATEGY	SOME BASIC FUNCTIONS	EXAMPLES OF RELATED TACTICS, AS REPORTED BY LEARNERS
Obtaining Resources for Cognition	Identifying and finding technological resources for cognition	I find out which CDs and tapes in Mandarin would be the most helpful. My friend tells me that while I am in Moscow I should visually capture Russian language in use – like billboard advertising – so I might use the camera in my cell phone. I make a list of the printed and audio-recorded material for my individualized study plan (ISP) so I can move on as efficiently as I can in learning Polish.[3] I find the best online dictionary and online thesaurus for English. I can practise my downloaded Korean lessons on the iPod no matter where I am.
	Identifying and finding print resources for cognition	I look for an etymology dictionary so I can understand where the words came from. I identify the books of stories I need for further reading in Yiddish. I go to bookstores and buy up sale books in the language so I will always have enough to read and practise with. I find a useful Russian verb wheel.
Organizing for Cognition	Prioritizing for cognition	I prioritize my bookmarked websites according to the degree of relevance to my Japanese learning.
	Organizing the study environment and materials for cognition	I organize my computer files so I can find all my Hungarian homework and notes easily. I organize my English language notebook with colors for the tabs. For studying Laotian, I organize my desk by clearing off everything except what I need. I think about the temperature of the library carrel and bring a sweater or light coat with me. I need bright light to study, so I sit in the brightest place in the apartment when I study Arabic. I make sure to bring something to eat while I am studying, because I always learn better that way.

Implementing Plans for Cognition	Thinking about the plan	I remember my plan to take notes about the key characters as I read Pushkin's *Pikovaya Dama* (*The Queen of Spades*). This will help me with my paper.
	Putting the plan into action for affect	While reading *Pikovaya Dama*, I take notes about the appearance, emotions, actions, and major statements of each of the key characters.
Orchestrating Cognitive Strategy Use	Orchestrating cognitive strategy use for fluency	When I try to go for communicative fluency, I consciously choose a bunch of strategies or tactics that all work together, such as identifying relevant vocabulary in advance, thinking of topics I am likely to discuss, and identifying collocations that I can recognize and use.
	Orchestrating cognitive strategy use for accuracy	When I am doing a task that focuses on accuracy, I switch over my strategies to those that work for precision. I especially like to use two types of reasoning: figuring out the grammar rule from examples and applying a rule to new situations.
	Orchestrating cognitive strategy use for balance	If I focus only on strategies for accuracy in Turkish, I can hardly communicate because I try to be perfect; so then I must try to readjust the strategy balance in favor of both fluency and accuracy. I have to think about which strategies to use for what purposes, and I try to tie them together in a balanced way so I can do what I want to do with the language.
Monitoring Cognition	Monitoring cognitive performance during a task	I look for mistakes while I am writing in French by using the spelling and grammar checker on the computer.
		I monitor my clarity of thought after half an hour of studying Cantonese.
		I check to see whether the generalization I made (using the grammar rule in a new situation) turned out to be correct.
		As I continue reading the short story in Lithuanian, I assess whether I was right in making a prediction that the main character would take a certain action.
		I monitor to see whether my guess was correct, that is, the meanings are basically the same between the proverb in Spanish and a similar-seeming proverb in English.
		I identify any time I am getting mentally off-task and quickly return to the task.
		I check whether I am mentally overwhelmed while I am reading a long novel in French. I know when this happens: it's when I read the same paragraph several times without remembering anything I read. If this happens, I have a good solution.

³ See Leaver (2003b) for ISP.

Appendix I.A   Metacognitive strategies and examples of related tactics (continued)

STRATEGY	SOME BASIC FUNCTIONS	EXAMPLES OF RELATED TACTICS, AS REPORTED BY LEARNERS
Monitoring Cognition (Continued)	Monitoring ease of learning (EOL)[4]	I consider whether the Farsi task will be easy or not. I predict which parts of the new Russian lesson will be easy and which will be difficult.
	Monitoring by making a judgment of learning (JOL)[5]	I think about whether I know the material well enough to do well on the next Russian test. During the exercise, I consider whether I know the vocabulary and structures well enough to do a good job in the next test or on an exercise that builds on this one.
	Monitoring via a feeling of knowing (FOK)[6]	After I have studied a lesson and done the exercises, I sense whether I will be able to recognize a certain Arabic sentence or phrase on the upcoming Arabic quiz.
	Monitoring cognitive strategy use	During the reading task, I determine whether the strategies I am using are working well for me. In other words, am I understanding what I am reading? If not, I try to think of other strategies that would help. When I am trying to speak, I sometimes find myself using too much analysis, so I realize that I will have to change my strategies.
Evaluating Cognition	Evaluating cognitive progress and performance	I compare my performance to goals the teacher set up for this Business Spanish simulation. I compare my pronunciation for this task to the pronunciation on the tape. I decide whether I have learned the material in one unit before I go to the next one. At the end of the week I listen to the recorded exercises I had listened to during the week to check whether I remember.

	I evaluate my progress in writing Ukrainian since the last essay.
	After every task I do a judgment of my learning: how much do I remember, what did I learn, why is it important?
	I compare my work to the course's official long-term objectives and goals and see whether I am making the progress that I need to make.
	I take an oral proficiency examination after every 300 hours of study and determine whether my proficiency has increased to the next step on the scale.
Evaluating cognitive strategy use	I evaluate whether the strategy of analysing worked well, that is, whether I figured out the correct meaning when I broke the information down into parts.
	At the end of every unit in my ESL textbook, there is a checklist that helps me think about the strategies I used. I consider whether they worked OK for me.
	I think about my learning strategies to see which ones have worked the best for me in the long run and which ones no longer support me at my level of proficiency.
	After three months, I look back at my studying to determine whether the spiraled reviewing strategy has worked for me.
	I have read several books on how to learn languages more effectively. To improve my overall performance, I sometimes check my strategy use against the strategies I find in those books.
	I figure out what I would do differently if I do a task like this one again.

4 Nelson and Narens (1994) would consider these two tactics, reflecting EOL, to be part of prospective monitoring. However, it could also be an aspect of Planning.

5 Nelson and Narens (1994) would have considered the above two tactics, reflecting JOL, to be part of prospective monitoring.

6 Nelson and Narens (1994) would have viewed FOK to be part of prospective monitoring.

Source: Typology and organization of learning strategies in this table are original. Learning strategies in the table were reported by learners in open-ended questionnaires, discussions, interviews, and conversations over two decades.

Appendix I.B Cognitive strategies and examples of related tactics (metaphor: "construction workers")

Names of cognitive strategies: *Using the Senses to Understand and Remember, Activating Knowledge, Reasoning, Conceptualizing with Details, Conceptualizing Broadly, Going Beyond the Immediate Data*

STRATEGY	BASIC FUNCTIONS	EXAMPLES OF RELATED TACTICS, AS REPORTED BY LEARNERS
Using the Senses to Understand and Remember	Using the visual sense to understand and remember	I understand better when I look at the visible structure of the article or story in Spanish.
		I examine any accompanying graphs and charts to help me understand what I am reading in German.
		When I am trying to understand what the newscaster is saying on TV, I always look at the screen.
		Sometimes I find it useful to go to YouTube to see whether there is a video on the topic I am reading about in French.
		I make charts, tables, and pictures to help me make mental associations in Norwegian.
		I remember based on where I first saw this word: it was on a huge billboard in Moscow.
		I use mental imagery to remember the parts of an airplane fuselage in Mandarin.
		I create a personal image to remember new words about food in Māori.
		I remember some Latvian adjectives by mentally "seeing" the Latvian government organizational chart in my mind and associating adjectives to each of the government offices. I try to make it as silly and funny as possible.
		I try to turn the conversation into a series of visual images so I can remember it.
	Using the auditory sense to understand and remember	The background noise on the Russian CD helps me understand the meaning.
		I memorize a common phrase in Middle English as a whole chunk, hearing it in my mind as though it were one word.
		I take both sides of the dialogue and remember them using different-sounding voices, which I associate with each character in the dialogue.

I use Spanish language hip-hop songs to help me remember the words. I especially remember better when I sing.

I say the dialogue in Czech out loud to myself many times so it will stick in my mind.

I use my "mental voice" to repeat the French dialogues to myself. This helps me remember them.

I memorize all the lines of the story by saying it into the recorder and listening to it repeatedly, until I can say it word for word.

I say the new Tsongan words aloud until they sound natural, and then it's easier to remember them.

Using the haptic (tactile/kinesthetic) sense to understand and remember	I write a new word many times in order to remember it.
	I find sentences on the Internet that use the words I'm learning. I copy the sentences down several times. This helps me understand the words and remember the real contexts for using the words.
	My friend and I create a Total Physical Response game to learn and practise transitive verbs. We connect the verbs to the movements and make up new sentences with the verbs.
Using combined senses to understand and remember	I walk around the apartment and post (on furniture, walls, and mirrors) a lot of colored sticky notes with words and sentences on them. I walk around later, several times a day, looking at the notes. This way I can understand what I am learning and have fun as I integrate it in my mind.
	As a memory aid, I say the new Finnish vocabulary expressions to myself while I run the track every morning.
	To remember what I am learning in Nepali, I associate the sights and sounds with personal experiences and with places I have been.
	I watch foreign films using closed-captioning, so I get sounds, images, and print at the same time to help me understand.
	I audio-record anything that seems important to me in class so that I can listen to it later and improve my comprehension.

Appendix I.B Cognitive strategies and examples of related tactics (continued)

STRATEGY	BASIC FUNCTIONS	EXAMPLES OF RELATED TACTICS, AS REPORTED BY LEARNERS
Activating Knowledge	Brainstorming	I brainstorm what I already know about the topic by writing notes on a page.
		I brainstorm aloud with a small group what we know about the topic.
	Using visual images to activate knowledge	I mentally scan what I already know about the content. To do this, I see it in my mind as linked pieces of information.
		I use a KWL chart to identify what I *know* and what I *want* to know; and I complete it later by indicating what I *learned*.
		I find out the new topic or new information I am supposed to learn. I mentally envision a lasso in my hand. I spin the lasso in my mind once or twice, and it grabs everything that I already know that might relate to the new information.
	Using information-internalization in reverse	To activate or retrieve knowledge when I need it, I go into reverse by remembering how I got it into my memory in the first place: image, sound, movement, or some other way.
		When I think of how I learned it, the information appears.
		When I need to use a phrase or idiomatic expression, I try to remember the original associations I made when I learned the material.
Reasoning	Using inductive reasoning	I try to figure out the grammar rules in Russian based on the evidence from my newspaper readings in *Izvestiya*, even before the teacher explains.
	Using deductive reasoning	I learn the rule and immediately try to apply it when I write out sentences in Farsi.
		I generalize a Guajarati grammar rule to another situation if it seems like it fits.
		I am careful about generalizing from English to German, because the languages don't work the same way.

Conceptualizing with Details	Making distinctions	I distinguish between more important and less important information that I read in Hungarian.
		When listening in Spanish, I distinguish between arguments that sound persuasive but are not based on facts and those that are persuasive because they are objective.
		I distinguish between more important details (who, what, when, where, why, and how) and other information when I read an article on the front page of the San Juan paper.
		I differentiate between what the words say on their own and what they really mean in the social setting. There is often a big difference.
		I distinguish between what I already know and what I still need to learn about using the *preterit* tense in Spanish.
		I distinguish between situations, as when it's useful to translate word-for-word and when it's better to translate more flexibly or interpret.
		I figure out when it is appropriate to directly transfer knowledge across languages and when not.
	Sequencing	I put ideas in order by chronological sequence, alphabetical order, or any other logical order.
		I list information in my notebook according to the date that the teacher provided it. This helps me remember it.
		I draw a storyline so I can remember the order of events in the Russian short story.
	Analysing and decoding	I decode letter by letter, word by word, and then the meaning starts to make sense to me.
		I break down words into their parts, especially focusing on prefixes and suffixes that are common.
		I break sentences into subjects, verbs, adverbs, and so on to get the meaning.
		I analyse the logical flow and argument of the news article in *Le Monde*.
		I analyse the Chinese character so I can understand the different parts.

Appendix I.B Cognitive strategies and examples of related tactics (continued)

STRATEGY	BASIC FUNCTIONS	EXAMPLES OF RELATED TACTICS, AS REPORTED BY LEARNERS
Conceptualizing with Details (Continued)	Classifying/categorizing	In my notebook I classify words by their features (e.g., nouns, verbs, adjectives) and by their topics and write labels so everything is clear.
		I categorize the material I find about social discrimination in the U.K., the U.S., Australia, and Japan and put it into various files so I can read it later. I want to compare the persuasive language styles, defensiveness, and other aspects.
		I classify the magazine articles according to whether they are useful for my learning of the language.
		I classify L2 films according to how interesting and difficult they seem; then I decide whether to watch.
	Comparing/contrasting across languages	I compare how I use my native language, English, with the literary language in Spanish novels.
		I compare the sound systems of Spanish, French, and Italian.
		When I read the Brazilian papers online, I compare what I read in Portuguese to what I know in Spanish.
		I contrast the Cyrillic writing system with the Roman alphabet.
	Making hierarchies of ideas	I organize my knowledge, starting with the details and going to the main categories.
		I use a T-line to outline the main points and the details of the plot.
		I draw stars by the most important information.
		I underline or circle the things that I need to study the most.
		I take notes verbatim, but I go back later and highlight the key points with different color ink.

Category	Strategy	Description
Conceptualizing Broadly	Synthesizing across several sources	I synthesize the main points of what I have learned from multiple sources before the weekly test.
	Summarizing/getting the gist	To make a summary of the scientific essay on the effects of Chernobyl on deaths in Baltic region, I first look for the key sentences or topic sentences of the various paragraphs in the essay.
		I skim the article briefly before reading it to get the gist of what it's about.
		I read the beginning and the end of the text and then some of the topic sentences (in the paragraphs) so that I can get the main idea before reading the whole text.
		I use pictures, headings, and all other clues to help me get the gist of the newspaper article I am reading.
	Combining/linking similar things	I combine the Spanish phrases to make sentences and then recombine them to make different sentences, creating as many as I can.
		In a conversation I notice all the words that are used to mean the same thing or are about the same topic. This helps me create mental links and build up a bank of synonyms.
		I create a semantic map linking the ideas about the economic system, such as inflation, interest rates, macroeconomics, microeconomics, downturn, and so on, in Korean.
Going Beyond the Immediate Data	Predicting	I set up a prediction about what the Telugu speaker will say based on all possible clues, then I check my accuracy as the speaker goes further. I predict what will be said on the TV based on facts I have picked up in the newspaper.
	Inferring	To infer the meaning when I am listening, I use all the background clues – ambient noise, how fast the person is speaking, the tone of voice (humorous, stern) – and combine it with what I already know.
		I use the situation and linguistic clues to help me understand the meaning of what is being said: background noise, politeness register, length of sentences, and so on.

Source: Typology and organization of the learning strategies in this table are original. Learning strategies in the table were reported by learners in open-ended questionnaires, discussions, interviews, and conversations over two decades.

Appendix I.C   Meta-affective strategies and examples of related tactics (metaphor: "electricity manager")

Names for meta-affective strategies: *Paying Attention to Affect, Planning for Affect, Obtaining and Using Resources for Affect, Organizing for Affect, Implementing Plans for Affect, Orchestrating Affective Strategy Use, Monitoring Affect, and Evaluating Affect*

STRATEGY	BASIC FUNCTIONS	EXAMPLES OF RELATED TACTICS, AS REPORTED BY LEARNERS
Paying Attention to Affect	Paying affective attention more broadly (floodlight, general attention)	I consider my attitude toward the language course and the teacher. When I am fatigued, my attitude is not positive.
		I think about my motivations for taking the course – why I am here in the first place.
		I focus on why I am learning Russian and what my hopes and dreams are about it.
		My affective style of learning is very relaxed, so I have to push myself to meet deadlines and take things more seriously.
	Paying affective attention more sharply (flashlight, focused attention)	I notice that I get really annoyed when my little sister and her friends come in the living room when I am trying to study my Swedish. They make so much noise!
		I watch for physical signs of stress or anxiety regarding language studies so I can take care of the situation.
		Before starting my homework, I think about how I feel: Am I happy, contented, interested, anxious, angry? Are there any barriers to my motivation right now?[1]
Planning for Affect	Setting affective goals	One of my goals is to figure out how to become less anxious when I have to make an oral report in German next Friday.
		I want to learn to relax when doing the listening exercises in this lesson.
		I set a double goal: what I want to accomplish in the task and how I want to feel about myself as a learner of Arabic.
		My goal is to find something valuable in this lesson so that I can feel motivated.

In the long haul, I want to be motivated to learn Czech all the way to the advanced-high proficiency level or beyond. I want to find ways to stay motivated the whole time. As it is, I feel my motivation wavering.

I have seen too many people who run out of steam or get very frustrated around the seventh month of the intensive Japanese course, when things get really difficult, so I set the goal of finding ways to stay engaged and interested during the hard times.

I want to keep on finding things that make me excited about learning Spanish.

I want to discover how to stop being embarrassed about my level of competence when I talk to native speakers of Portuguese.

Planning ahead for affect	When I am getting ready to do a task, I start by thinking whether I have done anything like this before, so that I can become calmer and more confident.
	When I plan by breaking the task down into steps or parts, I automatically feel more confident.
	Considering the emotional load of this task (Is it stressful or anxiety-provoking for me?) helps me plan ways to deal with that load.
	I consider steps I can take to lower anxiety about doing this speaking activity in Romanian.
	To feel more self-assured in learning French this year, I plan to make a "can-do" chart of my progress (what exactly I can do in French) every two weeks.
	Using my year-long individualized study plan is a good way for me to gain confidence that I am on the right track and making rapid progress toward distinguished proficiency in Polish.
	I plan to try out a new affective tactic every week for the next month to help myself let go of my perfectionist tendencies and start enjoying the course in Mongolian.

[1] This is like "taking one's emotional temperature" (in Oxford, 1990).

Appendix I.C Meta-affective strategies and examples of related tactics (continued)

STRATEGY	BASIC FUNCTIONS	EXAMPLES OF RELATED TACTICS, AS REPORTED BY LEARNERS
Obtaining and Using Resources for Affect	Obtaining and using technological resources for affect	I look for CDs of Latino hip-hop in order to motivate myself for learning Spanish. I search for relaxing music to play in the background while I study Catalan. My iPod comes in very handy when I want to relax between study sessions. I find blogs and websites to learn more about reducing my anxiety in language learning. I discovered the website at the Hong Kong Polytechnic University about independent language learning, and it helps me know how to deal with my motivational issues.
	Obtaining and using print resources for affect	I read books about how to become a better language learner to get tips on how to handle the stress of learning a language and how to stay motivated.
Organizing for Affect	Organizing the study environment for affect	I arrange for ways to minimize disruptions that annoy and upset me while I try to write an essay in Italian. For instance, I turn the cell phone off. I make sure to have music on in the background, because it helps relax and motivate me.
	Organizing for anxiety reduction	I feel very anxious about my baby when I am trying to study Tagalog. I can't learn when I am anxious like that, so I get my husband to take care of the baby when I'm studying.
	Organizing for entertainment and relaxation	I entertain myself by using colour and Google images to decorate my Russian notebook and my homework. I have images of Russian cities, the Siberian steppes in winter, cultural symbols, and Russian people – whatever I can find that interests me. I ask myself how I can have fun with the task and then organize things that way.

Implementing Plans for Affect	Thinking about the plan	I think about how I planned to calm myself down before the German test, and I used the plan.
	Putting the plan into action for affect	I implemented my plan to do some meditation before I have to make a major presentation. It helped me relax and enabled me to remember what I wanted to say.
Orchestrating Affective Strategy Use	Orchestrating strategies for current interest and future instrumental needs	In order to develop speaking skills in Laotian, I personalize the lessons to make them interesting for now, and I think about my future job.
	Orchestrating positive strategies and "threat" strategies for motivation	I needed to stay motivated and on task in French, so I intentionally created a combination of positive strategies (telling myself why I want to learn this language) and "scare" or "threat" strategies (telling myself what will happen if I don't keep trying). I responded better to a combination than to either one or the other.
Monitoring Affect	Monitoring affective state during a task	I judge how confident I am about the answers I gave on the German test.[2] When I make errors, I tend to get upset with myself. This makes it worse.
		I especially monitor my motivation several times during a very long reading.
		I monitor how I am feeling when my thoughts wander. Am I uninterested? Am I unmotivated? Am I physically fatigued? Am I feeling overwhelmed? Am I depressed about something that has nothing to do with language learning?
		I think about whether my wandering thoughts mean I need a break to relax for half an hour.
	Monitoring use of affective tactics and strategies	While doing a very challenging task in Somali, I monitor my affective tactics for staying calm and involved. If they are not working, I need to find others.
		If I start getting bored, it means I need to come up with a new strategy to keep me interested or that I need to take a break.

[2] Nelson and Narens (1994) consider this to be retrospective monitoring.

Appendix I.C   Meta-affective strategies and examples of related tactics (continued)

STRATEGY	BASIC FUNCTIONS	EXAMPLES OF RELATED TACTICS, AS REPORTED BY LEARNERS
Evaluating Affect	Evaluating affective progress and states	At the end of the week's effort of learning Swahili, I consider whether I feel confident and contented, which is based on whether I feel I have met my own high personal expectations.
		I consider whether the good result of the German exam was due to an easy exam, easy grading on the part of the teacher, or my own preparation and knowledge. I feel I can take credit for the result.[3]
		In considering how well I did in writing the essay, I thought about how much was in my control and how much was out of my control.[4]
		I was a nervous wreck before starting this series of listening activities, but the strategies I used to calm down and focus helped me a lot.
		I feel much happier and more relaxed when using Berber than I did six months ago.
		I notice that my anxiety level just keeps going up as the lessons get more difficult and I am forced to speak more often in Bengali.
	Evaluating effectiveness of affective strategy and tactic use	As I discussed my progress with the teacher, I considered whether my affective strategies were working to keep me motivated, interested, and not so anxious.
		So far in the Russian course, the best affective tools for me have been the ones that help me relax, like laughing and breathing deeply.
		After a very difficult Farsi listening task, I evaluate the degree to which the positive things I told myself earlier had helped me on the task.[5]

[3] This relates to attribution theory.
[4] This relates to local of control theory.
[5] This tactic is known as evaluating positive self-talk.

Source: Typology and organization of the learning strategies in this table are original. Learning strategies in the table were reported by learners in open-ended questionnaires, discussions, interviews, and conversations over two decades.

Appendix I.D   Affective strategies and examples of related tactics (metaphor: "electricity workers")

Names of affective strategies: *Activating Supportive Emotions, Beliefs, and Attitudes; Generating and Maintaining Motivation*

STRATEGY	BASIC FUNCTIONS	EXAMPLES OF RELATED TACTICS, AS REPORTED BY LEARNERS
Activating Supportive Emotions, Beliefs, and Attitudes	Expressing feelings or being in touch with feelings	I talk to my husband if I feel upset with myself about my progress in Japanese; and if that doesn't help, I talk to my distance tutor.
		I write in my journal almost daily to describe my language learning experiences and express my feelings about them.
	Relaxing	I relax with music so I can become less anxious and get the most out of the eTandem phone session this afternoon.
		I use deep breathing as a way to relax before I have to give my talk in Belarussian.
		I take a short break if I am feeling too tense while I am getting ready to do a talk in Romanian.
		I read something funny to relax before getting to my Hindi homework.
		Joking helps me to relax in class, and my classmates say that my joking relaxes them, too.
	Creating a positive emotion via thoughts and statements	I put myself in a good mood for studying Khmer by thinking of something good I have done today.
		I think of my Mexican girlfriend as I study Spanish, and this helps me feel positive.
		I say a word of gratitude to someone. That helps me feel better before I study Hausa for today.
	Creating a positive emotion with colours	I am happier when I am wearing bright colours, so I wear these when I study Turkish. I also have my desk decorated with Turkish items that have bright colours.
		I have happy pictures on the wall above my desk.

Appendix I.D   Affective strategies and examples of related tactics (continued)

STRATEGY	BASIC FUNCTIONS	EXAMPLES OF RELATED TACTICS, AS REPORTED BY LEARNERS
Activating Supportive Emotions, Beliefs, and Attitudes (Continued)	Substituting positive emotions, beliefs, and attitudes for negative ones	When I hear a negative voice in my mind telling me that I just can't do it, I switch off the voice as if it were a TV or iPod.
		If I start feeling angry about all the homework, I recognize it but immediately substitute a feeling of harmony and peace.
		When the Greek lesson is difficult, instead of feeling down I think how privileged I am to be studying Greek.
		When I am feeling negative about my ability in Italian, I think about the time I was at the Plaza d'Espana and talked all night over Italian ices.
		Instead of getting threatened by contradictory or incomplete information, or thinking this language is too strange, I think of the contradictions as interesting.
	Using positive self-talk for the short term (at the task level or just above)[1]	I tell myself that if I study hard now, the next Korean test will be easier.
		When I compare my Danish pronunciation to the native pronunciation on the tape, I say to myself that my pronunciation is fairly good, and this helps me stay motivated and keep trying.
		I tell myself it's OK to feel anxious about a speaking task. This ironically makes me feel calmer.
		I say that is fine for me not to understand everything I hear in Amharic. Accepting this makes me able to understand better.
		I use positive self-talk ("I know I can do this") to get started on the next Hebrew task.
		Because I did so well on the Thai exam, I tell myself, "All that hard work paid off," and that pumps me up for more work.
		I encourage myself to take risks during the speaking task and tell myself I can learn from mistakes.
		When I communicate on the discussion board in Russian, I tell myself that others will be interested in what I have to say.
		To keep myself going while I am going over the Greek vocabulary for the new lesson, I say positive things to myself, like "I've done well so far, and I can finish the rest," or "This is interesting to me," and "I can do it!"

	I remind myself that I did well on tasks like this one when I studied French, and that keeps my spirits up for doing the Serbian task.
	While I am doing the task, I remind myself of how much I enjoy studying Bahasa Indonesia.
	While I am doing a task in Turkish and starting to question my ability, I think to myself, "My friend Madeline could do this, and I did something like this last week." Then I feel comfortable again.
Using positive self-talk for the long-term	I tell myself how good I will feel when I reach the intermediate level in Portuguese.
	I tell myself how useful it will be to do well in this course, because it brings me one step closer to going to Rome for my study-abroad year.
	I tell myself that I am building this "language house" bit by bit, and doing well on this part will help me with the next.
	I tell myself that that every hour I study for the English entrance exam will be worth it, because I will pass and be accepted at the university I want.
	The language experts wrote that it was helpful for students like me to use self-encouragement and positive self-talk, and I find that this works well when I am experiencing difficulties with the language.
Using paradoxical intention to reduce anxiety	I intentionally make a mistake, or make a joke about a mistake, so that I will not be so anxious about making one. It's like scratching my new car on purpose so that I won't get upset when I do it by accident.[2]
Setting low expectations	I intentionally expect to do poorly, so that when I do better, I can feel good about myself.[3]
Using self-handicapping to provide a failure excuse and improve self-esteem	I make the Korean task much harder than it has to be by adding extra steps or more details. That way, if I bomb the task, I will have a good excuse, but if I do well, I will feel great about myself and what I achieved.[4]

[1] Positive self-talk is functional for both affective strategies, i.e., Activating Supportive Emotions, Beliefs, and Attitudes and Generating and Maintaining Motivation.
[2] This is a pre-emptive negative behaviour to reduce anxiety.
[3] This goes with defensive pessimism. See later in this table.
[4] Self-handicapping can be used as an excuse for possible failure, as shown immediately above, or for increasing challenge and interest, as shown later in this table.

Appendix I.D   Affective strategies and examples of related tactics (continued)

STRATEGY	BASIC FUNCTIONS	EXAMPLES OF RELATED TACTICS, AS REPORTED BY LEARNERS
Generating and Maintaining Motivation	Using positive imagery for expectations	I envision that I will perform well on the English entrance examination. Since this exam is so important, it helps to have a positive image.[5]
	Using self-handicapping as a positive challenge	I challenge and interest myself by writing a comparison-and-contrast essay in Slovak, even though the essay could have just been a simple description instead.[6]
	Using self-entertainment to stay motivated	I always write my homework sentences in Serbo-Croatian with silly or crazy-sounding statements. It takes more work, but I never get bored![7]
	Increasing extrinsic motivation by considering instrumental use of the L2	I think of all the ways I can use Chinese after I graduate. When I am getting tired and want to quit doing my English homework, I tell myself how much this means to my future career. I think about how important it is for my GPA – and my chances for graduate school – for me to earn an "A" in this Latin class.
	Increasing extrinsic motivation by considering future rewards or future good feelings	I remind myself that I will get to watch a film when I finish this task, and that keeps me motivated. I promised my wife I would finish this Cantonese homework and go out to dinner with her, so I think of her (and dinner) when I need inspiration. I motivate myself by planning to go swimming after I finish the lesson. I am sometimes overwhelmed by all those words to remember, but I think how good it will feel to reach a Level 2+ in June.

Increasing extrinsic motivation regardging integration into the culture	I inspire myself by realizing that I can use the language in order to get to know Italian people, create deep friendships, and immerse myself in Italian culture and life.
Increasing intrinsic motivation	I think about all the things I like about the Spanish language and literature: the sounds, the idioms, the poetry. This motivates me. I listen to CDs of poets reading in the language, and this makes me very excited and happy. I get into a real flow. I always look for something of cultural interest in the Spanish homework. I personalize the German tasks to make them more interesting.
Using defensive pessimism as a motivator	I tell myself that I will do poorly in the debate in German, so that I will not lose my motivation entirely if this happens. If I do better, that's great. I tell myself that there's no chance to do really well in Russian, so when I get a C grade I will not be discouraged or demotivated.
Using positive self-talk for motivation[8]	I remind myself that it helps my motivation to meditate fifteen minutes before starting to study Farsi each day.

[5] This reflects the expectancy part of Expectancy x Value theory, Rheinberg, Vollmeyer, and Rollett (2000).
[6] Self-handicapping can be used for increasing challenge and interest, as shown above, or as an excuse for possible failure, as shown earlier in this table.
[7] This is viewed as a satiation strategy.
[8] See all of the tactics for positive self-talk under Activating Supportive Emotions, Beliefs, and Attitudes. Note the close ties among emotion, attributes, and motivation.

Appendix I.D Affective strategies and examples of related tactics (continued)

STRATEGY	BASIC FUNCTIONS	EXAMPLES OF RELATED TACTICS, AS REPORTED BY LEARNERS
Generating and Maintaining Motivation (Continued)	Strengthening motivation through counter-discourses	I was a lawyer in my country before coming here. Now I drive this taxi, but my mind says I am a lawyer. I will learn English, take exams, and be a lawyer here. I will help immigrant families like mine.
	Using negative self-talk or negative self-assessment as a prod to improve	I tell myself that even if I do very badly when I speak, at least it won't be too long a time, and I can survive anything for a little while.
		I tell myself that I cannot possibly make more of a fool of myself than I did last time I spoke Yoruba, so I might as well not worry and just do it.
		While I am doing my Spanish homework, I keep chiding myself for being lazy, and that makes me stick to the task.
		I picture myself as having been really stupid on my last exam in Dutch, and that inspires me to try harder this time.
	Posing a negative outcome and working to avoid it	The only way I can keep on task is to remind myself how terrible it will be if I don't finish.
		I study hard in French so that I will avoid bad grades and will not feel bad about myself.
		I work very hard in my German studies, because I don't want my teacher or classmates to think badly of me.

Note: In this table, some of the tactics reflect "reverse psychology," in which a seemingly "negative" step is taken to create a positive psychological outcome. Some students felt their reverse psychology tactics were useful, although obviously not all these tactics would work for all students.
Source: Typology and organization of the learning strategies in this table are original. Learning strategies in the table were reported by learners in open-ended questionnaires, discussions, interviews, and conversations over two decades.

Appendix I.E   Meta-sociocultural-interactive (meta-SI) strategies and examples of related tactics (metaphor: "community manager")

Meta-SI strategy names: *Paying Attention to Contexts, Communication, and Culture; Planning for Contexts, Communication, and Culture; Obtaining and Using Resources for Contexts, Communication, and Culture; Organizing for Contexts, Communication, and Culture; Implementing Plans for Contexts, Communication, and Culture; Orchestrating Strategies for Contexts, Communication, and Culture; Monitoring for Contexts, Communication, and Culture; Evaluating for Contexts, Communication, and Culture.*

STRATEGY	BASIC FUNCTIONS	EXAMPLES OF RELATED TACTICS, AS REPORTED BY LEARNERS
Paying Attention to Contexts, Communication, and Culture	Paying attention to contexts, communication, and culture more broadly (floodlight, general attention)	As I am finding out about courses, I stop to consider how much each course would require me to talk with other people. I look forward to courses with real communication.
		I consider the different social identity I seem to take on when speaking in German. Because of my communication skills, I feel like a little child again – a great reduction of who I really am.
		Before deciding whether to say anything, I generally take the pulse of the group to see whether I, as a foreigner and language learner, would be accepted if I opened my mouth. Sometimes I just stay silent.
		If I have not been in a particular group before, I identify who has the greatest power in the group.
		I studied "communities of practice", so now I look for the experts or old-timers in any community I am in. This is valuable in my language classes and when I study abroad.
		My learning style is normally rather introverted, but the communicative course in Hungarian will require me to interact with many people. I realize I will have to stretch my style a bit.
		I prefer to work with others, and this fits well with the steps I have to take to improve my Arabic within the distinguished level.
	Paying attention to contexts, communication, and culture more sharply (flashlight, focused attention)	I consider whether the task will require me to interact with others and how to deal with that.
		I consider how difficult it was last time not to be able to understand and converse in German with Herr Finkelstein, and I know something needs to improve very soon in my listening and speaking.

Appendix I.E   Meta-SI strategies and examples of related tactics (continued)

STRATEGY	BASIC FUNCTIONS	EXAMPLES OF RELATED TACTICS, AS REPORTED BY LEARNERS
Planning for Contexts, Communication, and Culture	Setting goals for communication in specific cultures and contexts	While preparing for a task that requires speaking, I prioritize my goals: to make the task humorous and fun, help my class partner to relax, and practise my Spanish vocabulary.
		My objective is to work very hard to become a better listener so I can work more effectively with Alberto Marcos on the upcoming investment plan in three weeks.
		Even though the teacher emphasizes perfect grammar when we speak aloud in Slovak, I really feel that getting to know the pragmatics – how to act and what to say in any social situation – is a more important long-range goal for me.
		Because my business career will involve a lot of international travel to China, I must develop a strong command of speaking and must be able to say the tones correctly, because these things can help me make a good social impression when I'm interacting with the Chinese.
		I want to reach level 3+ in speaking proficiency before I graduate, so that I can communicate and be understood by most people for most ordinary social and work situations.
		My goal is to become fluent enough to communicate with my Estonian fiancé's family in Tallin so they will welcome me as part of the family.
		My aim is to become comfortable with communicating orally in French and develop sufficient skill to work with a French-speaking real estate agent, who can help me buy a *pied-à-terre* in Nice. I need to listen and speak well enough, and also be able to read the contract adequately, so that the deal will go well.
		I am a lawyer from Egypt studying for an international law certificate at ____ School of Law in Washington, D.C. My goal while I am here is to publish a legal paper in an international law journal, which signifies acceptance in the international law community. The power is in the hands of legal scholars in that community. I prepare myself to join it through my English writing.
		I want to become accepted as a scholar and programme administrator here in the U.S. I study how others do their research and writing so I can match it or surpass it. I am learning very different English genres from what I learned in China. I am gaining a new identity here.

Planning ahead for communication in specific cultures and contexts	In preparation for the role-play in Portuguese, Roberta and I plan to create role cards[1] and use them for practicing.
	I plan to work on the appropriate speech acts so that when I meet the new Japanese visiting scholar next week I will be properly respectful and polite.
	An activity in Korean class involves appropriate addressing of females who are of different ages, some younger and some older than I am. I need to learn the rules for how to address women according to their ages and other factors. I plan to read all I can find about this and then check my understanding with a Korean native speaker.
	Once I know whether I want to emphasize fluency or accuracy for a given task – or both of them – then I can plan the strategies to use for the task.
	My automatic computerized reminders tell me the days and times I have scheduled to meet with my friend Vaclav and speak Czech this month.
	Even though the teacher emphasizes perfect grammar when we speak aloud in Slovak, I really feel that getting to know the pragmatics – how to act and what to say in any social situation – is a more important long-range goal for me.
	Because my business career will involve a lot of international travel to China, I must develop a strong command of the oral language and must be able to say the tones correctly, because these things can help me make a good social impression when I'm interacting with the Chinese.
	I want to reach level 3+ in speaking proficiency before I graduate, so that I can communicate and be understood by most people for most ordinary, not-too-difficult social and work situations.
	I decide to go to the town meetings where Hispanic issues are discussed, and then I can meet many people speaking Spanish.
	I plan to seek a mentor who is a native speaker, someone who has a lot of free time, preferably a retired person who does not have too many pressures.

[1] Role cards describe the person's role without providing a script.

Appendix I.E Meta-SI strategies and examples of related tactics (continued)

STRATEGY	BASIC FUNCTIONS	EXAMPLES OF RELATED TACTICS, AS REPORTED BY LEARNERS
Obtaining and Using Resources for Contexts, Communication, and Culture	Obtaining and using technological resources for contexts, communication, and culture	I look for opportunities to practise my Italian with other people online. I have made connections so that I can participate in a telephone eTandem learning project with a student in Norway. I will teach him English and he will teach me Norwegian. I have great communication practice by playing massively multiplayer online role-playing games (MMORPGs) in French, especially *Dofus* and *Dragonica*. It is great to know that people are playing these games in different parts of the world and that I can participate.
	Obtaining and using print or in-person resources for context, communication, and culture	In Germany, I seek out chances to interact with people in German. This is sometimes hard in the cities, because many people just want to practise their English with me. I travel a lot, and I look for people with whom to practise my Yiddish. When I travel to London I go to Golders Green to speak Yiddish, and when I am in New York State I go to Williamsburg or Kiryas Joel. I make friends, and I visit their homes. I learn the culture, too. I ask my older friend, Señora Sanchez, to help me gain access to Spanish-speaking communities where I might otherwise not be allowed or might not feel comfortable. She takes me to community events and introduces me to people so I can speak Spanish. I have a pen-pal in Mexico with whom I exchange letters in Spanish. I ask my friend in Pakistan to send me packages of political news clippings in Urdu. I read everything I could about the country. This did not help me with producing the language, but it made me more comfortable talking with native speakers. My friend from Germany and I talk about books a lot and share books in each others' languages.
	Obtaining and using hybrid resources for contexts, communication, and culture	I have joined a new hybrid language-learning program at the Open University that provides print textbooks and workbooks, online communications with a tutor, and the possibility of a meeting with other students on a regular basis. This allows me to have a lot of freedom while still getting social support and interaction.

Organizing for Contexts, Communication, and Culture	Organizing for communication in specific contexts	I set the schedule so that I have time to visit my grandmother's friend. I like to speak Hungarian with her once a week. I find a place where it is easy to talk in Russian. The bars are often too loud, but the city park is perfect. When I want to communicate with my eTandem partner by phone, I have to ask my brother to turn off the TV and the videogames so that I can hear better. I make and post a list of the names and email addresses of my teacher and the other students in the Urdu class. This helps to build our community and heightens our interaction outside of class.
	Organizing for cultural understanding in specific contexts	I tape all of the eTandem discussions and then listen to them several times. This gives me a lot of understanding about the culture of my Norwegian friend. I have a place for all of my books filled with dialogues and conversational materials, and I take time to review them to find cross-cultural differences.
Implementing Plans for Contexts, Communication, and Culture	Thinking about the plan	I remember my plan to work on some key Japanese speech acts before I meet the new Japanese visiting scholar.
	Putting the plan into action	I deliberately put my plan into action, so that I am comfortable talking with the Japanese visiting scholar when he arrives.
Orchestrating Strategy Use for Contexts, Communication, and Culture	Orchestrating strategy use for contexts, communication, and culture at different levels of proficiency	When I am trying to interact with someone in Pashto, I use techniques for staying in the conversation, for helping the person give me information without my asking, and for noticing and learning from subtle social clues in high-level interactions. When I try to go for fluency, I consciously choose a bunch of tactics that all work together, such as overcoming my lack of vocabulary by using circumlocution, gesturing to act out what I mean, and stalling for time.
	Orchestrating strategy use for contexts, communication, and culture for different purposes at the same time	I find that I have to balance my efforts to show respect to the teacher with my need to ask lots of questions and learn from the teacher.

Appendix I.E Meta-SI strategies and examples of related tactics (continued)

STRATEGY	BASIC FUNCTIONS	EXAMPLES OF RELATED TACTICS, AS REPORTED BY LEARNERS
Monitoring for Contexts, Communication, and Culture	Monitoring cultural understanding and communication in specific contexts	I monitor my accuracy and cultural understanding during conversations in my Arabic class.
		I check whether I am understanding what the speaker says, particularly if it is in a slightly different dialect from the one I know.
		I listen well to my distance tutor's phone response to determine whether she has understood what I am saying.
		I monitor whether I still have the trust of the native speaker throughout the conversation, and this tells me whether I am effectively using my understanding of the social situation.
	Monitoring strategy use for culture and communication in specific contexts	I monitor whether I am using "communication strategies" too much. At my level of proficiency, I shouldn't be overly relying on circumlocution and things like that.
		I check how well I am imitating the native speaker, especially in terms of accent, posture, and stance.
		I consider whether I am relying too much for help on my study partner and whether I should be more self-reliant.
Evaluating for Contexts, Communication, and Culture	Evaluating communication in specific contexts	Given the general topic and the person with whom I am speaking, I predict what will happen in the conversation (for example, my friend will invite me to go see an Indonesian film). Naturally I check whether I was right.
		I judge that I did better in this conversational task than I did in the last one.

	I evaluate my performance on this communication task by checking it against that of the best student in the Swahili class.
	I evaluate the progress I have made in the last six months in communicating in Turkish. I no longer feel the massive confusion that I experienced at first.
Evaluating cultural understanding in specific contexts	I reflect on what I have learned so far about Thai culture and all the things I still need to learn.
	In evaluating where I am now in Chinese, I feel that I am finally "gaining a voice." It is not like my old voice in my country. This seems like a whole new cultural way of being and thinking.
Evaluating effectiveness of strategy use for communication and understanding in specific contexts	I ask myself whether I relied too much on masking, gestures, and asking for repetition during the last task I did in Tongan.
	I think about the strategies I have been using to communicate in Yoruba. I think they help me understand more and be more understood. But will they be useful for the long run or will they eventually get in the way?
	The strategies I have used for communicating in Russian seem be helpful. They have helped me stay in conversations so I can learn more, rather than going silent or being afraid. They have helped me understand more about Russian culture because of the extended discussions.
	I think about the strategies I have been using to become a recognized international legal scholar in English. It is difficult for a native Arabic speaker. I realize that I have been doing very well and that my mentor, Dr Butler, has given me very good advice.

Source: Typology and organization of the learning strategies in this table are original. Learning strategies in the table were reported by learners in open-ended questionnaires, discussions, interviews, and conversations over two decades.

Appendix I.F   Sociocultural-interactive (SI) strategies and examples of related tactics (metaphor: "community workers")

Names of SI strategies: *Interacting to Learn and Communicate, Overcoming Knowledge Gaps in Communicating, Dealing with Sociocultural Contexts and Identities*

STRATEGY	BASIC FUNCTIONS	EXAMPLES OF RELATED TACTICS, AS REPORTED BY LEARNERS
Interacting to Learn and Communicate	Interacting online or in person	When online with my instructor and the other students, I ask if anyone has heard about the new Chinese film.
		I read all the postings on the discussion board so I can get different ideas and learn the language better.
		I go to the chat room in Italian to see what people are saying and keep up with any new jokes.
		I go to the chat room even if I don't have much to say, because it allows others to know I am interested.
		I meet every two weeks with a small group of independent learners of modern Greek so we can speak the language together.
		I form a study group with two friends so we can study before tests in advanced German.
		I meet with Uyghur refugees to find out about the political situation and speak the language.

Working with a mentor or tutor	I work with a mentor who is a native speaker of Hungarian and who has lots of patience with me.
	I have an "apprenticeship" with the Dean of Foreign Languages at ___ University in Nanjing. He helps me understand Chinese culture, takes me to see the sights, invites me to visit his family home, and introduces me to students and teachers who speak Chinese with me.
	I work with a mentor who knows a different dialect. My mentor can teach me the new dialect. It is important at my high proficiency level to be flexible and fluent in different dialects.
	I have a person who tutors me in French, and I tutor him in English.
Asking for explanation, clarification, verification, or repetition or asking a question nonverbally	If I do not understand what the teacher is saying about today's assignment, I ask my friend to explain it to me.
	I ask for help to understand the meaning of "acid rain" in the article.
	I write down questions to ask the distance tutor, and then I go over them one by one with the tutor to get explanations.
	I email my teacher or another student to get clarification when I am confused about this week's Romani homework, especially about the difficult grammar points.
	I ask my colleague whether I have correctly understood what she said in Gujarati.
	I ask whether I used the clicks correctly when speaking in Xhosa.
	I ask the person to say it again when I don't understand the Serbian statement the first time.
	I never let the Bengali speaker know that I don't understand. I just repeat what he or she said in a way that sounds like a question, and then the person starts telling me more. It works every time.

Appendix I.F Sociocultural-interactive (SI) strategies and examples of related tactics (continued)

STRATEGY	BASIC FUNCTIONS	EXAMPLES OF RELATED TACTICS, AS REPORTED BY LEARNERS
Overcoming Knowledge Gaps in Communicating (in order to continue to speak, listen, and learn)	Using other words to continue to communicate, despite the gap in knowledge	I make up a new word while I am talking if I don't know the right one, just so I can stay in the conversation. Often it is the right word.
		If I don't know a word, I "talk around it." For instance, if I didn't know the word metro (underground or subway) in English, I could say, "It is long, it has wheels, and it goes from Greenbelt all the way downtown." I would describe it by its features or what it does. [circumlocution]
		I use a synonym or even an antonym ("it's not this," "the opposite of this") if I cannot think of the word I need.
		If I cannot think of the right word, I sometimes slip back into English [native language], but then I immediately go back into Romanian.
		I might not know for certain what the other person said, but if I have any idea, I add new combinations to what I think he said and then look for reactions.
	Using physical cues to continue to communicate, despite the gap in knowledge	If I don't know a word, I use gestures to signify the word physically.
		If I don't know the word I need, I raise my eyebrows or otherwise indicate physically that I do not know but want to continue to talk.
	Changing the topic (topic avoidance)	I change the topic to something that I find easier to talk about.
	Pretending to understand (masking)	I pretend to understand so that the conversation will continue. This often helps me learn more.
		I nod my head rapidly to indicate that I understand, even though I do not.

Dealing with Sociocultural Contexts and Identities	Imitating cultural behaviors	I imitate the cultural behaviours of others who are of my same gender and general age.
		I imitate the gestures, posture, pronunciation, and speaking-distance of my teacher and recognize how he communicates with people older, younger, and of the opposite sex.
	Exploring the meaning of social roles, identity, power, and the media	I think about the position of women in the countries whose language I am studying and think about how I, as a foreign woman, am viewed in those countries.
		I compare the attitudes toward old age and family in China and the social roles of the elderly with such attitudes and roles in my country, and I try to understand the reasons for and meaning of the differences.
		I compare my feelings here in the new school, in the new country, with those back home. I feel afraid and silenced and helpless here. I used to be intelligent. Here I feel stupid. Or I think that is how others see me.
		I write down what was new to me in the culture (calling the teacher by first name) so I can think about what it means about teacher-student relationships.
		I think about how some very common political metaphors in English and in Bosnian both reflect and spread attitudes toward war or peace – like alien, opponent, enemy, disloyal, unstable, weak, sick man of Europe, and so on. I understand the language and culture simultaneously.
		I analyse logic or truthfulness of what the TV news commentator is saying in German and try to identify the real purpose (to inform, persuade, exhort, and so on). I also try to understand the cultural beliefs in the statements.
	Considering what is expected for entry into the "imagined community"	I think about wanting to be treated like a professional while I am on my business internship in the U.A.E., and I consider all the social and linguistic competencies I will need to make this happen.

Appendix I.F Sociocultural-interactive (SI) strategies and examples of related tactics (continued)

STRATEGY	BASIC FUNCTIONS	EXAMPLES OF RELATED TACTICS, AS REPORTED BY LEARNERS
Dealing with Sociocultural Contexts and Identities (Continued)	Using "counter-discourses" (opposite stories) to gain sociocultural acceptance	When people judged me negatively in France because I was an American, only a middling French speaker, and new to Paris, I subtly but confidently communicated my own positive view of myself that contradicted their picture: how I was different from many Americans they had met, why I was interesting, and why we should get together to talk. Many negative views dropped away, and I gained friends and spoke in French all the time, increasing my French skills significantly.
	Exploring sociocultural meanings about silence, body language, and social customs	I especially focus on the amount of silence (waiting times or just peaceful silence) and the presence or absence of interruptions (by whom? between whom?) that is expected in conversations and try to figure out more about the culture based on this.
		Whenever I imitate someone's posture and standing-distance, I try to think of the cultural meanings.
		I ask myself the social significance of the ubiquitous vodka-drinking tradition in Russia. Tonight what would happen if I do not participate, or if I participate for one vodka round and "fake it" (or even refuse) for all the other rounds? How would I (and my country) be viewed?
		I consider the cultural implications of the Japanese bathhouse and spa traditions, especially the values that are involved.

Source: Typology and organization of the learning strategies in this table are original. Learning strategies in the table were reported by learners in open-ended questionnaires, discussions, interviews, and conversations over two decades.

II Authentic Uses of Strategy Assessment and Strategy Assistance

Chapter 5

Strategy assessment in the S²R Model

Measure for Measure

Title of Shakespeare's 1604 play

Preview questions

1. In the S²R Model, which tools are used for assessing the L2 learning strategies a given student is using for a specific task?
2. How can we discover a learner's general or typical strategy use?
3. What are the advantages and disadvantages of actual-task strategy assessment versus general strategy assessment, according to the S²R Model?
4. What are the comparative advantages of quantitative and qualitative strategy assessment?
5. How do cultural beliefs and values relate to strategy assessment?

The two chapters in Section II highlight some of the issues raised in Section I (e.g., strategy-tactic relationships, strategy chains, and the various dimensions of L2 learning), applying these to *strategy assessment*, or identifying students' strategies (Chapter 5), and *strategy assistance*, or helping students optimize their strategy use (Chapter 6). Section II also looks forward to the research options in Section III. Strategy assessment is a key component of both strategy research and strategy instruction.

Strategy assessment can heighten learners' and teachers' awareness of strategies. Students develop L2 learning strategies more easily when they and their teachers are aware of these strategies. However, research shows that teachers are often unaware of or mistaken about their students' strategy use, and learners differ in their degree of awareness about their own learning strategies (Oxford, 1996b). Effective assessments of L2 learning strategy use are necessary to clarify the picture. This chapter presents a selection of strategy assessment techniques and explains their pros and cons. Table 5.1 on the next page is an overview of the chapter.

5.1   Purposes of strategy assessment

Strategy assessment can serve as a baseline description, a source of predictions, a diagnostic tool, a foundation for deciding what strategies to teach, or a pre- and post-instruction measure to evaluate strategy instruction. *Strategy assessment* is a shorthand term in the S²R Model. I will use the term *strategy assessment*, although actual-task strategy assessment usually measures the use of tactics responding to real-time, specific learning purposes.

5.2   Key issues at the outset

Four basic questions must be answered before using any form of strategy assessment:

* Should assessment of L2 strategy use involve self-report or observations by others?
* Should self-report strategy assessment be oriented to specific L2 tasks, or should it be more general?
* How can cultural appropriateness be ensured in strategy assessment?
* Should strategy assessment be qualitative, quantitative, or both?

5.2.1   Key issue A: Self-report versus other-report

The first key assessment issue is whether strategy assessment should be done by the learner (self-report) or by someone else (other-report). *Self-report* means the learner's reporting, regardless of whether this occurs orally or in writing. Self-report can be highly directed, as in a structured questionnaire, or highly flexible, as in an open-ended consultation or discussion. It can occur during a learning task (*introspection*) or can involve looking back (*retrospection*). Researchers have shown great interest in self-report for uncovering readers' mental processes (Ericsson and Simon, 1993). *Other-report* refers to someone else's observations of the learner's learning, and this chapter provides an array of observational options. Concept 5.1 on page 142 presents positive and negative factors concerning self-report and other-report.

Table 5.1   Overview of this chapter

Concept 5.1   **Positive and negative factors in self-report and other-report**

Potential factors	Type of report	
	Self-report	Other-report
Positive	• Self-report is one of the very few ways that we can gain access to the learner's thoughts, feelings, attitudes, and strategies. • Self-report may be needed as a check on the findings of other-report. • Social desirability response bias (tendency to report what the participant thinks the researcher wants) is not an issue in L2 learning strategy studies (a) if it is made clear that there are no right or wrong answers and that what participants say will not influence evaluations of the individual by others, and (b) if, in formal studies, anonymity and confidentiality are established.	• Many kinds of other-report exist, largely via observation (live observation in the classroom, computer tracking, neurological observation). • Other-report can be a check on the findings of self-report. • Social desirability response bias is not present in other-report. • Other-report in the classroom and via computer tracking is not generally intrusive. • Other-report is not clouded by participant memory loss, irrelevant comments, inarticulateness, or inability to generalize across tasks.
Negative	• Interpretations of retrospective self-report might be clouded by memory loss; automaticity of the behaviour, making it unconscious; or complexity (Anderson and Vandergrift, 1996). • Interpretations might be marred by a participant's irrelevant comments about "epiphenomena," inarticulateness, or inability to generalize over a number of recent task performances (see White et al., 2007). • Interpretations can be hampered by the researcher's lack of understanding or cultural assumptions too distant from or too similar to those of the participant. • If a self-report occurs during an L2 task, this can be experienced as intrusive (Cohen and Scott, 1996) or burdensome (Branch, 2000). • Self-report can have social desirability response bias under some circumstances.	• Other-report might miss the internal aspects of L2 learning that could be reported by the learner, so self-report is needed. • Even if good observations are possible by the teacher or researcher, the correct interpretation of what the observations mean might be difficult or elusive. • Other-report can be hampered by the researcher's lack of understanding or cultural assumptions.

5.2.2 Key issue B: Closeness to an actual, current L2 task during self-reported strategy assessment

The second assessment issue is the closeness to an authentic, current L2 task during self-reported strategy assessment (Concept 5.2). *Actual-task strategy assessment* (also known as *task-oriented strategy assessment*) involves reporting the strategies for an authentic task, e.g., reading a passage in the L2. The learner identifies strategies he or she is using (or has finished using) to accomplish the L2 task. The information is highly detailed.

In *hybrid strategy assessment*, the learner responds to a task description (scenario) by saying – in an interview or questionnaire – which strategies he or she would use if doing the task in reality. Depending on the purposes, several scenarios can be presented sequentially during any single data-gathering session. The questionnaire or interview can be structured or open-ended.

In *general strategy assessment*, the learner identifies the strategies he or she typically uses now or usually employed in the recent past. Benefits are that general strategy assessment (a) provides a more sweeping view of strategy use than do actual-task and hybrid strategy assessment and (b) can frequently be linked to long-term proficiency or achievement in ways that actual-task or hybrid strategy assessment cannot. General interviews, discussions, questionnaires, and written *recollective techniques* (e.g., diaries, dialogue journals, learning histories, and other narrative forms) are useful for general strategy assessment.

None of the three modes of strategy assessment – actual-task, hybrid, or general – is better than the others. Value depends on the purpose. To discern learners' immediate strategy use, employ actual-task strategy assessment. To discover probable strategy use over several pre-developed task scenarios, hybrid strategy assessment is useful. To gain general information on strategies typically used, employ general strategy assessment. Pros and cons of these formats are given later.

5.2.3 Key issue C: Cultural appropriateness

The S²R Model says that strategy assessment must be culturally attuned to learners' sociocultural situation. Strategies that are relevant in one culture might not be valued in another culture. Therefore, some strategy questionnaire items must be adapted, omitted, or added (see later).

Concept 5.2   **Strategy assessment in relationship to an actual L2 task**

Type of strategy assessment	Relationship to an actual, current L2 task	Summary	Example
Actual-task strategy assessment	L2 learner does an L2 task during the strategy assessment and names or describes strategies used while doing the task	DOING AN ACTUAL TASK	Strategy assessment through a think-aloud protocol
Hybrid strategy assessment	L2 learner receives a description or scenario of an L2 task and cites the strategies he or she would use with such a task	THINKING ABOUT AN ACTUAL TASK	Strategy assessment through a "Detailed Task-Scenario"
General strategy assessment	L2 learner cites the strategies he or she usually or typically uses now (or has typically used in the past)	NO ACTUAL TASK REQUIRED	Strategy assessment through a general strategy questionnaire asking about typical strategy use

> **Quote 5.1** Context sensitivity
>
> Since strategies are always used in a particular context and since contextual differences are likely to influence strategy use, [assessment techniques and] research methods must be context-sensitive.
>
> Koyo Yamamori, Takamichi Isoda, Tomohito Hiromori, and Rebecca L. Oxford (2003, p. 383)

Cultural appropriateness is important in choosing assessment tools. As a strategy assessment tool, keeping a learner diary or writing an L2 learning history might be useful in some settings but culturally awkward in others. In any strategy assessment, the researcher should describe carefully cultural beliefs and values that might influence strategy use.

5.2.4 Key issue D: Qualitative, quantitative, or both

In the S²R Model, strategy assessment can be qualitative or quantitative. The practice of using both types in a single study is currently becoming more popular. Now I turn to various types of strategy assessment tools, starting with strategy observations.

5.3 Strategy observations

Teachers and researchers often observe students' strategies and tactics. Videotaping of observations allows repeated review of videotapes later, which provides further detail. One major difficulty with any observational technique is that many strategies occur mentally and cannot be seen through ordinary observation. Hence it is helpful to combine observation with querying learners about their strategies through an interview, questionnaire, or a simple "member check" (Chapter 7). Macaro (2001a, 2001b) contends that strategy observations are valuable, despite limitations.

> **Quote 5.2** Observations of strategies
>
> Observing task performances without asking the learners . . . cannot give a full picture of the strategies used.
>
> Annamaria Pinter (2006)

5.3.1 Live observations by teachers or external researchers

Teachers or external researchers can notice which students collaborate, take notes, ask questions, request help, ask for extra work, and so on. A good way to systematize these observations is by keeping "classroom field notes" or a journal. If a student has a problem or is doing very well, some teachers or researchers keep track of the strategies or tactics the student uses.

5.3.2 Live co-teaching observations

Systematic strategy observations occurs during the "One Teaches, One Observes" model of co-teaching (Friend and Cook, 2007; Oxford, 2007). The co-teachers decide the following. Should the strategy observation focus on a particular student, a small group, or the class? Should the observer look at strategies for one task or many? Should the observer take notes or use a strategy observation scale or checklist (for examples, see O'Malley, Chamot, Stewner-Manzanares, Küpper, and Russo, 1985; Oxford, 1990; Rubin, 1981). How can classroom dynamics be noted? After these decisions, one teaches and one observes, and they can switch. Together they analyse the data and consider various interpretations. For instance, does student question-asking signify high interest, task difficulty, or something else?

5.3.3 Trace measures: a different kind of strategy observation

Computer tracking offers "trace measures" or "trace logs." Baily (1996) employed trace measures to identify computer-aided writing strategies employed by university French learners. Zimmerman (2008) used trace measures to identify self-regulated strategies during computer-assisted science learning. Other strategy assessments, such as interviews, should accompany trace measures (Winne and Perry, 2000). In investigating effects of online strategy advice, Meskill (1991) not only tracked students' computer navigation and time on task but also interviewed students and queried them by questionnaire.

5.3.4 Neurological brain observations

Chapters 2 and 3 briefly explored neurobiology in relation to L2 strategies. *Brain-mapping* produces images showing increased oxygen use or heightened electrical currents in certain brain regions during a task. If students used certain task-related strategies during brain-mapping, this could verify hypotheses about which brain areas assist which strategies.

5.3.5   Advantages and limitations of observations

See Concept 5.3 for advantages and limitations of strategy observation options. I discuss below actual-task verbal reports.

5.4   Actual-task verbal reports

Actual-task verbal reports provide rich strategy information. *Verbal report* implies orally reporting task-related strategies and other mental processes, although *verbal* originally meant "in words," without indicating oral or written responses. Newell and Simon (1972) initiated verbal reports by asking for students to report cognitive mathematics strategies, but verbal report techniques are now widespread in many subjects.

Quote 5.3   Necessity of asking

In almost all learning contexts, the only way to find out whether students are using learning strategies while engaged in a language task is to ask them. Verbal report data are used to identify language learning strategies because observation does not capture mental processes.

Anna Uhl Chamot (2004, p. 14)

5.4.1   During-task verbal reports (thinking aloud)

When an actual-task verbal report occurs during the task (Afflerbach, 2000; Feyton, Flaitz, and LaRocca, 1999; Matsumoto, 1994) it is called a *think-aloud*. This relatively time-intensive tool gathers detailed data from an individual about strategies or processes used during a task (Pressley and Afflerbach, 1995). For reading, one think-aloud technique asks learners to (a) locate visual prompts in various places on a text while reading (e.g., red dots placed after every sentence, every paragraph, and the whole text) and (b) verbalize strategies or processes at each visual prompt (see Afflerbach, 1990). Another technique asks learners to verbalize strategies or processes at certain time intervals. Still another technique asks learners to "think aloud" spontaneously (called *self-revelation*, Cohen and Scott, 1996), without any prompts unless the student stops verbalizing. If verbalization stops, prompts are "What are you thinking now?", "Why did you stop here?", or "Please keep talking." The prompt "What made you think so?" offers deeper information by pushing learners to analyse, but this might deter task progress.

Concept 5.3   Advantages and limitations of observations of L2 learning strategies

Type of strategy observation	Advantages	Limitations
Live observation without video support	• Easy and efficient • Does not always require an outside observer; teacher can often do it • Can be done informally or formally • Does not have to upset the normal activities of the class or the student. • Some L2 learning strategies are observable by the human eye and ear.	• Live observer is often drawn to learners who appear to be more active or extroverted in class, even though others might be using observable strategies that are equally interesting (Cohen and Scott, 1996). • When a live observer is physically present, learners' behaviour often changes, at least initially (Cohen and Scott, 1996). • Observer might be biased in what he or she looks at or might be limited by a strategy observation scale or checklist (Cohen and Scott, 1996). • Some L2 learning strategies are mentalistic, i.e., they occur in the mind and are not observable. • Better to gather strategy data with other techniques in addition to observations.

Live observation with video support	• Same as for live observation above. Also: • "Recording groups and pairs working together on a task can later on lead to classroom discussions about different approaches to language tasks . . ." (Pinter, 2006). • This can be a basis for later task-related strategy instruction.	• Video equipment can change learners' behaviour until they get used to it. • Possible observer bias, though this can be reduced by video-recording and by more than one observer. • Cannot see all possible strategies; some are mentalistic. • Better to use additional forms of data gathering along with observations.
Computer-trace strategy log	• Data collection (traces) is efficient, easy, and accurate • Provides data that might not be seen through live observation	• Only tracks what it is programmed to track. • Better to use additional sources of data, such as learner interviews, to verify the researcher's explanation of the traces at any given point.
Neurological imaging	• Would fit what we know about the workings of the brain • Would show important applications to strategy use	• Not yet developed for L2 learning strategy observation • Not yet widely discussed in the L2 field • Would necessitate proper imaging equipment, competent neurologists to set up the observations and read the results.

A criticism is that think-alouds cause the learner do two things (orally report strategies and do a language task) simultaneously, making the effort awkward or artificial. Verbal report might be easier for those who like multitasking than for those who do not. However, think-alouds have provided exceptionally interesting and useful data.

Actual-task verbal reports for reading can be used informally in small groups or in the whole class to sharpen strategic awareness or provide practice before formal research. Each student reads one sentence, then verbalizes the strategies used. The next student does the same with the next sentence. Alternatively, during silent reading, students stop reading on signal and report their strategies.

During-task verbal reports can also be used to identify strategies for L2 listening (Anderson and Vandergrift, 1996). One technique asks learners to halt an audiotape or CD at certain intervals to verbalize strategies, or the student can simply interrupt the tape or CD spontaneously to verbalize. Students can also interrupt writing tasks for the purpose of thinking aloud, either at intervals or spontaneously. If intervals of time or material are used as a signal, these should be short enough so memory load does not become a factor. The key to any "thinking aloud" is advance training and practice (Concept 5.4).

Concept 5.4   **Teaching students to think aloud for reading strategy assessment**

- The teacher or researcher models how to think aloud while doing an L2 task, such as reading an unfamiliar passage.

- The students follow along silently while the teacher or researcher reports aloud what is going on in his or her mind. This demonstration allows students to understand what is involved in thinking aloud.

- The students are invited to mention aloud any mental processes they used while they read the material silently.

Note: For detailed additional guidelines relevant to different age groups, see White, Schramm, and Chamot (2007) and Anderson and Vandergrift (1996).

5.4.2   Videotaping during-task verbal reports

During-task verbal reports can be enhanced by videotaping and then asking learners to review the videotape after the task. A video-aided verbal report is a form of a "stimulated recall" protocol, because the video stimulates the individual to recall strategies or processes used during the task.

5.4.3 Pre-task (prospective) and post-task (retrospective) verbal reports

Pre-task and post-task (pre-actional and post-actional) verbal reports are becoming popular (White *et al.*, 2007). Pre-task or prospective verbal reports allow learners to report on the strategies they plan to use in doing the task. Post-task verbal reports reveal strategies that were used and are of two types: (a) initial reporting of strategies (with no during-task report) and (b) "think-after" (Branch, 2000), i.e., a retrospective follow-up in which learners evaluate the utility of strategies they reported during the task.

5.4.4 Issues in verbal report

Should the L2 learner be asked to report in the L2 or in the L1? A rule of thumb is for learners, at least at the beginning and intermediate level, to think aloud in the language in which they are the most fluent, even if it is not the language of the task. Research indicates that learners have been allowed to report in either the L1 or L2, whichever is more comfortable, and that learners have most often produced verbal protocols in their native languages (Young, 1993). Upton (1997) also found that only highly proficient ESL students preferred to use the L2, and only in some cases. Seng and Hashim (2006) reported that L2 learners tended to use the L1 especially when facing difficult parts while reading, which supported the important role of L1 use in L2 readers' comprehension processes (see Garcia, 2000). However, it can sometimes be confusing for the learner to think aloud in the L1 while doing the task in the L2.

Kuusela and Paul (2000) stated that reporting retrospectively provides less and worse information than reporting concurrently with a task. However, reporting after the task is especially helpful for L2 speaking tasks, which are too disrupted if reporting occurs during the task.

5.5   Colour-coding of actual-task strategies

Lee (2007) invented colour-coding for actual-task reading strategy assessment in a quasi-experimental study of students at a Korean university (see Chapter 7). The control group received traditional English reading instruction in (grammar and translation), while the treatment group received instructions in these strategies: predicting, making inferences, summarizing, finding patterns, and clarifying. As part of both strategy assessment and strategy-awareness-raising, Lee asked treatment-group students to colour-code the reading strategies they used. For instance, while reading about the caste system in India, treatment-group students were to use a red sticky-tab at the text spot where they used predicting and a yellow tab to signify any text location where they made inferences. Treatment-group students used colour-coding four times during the semester, and in the fourteenth week they colour-coded on texts all of the strategies they had learned. Strategy use was verified through strategy journals.

Results showed that presence or absence of strategy instruction was significantly associated with students' performance on reading comprehension tests. Reading comprehension scores improved significantly between the midterm and the final test for the treatment group, but not for the control group. Colour-coding was very useful. It helped treatment-group students to assess their own strategies by providing visible strategy-use patterns, which, along with fine motor movement involved in colour-coding, made the strategies more memorable for the long term.

5.6   Learner portfolios that include task-related strategy assessment

Portfolio assessment is a powerful way to assess L2 performance and strategy use for multiple levels of proficiency and varied cultures. To assess strategies with portfolios, ask students to report their strategy use on regular tasks.

Quote 5.4   About portfolio assessment

Portfolio assessment develops a longitudinal portrait of what the student can and cannot do in the area(s) identified. Portfolios include rubrics to evaluate when a student is at a particular academic level, comSectionments where students and teachers can place exemplary work . . ., [and] a student reflection about his or her own learning (metacognitive tasks) . . .

Jacqueline Vialpando, Caroline Linse, and Jane Yedlin (2005, p. 41)

A study with university French-conversation students involved portfolio-based self-assessment (Donato and McCormick, 1994). Every three weeks throughout the semester, students provided tangible evidence (e.g., recordings, creative writing, homework, and activity reports) to document L2 development. "The students were empowered with opportunities to create and reflect upon personally-meaningful activities and strategies for learning" (Donato and McCormick, 1994, p. 457). The instructor responded in writing to student portfolio reflections and encouraged students who mentioned strategies. The portfolio helped students (a) use and evaluate strategies, (b) reflect on L2 performance, and (c) plan improvements. Instead of giving overt strategy instruction, the instructor offered a strategic classroom culture (Donato and McCormick, 1994). See Chapter 6 for more on portfolios.

> **Quote 5.5** Contributions of portfolio assessment
>
> Through the use of the portfolio, the classroom became a context for self-investment, critical analysis, and the discovery of new strategic orientations to language learning.
>
> Richard M. Donato and Dawn E. McCormick (1994, p. 462).

5.7   Individual interviews for strategy assessment (not based on immediate tasks)

Another strategy assessment tool is individual interviews without a task. Here are three options: (a) interviews about described tasks, (b) interviews about an activity grid, and (c) open-ended interviews.

5.7.1   Structured or semi-structured individual interviews

This option involves structured or semi-structured interviewing. The interview is based on one or more contexts, situations, or task-scenarios. It does not demand the time and resources of a procedure such as think-alouds, which require the learner to do the actual task and reflect on strategies used in the task.

Self-Regulated Learning Interview Schedule

The *Self-Regulated Learning Interview Schedule* (*SRLIS*, Zimmerman and Martinez-Pons, 1986, 1988) is a structured interview that asks students to provide open-ended responses, later coded into categories. Students are given six "problem contexts," such as preparing for a test or writing an essay, and are asked to say the strategies they use. Transcriptions are organized into categories focusing on metacognition (goal setting and planning, organizing and transforming, seeking information, and rehearsing and memorizing – primarily mental strategies), observable behaviour (environmental structuring; keeping records and monitoring; reviewing texts, notes, and tests; and seeking assistance from peers, teachers, and parents), and motivation (self-evaluation reactions and self-consequences). Students' strategy answers are rated for frequency of being mentioned during the interview, and students are asked to rate the frequency ("consistency" on a four-point scale) with which they use these strategies.

Student Interview Guide

A similar tool is the *Student Interview Guide* (O'Malley *et al.*, 1985). That guide "asks learners to think about what they usually do when faced with familiar language tasks, such as pronunciation, oral grammar exercises, vocabulary learning, following directions, communicating in a social situation, and two levels of listening comprehension in class" (Oxford, 1990, pp. 195, 197).

Detailed task-scenario interview

The detailed task-scenario interview is a hybrid form, halfway between a during-task strategy interview (e.g., a think-aloud) and a general strategy interview. The learner receives the task-scenario (a description of a possible L2 task) orally and in writing in his or her native language. Sometimes the task-scenario involves multiple language skills, such as reading and writing, just as in real life. The scenario also mentions the *task difficulty* in degree of (un)familiarity or complexity; the *resources*, such as presence or absence of a phrase book or an online dictionary; and the *setting*, including the presence of other people. Naturally, the scenario must refer to the language the learner is studying. The learner then answers two questions: (a) How difficult does this task seem to you? (b) What strategies or tactics would you use? This format allows learners to respond to several detailed scenarios in a relatively short time, but a given learner's ability to identify probable strategies to use depends on self-awareness.

5.7.2   Semi-structured individual interviews based on a grid of daily activities

This is a semi-structured interview following the learner's completion of a weekly grid showing day-by-day activities and strategies used in those activities. During the interview, the interviewer asks broad questions, and the learner responds based on the grid (Wenden, 1987). The grid records authentic experiences and strategies and stimulates self-reflection. This interview is most successful when the learner has multiple opportunities to use the L2 during the week.

5.7.3   Open-ended individual interviews

Open-ended, individual strategy interviews or discussions can occur during consultation or counseling. The School of Language Studies at the U.S.

Foreign Service Institute (FSI) provides a formal Learning Consultation Service (LCS) involving learning strategies in the context of the learners' overall learning style, attitudes, and motivation (Ehrman, 1999).

5.8   Group strategy assessment interviews or discussions

Open-ended, group interviews or discussions can assess strategy use. The teacher can encourage the students, in a group, "to think about what they are doing and why, how they would evaluate their performance on a particular task and how their performance can be improved on a subsequent occasion" (Pinter, 2006). These discussions enable students to articulate the strategies they have been using, thus combining informal strategy self-assessment with strategy consciousness-raising (Yang, 1996, 1998). Such discussions also help pinpoint learning problems and the need for strategy instruction.

5.9   Discourse analysis for strategy assessment

Think-alouds and other strategy assessment interviews can benefit from discourse analysis – analysis of language in sociocultural contexts – as a tool for transcribing, analysing, and interpreting the data. Chapter 4 mentions discourse as a key to L2 learning. Critical discourse analysis additionally takes into account power, oppression, resistance, opposition, and identity. For strategy assessment, discourse analysis has several possible uses:

- Analysing what the learner directly says about L2 learning strategies in a given sociocultural setting or situation.
- Analysing cultural models or sociocultural issues related to learning strategies or the teaching of learning strategies (Chapter 4).
- Analysing learners' ordinary spoken or written production to infer the strategies being used, though it is necessary to ask learners about the validity of these inferences.

In a study of content-based learning strategies, Schramm (2001) gathered actual-task strategy data and other data from German university students who were learning psychology from an English-language textbook. The study produced a wealth of verbal and nonverbal data, which Schramm transcribed. She then used standard discourse-analytic conventions. See Rogers (2004), Schiffrin, Tannen, and Hamilton (2003), and White *et al.* (2007) for more on how to use discourse analysis.

5.10   Strategy questionnaires

Strategy questionnaires are widely used outside of the L2 area (Table 5.2) and for assessing L2 learning strategies (Tables 5.3 to 5.5). Categories of L2 learning strategy questionnaires are: actual-task strategy questionnaires, hybrid strategy questionnaires, and general strategy questionnaires. See Concept 5.5.

Table 5.2   **Two well known learning strategy instruments outside of the L2 field**

The Learning and Study Strategies Inventory (LASSI; Weinstein, Schulte, and Palmer, 1987; see also Weinstein, Goetz, and Alexander, 1988)
- 80-item self-report inventory
- 5-point Likert scale
- Assesses students' strategies for enhancing their learning and study practices.
- 10 scales corresponding to a rather comprehensive concept of self-regulation (metacognitive strategies, "will-related" motivational strategies, and "behavioural" self-regulation strategies).
- Metacognitive strategy scales = Concentration, Selecting Main Ideas, and Information Processing
- Self-regulation (behavioural) strategy scales = Time Management (included in Planning and Organizing in my own strategy system), Study Aids, Self-Testing, and Test Strategies
- Motivational (will-related) strategy scales = (strategies for) Motivation, Attitude, and Anxiety.
- Reliability and validity acceptable

Motivated Strategies for Learning Questionnaire (MSLQ; Pintrich, Smith, Garcia, and McKeachie, 1991; see also Dörnyei, 2005, p. 181)
- 81-item questionnaire
- 7-point Likert scale
- Assesses motivated learning strategies
- Two major sections: Learning Strategies and Motivation
- Learning Strategies section includes two scales: (a) Cognitive-Metacognitive strategies, e.g., rehearsal, elaboration, organization, critical thinking, and metacognitive self-regulation; and (b) Resource Management strategies, e.g., managing time, study environment, and effort as well as learning with peers and seeking help.
- Motivation section involves three scales: Valuing (Intrinsic–Extrinsic Goal Orientation and Task Value), Expectancy (Self-Efficacy and Control of Learning), and Affect (Test Anxiety).
- Reliability and validity acceptable

See also Mokhtari and Reichard (2002) and Pereira-Laird and Deane (1997).

Concept 5.5   **L2 learning strategy questionnaires: a conceptual framework**

Type of Instrument	Description
Type A. Actual-task strategy questionnaire A1. Structured actual-task strategy questionnaire A2. Less structured actual-task strategy questionnaire	Questionnaire asks learners to indicate the strategies they used in a L2 task they just performed
Type B. Hybrid scenario-based strategy questionnaire	Questionnaire asks learners to write down strategies they would use if facing a given set of L2 tasks
Type C. Structured general strategy questionnaire C1. Well known structured general strategy questionnaire C2. Structured general strategy questionnaire for specialized areas C3. Structured general strategy questionnaire as part of a major diagnostic battery	Questionnaire asks learners to identify typically used strategies

5.10.1   *Type A*: Actual-task strategy questionnaire

Some researchers use strategy questionnaires to assess the strategies that students used in a newly completed task, so forgetting is not an issue. A limitation of actual-task questionnaire studies is that there has been no standardization of either the tasks or the questionnaires, making it impossible to compare results across studies (Chamot, 2004). An obvious next step for investigators might be to work in teams to standardize classic sets of L2 tasks for different language purposes at several proficiency levels and create simple, actual-task strategy questionnaires for validation.

Type A1: Structured actual-task strategy questionnaire

For detailed assessment of strategy use, structured actual-task strategy questionnaires are among the most relevant and efficient modes (Hsiao and Oxford, 2002). The actual-task questionnaire is filled out immediately after the task is completed. Oxford *et al.* (2004) employed a structured questionnaire first without a reading task (general strategy assessment) and then with two reading tasks (actual-task strategy assessment with two levels of difficulty) in a study of reading strategies of adult English learners in the

U.S. Results indicated that the students used somewhat different reading strategies for different difficulty levels and that there was value in both general and actual-task strategy assessment.

Type A2: Less structured actual-task strategy questionnaire

This mode consists of a very short checklist of four or five potentially task-relevant strategies, with space for students to write in their own strategies if they do not appear on the list. It is easy to use and tabulate.

5.10.2   Type B: Hybrid strategy questionnaire

In a hybrid strategy questionnaire, the learner reads scenarios of various L2 tasks, such as writing a summary of a story, listening to a lecture on a new topic, or writing a letter to the editor. For each task-scenario, the learner writes down or checks the strategies he or she would use if doing the described task.

5.10.3   Type C: Structured general strategy questionnaire

Many researchers and teachers use structured questionnaires to identify students' typical or general use of L2 learning strategies. Quantitative, general strategy questionnaires are popular for several reasons. First, they are among the "most efficient and comprehensive ways to assess frequency of language learning strategy use" (Oxford, 1996a, p. 28), allowing assessment of a number of strategies for many students in a relatively short time. Second, these questionnaires can serve as the basis of standardized, general strategy profiles (Winne and Perry, 2000) for individuals or groups, allowing comparability. Third, strategy data from these questionnaires can be analysed in relation to different variables, such as gender, age, proficiency level, and learning style (Oxford, 1996a and 1996b). Fourth, these questionnaires are easy to administer and score. When a general strategy questionnaire is given online, the scoring and interpretation can be instantaneous. Some general strategy questionnaires allow respondents to tabulate their scores by hand and immediately read score interpretations. Clear score interpretations offer "lessons" about strategies that can be followed up by serious strategy instruction. Many students have said that taking and self-scoring a strategy questionnaire alerted them to new strategies they could use.

General quantitative strategy questionnaires have limitations, however. A student might not remember what strategies he or she used in the past or might not understand what a strategy item means (Chamot, 2004). In addition, respondents might interpret the scales differently.

Type C1: Well known structured general strategy questionnaire

"The greatest numbers of descriptive studies have utilized a questionnaire developed by Oxford (1990), the *Strategy Inventory for Language Learning (SILL)*" (Chamot, 2004, p. 16). "The basic purpose of the *SILL* is to provide a general picture of the individual learner's typical strategy use, rather than a specific portrayal of the strategies used by the learner on a particular language task" (Oxford, 1999b, p. 114). This questionnaire has been used by approximately 10,000 learners around the world and has been translated into Cantonese, English, Finnish, French, Dutch, German, Japanese, Italian, Korean, Mandarin, Portuguese, Russian, Serbo-Croatian, Spanish, Swedish, Thai, Ukrainian, and other languages (often with back-translation to check for accuracy).

Though the *SILL* has been called atheoretical, the strategies in the *SILL* were actually based on several complementary sets of learning theories included in my first book (Oxford, 1990), in which the *SILL* was published. The theories were: (a) cognitive information-processing theory (Anderson, 1985; O'Malley, Chamot, and Walker, 1987); (b) metacognition theory (Flavell, 1978, 1979); (c) theories of long-term and short-term memory (Begley, Springen, Katz, Hager, and Jones, 1986); (d) theories of L2 motivation, anxiety, and other affective aspects (Bailey, 1983; Gardner, 1985, 1988; Gardner and Lambert, 1972); and (e) theories of L2 learning through communication (Færch and Kasper, 1983; Tarone, 1983). Thanks to a developmental editor dead set on making the book "practical," many fundamental theories and research issues were shown only in an intensive notes section toward the end (see Oxford, 1990, pp. 237–259). Subsequent work (Oxford, 1996a, 1999a, 1999b; Oxford and Burry-Stock, 1995) more accessibly emphasized theoretical and research-related aspects of the *SILL*.

The *SILL* has two basic forms: a 50-item questionnaire for those learning English as a second or foreign language and an 80-item form for native English speakers learning other languages. The *SILL*'s Likert-scaled ratings for each strategy item range from 1 to 5, with the poles being "never or almost never" to "always or almost always." An example of a *SILL* item is, "I try to find patterns in the language." The *SILL* format is similar to that of the *Learning and Study Strategies Inventory (LASSI)* (Weinstein *et al.*, 1988), except that items in the *SILL* are grouped into six strategy categories based on an initial factor analysis: memory-related, cognitive, compensatory, metacognitive, affective, and social. Many of the memory-related strategies were sensory-mnemonic devices (e.g., remembering through rhyming or flashcards) and, statistically speaking, operated quite differently from the cognitive strategies, aimed at deep processing (Chapter 2). Across many studies, the *SILL*'s cognitive strategies were usually significantly related to proficiency, unlike the memory-related strategies.

Hsiao and Oxford (2002) tested 15 strategy classification models, each reflecting a somewhat different theory of language learning strategies. Based on Hsiao's confirmatory factor analysis involving 517 university-level English language learners, the researchers found that Oxford's six-factor system in the *SILL*, compared with other L2 strategy taxonomies, was the most consistent with the students' patterns of strategy use. An early report on the factor-analytic development and testing of the *SILL* (Oxford, 1986) and later studies (e.g., Hsiao and Oxford, 2002; Oxford and Burry-Stock, 1995) provide substantial psychometric information (see also Table 5.3).

Many studies have shown significant linear relationships between *SILL*-gauged strategy use and L2 proficiency, meaning that the more frequently learners used L2 strategies, the higher their proficiency. Some other *SILL* studies showed significant curvilinear relationships, in which learners at the intermediate level showed significantly higher strategy frequency than did those at the lower and higher levels. One reason is that people at the higher proficiency levels might have automatized many of their cognitive or meta-cognitive strategies, creating unconscious habits (Chapter 2) that are not necessarily reported on strategy questionnaires. Leaver (2003a) suggested that high-level learners should be interviewed rather than responding to a questionnaire because of their very individualized strategies.

Parametric statistical tests, such as analysis of variance (ANOVA) and multiple ANOVA (MANOVA), are typically used for interval-level (equal interval) data or ratio-level data. Although the *SILL* uses an ordinal-level scale for the frequency of use of each strategy, many researchers analyse *SILL* data with parametric tests. This is because "for many [parametric] statistical tests, . . . [even] severe departures (from equal-intervalness) do not seem to affect Type I and Type II errors dramatically" (Jaccard and Wan, 1996, p. 4), especially if the participant sample is large (Briand, El Emam, and Morasca, 1996; Ferguson and Takane, 2005; Niness, Rumph, Vasquez, Bradfield, and Niness, 2002) or if the scale has at least five categories, as the *SILL* does (Jaccard and Wan, 1996). The lesser statistical need for equal intervals for using parametric tests – as long as the sample is large and the scale has enough categories – might ease Dörnyei's (2005) concern about the cumulativity of *SILL* responses across strategy items and categories. Nonparametric statistical alternatives are not always good. Non-parametric tests "unfortunately . . . have notoriously weak sensitivity to treatment effects [as in a strategy instruction study] with small-n [small sample size] data" (Niness *et al.*, 2002, p. 65). Niness *et al.* offered a different and more positive alternative for small samples: multivariate randomization tests.

The *SILL* has been successfully applied for discerning factor analytic profiles of strategy use among samples of L2 learners from cultures as divergent as Puerto Rico, Taiwan, and Egypt (Oxford and Burry-Stock, 1995). It has worked reliably and validly in these instances, and the general cultural differences in factor structures were interesting (Chamot, 2004).

Table 5.3   Features of the *SILL*

Strategy Inventory for Language Learning (*SILL*, Oxford, 1989)

- 80-item version (for native English speakers learning an L2), Cronbach alpha reliability: 96 (for a sample of 1,200 university learners) (Oxford and Nyikos, 1989) and .95 (for a sample of 423 learners at government language institute) (Ehrman and Oxford, 1995, Oxford and Ehrman, 1995), .94–.98 in other studies (Oxford and Burry-Stock, 1995; Bedell and Oxford, 1996).

- 50-item versions (for non-native English speakers learning English), Cronbach alpha reliabilities .91–.95 when used in translation (Chinese in Taiwan, Japanese in Japan, Korean in Korea); .89–.90 when administered in English to non-native English speakers (Oxford, 1999b).

- Confirmatory factor analysis (N = 517 college learners): 50-item SILL showed most consistent fit with learners' strategy use compared with other classifications of strategies (Hsiao and Oxford, 2002).

- Ku (1995, N = 904) and Yang (1992, N = 505) empirically found that the SILL did not have social desirability response bias.

- In regression studies, *SILL*-reported strategies predicted the following: 56% of the variance of English proficiency in a Japanese study (Takeuchi, 1993), 51% for Kanji proficiency in Australia (Kato, 1996), 46% for English proficiency in South Africa (Dreyer and Oxford, 1996), and 21% for English proficiency in Taiwan (Ku, 1995). These *SILL* predictive findings can be compared to those for the *Learning and Study Strategies Inventory* (*LASSI*), which, when combined with the *Preliminary Scholastic Aptitude Test*, predicted 38% of the variance in high school grade point averages of 1,650 students in the U.S. (Evertson, Weinstein, Roska, Hanson, and Laitusis, 1998).

- Correlations between *SILL* and proficiency: r = .73 (canonical correlation between *SILL* and *TOEFL* sections in South Africa, Dreyer and Oxford, 1996), r = .61 (both cognitive and metacognitive strategies as correlated with L2 proficiency, U.S. government language school, Oxford and Ehrman, 1995); r = .30–.50 in studies in five other countries (Oxford, 1999b). Usually linear relationships between *SILL* and proficiency measures, but two studies showed curvilinearity, supporting the theory that many higher-level students have automatized their learning strategies or no longer need them.

- Concurrent validity is shown by the predicted statistically significant relationships with other strategy instruments (e.g., the *LASSI*), with an L2 aptitude test (the *Modern Language Aptitude Test*), and various questionnaires for psychological type, learning style, and motivation/affect questionnaires (*Myers-Briggs Type Indicator, Style Analysis Survey*, and *Learning Style Profile*) (see Dreyer and Oxford, 1996; Ehrman and Oxford, 1990; Oxford and Ehrman, 1995).

- Used for multiple purposes:
  ○ For research and theory-building
  ○ As practical information for teachers, students, and language counsellors.

Researchers have used the *SILL*, along with other instruments, in path-analytic studies to determine lines of causality among strategy use, proficiency, motivation, and other variables (McIntosh and Noels, 2004; Yin, 2008). *SILL* results have significantly predicted proficiency in a number of regression studies (Table 5.3).

A number of structured general L2 learning strategy questionnaires have been developed for children using the *SILL* model. The first was the *Children's SILL* (Gunning, 1997), followed by the *Taiwanese Children's SILL* (see Lan and Oxford, 2003). See these and other children's strategy questionnaires in Table 5.4 on page 163.

Despite its widespread use in different cultures, the *SILL* was criticized for being a standardized instrument which includes some items that might not fit all sociocultural settings (LoCastro, 1994). Learning from this criticism, since 1995 I encouraged researchers to adapt *SILL* items to the culture and to leave space for students to write in additional strategies. The study by Lee and Oxford (2008) is a good example of using additional, open-ended questions along with the standard *SILL* strategy items. Many researchers (e.g., Gunning, 1997, in Canada; Lan and Oxford, 2003, in Taiwan; Yamamori *et al.*, 2003, in Japan) have made adjustments to *SILL* items to meet cultural and age needs while retaining the general structure and format of the questionnaire. In pilot tests in various cultures, researchers have found that major overhauls of the *SILL* have not been necessary to meet cultural needs, although I would have welcomed such revisions based on culture. Pilot tests have caused researchers to eliminate certain strategy items (e.g., keeping a diary or journal, using flashcards, and talking about learning-related feelings) that were rarely used spontaneously in any culture and to add items about rote learning or other strategies used in specific cultures. *SILL* users are encouraged to make cultural adaptations and re-assess *SILL* reliability and validity in each study and each sociocultural context.

Type C2: Structured general learning strategy questionnaire for specialized areas

A number of structured general L2 learning strategy questionnaires have been developed to assess strategy use in specialized areas: reading, listening, and metacognition. See Table 5.5 on page 164.

Type C3: Structured general strategy questionnaire as part of a diagnostic battery

A bold project for diagnosis and counselling has been created by Ma Xiaomei of Xi'an Jiaotong University, in cooperation with other Chinese universities. Ma and colleagues have developed the "Online Personalized English Learning Diagnosis and Advice System" (Figure 5.1) which links strategy assessment and strategy instruction and allows large-scale, efficient,

Table 5.4 Structured, general learning strategy questionnaires for children

Children's Strategy Inventory for Language Learning (*Children's SILL*, Gunning, 1997)
- 30 items
- 5-point Likert scale
- In French for francophone learners of English in Canada
- Administered by English teachers
- Field tested with 115 students
- Used with different sample of 107 fifth graders
- Reliability: .96
- High proficiency students used significantly more affective strategies than medium or low proficiency students
- No gender effect in 107-student francophone sample
- Frequency of use pattern: Compensation strategies > affective > metacognitive > cognitive/social/memory

Taiwanese Children's Strategy Inventory for Language Learning (*Taiwanese Children's SILL*, Lan and Oxford, 2003)
- 30 items
- 5-point Likert scale
- Adapted from *Children's SILL* (Gunning); translation and other features checked by panel of experts
- Used with 379 sixth graders in north Taiwan
- 4 categories of strategies (cognitive, compensation, metacognitive, and affective) out of 6 were associated significantly with proficiency, with higher proficiency learners using these categories more frequently than low or medium proficiency
- 5 categories out of 6 were significantly associated with gender, with females > males in strategy use
- Liking of English was significantly associated with strategy use
- Later used with 1,991 students in different regions of Taiwan (Lan, 2008, see Chapter 7)

Singapore Children's Listening Strategies Questionnaire (Gu, 2008)
- 5-point scale
- Included metacognitive, cognitive, and social/affective strategies
- Validated by team of experts to ensure construct validity
- Validated by teachers and small sample of children
- Field tested with N = 300 upper elementary students in Singapore, then revised
- Given to 3,216 students in upper elementary grades (4–6) in Singapore
- Found that listening strategies were used but not at a high level
- All strategies were significantly associated with English learning performance (course grades) but at low levels
- Children in different grades used somewhat different strategies
- Most frequently used strategies were monitoring and evaluating strategies

Strategy Inventory for Children (SIC) (Park, 2006)
- 7 factors
- One factor includes strategies for using a variety of resources commonly used in Korea, such as computers, online learning, video, worksheets, private tutoring and so on.
- Results have showed how Korean children use learning strategies
- Research has shown how strategies (on the *SIC*) are related to children's learning styles.

Also see: Cohen and Oxford (2001b). *Young Learners' Language Strategies Survey.* http://www.carla.umn.edu/about/profiles/Cohen; Cohen and Oxford (2002), *Young Learners' Language Strategy Use Survey* http://www.carla.umn.edu/about/profiles/CohenPapers/Young_Lg_Strat_Srvy.html

Table 5.5 **Structured general learning strategy questionnaires for reading, listening, writing, speaking, vocabulary learning, translation, and metacognitive awareness**

Metacognitive Awareness of Reading Strategies Inventory (MARSI, Mokhtari, 1998–2000)
- Assesses metacognitive awareness and reported use of reading strategies
- Validated with native speaker population (N = 825)
- Overall reliability = .93
- Subscale reliabilities: metacognitive strategies .92, cognitive strategies .79, support strategies .87

Source: White *et al.* (2007)

Survey of Reading Strategies (*SORS*, Sheorey and Mokhtari, 2001)
- Assesses metacognitive awareness and reported use of reading strategies
- Adapted from MARSI for non-native speakers of English; changes included removing redundant items and modifying some wording
- Overall reliability = .89

Source: White *et al.* (2007)

Learning Strategies Survey (*LSS,* Cohen, Oxford, and Chi, 2003)
- 89 items
- 5-point Likert scale
- Covers L2 learning strategies organized according to these areas: listening, speaking, reading, writing, vocabulary learning, and translation
- 5 factors: Learning Structure and Vocabulary, Speaking, Listening, Reading, and Asking for Clarification (reliabilities .67 to .85)
- Confirmatory factor analysis showed fair fit with the data (Paige *et al.,* 2004)
- Found to be very useful for study abroad students (Paige *et al.,* 2004)

Source: White *et al.* (2007).

Metacognitive Awareness of Listening Questionnaire (*MALQ,* Vandergrift *et al.,* 2006)
- 21-item questionnaire
- 5 factors: problem-solving, planning and evaluation, mental translation, person knowledge, and directed attention
- Assesses metacognitive awareness and reported use of L2 listening strategies
- Trialed and validated with approximately 1,000 learners in different countries and contexts
- Reliabilities with a large sample (N = 425): .68 to .78
- Confirmatory factor analysis
- Significant relationship between reported listening strategies and actual listening performance

Source: White *et al.* (2007)

Also see structured strategy questionnaires (actual-task or general) by: Anderson and Vandergrift (1996); Chamot and El-Dinary (1999); Chamot and Küpper (1989); Cohen, Oxford, and Chi (2005); Fan (2003); Kojic-Sabo and Lightbown (1999); Li and Qin (2006); National Capital Language Resource Center (NCLRC, 2000a, 2000b); O'Malley and Chamot (1990); Oxford, Cho, Leung, and Kim (2004); Ozeki (2000); Politzer and McGroarty (1985); Rubin and Thompson (1994); and Weaver and Cohen (1997).

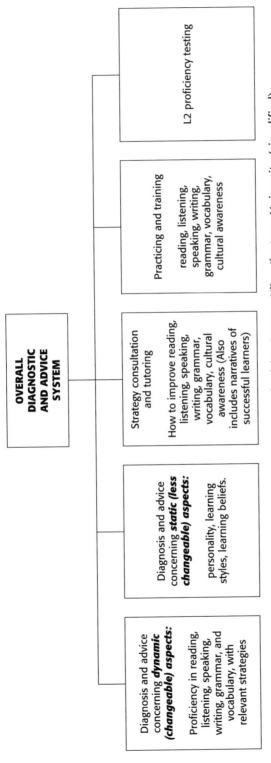

Figure 5.1 The framework for the Diagnostic Assessment and Advice System, Xi'an Jiaotong University (simplified)

Note: Diagnostic elements guide strategy consultation/tutoring and practising/training.

Source: Adapted from material provided by Ma Xiaomei

and useful assistance to L2 learners. The system aims to identify learning strategies relevant to individual learners' characteristics (e.g., personality, styles, and motivation), provide advice on how to strategically address any EFL learning problems, and foster learners' self-regulation. The system has four modules: (a) a reading dynamic diagnostic module which assesses learners' reading behaviours and skills; (b) a learners' static diagnostic module which diagnoses learners' personal characteristics, such as personality, learning style, learning strategies, learning motivation, and learning beliefs; and (c) two strategy instruction modules.

At the same time, Yang Nae-Dong at National Taiwan University has developed an online strategy diagnostic system (Yang, personal communication, November 15, 2007). Madeline Ehrman (1999) described a diagnostic assessment battery used for adult students entering the U.S. Foreign Service Institute's School of Language Studies.

5.10.4 Current dynamics regarding L2 learning strategies questionnaires

Several dynamics are evident in the area of strategy questionnaires at present. First, many questionnaires are becoming more standardized, using common formats built on the same Likert scale used in the *SILL*, which was modelled on the *LASSI*. Second, some researchers are using strategy questionnaires with very large samples, surpassing that of Nyikos and Oxford (1993), N = 1,200. Gu's (2008) study in Singapore involved administering a questionnaire to 3,216 children. Third, strategy questionnaires are often used with smaller samples for classroom action research. Fourth, some researchers developed more specialized strategy questionnaires in one or more particular language areas, while others developed strategy questionnaires for children. Gu (2008) did both types of specialization with his children's listening strategy questionnaire. Fifth, path analysis has been more widely used to identify causality. Finally, confirmatory factor analyses are becoming more common for establishing with greater certainty the latent structure of quantitative strategy questionnaires.

5.11   Narratives for strategy assessment

Narratives, such as learner diaries or learner histories, often provide much more contextualized information than many other strategy assessment techniques. Learners tell their own stories of L2 learning in specific sociocultural situations, describe the strategies they used to handle specific learning challenges or needs, and explain how they felt in various episodes and instances. Examples of narrative strategy assessment tools are diaries, journals, L2 learning histories, and more general strategy narratives. In addition to being a strategy assessment tool, a narrative is also a well recognized, respected research method (see Chapter 7).

5.12   Quality of strategy assessment tools

Quality of assessment (measurement quality) is very important, and it is therefore the capstone of this chapter. I start with criteria for quality of quantitative strategy assessment tools, validity and reliability, and then discuss quality of nonqualitative strategy assessment tools.

5.12.1   Measurement validity – quantitative

Concept 5.6 on pages 168–169 refers to *measurement validity*. The main question to ask about measurement validity is, "To what degree does the instrument actually measure what it purports to measure?" A number of subquestions address different aspects of measurement validity.

A given measure is not proven to be valid in all settings or for all time. Measurement validity should be viewed in relation to a given sociocultural setting and its participants at a given time in history. If an instrument from one culture is to be used in another, it is very important to recheck the validity. If an instrument is applied to an age group for which it was not intended, validity needs to be rechecked.

As noted by Adcock and Collier (2001), measurement validity is not the same as the validity of the concept being measured. For instance, an interview might measure what it purports to measure, but the concept itself might be off-base; or the concept might be meaningful but the measure might be non-valid.

5.12.2   Measurement reliability – quantitative

Measurement reliability refers to accuracy, precision, or consistency of measurement. Concept 5.7 on page 170 presents possible reliability criteria for a quantitative instrument, such as a highly structured questionnaire, interview, or rating scale. At the top of the box is the main question, "To what degree does the quantitative instrument measure accurately, precisely, or consistently?" Below the main question are specific questions about different types of reliability for a quantitative measurement instrument. A quantitative strategy instrument must show reliability, but reliability is not meaningful unless validity is also present. For instance, Michaela's use of L2 writing strategies can appear identical each time (perfect test–retest reliability), but if the writing strategy measure actually requires considerable L2 reading as well as writing, it might not be a valid measure of L2

Concept 5.6   Questions to ask about quantitative measurement validity (i.e., validity of a specific quantitative measure), with possible L2 learning strategy research examples

Main question: To what degree does the quantitative instrument measure what it claims to measure?

Relevant questions and strategy research examples	Type of evidence of instrument (measurement) validity
To a non-expert, does the instrument intuitively *appear*, on the face of it, to measure what it claims to measure? (An intuitive judgment of appearance should never be used as the only or main basis for judging the validity of an instrument.)	Face validity (inadequate)
How was the content of the instrument selected? 1. Were the items or aspects of the instrument randomly selected to represent all aspects of the domain to be measured? *Example*: Random selection of L2 learning strategy items from a larger set of L2 learning strategy items. **Or:** 2. Were the items or aspects of the instrument purposefully selected to represent all key parts of the domain to be measured? *Example*: Purposeful selection of L2 learning strategies so that there is adequate representation of various types of strategies: metacognitive, cognitive, affective, and sociocultural-interactive strategies.	Content validity

To what degree does the instrument correlate with other instruments that claim to measure the same construct? *Example:* A strong correlation exists between the strategy use questionnaire in question and a different (well validated) strategy use questionnaire.	Concurrent validity	*Criterion validity*
To what degree do results on this instrument successfully predict results on some other instrument that is theoretically related to this instrument? *Example:* A high score on a strategy use questionnaire predicts a moderate to high score on a reading proficiency test.	Predictive validity	
Does the instrument correlate well with other instruments measuring theoretically similar constructs/concepts? *Example:* A strongly positive correlation exists between a strategy use measure and an autonomy measure.	Convergent validity	*Construct validity*
To what degree does the instrument have a low correlation with other instruments designed to measure theoretically different constructs/concepts? *Example:* A strongly negative correlation exists between strategy use scores and scores on a scale of passivity in learning.	Discriminant validity	
To a group of professionals who are experts on this theoretical construct, to what degree does the instrument effectively measure the theoretical construct? *Example:* A team of experts agrees that the theoretical construct in a strategy instrument is measured appropriately.	Expert-judgment validity	

Source: R. Oxford, Presentation Notes, EDCI 798, Research Methods, University of Maryland.

Concept 5.7   Questions to ask about quantitative measurement reliability (i.e., reliability of a specific quantitative measure), with possible L2 learning strategy research examples

Main question: To what degree does the quantitative instrument measure accurately, precisely, or consistently?

Relevant questions and strategy research examples	Type of evidence of instrument (measurement) reliability
To what degree does the instrument measure consistently from one time to the next for the same group of participants? *Example:* Strategy use questionnaire given to a group once and then a week later.	Test-retest reliability (2 or more different times)
To what degree do different raters or scorers give consistent ratings to the same construct using the instrument with the same participant or group? *Example:* Two raters rating the strategy awareness of a given student based on a video of an interview with the student.	Inter-rater reliability (2 or more raters/scorers)
To what degree do different forms of the same instrument measure the same construct consistently for the same group of participants? *Example:* Two supposedly equivalent forms of the same strategy questionnaire given to the same group.	Parallel forms reliability, also known as alternate forms or equivalent forms reliability (2 or more forms of the instrument)
Using one measurement instrument administered once to a group of participants, to what degree do the items measure the same construct within the instrument? *Example:* Consistency within a single questionnaire measuring strategy use.	Internal consistency reliability (1 time, 1 form of the instrument) Subtypes: Average inter-item correlation; average item-total correlation; split-half reliability; Cronbach alpha (α)

Source: R. Oxford, Presentation Notes, EDCI 798, Research Methods, University of Maryland.

writing strategy use. In that case, the L2 writing strategies measure would be reliable but not valid. This is analogous to having a broken bathroom scale that reliably measures the same incorrect weight every time.

5.12.3   Quality of a qualitative measurement instrument

Quality of particular qualitative measurement tools, such as an open-ended questionnaire or interview, is not discussed as much as the validity of entire qualitative study designs (Chapter 7). However, Adcock and Collier (2001) argued that qualitative measures must have the same standards of quality as quantitative measures. Concept 5.8 on the next page provides some guidelines to consider.

5.12.4   Difference between quality of a measurement tool and quality of an entire research study

So far the discussion of quality has focused on a given measurement tool, not on the rigour of an entire study of L2 learning strategies. Criteria for rigour or quality of entire studies is found in Chapter 7.

5.13   Conclusion

The S²R Model honours many forms of L2 strategy assessment: observations, verbal reports, semi-structured interviews, discussions, colour-coding, questionnaires, and narratives. Strands running through this chapter have included purposes, advantages, limitations, quality, and cultural issues.

This is a potentially rich time for L2 learning strategy assessment. Discourse analysis is used to transcribe and interpret qualitative data on strategies. Hybrid strategy assessments and colour-coding have become realities for strategy assessment. Greater standardization and rigour of some instruments has occurred. Greater sensitivity regarding culturally relevant strategy assessment is growing. Diagnostic assessment systems are being developed. The door is even open for development of neurological observations of strategy use. Clearly L2 strategy assessment can develop much further, and deficiencies can always be noted with any measurement technique, but there are significant signs of hope in strategy assessment.

To understand precisely how self-regulated strategy use develops and how to help learners, proper strategy assessment is essential. Constant work is necessary to develop optimal tools to measure learners' strategy use patterns. Using reliable and valid assessments, we can gauge the relationship of strategies to proficiency and a host of other variables in different sociocultural contexts.

Concept 5.8   Questions to ask about the quality of qualitative measures (e.g., open-ended interviews) with possible L2 learning strategy research examples

Main question: To what degree does the qualitative instrument measure the phenomenon effectively?

Relevant question and strategy research example	Type of evidence of instrument (measurement) quality
To a group of professionals who are experts on this theoretical construct, to what degree does the instrument effectively measure the theoretical construct? *Example:* A team of experts agrees that the theoretical construct in the strategy interview is measured appropriately.	Expert-judgment validity
To what extent do the instrument's results appear to cohere well with results from other instruments that claim to measure the same construct in the same study? *Example:* Similar qualitative patterns of results appear for an open-ended strategy use questionnaire and an open-ended strategy use interview.	Cross-measure/same-construct agreement
To what degree do the instrument's results appear to cohere well with the results of other instruments measuring theoretically similar constructs/concepts? *Example:* Similar qualitative patterns of results appear for an open-ended strategy use interview and an autonomy measure.	Cross-measure/similar-construct agreement
To what degree does the instrument have good structural coherence? *Example:* An interview's questions are all in the same register (e.g., personal, friendly, and welcoming for an interview in a narrative study), rather than shifting registers midway.	Structural coherence
Do the data from the measure obtain similar interpretations from different researchers? *Example:* Responses on a think-aloud measure receive similar interpretations from two researchers.	Inter-coder reliability
Do the data from the measure obtain similar interpretations from the same researcher at different times? *Example:* Responses on a think-aloud measure receive similar interpretations from the same researcher who looks at the videotape a second time.	Intra-coder reliability

Further reading

Carson, J.G., and Longhini, A. (2002) Focusing on learning styles and strategies: A diary study in an immersion setting. *Language Learning*, *52*: 401–438. This useful diary study shows the influence of learning style and sociocultural environment on the choice of an adult learner's strategies.

Schumann, J.H. (ed.) (2004). *The Neurobiology of Learning: Perspectives from Second Language Acquisition*. London: Routledge. This book covers the neurobiology of motivation, of declarative and procedural memory, and of memory consolidation, attention, and aptitude. It does not focus on strategies but can serve as a springboard for later strategy research, assessment, and theory-development.

White, C., Schramm, K., and Chamot, A.U. (2007) Research methodology. In Cohen, A.D. and Macaro, E. (eds), *Language Learner Strategies: Thirty Years of Research and Practice*: 92–116. Oxford, UK: Oxford University Press. Though labelled as research methodology, this chapter also stresses various techniques for assessing L2 learning strategies, with an emphasis on qualitative assessment.

Zimmerman, B.J. (2008) Investigating self-regulation and motivation: Historical background, methodological development, and future prospects. *American Educational Research Journal*, 45 (1): 166–183. In addition to discussing motivation, Zimmerman reviews research on self-regulated learning strategies and current means of assessing strategies: questionnaires, computerized trace measures, diaries, think-alouds used with hypermedia, portfolio assessment, microanalytic measures with cyclical analyses, and others.

Chapter 6

Strategy instruction and other forms of strategy assistance

Give light, and the darkness will disappear of itself.

Desiderius Erasmus

Preview questions

1. How does the S²R Model expand ideas about assistance for self-regulated learning strategy use?
2. How does culture relate to the teaching of L2 learning strategies in this model?
3. Should the teaching of strategies be integrated into a regular language course or handled separately?
4. Does the S²R Model have specific, accepted steps to follow in helping students develop more optimal strategy use?
5. Why do distance learners require special strategy assistance?

Direct strategy instruction by teachers, as in the Cognitive Academic Language Learning Approach (CALLA), is a very important form of strategy assistance. However, according to the S²R Model, strategy assistance is far broader than direct, teacher-led strategy instruction. This chapter presents a variety of forms of strategy assistance for L2 learners of different ages and cultures, with the goal of increased L2 proficiency and greater self-regulation. Varied types of strategy assistance include strategy-rich L2 textbooks, strategic learner guidebooks, learner consultation services, meta-scripts, and other modes to help learners in improving their strategy use. "Improving strategy use" does not imply any single formula for optimal L2 learning. Different learners, given their varied learning needs and proficiency levels, often require different sets of strategies and different kinds of strategy assistance. Distinguished language learners use strategies that are not identical to those of beginners, and they require a different strategy assistance approach, often one-to-one consultation. Strategy assistance is useful at all levels as long as it is tailored to learners' needs. Table 6.1 previews the topics in this chapter.

Table 6.1 **Overview of this chapter**

6.1   Key terms

The term *learning strategy instruction* (Oxford, 1990) (also *learning strategies instruction*, Chamot, 2004) has been used for many years to refer to ways by which teachers can help students become more effective learners. Most often this help is viewed as being directly woven into regular L2 teaching as a primary component. More specifically, the image evoked by the term *learning strategy instruction* is generally that of the teacher directly teaching learning strategies to a group of students in a language classroom.

Strategies-based instruction (SBI) and *styles- and strategies-based instruction (SSBI)* have emerged more recently (Cohen and Weaver, 2006). These terms refer to forms of L2 instruction in which learning strategies (or learning styles and strategies) are absolutely foundational to L2 instruction. In SBI or SSBI, direct strategy instruction typically occurs.

Self-regulated strategy instruction is the teaching of strategies with the ultimate goal of self-regulation, which is viewed as a key to L2 proficiency. This term simply emphasizes the ultimate purpose. *Self-regulated learning (SRL)* is an umbrella expression that encompasses a variety of different techniques and modalities for teaching students to become more self-directed in their learning, as discussed in Chapter 1. Models of self-regulated learning almost always involve learning strategies. They also typically involve the implicit or explicit teaching of such strategies.

The S^2R Model defines *strategy assistance* as *any* type of help (a) that is appropriate to the learner's culture and relevant to his or her needs and (b) that the learner receives to improve the use of self-regulated L2 learning strategies. The goal of strategy assistance is to help students become more effective L2 learners and take greater control over their learning through self-regulated learning strategies. This type of assistance can include direct classroom teaching of strategies, course materials and textbooks that emphasize strategies and autonomy, general guidebooks on how to become a better language learner, a learning consultation service or similar model, and other forms of assistance.

6.2 Culture as a factor in excellent strategy assistance

According to the S^2R Model, excellent strategy assistance, whether provided by a teacher, a textbook, a website, or some other means, embodies both cultural appropriateness and cultural openness. Strategy assistance should be culturally relevant to learners in given sociocultural contexts. It should pay positive attention to culturally valid strategies that learners already use but should also offer help regarding other potentially useful strategies, which might or might not be part of the learners' home culture (Holliday, 2003).

In presenting new strategies, strategy assistance providers should never imply that a learner's current, culturally valid strategies are "wrong" or "useless." In the paper entitled "When Is 'Rote' Not Really Rote?," Tsai, Kim, and Kim (2000) noted that non-Asian L2 teachers often disparaged Asian learners' L2 memorization strategies as being "rote," i.e., reflective of memorization without understanding or meaning. However, Tsai *et al.*

displayed many examples of memorization strategies that involved highly sophisticated, meaningful mental associations on the part of many Asian students; in other words, the strategies were not rote at all. The uninformed, negative judgments against culturally-promoted strategies, such as these, exhibited what Holliday (2003) viewed as cultural discrimination or "culturism." A better route for teachers and other strategy assistance providers is to be aware of their own cultural biases, try to move past those biases, learn from other cultures, and discern the value of strategies used in other cultures, while also offering new strategies that might be useful. New strategies can expand learners' repertoire without being used as substitutes for existing strategies. This does not imply that those who offer strategy assistance should accept the dysfunctional strategy use of clearly unsuccessful language learners, who typically display random, desperate grasping at strategies that are irrelevant to the task and situation (Reiss, 1981, 1983). Such strategy use relates to the individual's learning problems and is not cultural.

The following sections offer an array of strategy assistance options, all of which are honoured as part of the S²R Model. The first option consists of separate learning-to-learn courses or programmes.

6.3 Strategy instruction in separate learning-to-learn courses or programmes

Some experts have had good success with providing strategy instruction as part of separately-taught "learning to learn" courses and training programmes, rather than direct strategy instruction integrated into regular L2 instruction. Andrew Cohen (personal communication, May 15, 2007) shared his views about a separate, very popular course on language learning at the University of Minnesota entitled "Practical Language Learning for International Communication," which he has taught since 2001. The course addresses L2 learning strategies, learning styles, motivation, culture, L2 tasks, instructional methods, and other themes. Its goal is to increase awareness and equip students to succeed at learning language and culture in their home institution or abroad. The course requires students to do background readings, assess their own learning styles and strategies, gather data about L2 learning from three other students, and participate in classroom simulations and reflections. The main book is *Maximizing Study Abroad: A Students' Guide to Strategies for Language and Culture Learning and Use* (Paige, Cohen, Kappler, Chi, and Lassegard, 2006). Many classroom exercises come from *Styles and Strategies-Based Instruction: A Teachers' Guide* (Cohen and Weaver, 2006). The effectiveness of this course seems to lie in its clear goals and detailed, practical materials and exercises. In addition, learners who choose to take the course – especially those who are study-abroad students before or after the course – have a sense of purpose and are therefore motivated to transfer the information to their own L2 learning.

An interesting example of a separate "learning to learn" training programme is provided by Flaitz and Feyten (1996). They conducted a study that involved consciousness-raising and strategy use for foreign language learners at a U.S. university. A treatment group of 130 students of Spanish I and II (in six groups) received "metacognitive awareness raising" (MAR), a single 50-minute session which involved students in developing a general awareness of strategies without being exposed to any actual strategy practice, while the control group of 99, similar in characteristics, received a "placebo" questionnaire on language learning myths. The treatment group received a brief strategy presentation, performed a brainstorming activity about their current strategies, and received a lively, visually interesting handout entitled "How to Survive Spanish I or II," outlining 26 learning strategies, each keyed to a letter of the alphabet. Students performed a jigsaw activity that helped them organize this information, gave them ownership of it, and encouraged them to refer to the strategies they had brainstormed earlier as they discussed strategies on the handout. The only other treatment these students received after the MAR session consisted of: (a) a strategy assessment (checklist format) at midterm and (b) one strategy-reminder activity given by the teacher. Nevertheless, when grades were tallied at the end of the course, Spanish achievement for the treatment group was significantly higher than achievement for the control group. In a questionnaire, classroom teachers of the treatment-group students said the treatment had a discernible effect on their students' learning. These findings suggest that a separate strategy instruction session can do a world of good if properly conducted.

Joan Rubin (1996) created an hour-long videodisc and eight hours of additional instruction called the Language Learning Strategies (LLS) Programme. This programme helps learners work on strategies for three major language skills: listening (use knowledge of the world, listen for familiar places and names, and use key words to narrow predictions), reading (integrate text and pictures, use discourse markers to organize text and predict content, and use the topic to narrow predictions), and speaking (asking for clarification and managing conversations). For the reading and speaking sections, learners can choose to do tasks in either English or another language. The programme is based on research showing that learning performance improves with instruction in using cognitive and metacognitive strategies. It is also based on the concept that learners already know much more than they think they do about how to learn. "An important component of strategy instruction is the increase in students' awareness of the background knowledge they bring to the task" (Rubin, 1996, p. 152).

Rubin noted that semester-long courses on strategies have been taught at the University of Michigan and the University of Arizona.

One of the best known courses for learner development is Ellis and Sinclair's (1989) *Learning to Learn English: A Course in Learner Training*. This course, which has won praise from learners and teachers, has been used worldwide to teach how to optimize English-learning. Sinclair (n.d.) called this version of learner training "teacher-guided/learner-decided." In this course, the teacher is an active guide, informant, and counsellor, but the learner decides what to do by using reflection and metacognitive strategies. Ellis and Sinclair's learner training mode does not try to impose a particular set of strategies on learners; it is founded on constructivism and therefore asserts that learners decide for themselves the optimal way for them to learn languages. This variety of learner training is aimed at helping learners to (a) consider factors (psychological, physiological, and educational) affecting their English learning and (b) identify relevant strategies for becoming more responsible and effective learners. Later Sinclair (2000) specifically expanded the definition of learner training to include helping the learner consider social, cultural, and political factors that affect English learning. See also Sinclair and Ellis (1992).

Chamot (2004) noted advantages of presenting direct strategy instruction in separate courses for "learning to learn" as compared to offering direct strategy instruction that is interwoven into an ordinary L2 class. First, strategies learned within a language class for certain tasks might be less likely to transfer to other tasks (Gu, 1996). Second, some L2 teachers are not prepared to integrate strategy instruction into their courses, and it takes significant time and effort to teach them how to do so (Vance, 1999; Weinstein and Mayer, 1986). Third, strategy instruction that is unintegrated with L2 instruction might actually be preferred by motivated, adult learners whose time is limited and who are capable of applying the principles and practices on their own (Wenden, 1986). Even with these potential advantages, if the learner is taking an L2 course at the same time as a separate "learning to learn" course, it would be helpful if the two teachers communicate and provide scaffolding across courses for the necessary application to take place.

6.4   Direct strategy instruction integrated into regular L2 courses

The value of separate "learning to learn" courses has been mentioned. However, many experts promote the direct teaching of strategies within the context of the L2 curriculum, because this gives students the chance to practise the strategies with real L2 learning tasks (Chamot, 2004; Grenfell and Harris, 1999). Unless learners have clear awareness of their L2 learning process, they might not be able to transfer what they learn in a separate "learning to learn" course. In such instances, learners benefit from having direct strategy instruction woven into their regular L2 course.

6.4.1   Some factors in successful direct strategy instruction in L2 courses

For direct, classroom-based, integrated strategy instruction, research suggests that it is helpful to identify when a given strategy might be useful, model the strategy with a specific L2 task, provide learners time to practise the strategy, and teach learners how to evaluate whether the strategy is useful and when it should be transferred to other tasks and situations. For this process to work optimally, teachers should also find out which strategies the students are already using.

Direct strategy instruction in L2 classes can significantly reduce the amount of time needed for acquiring high levels of L2 proficiency (Leaver, 2003a). Such instruction should address affective issues such as anxiety, motivation, and interest and should help students understand why they often choose strategies that match their own preferred learning styles (Oxford and Leaver, 1996). It should also deal with strategies students really need to know (O'Malley, and Chamot 1990) and should be as relevant as possible to learners' interest and concerns (Cohen and Weaver, 1998).

Chamot (personal communication, May 19, 2007) indicated that learner-centered L2 teachers can successfully integrate learning strategy instruction into their teaching but that transmission-oriented L2 teachers find it difficult to be effective in strategy instruction. Effective L2 strategy instruction never involves merely transferring or transmitting the strategies of "good learners" to poor learners; instead, it calls for learners to be active, not passive. It involves teachers in the following: (a) developing meta-cognitive awareness of their own learning and their students' learning, (b) practicing and encouraging self-reflection, (c) observing and questioning students regarding learning, (d) modelling learning strategies, and (e) identifying a given student's strategies and encouraging other students to try it out (but not with the idea that every strategy fits every student).

Quote 6.1 Explicit strategy instruction

Explicit strategy instruction is more effective than implicit instruction embedded in classroom activities without explanations and modelling.

Anna Uhl Chamot (2008)

Various levels of explicitness are possible in strategy instruction (adapted from Hajer, Meestringa, Park and Oxford, 1996). Most research indicates that the more explicit the strategy instruction, the more successful it is. Here are the levels, the last of which is the most valued:

- *Level 1. Blind (covert) strategy instruction*: Some learning strategies are integrated into L2 textbooks or teaching but are not explicitly or overtly mentioned. Learners are merely told what to do but might think the strategy is just part of the L2 task.

- *Level 2. Somewhat informed strategy instruction*: The teacher (or textbook) names the strategy, says what it is for, and asks students to apply the strategy.

- *Level 3. Informed strategy instruction*: The teacher (or textbook) names the strategy, demonstrates how to use the strategy, explains when the strategy is useful and its purpose, and asks students to use the strategy.

- *Level 4. Completely informed strategy instruction (strategy-plus-control instruction)*: The teacher (or textbook) names the strategy, demonstrates how to use the strategy, explains when the strategy is useful and its purpose, and asks students to use the strategy. In addition, learners receive practice in how to reflect on the strategy, how to evaluate their success, and when and how to transfer the strategy to new tasks.

Quote 6.2 Successful strategy instruction

Research shows that strategy [instruction] that fully informs the learner (by indicating why the strategy is useful, how it can be transferred to different tasks, and how learners can evaluate the success of the strategy) is more successful....

Rebecca Oxford (1990, p. 207)

Explicit, informative strategy instruction is supported by years of research in L1 literacy (Graham and Harris, 2000) and in the L2 field (Grenfell and Harris, 2004). In five different evaluations in various school settings with different content emphases, Chamot's CALLA model has resulted in significant gains in content knowledge and skills, English proficiency, and learning strategies (Chamot, 2007), at least partly because it includes explicit strategy instruction. Excellence in the design of strategy instruction is important to the success of the effort (Lee, 2007). Other success factors in strategy instruction include teachers' interest and motivational approaches (Chamot and Küpper, 1989), instructional flexibility, and overt attention to learners' specific needs (Lee, 2007).

The selection of strategies is important, Chamot explained. "Metacognitive strategies . . . are applicable to all sorts of language and non-language tasks. The same holds true for strategies like using one's prior knowledge and cooperating with others. Other learning strategies are more suitable for specific kinds of tasks. For instance, making inferences . . . is useful for reading and listening tasks, while substituting/paraphrasing is helpful for speaking and writing tasks" (Chamot, personal communication, May 19, 2007). Foreign language students benefit from strategies that help with speaking and understanding the language, while second language students often need strategies for academic tasks, she stated.

Chamot (2004) presented a template for creating a model L2 activity incorporating strategies: (a) activity title, (b) strategy or strategies to be taught, (c) learning standards, (d) language and proficiency level, (e) brief description of the activity, (f) objectives, (g) materials, (h) procedures (linking the strategy to the activity, introducing and modelling the activity, practicing), (i) expansion, (j) adaptation, and (k) teacher resources to enhance the activity.

6.4.2   Learner variables to consider in integrating learning strategies directly into L2 instruction

Learner variables to consider in integrating strategies into regular L2 instruction include:

- demographics (age, gender, and status as minority, majority, refugee, or immigrant),
- education (interrupted schooling, years of formal and informal education, when, and where), and
- L2-learning factors (native language, differences between L1 and L2 in terms of language characteristics, proficiency in L1 and L2, language learning styles, L2 learning motivation, length of time studying the L2 and under what circumstances, strategies currently used, and attitudes and beliefs about the L2, about L2 learning, and about the culture).

Learners' attitudes and beliefs are especially important for the success of strategy instruction. Self-regulated L2 learning involves the learner as an active co-constructor of knowledge, taking responsibility for learning. Some learners come from cultures that encourage a less overtly active role, and these learners sometimes need to develop new attitudes and beliefs. Classroom strategy instruction can help by identifying ways in which learners already take responsibility for their learning, the strategies they currently use, and ways that an expanded range of strategies – and greater learner responsibility and control – can help them become more confident and proficient.

The teacher must be aware of the many types of learning strategies that are useful for different learners. The teacher must not have a narrow view but should instead look widely at the following: Who has strategies that are working perfectly well for accuracy and vocabulary learning but needs to expand strategies for fluency? Who is progressing very well in fluency but could make still greater strides through strategies promoting accuracy necessary for higher-level proficiency? Who is struggling because of lack of focus? Who does not understand strategies and needs basic help? Who needs assistance in knowing what a given L2 task requires (task analysis) and how to identify task-relevant strategies? Who needs help with strategies for longer-term planning and self-evaluation beyond the task level? Understanding individual learners' strategy needs in the classroom is crucial as a precursor to classroom-based strategy instruction. It is because of this that strategy assessment is a welcome part of (or precursor to) strategy instruction. (See Chapter 5 regarding strategy assessment.)

6.4.3   Language of direct strategy instruction

Beginners in a language cannot necessarily comprehend strategy instruction in the L2, as shown in a study by Chamot and Keatley (2003). In that study, teachers of beginning English learners (native Spanish speakers) were unsuccessful in trying to teach learning strategies completely in English. Greater success occurred for other teachers, who taught the strategies first in the L1 (Spanish), had students practise them in Spanish, and then asked students to transfer these strategies to English language tasks. Chamot (2004) advised that if the whole class shares the same L1, strategy instruction at the beginning level of L2 learning should be conducted in the native language. Grenfell and Harris (1999) suggested conducting strategy instruction in the L2 as much as possible but recognize that this is difficult at the beginners' level.

Other studies successfully used a combination of the native and target languages for strategy instruction (Chamot, 2004). Secondary foreign language (French and German) teachers in London used some strategy instruction materials in English, the L1, but also successfully employed checklists, strategy descriptions, and strategy activities in a simplified version of French and German, so that strategy instruction would not take away from L2 use in instruction (Grenfell and Harris, 1999). Ozeki (2000) taught learning strategies through simple English to her Japanese students in Japan but allowed students to respond in their native language. These combinations worked effectively.

However, teaching learning strategies in the L1, or in a combination of the L1 and the L2, becomes complicated or impossible in a classroom in which the learners come from many different L1 backgrounds. Chamot (2004) advised providing an L2 name for the strategy, explaining the strategy simply in the L2, and repeatedly modelling the strategy. Visual and tactile effects often help when language is a problem in classroom-based strategy instruction. Pictures, gestures, posters, and strategy cards are useful. In addition, in teaching strategies to elementary school children, Chamot and her colleagues effectively used stuffed animals representing various types of strategies (Robbins, n.d.). This not only overcame language barriers but also relaxed young learners and helped them remember strategies.

6.4.4   Practical classroom models for direct strategy instruction

The entire strategy instruction process is a cycle (Macaro, 2001a, 2001b; Oxford, 1990), as shown in Figure 6.1. Concept 6.1 on pages 185–187 compares various models and reveals the cycle in a linear, detailed, step-by-step format. All strategy instruction models in that table involve direct teaching, but some also include a discovery segment, in which learners perform an L2 task without any strategy instruction and discuss it as a means of revealing the need for strategies (also Oxford, 1990; Grenfell and

Figure 6.1   **A generic, flexible, cyclical model of direct strategy instruction**
Note: The elements of the model can be flexibly adapted to the needs of learners and teachers in specific situations.
Source: Thanks to Ernesto Macaro for initially drawing a cyclical representation.

Concept 6.1 Comparison of strategy instruction models

Phase	Oxford (1990, updated 2006)	O'Malley and Chamot (1990)	Chamot (2004, 2005); Chamot, Barnhardt, El-Dinary, and Robbins (1999)	Grenfell and Harris (1999)	Macaro (2001a, 2001b) Note: His phase numbers are shown as letters below for clarity.
			Models by different theorists		
1	*Prepare: Identify Current Strategies, Raise Initial Awareness:* Students identify current strategies for familiar tasks. Optional: Strategy awareness games. Teacher considers motivational and cultural issues regarding strategy instruction.	Students identify their current learning strategies	*Preparation:* Teacher identifies students' current learning strategies for familiar tasks.		
2	*Continue to Raise Awareness:* Learners do a task "cold," i.e., without any strategy instruction. They discuss how they did it (strategies). Brainstorming of strategies that work for learners on common types of tasks.			*Awareness Raising:* Learners do a task "cold." They brainstorm the strategies used. Class shares strategies that work for them.	A. Raise the awareness of students B. Explore possible strategies available
3	*Model and Name Strategies:* Teacher (or a strategic learner) names and models (demonstrates) and explains new strategies, stressing the potential benefits.	Teacher explains additional strategies	*Presentation:* Teacher models, names, explains new strategy; asks students if and how they have used it.	*Modelling:* Teacher demonstrates new strategies, emphasises their value and draws up a checklist of strategies for subsequent use.	C. Modelling by teacher and/or by other student

Concept 6.1   **Comparison of strategy instruction models** (continued)

Phase	Oxford (1990, updated 2006)	O'Malley and Chamot (1990)	Chamot (2004, 2005); Chamot, Barnhardt, El-Dinary, and Robbins (1999)	Grenfell and Harris (1999)	Macaro (2001a, 2001b) Note: His phase numbers are shown as letters below for clarity.
			Models by different theorists		
4	*Practise: Use, Combine, and Monitor Strategies:* Learners practise the new strategies and make strategy combinations (strategy chains) as needed for tasks; they simultaneously monitor use.	Teacher provides opportunities for practice	*Practice:* Students practise new strategy; in subsequent strategy practice, teacher fades reminders to encourage independent strategy use.	*General practice:* Learners are given a range of tasks to deploy new strategies.	D. Combining strategies for a specific purpose or task E. Application of strategies with scaffolded support
5a	*Evaluate and Transfer:* Learners evaluate effectiveness of strategies. Teacher or learner shows how strategy can be transferred to other tasks.		*Self-evaluation:* Students evaluate their own strategy use immediately after practice.		F. Initial evaluation by students

5b	*Expand and Adapt:* Learners apply strategies to further tasks, making choices about which to use, how to link them into strategy chains. Teacher releases control, fades strategy reminders.	Teacher assists learners in evaluating their success with the new strategies	*Expansion:* Students transfer strategies to new tasks, combine strategies into clusters, develop repertoire of preferred strategies.	*Action Planning:* Learners are guided to select strategies that will help them address their particular difficulties. *Further practice and fading out of reminders to use strategies.*	G. Gradual removal of scaffolding
6 (leads back to 1)	*Learners Continue to Increase Ownership:* Learners continue to monitor use and evaluate success. Phase can also include formal assessment and impact on performance. Increase learner ownership via discussions, bulletin board, think-pair-share. (Continue cycle)		*Assessment:* Teacher assesses students' use of strategies and impact on performance.	*Evaluation:* Teacher guides learners to evaluate progress and strategy use and to set themselves new goals.	H. Evaluation by students (and teacher) I. Monitoring strategy use and rewarding effort (Continue cycle)

Sources: Adapted from Chamot (2005) and Harris (2003) with additions by R. Oxford.

Harris, 1999). Some of the models have left out a phase, early preparation, which occurs before identifying any strategies to be taught and which I believe to be important.

The S²R Model can include many types of strategy assistance. One of them is direct strategy instruction. The S²R Model's approach to direct strategy instruction – which is one of the many options for strategy assistance in the overall S²R Model – includes the following phases, which have been built on years of experience. Phase 1 is *Prepare: Identify Current Strategies, Raise Initial Awareness*. When time permits, this phase includes a variety of strategy-awareness games, such as the *Strategy Search Game* and the *Embedded Strategies Game* (both in Oxford, 1990) and *The Best and the Worst Game* (Oxford, 1989). These games, which are in English but could be translated, are designed to help learners discover learning strategies in an enjoyable way while assessing their own strategies informally. In this phase, more formal strategy assessment (Chamot, 2004, 2005) is also possible to determine typically used strategies (via a questionnaire, open discussions, or other means). Lee (2007) initiated reading strategy intervention with assessment of current strategies.

The second phase is *Continue to Raise Awareness*. In this discovery-based phase, learners do a task without any strategy instruction, discuss how they did it, and reflect on how their strategies might have facilitated their accomplishing of the task. Grenfell and Harris (1999) included a similar phase, including doing the task "cold" and brainstorming strategies used. Macaro similarly included here raising awareness of students and exploring possible strategies available. This was not part of the models of O'Malley and Chamot (1990) or Chamot (2004, 2005).

The third phase is *Model and Name Strategies*. In this phase, there is some type of overt demonstration (modelling) of one or more relevant strategies. The strategies are given simple, easy-to-remember names. This phase is present in virtually all strategy instruction models. In most of the models the demonstration and naming are conducted by the teacher, but Macaro and I opened the door for a student to lead this part.

The fourth phase is *Practise: Use, Combine, and Monitor Strategies*. Learners practise the new strategies and make strategy combinations (strategy chains) as needed for tasks; they simultaneously monitor use. Like me, Macaro specifically mentioned possibilities of students practising combining strategies; I called combined strategies a "strategy chain" (Chapter 1). Active learners start monitoring their strategy use in this phase by determining whether they are using a strategy the way it was demonstrated. The scaffolding that the teacher has provided is gradually removed (faded), which Chamot (2004, 2005) showed as occurring in the practise phase, but for others (Grenfell and Harris, Macaro, and Oxford) it is slightly later.

In the first part of the fifth phase, *Evaluate and Transfer*, learners evaluate the effectiveness of strategies and learn how to transfer them to other related tasks or situations. Grenfell and Harris specifically mentioned action-planning at this phase, in which learners are guided to think about strategies for addressing specific problems. In the second part of the fifth phase, *Expand and Adapt*, learners apply strategies to further tasks, making choices about which to use and how to link them into strategy chains. The assistance by the teacher fades out.

In the sixth phase, *Learners Continue to Increase Ownership*, learners continue to monitor use and evaluate success (possibly through formal assessment of performance and learning strategies led by the teacher). Learners also increase ownership through open discussion, targeted focus groups, think-pair-share activities, peer mentoring, and a bulletin board of favourite strategies, techniques that I have used successfully. Recycling of the process was specifically highlighted by Macaro (2001a, 2001b) and Oxford (1990).

In short, the comparison shows that these direct instruction models are very similar in their general flow, with only a few distinctions among them. They are all guided by the principle of increased responsibility and authority for strategy use being taken by the learner. I have highlighted the S^2R Model of direct strategy instruction, one of many strategy assistance options in the overall S^2R Model, but other direct strategy instruction models are not too different.

6.4.5 Guidebooks for direct strategy instruction

The National Capital Language Resource Center (NCLRC, 2003, 2004a, 2004b) developed guidebooks to help teachers integrate strategy instruction into L2 instruction at the following levels: elementary school (for immersion), secondary schools, and postsecondary education. These materials not only explain the rationale for integrated strategy instruction but also provide very useful tools and techniques. For instance, in the higher education (postsecondary) guidebook (NCLRC, 2004b), there are 20 strategies divided into two categories, "metacognitive" and "task-based." The metacognitive strategies are identified as being useful for virtually all tasks, while the task-based strategies are determined by the particular nature of a given task and the students' own resources.

6.4.6 Portfolios for direct strategy instruction

Chapter 5 showed that learner portfolios can be used for strategy assessment, but portfolios are valuable for strategy instruction as well. Yang (2003) used learner portfolios to integrate strategy instruction into a university freshman English course and into English composition courses. She developed a Web-based Learning Portfolio system, which incorporated all the learning strategy instruction components, such as learning strategy diagnosis, assessment, goal-setting and planning, record-keeping and self-monitoring, and final self-evaluation, to support teacher-provided strategy-based instruction in freshman English and in an online English programme (Yang, 2005, 2006).

6.4.7   Metascripts for direct strategy instruction

A unique way to integrate strategy instruction is through *strategy metascripts*, which help learners organize, coordinate, and use strategies and tactics to accomplish a particular L2 task. A strategy metascript is a detailed, step-by-step plan for employing L2 learning strategies. Lavine and Cabal Krastel (1994) developed the idea of strategy metascripts for Spanish language learners experiencing learning difficulties, based partly on the work of Harris and Graham (1992) and Oxford (1990). Later strategy metascripts were understood as useful for all types of L2 learners.

Strategy metascripts can be created in three different ways: (a) by the teacher, who models it and helps students rehearse it; (b) by the individual learner, who uses self-questioning, such as "What is the task? How can I approach it? What is the topic?"; and (c) by learners who collaborate to create the metascript. In the collaborative mode, if one student is more proficient than another, that student can serve as a model and can "think aloud" about steps in how he or she does a given language task, while other students write down what the more proficient student "thinks aloud." Finally, the students collaboratively adapt the metascript. Students especially like strategy metascripts created by their classmates.

Quote 6.3   Strategy metascripts

No matter who creates the strategy metascript, when students use it, they learn to guide themselves, take charge of their own actions, improve their L2 proficiency, and develop desperately needed self-confidence. Learners rehearse strategy metascripts and can even memorize them until the metascripts become automatic. Rehearsal is a valuable strategy in itself.

Roberta Lavine (2008, p. 7)

Lavine and certain students developed the following strategy metascript to help other classmates learn weather vocabulary in Spanish. "The students navigate the following process, out loud or silently. This can, of course, be adapted for use at many levels of proficiency and in any language," said Lavine.

Step 1
I need to learn the new Spanish vocabulary. What should I do?
I see the pictures in the book, but that's not enough.

- *How does this vocabulary relate to me?*

Step 2
I know a technique I can use. It's called a semantic map.

- *First I choose the vocabulary I want to remember.*
- *Then I need a picture of the main idea. [Something about winter]*
- *The picture goes in the middle of the map.*

Step 3
Next, I need to fill in the semantic map.
To do that, I'll think of some questions:

- *How is the weather?*
- *What season is it?*
- *What do I like to do in this kind of weather?*
- *Where do I like to go in this kind of weather?*
- *What special occasions are there?*
- *What clothes should I wear in this weather?*
- *How does this weather make me feel?*
- *Those are enough questions.*

Step 4
Now I have to answer the questions.

- *I will fill in one answer per box on the semantic map.*

Step 5
Now I need to check my spelling.

- *If I need help I can look for these words in my textbook.*
- *These words are in the glossary.*
- *The glossary is in the back of the book.*

Step 6
Now I have to check my work.

- *Is my picture in the middle?*
- *Did I answer all of the questions?*
- *Do I have one answer in each box?*
- *Did I check my spelling?*

Step 7
Here is my final semantic map. (See Figure 6.2.)

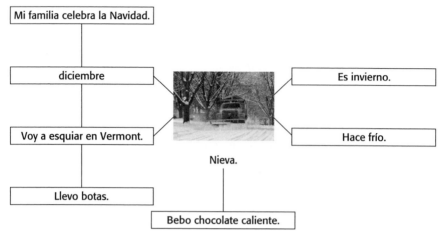

English translation: [In the centre] It's snowing. Clockwise from the top: It's winter. → It's cold. → I drink hot chocolate. → I wear boots. → I go skiing in Vermont. → December. → My family celebrates Christmas.

Figure 6.2   **Semantic map from metascript**
Source: Metascript, Roberta Lavine; photo, POD/Digital Vision.

Lavine indicated that students are generally receptive to strategy metascripts for strategy instruction and L2 learning. In more advanced classes, the metascripts are totally in Spanish.

6.5   Integrating strategy instruction into L2 textbooks and course materials

Textbook companies now provide strategy instruction, usually task-based and integrated into L2 textbooks, in order to increase proficiency, strategy awareness, and self-regulation. According to Bourdieu and Passeron (1977), textbooks reproduce social and cultural ideals. Strategies, strategy instruction, and self-regulation appear to be among those ideals in many L2 texts. Most major international publishers of L2 student books and teacher editions of student books incorporate learning strategies, whether they are called "strategies," "tips," "tactics," or any other name. An example is the *Tapestry Series* (see, e.g., Fellag, 2004; Fragiadakis and Maurer, 2000), developed for English learning among college-age students in North America, Asia, and the Middle East. This series has included learning strategies as a primary feature of the materials since its inception. *¡Avancemos!* (Gahala, Carlin, Hening-Boynton, Otheguy, and Rupert, 2007), McDougall Littell's three-level middle school textbook series for Spanish as a foreign language, employs learning strategies at every level for particular uses, such as listening and reading comprehension, writing, speaking, and cultural understanding.

Gunning and colleagues integrated learning strategies into excellent textbooks and materials for Québec's ESL learners and teachers. For instance, see *The Spinning Series* (Gunning and Lalonde, 1997), *A Tiny Twist to English* (Gunning, Lalonde and Watts, 2007), and *A New Twist to English* (Gunning, 2001, 2002, 2003; Gunning, Lalonde, Schinck, and Watts, 2001). These works use attractive mascots and assessment tools for young children, as shown in Figures 6.3 (below) and 6.4 (on page 194).

Use resources   Practice

Figure 6.3   Genie and Tiny Twist, elementary school strategy mascots
Note: Genie is the elementary school strategy mascot for Cycle 2 in *A New Twist to English*, and Tiny Twist is the elementary school strategy mascot for Cycle 1 in *A Tiny Twist to English*.
Source: Pamela Gunning. Reproduced by authorization of Lidec, Inc. © Lidec, Inc.

6.6   The learning consultation service model

Several governmental language schools and institutes have created learning consultation services (LCS). One of the best developed of these services is in the Foreign Service Institute (FSI) of the U.S. Department of State. Ehrman (1999) described it as a means of "bringing learning strategies to the student" (Ehrman, 1999, p. 41). According to Ehrman's 1999 description, a small cadre of LCS counsellors working in the central administration administered and interpreted the learning style questionnaires when students arrived. In addition, many language sections also had specialists called learning consultants, i.e., experienced teachers or language training supervisors who were well trained in learning assistance and who advised students and advocated for them. The learning consultants helped the student understand how to use diagnostic learning style questionnaire results, conveyed

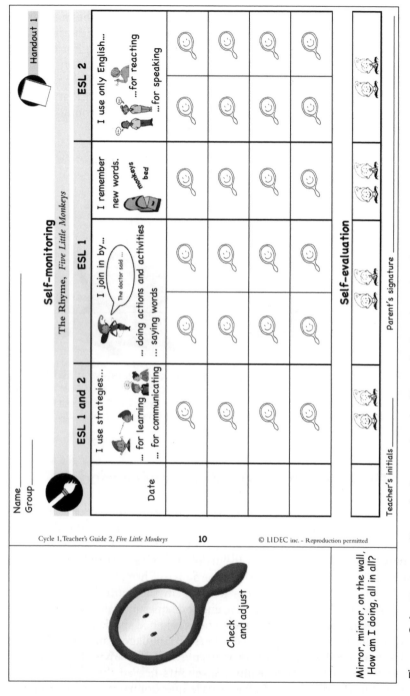

Figure 6.4 Strategy self-monitoring card and self-monitoring sheet for elementary school students
Source: Pamela Gunning. Reproduced with authorization of Lidec, Inc. © Lidec, Inc.

information to the student's teachers as permitted, and consulted periodi-
cally with the student and the teaching staff. Work of the section-specific
language consultants thus complemented that of LCS counsellors, who
provided individual feedback and special, expert consultations on L2 learning strategies or anxiety management. Learner counselling fits coherently
with the learner consultation service model. An entire special issue of *System*
(Rubin, 2007) has been devoted to learner counselling.

6.7   Strategy instruction through learner guidebooks

A number of general (non-course-related) guidebooks have been published
in English, such as those in Table 6.2 on page 196. Each of these offers
something slightly different. These books are helpful to learners who are able
to initiate and sustain learning on their own. Such books can also be used
by teachers who want to help their students become better L2 learners.

6.8   Strategy instruction in distance learning

Distance learners face many challenges, one of which is staying motivated.
However, they might not know how to maintain motivation or develop
motivation-enhancing strategies (Harris, 2003; White, 1995).

> **Quote 6.4** Motivational issues in distance learning
>
> In order to successfully complete a distance learning programme, learners
> have to maintain their motivation while working alone and develop a series of
> strategies that will enable them to work individually.
>
> Stella Hurd, Tita Beaven, and Ana Ortega (2001, p. 344)

Therefore, distance learners often need strategy assistance in order
to organize, prioritize, take initiative, and figure out their own needs.
Fortunately, some distance education programmes help their students
learn how to learn. For example, the U.K.'s Open University, which enrolls
approximately 8,000 students in distance courses in French, Spanish, and
German, specifically encourages strategy use, and at the Shantou Radio
and TV University in China, EFL course books are designed to encourage
learners to use self-study strategies (Hurd and Xiao, 2006). Harris (2003)
reported on the INSTAL (Individualising Strategies for Adult Learners

Table 6.2 A selection of learner guidebooks to teach strategies

- *How to Learn a Foreign Language* (Fuller, 1987) – one of several learner guidebooks for foreign language students in the 1980s
- *Learning to Learn English: A Course in Learner Training* (Ellis and Sinclair, 1989) – well known course, which can also be used in flexible ways as a resource guidebook for learners
- *Practical Guide for Language Learning: A Fifteen-week Program of Strategies for Success* (Brown, 1989) – organized for semester-long guidance to L2 learners but can be used in other ways
- *Navigating the DSL Czech Course: A Guide for Students* (Leaver, 1990) – one of many learner guidebooks in the "navigating" series, oriented to those in a particular type of language course
- *Breaking the Language Barrier: Creating Your Own Pathway to Success* (Brown, 1991) – useful and includes a range of strategies
- *How to Become a More Successful Language Learner* (Rubin and Thompson, 1994) – contained the greatest number of strategies of all L2 learner guidebooks examined in a study by Hajer *et al.* (1996)
- *How to Study a Foreign Language* (Lewis, 1999) – practical references for university and secondary school students
- *Individualized Study Plans for Very Advanced Students of Foreign Languages* (Leaver, 2003b) – for highly advanced learners in classrooms, self-study, or informal learning; see strategy chapter
- *Strategies for Success: A Practical Guide to Learning English* (Brown, 2001) – easy to read for learners of English, connects learning strategies with learning styles (general preferences)
- *How to Improve Your Foreign Language Immediately: Foreign Language Communication Tools* (Shekhtman, 2003a) – talks about strategies for "organizing, fostering, controlling, and learning from whole communications" (p. ix)
- *Keys to Learning: Skills and Strategies for Newcomers* (Keatley, Anstrom, and Chamot, 2004) – useful guidebook for middle school learners
- *Maximizing Study Abroad: A Student's Guide to Strategies for Language and Culture Learning and Use* (Paige, Cohen, Kappler, Chi, and Lassegard, 2006) – well-researched, usable, detailed guide for students who want to get the most out of studying abroad; some information can also be used for learning in classrooms

in Language and ICT-Learning) Project, which was established in 2000, under the European Commission's Grundvig Programme for Adult Education. In this project, 23 researchers from across the EU met regularly to find ways to support adult distance learners at diverse levels of competence in a range of different languages, including learners whose access to computer technology and current textbooks might be limited. They created a handbook and a CD-ROM to help adult learners become more strategic. For learning strategies and strategy instruction to assist distance learning in general, see O'Neil (2005, 2008).

6.9 Conclusion

This chapter has focused on culturally-relevant strategy assistance for self-regulation in the S²R Model, which encompasses many methods, techniques, and materials exist for providing strategy assistance. Some of the examples discussed here are traditional, while others are highly innovative. Teachers can use these means to improve and expand the ways they help L2 learners become more strategically self-regulated. Additional research is welcome on all aspects and types of strategy assistance for L2 learning.

Further reading

Chamot, A.U. (2005) Language learning strategy instruction: Current issues and research. *Annual Review of Applied Linguistics*, 25: 112–130. This chapter raises important and thorny questions about L2 strategy instruction and is therefore very valuable. It does not deal with the full array of strategy assistance options found in Chapter 6 of the current book.

Chamot, A.U. (2009) *The CALLA Handbook: Implementing the Cognitive Academic Language Learning Approach*. Second edition. White Plains, NY: Pearson Education/ Longman. This handbook concerns one of the most widely used models for strategy instruction around the world. The three-pronged model combines instruction in language, content, and strategies.

Cohen, A.D. and Weaver, S. (2006) *Styles and Strategies-Based Instruction: A Teachers' Guide*. Minneapolis, MN: National Language Resource Center, University of Minnesota. This is a detailed guide that teachers can use to help students understand and optimize learning styles and strategies. It is full of activities, explanations, and resources.

Oxford, R.L. and Leaver, B.L. (1996) A synthesis of strategy instruction for language learners. In Oxford, R. (ed.), *Language Learning Strategies around the World: Cross-cultural Perspectives*. Manoa: University of Hawaii Press: 227–248. This remains one of the most thorough analyses of highly varied modes of L2 learning strategy instruction.

Rubin, J. (ed.) (2007, Mar.) *Learner Counseling*. Special issue. *System: An International Journal of Educational Technology and Applied Linguistics*, 35(1). This special issue provides an array of theoretically sound ideas and practical factors in learner counselling as a means of helping individual students use strategies that work effectively for them.

Section

III Researching Learning Strategies

Chapter 7

A guide to conducting research on self-regulated L2 learning strategies

That is the essence of science: Ask an impertinent question, and you are on the way to a pertinent answer.

Jacob Bronowski (1973)

Preview questions

1. What worldviews exist regarding research, and how are they similar and different?
2. What are the chief research methods relevant to self-regulated L2 learning strategies?
3. What are the advantages and disadvantages of quantitative research methods for investigating strategies?
4. How do qualitative and mixed methods research address the vast range of sociocultural contexts in which learners use L2 learning strategies?
5. What quality criteria are relevant for quantitative, qualitative, and mixed methods research?

A key purpose of Section III is to encourage and enable readers to plan, carry out, report and use research on learning strategies. Therefore, Chapter 7 offers an array of research methods for investigations involving L2 learning strategies, with specific examples or models that readers can follow. The S²R Model honours multiple ways to conduct strategy research, as long as studies are of high quality. This chapter presents important questions that can be asked about research quality. Chapter 8 presents a synthesis of existing strategy research studies, which have employed a wide range of research methods ever since the L2 learning strategy research field was born in the 1970s.

Written for novice researchers as well as experienced investigators, this chapter draws on knowledge from inside and outside the L2 field. Table 7.1 reveals the key topics in this chapter. Data elicitation is not strongly emphasized in this chapter except for comments about narrative research. For data elicitation, see Gass and Mackey (2007) and Dörnyei (2003b).

This chapter offers specific models for conducting different types of strategy research. These are shown in the chapter text and in the "how to" tables, but for full details on how to conduct such studies, consult the research methodology books listed under "Further reading."

Table 7.1 Overview of this chapter

7.1 Worldviews underlying various research methods

7.2 Overview of methods for research on self-regulated L2 learning strategies

7.3 Quantitative research methods, models of quantitative L2 studies, and validity of quantitative studies
    7.3.1 Experimental and quasi-experimental studies
    7.3.2 Non-experimental quantitative studies

7.4 Qualitative research methods, models of qualitative L2 studies, and validity of qualitative studies
    7.4.1 Phenomenology
    7.4.2 Grounded theory
    7.4.3 Case study
    7.4.4 Ethnography
    7.4.5 Narrative research
    7.4.6 Validity of qualitative studies

7.5 Mixed methods, a model of a mixed method L2 study, and validity of mixed methods studies

7.6 Action research, a model of an action research L2 study, and validity of action research studies

7.7 General thoughts about research quality

7.8 Ethics in L2 learning strategy research

7.9 Conclusion

    Further reading

7.1   Worldviews underlying various research methods

People have largely unexamined, fundamental beliefs (*doxa*) influenced by cultural contexts, institutions, and other people. Doxa are experienced as self-evident universals or worldviews that guide conscious thoughts and actions (Bourdieu, 1977). Worldviews can change through reflection or through crises.

Every research study involves a worldview reflecting what the researcher views as knowledge (epistemology) and as reality (ontology). Questions of *epistemology* include: What do we know, and how do we know it? What is evidence? *Ontology* is related to these questions: Does a single, universal reality exist outside of the mind of the researcher? Are there multiple realities in a pluralistic world? Concept 7.1 on page 204 shows worldviews relevant to L2 learning research. Postpositivism, a revision of positivism, pervades most quantitative research. Constructivism and poststructuralism are "interpretivist" worldviews influencing most qualitative research. Pragmatism infuses mixed designs and action research. While some researchers label themselves by their worldviews as positivists, constructivists, poststructuralists, or pragmatists, others want to go beyond labels.

Quote 7.1   Beyond labels

I no longer want to be labeled as a positivist researcher or an interpretivist researcher. It is time for us to move beyond labels and see the underlying unity in what we are trying to achieve via our research methods. The commonalities in my view are compelling and paramount. . . . The differences, on the other hand, are ancillary. We should understand them, but they should not divide us.

Ron Weber (2004, p. xii)

7.2   Overview of methods for research on self-regulated L2 learning strategies

This chapter presents the following methods for research on self-regulated L2 learning strategies: (a) experiments and quasi-experiments, (b) nonexperimental quantitative surveys, (c) phenomenological studies, (d) grounded theory studies, (e) case studies, (f) ethnographic studies,

Concept 7.1   Primary beliefs of various worldviews

Worldview	Beliefs
Positivism	Single, universal truth/reality exists outside of the mind of the researcher and can be *positively, i.e., with certainty*, identified through the "scientific method." This method involves: objectivity (claimed, at any rate), reductionism (reducing complex situations or people to a few measureable variables), quantification, deductive testing of hypotheses established in advance, and typically experiments/quasi-experiments. Positivism has been discredited; few now believe the scientific method can positively identify truth.
Postpositivism	Single, universal truth/reality exists outside of the mind of the researcher. Uses the "scientific method" (see above) but argues that the "scientific method" cannot demonstrate *with certainty* whether the reality has been identified, so postpositivism admits fallibility and emphasizes testing for statistical significance. Postpositivism is the foundation of almost all quantitative L2 research at the present time.
Constructivism	Instead of a single, universal truth/reality, multiple realities exist; people construct their own subjective realities to a great extent. Meaning is an active social construction. In constructivism, subjective realities are discovered through induction, i.e., letting meaning evolve from the data. Knowledge is complex and individual, so reductionism is dangerous; better to maintain the contradictions, ambiguities, and richness of the data. Significant focus on qualitative research.
Poststructuralism	Holds many of the beliefs of constructivism. In addition, the focus is on structural violence, inequity, power struggles, multiple identities and roles, and agency, all within specific sociocultural contexts. Goal of research is empowerment and social/cultural/educational transformation. All knowledge is political, founded on human interests in particular sociocultural-historical settings. Asserts that there is no such thing as a stable, free, coherent, autonomous, rationally aware person who is not influenced by the surrounding context. Poststructuralism often decentres and destabilizes assumptions about meaning. Significant focus on qualitative research.
Pragmatism	Pragmatism is open to multiple worldviews. Meaning of concepts is revealed in practical outcomes. No universal overarching truth/reality. Truth/reality relates to practical consequences. It is not necessary to pledge allegiance to a given way of doing research. Qualitative, quantitative, and mixed research designs are all helpful for various purposes.

Source: Poststructuralism was summarized from Peters and Burbules (2003).

(g) narrative studies, (h) mixed designs, and (i) action research. Concept 7.2 on pages 206–207 presents an overview of each of these methods.

Grotjahn (1987, p. 59ff) placed forms of research inquiry on a continuum, rather than considering them in isolation. The continuum is related to three aspects of research: research design type, data type, and analysis type. Figure 7.1 below adapts and clarifies Grotjahn's continuum.

Criteria ↓	**Form A** (pure form) Experimental/ quantitative/statistical	**Mixed forms**	**Form B** (a pure form) Exploratory/ qualitative/interpretive
Type of overall study	Experimental	Depends on study	Exploratory
Type of data	Quantitative	Depends on study	Qualitative
Type of analysis	Statistical	Depends on study	Interpretive

Continuum of research forms

Figure 7.1   Continuum of forms of research based on three criteria
Source: Adapted from Grotjahn (1987).

7.3   Quantitative research methods, models of quantitative L2 studies, and validity of quantitative studies

Here I discuss experimental and quasi-experimental studies and non-experimental quantitative studies, provide models of study designs, and discuss validity of studies.

7.3.1   Experimental and quasi-experimental studies

Experimental and quasi-experimental designs are postpositivist in worldview. In an experiment, the experimental or treatment group receives a treatment, while the control or comparison group does not, so experiments involve manipulation. The term *independent variable* refers to the treatment, such as L2 strategy instruction, hypothesized to influence the outcome. *Independent variable* can also refer to other variables, such as age, gender, amount of prior language study, or type of institution, also hypothesized to affect the outcome. *Dependent variables* are the measured phenomena, such as L2

Concept 7.2   Overview of various research methods

Column A Method as used in the L2 field	Column B Some major features (not complete list of steps)	Column C Type of data: Quantitative or qualitative/reductive or rich	Column D Main purpose (see key)
Experiment	Randomly assign individuals to treatment and control groups. Give treatment to treatment group. Test hypotheses with quantitative data and statistical analyses. Reveal degree of statistical significance.	Quantitative/reductive	Deductive explanatory
Quasi-experiment	Do same as for experiment, except no random assignment is possible.	Quantitative/reductive	Deductive exploratory
Nonexperimental Quantitative	Gather data using survey (questionnaire or interview). Test hypotheses and/or answer non-directed research questions.	Quantitative/reductive or rich	One or more of these: exploratory, descriptive/atheoretical, classificatory, or deductive explanatory
Phenomenology	Identify the "essence" of the phenomenon for the participant(s), with essence = what participants experienced and how they experienced it. "Bracket" researcher's own experiences. Use intuition, imagination, universal structures, data from participants. Note: In this method, finding the essence is not meant to oversimplify the person's experience.	Qualitative/rich	Essentialist, inductive explanatory
Grounded Theory	Gather data. Use various kinds of coding (open, axial, selective) over different iterations of "constant comparison" to arrive at interpretations.	Qualitative/rich	Inductive explanatory, classificatory

Case Study	Select the "case" (the person, event, or process) that is "bounded" by various criteria, such as time, importance, space, context) or cases. Gather various types of data. Analyse data differently depending on type. Create integrated conclusions.	Usually qualitative (but can also be quantitative)/rich	One or more of these: Exploratory, descriptive/ atheoretical, classificatory, inductive explanatory, evaluative
Ethnography	Study an intact cultural group in natural setting. Use extensive fieldwork as participant observer. Give positionality statement. Triangulate with different kinds of data. Analyse iteratively to identify emerging themes/interpretations/theories. Conduct member check and peer debriefing.	Qualitative/rich	Inductive explanatory, classificatory
Narrative	Ask inviting questions that encourage the participant to share subjective feelings, thoughts, experiences orally or in writing. Use empathy to understand from participant's view. "Re-story" the participant's story to make it even more meaningful. Avoid abstraction.	Qualitative/rich	Inductive explanatory, might also include evaluative
Mixed Method	Recognize that the questions cannot be answered by quantitative or qualitative methods alone; mixed methods are needed. Decide on concurrent or sequential design. Gather quantitative and qualitative data. Identify when and how both kinds of results will be integrated.	Both quantitative and qualitative Could be both reductive and rich (different data have different features)	Combination determined by researcher
Action Research	Identify major problem and stakeholders. Gather data on perspectives of all stakeholders. Perhaps do an intervention as part of the research. Link findings to major problem. Plan further action based on results.	Quantitative or qualitative or both Could be reductive or rich or both	Rapid-answer, evaluative. Could be exploratory. Could be explanatory.

KEY for Column D (main purpose): *Deductive explanatory* = test an *a priori* theory. *Inductive explanatory* = develop a theory based on the data. *Descriptive/atheoretical* = describe, create picture, but do not involve theory. *Classificatory* = create interpretive classifications (can be a step toward theory). *Exploratory* = present initial, preliminary information. *Essentialist* = find essence. *Evaluative* = make value judgments of good/bad. *Rapid-answer* = answer immediate problem. *Reductive* = complexity has been reduced to a small set of variables, each of which is tightly defined. *Rich* = complexity or richness of the data is maintained, not reduced to a small set of variables.

performance, expected to be influenced by the independent variables. *Intervening variables*, such as teacher effects or time of day, must be ruled out or controlled, or they must be mentioned as factors potentially affecting the results.

True (i.e., randomized) experiments evidence cause-and-effect relationships (causality), meaning that the independent variable has a significant effect on the dependent variable (Pedhazur and Schmelkin, 1991). Causality requires: (a) *association* – the independent variable and the dependent variable must be related, (b) *sequence* – if changes in the independent variable cause changes in the dependent variable, the independent variable must occur first, and (c) *non-spuriousness* – an observed relationship between the independent variable and the dependent variable must not be plausibly explainable by an extraneous or intervening variable (Johnson and Christensen, 2000).

Here is an example. L2 learners were randomly assigned to two groups, with the same number of males and females in each group. In additional randomization, the treatment was then randomly assigned to one of the two groups. The experimental (treatment) group received listening strategy instruction, while the control group did not. The same teacher taught both groups to reduce possible extraneous variation. Both groups were assessed at the beginning and the end of the experiment for listening strategy use, the dependent variable. The pre-test showed no difference in listening strategy use: members of both groups used very few listening strategies. At the end of the experiment, the treatment group reported using significantly more listening strategy use than the control group, and listening strategy instruction can be said to be the cause. This experimental design, the Pre-test-Post-test Experimental and Control Group Design, is shown as:

Experimental (Treatment) Group   R (Pre-test)   **Treatment**   (Post-test)
Control Group   R (Pre-test)   _____   (Post-test)

Key: R = randomization

Another experimental design is called the Post-test-Only Experimental and Control Group Design (see Creswell, 2008). Without a pre-test, it is not as strong as the first experimental design but still includes randomization. The Solomon Four-Group design combines the Pre-test–Post-test Experimental and Control Group Design and the Post-test-Only Experimental and Control Group Design.

However, random assignment is often impossible in education programmes. Without randomization, an intended experiment can be only a "quasi-experiment," which opens the door to alternative explanations. For instance, if the two groups are two intact classes taught by different teachers, any change in the frequency of listening strategy use by the experimental group might be explainable by an extraneous "teacher effect" variable: a very enthusiastic, engaging instructor teaching the strategy instruction group and an uninteresting teacher teaching the control group, or vice versa. Other extraneous variables might exist. Perhaps the most motivated students register for the 8 a.m. section of the course (the experimental group), while the less motivated students register for the 2 p.m. section (the control group), an example of an extraneous "selection effect" (see Creswell, 2008).

Chapter 5 explained measurement reliability and validity as qualities of a good measurement instrument. When judging the quality of an entire experiment or quasi-experiment, we are interested in internal and external validity, not just measurement validity. Concept 7.3 on pages 210–211 presents questions to ask about *internal validity*, i.e., the extent to which the observed out-come can be related to a given independent variable while ruling out or reducing intervening, extraneous, or confounding variables. Concept 7.4 on pages 212–213 offers questions to ask about *external validity*, or generalizability (see also Chaloub-Deville, Chapelle, and Duff, 2006).

"How to:" a model of a quasi-experimental study

Table 7.2 on page 214 presents a model of a well-constructed quasi-experiment. This study concerned English reading strategies of students at a Korean university and employed colour-coding of reading strategies (see Chapter 6) and creative tracking of the treatment group's changing strategy awareness (Figure 7.2).

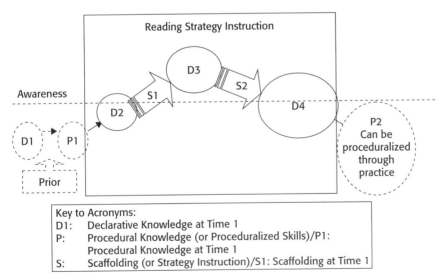

Figure 7.2   Students' changing pattern of strategy awareness during Lee's research
Source: Lee (2007, p. 108). Used with permission.

Concept 7.3 Questions to ask about the internal validity of an experiment or a quasi-experiment, with possible L2 learning strategy research examples

Main question: To what degree is the study free of extraneous variables that could cloud the interpretation of results? *Subsidiary question:* Are any potentially relevant variables not considered that should have been?

Column A Name of possible internal validity threat (Note: These threats can also be combined.)	Column B Questions to ask about this possible threat	Column C Possible examples in L2 learning strategy experiments or quasi-experiments
History threat	Did any unusual or unexpected events occur between the first and second measurements that could have affected the results?	A teacher's strike occurred in the middle of an experimental study on strategy instruction, and that influenced the study's results.
Maturation threat	Did any normal processes (e.g., growing older, more fatigued, more overloaded, or hungrier) occur for participants, unrelated to any specific study events but potentially influencing the results?	The control group classes were held at the end of the day, when the students were tired, but the treatment group classes were held at 10 a.m., when students were feeling fresh and alert.
Reactivity threat	Did the effect of taking the measurement instrument (e.g., questionnaire or interview) the first time affect the scores the second time?	Several students remembered their earlier strategy answers and used the same answer the second time.
Instrumentation threat	Was there any difference in how the instrument (e.g., questionnaire or interview) was calibrated or employed between the first or second times it was used? Were there changes in the observers or the rating scales?	The first time the strategy questionnaire was used during the study, the directions were not clear enough, but the directions were much clearer the second time. Results are therefore not comparable between time 1 and time 2.

Threat	Question	Example
Regression to the mean (a statistical fact) threat	Did the groups chosen for extremely high scores or extremely low scores tend to move toward the overall mean when they took the instrument again?	The highest-proficiency students in the strategy experiment tended to move toward the proficiency mean when retested.
Selection threat	Were groups selected in a way that would affect the scores? Were the treatment and control groups different from the outset?	The better teacher's classes were chosen to be the control group, while the less effective teacher's classes were chosen to be the treatment group.
Attrition (also called research mortality) threat	Did members of one of the groups drop out of the study more often than members of the other group?	For reasons unrelated to the strategy study, three control group members dropped out of the study, while none of the treatment group participants dropped out.
Researcher bias threat	Was the researcher unconsciously influenced by his or her beliefs or hypotheses so that he or she unintentionally biased the way the groups were treated?	The same researcher taught both the experimental (strategy instruction) and control groups but was far more enthusiastic when teaching the treatment group.
Design implementation threat	Did the treatment group and the control group realize they were being treated differently?	The control group realized that the treatment group was receiving strategy instruction, and the control group started sharing strategy ideas and competing against the treatment group.
Procedural threat	Are the statistical procedures misapplied?	The researcher used the wrong statistical procedure for nominal (categorical) data in one of the analyses.
Threat to comprehensiveness	Are any potentially important variables ignored or forgotten that might influence the results?	The researcher did not consider gender or socialization as a factor in the strategy results.

Source: R. Oxford's (2008) research methodology course notes, University of Maryland.

Concept 7.4 **Questions to ask about the external validity of an experiment or a quasi-experiment, with possible L2 learning strategy research examples**

Main question: To what degree are the results of the experiment (or quasi-experiment) generalizable to a larger population or to different environments, conditions, persons, and times?

Column A Name of possible external validity threat (Note: These threats can also be combined.)	Column B Questions to ask about this possible threat	Column C Possible examples in L2 learning strategy experiments or quasi-experiments
Population validity threat (threat to generalizability to larger population)	To what extent can the results be generalized to the larger population? (This relates to the question: Was the sampling done in a principled way or purely by convenience?)	The strategy experiment used convenience sampling only, so results are not generalizable to the larger population of L2 learners.
Ecological generalizability: treatment replicability threat	To what extent can the results be generalized if the treatment is unique to the initial setting and cannot be reproduced elsewhere?	The strategy experiment supported strategy instruction because the school head was very supportive and dropped by frequently, but a different result might be found for schools without such a school head.
Ecological generalizability: threat from multiple treatment interference	To what extent can the results be generalized if the treatment actually included several sub-treatments?	Results of a single part of the strategy instruction treatment, such as colour-coding instruction, might not be generalizable without the other parts.
Ecological generalizability: threat from novelty effect	To what extent can the results be generalized if the treatment was in fact novel (new, exciting, refreshing) in the original study but will not be novel in a later study?	The excitement of learning new L2 strategies might not generalize to other places where strategies are already discussed a lot.

Ecological generalizability: threat from Hawthorne effect (effect of being observed)	To what extent can the results be generalized if the study participants changed their behaviour simply because of being observed?	In the experiment, the control group (not receiving strategy instruction) changed its behaviour and paid more attention to learning because of being observed. This would limit generalization of the results.
Ecological generalizability: threat from interaction between treatment and group characteristics (called "treatment × group interaction")	To what extent can the results be generalized if differential treatment results occurred based on group characteristics?	Results of an L2 learning strategy experiment might not generalize across different cultural groups.
Time durability/time effect threat	To what extent are the results durable across time for the same group? To what extent are the results generalizable to the future for the same group?	More talented L2 learners often learn strategies very quickly, make them automatic (habits), and no longer use them consciously 6 weeks later. Other learners might still use them consciously.
Pretest or posttest sensitization threat	To what extent can the results be generalized if a pretest only or a posttest only is used?	Study results might differ if a proficiency pretest were not used and if students were not sensitized implicitly to a connection between strategies and proficiency.
Dependent measure threat	To what extent can the results be repeated if a different measure of the dependent variable is used?	If the dependent variable in a strategy instruction experiment (or other strategy study) is frequency of strategy use, the results might be different if a different strategy questionnaire were used.

Source: Typology in Columns A and B is adapted by R. Oxford from Martella, Nelson, and Marchand-Martella (1999). Column C (strategy applications) is original.

Table 7.2 "How to:" a model of a quasi-experimental study

Lee (2007) conducted a quasi-experiment of Korean university students' reading strategies.

Problem: Many Korean university students do not comprehend English reading materials as well as they might, so it is important to find out whether reading strategy instruction might help.

Procedures:
- A quasi-experiment was designed. The treatment group (receiving strategy instruction) and the control group (not receiving such instruction) were each an intact English reading class at a well known Korean university. A strategy pretest showed that both groups had low usage of strategies for English reading comprehension. The hypothesis was that the treatment group would have a significantly higher posttest reading comprehension mean than the control group.
- Extraneous variables that could threaten internal validity were controlled to the extent possible, given that random assignment of each student to the treatment group and the control group was impossible. The two groups were identified at the outset as being very similar to each other in all ways salient to the study (e.g., age, university, initial English reading comprehension, and general lack of strategy knowledge). The same teacher taught the treatment group and the control group. All students used the same interesting reading materials throughout the semester.
- Selected reading strategies were taught to the treatment group in a carefully sequenced programme. The researcher documented all strategy instruction, student responses, and classroom events. Treatment group students also documented their ongoing strategy use in multiple ways.
- In addition to learning reading strategies, treatment group students were taught how to colour-code places in the text at which they used certain reading strategies.
- Lee diagrammed the dynamic trajectory of reading strategy awareness for the treatment group (see Figure 7.2 earlier).

Results:
- Despite the initial similarity in English reading comprehension at the pretest, the treatment group significantly outperformed the control group in English reading comprehension at the posttest.
- Most of the growth in the treatment group's strategy use took place after the midterm, when this group had grown accustomed to reading strategies and had started, in their view, experiencing the value of these strategies.
- The sequential, organized strategy instruction procedures appeared to be quite successful.
- Colour-coding was not quantified for a statistical correlation with reading comprehension, although it seemed that students who took fullest advantage of colour-coding performed better in reading comprehension.

Conclusions:
- It took awhile for the participants to discover the utility of reading strategies for themselves, but once they did, they were very engaged in using these strategies. Their reading comprehension improved significantly in comparison to that of the control group.
- This study supported the contention, often found in the L2 strategy literature, that strategy instruction should be conducted over a long period of time and interwoven into classroom L2 teaching.
- Colour-coding of strategies proved to be an active, engaging way for students to raise strategy awareness and learn to assess strategy use.

Note: See Figure 7.2 on page 209
Source: Based on Lee (2007)

A paradox exists: Objectivity is one of the key claims of experiments and quasi-experiments, but these studies are not totally objective. Even experiments and quasi-experiments, like all other research, are influenced by social conditions, ideologies, and in-group language (Josselson, 1995). This implies that we must always look for a study's interpretive lens and not automatically believe everything the experimenter says. Experimenters must recognize their research design and interpretations are influenced by sociocultural factors.

Quote 7.2 **Surprising non-objectivity of experiments**

Data, after all, do not speak for themselves. They presuppose certain ways of asking questions and certain ways of interpreting results. The results of our experiments are never self-evident in their import. They are merely the occasion for us to try to weave a narrative in which obtaining a certain set of "significant'" results makes sense.... And "sense" is a product of interpretation ... [and] ideology...

Ruth Josselson (1995, p. 29)

7.3.2   Nonexperimental quantitative studies

Nonexperimental quantitative studies lack manipulation by the researcher. They are not randomized, so cause and effect are difficult to identify. Many survey studies are of this type. Johnson (2001) created a useful system to classify nonexperimental quantitative studies based on two factors: the *research objective* (descriptive, predictive, and explanatory) and the *time dimension* (retrospective, cross-sectional, and longitudinal), thus creating nine categories. Concept 7.5 on page 216 offers key questions to ask about the validity of nonexperimental quantitative studies.

"How to:" a model of a nonexperimental quantitative study

Table 7.3 on page 217 contains a model of a nonexperimental quantitative study, in which the researcher used a well-designed questionnaire to assess the English-listening strategies of Singaporean children.

We now turn to qualitative studies, which some researchers use to investigate L2 learning strategies.

Concept 7.5   **Questions to ask about the validity of quantitative studies that are neither experimental nor quasi-experimental**

Type of possible threat	Questions to ask
Instrumentation threat	Was there any difference in how any instrument was calibrated or employed at any time, particularly at different times in a longitudinal study, that might affect the results?
Maturation and/or history threat	Did any normal processes (e.g., growing older, more overloaded) occur for participants and/or did any major events occur, potentially influencing the results of retrospective or longitudinal studies?
Threat to comprehensiveness	Are any potentially important variables ignored or forgotten that might influence the results?
Procedural threat	Are the descriptive statistical procedures, multiple regression procedures, SEM procedures, or any other statistical procedures misapplied?
Regression to the mean threat	Was there any regression to the mean across time in the study?
Attrition/mortality threat	Was there any dropout during the study, and if so, what did it mean?
Explanatory reactivity threat	In the study, did taking the instrument the first time affect scores at any other time?
Selection threat	Were any groups selected in a way that would affect the scores?
Researcher bias threat	Did the researcher have any bias that might have affected the way he or she conducted the study or analysed the results?
Population validity threat (threat to generalizability to larger population)	To what extent can the results be generalized to the larger population or a different group?
Time durability/time effect threat	To what extent are the results durable across time for the same group? To what extent are the results generalizable to the future for the same group?
Dependent measure effect threat	To what extent can the results be repeated if a different measure of the dependent variable is used?

Table 7.3   "How to:" a model of a nonexperimental quantitative study

Gu (2008) explored the English language listening strategies of Singaporean children in upper elementary school grades.

Problem: Listening is a very important L2 skill area, but little information exists about children's L2 listening strategies. The researcher wanted to discover the frequency and patterns of use of listening strategies among Singaporean upper elementary school children.

Procedures:
- The researcher created and validated (with input from experts and from Singaporean children themselves) a listening strategy questionnaire and then pilot tested it with 300 Singaporean learners of English in upper elementary grades.
- He asked questions about whether English listening strategies would differ across grade levels among upper elementary English learners, whether listening strategies would be related to the grades teachers give students for their English performance, and whether certain types of strategies would be used significantly more often than other types of strategies.
- He then administered the questionnaire to 3,216 upper elementary learners of English in Singapore.

Results:
- The most frequently reported strategies were in the areas of metacognition (e.g., monitoring and evaluating) and processing. These were in the medium-use range.
- All strategies were significantly related to English language grades but not at high levels.
- Strategy use patterns significantly differed across grade levels. Significantly fewer socioaffective and processing strategies and more inferencing strategies were used by the higher-grade students in the sample.

Conclusions:
- It was possible to create and validate a pedagogically relevant L2 listening strategies instrument.
- It appears that listening is probably not emphasized very much in Singaporean schools, given the results of this study.
- Listening deserves far more emphasis if students are to develop communicative competence in English.

Source: Based on Gu (2008)

7.4 Qualitative research methods, models of qualitative L2 studies, and validity of qualitative studies

Qualitative research methods can richly depict individuals and groups in authentic sociocultural environments. This part presents qualitative research methods, including phenomenology, grounded theory, case study (which can also include quantitative data), ethnography, and narrative. Although these are presented here as somewhat distinct types, in practice they overlap significantly. I also discuss criteria for judging the validity of qualitative research studies.

7.4.1 Phenomenology

Phenomenology is focused on how people perceive their own experiences. Phenomenological research uses intuition, imagination, and universal structures to identify the "essence" (essential, invariant structure of lived experience across all study participants) concerning a phenomenon, such as L2 learning strategy use, multiple identities, or L2 anxiety. Phenomenology involves studying a few participants, usually through interviews, across an extended period to develop "clusters of meaning." Processes include: (a) *epoché* (also transcribed as *epochè* or *epokhé*), i.e., setting aside prejudgments; (b) phenomenological reduction, which includes bracketing the topic or question, giving each statement equal value (horizontalization), and focusing on invariant qualities of the experience for the individual and the group (textural description); (c) imaginative variation, i.e., varying the possible perspectives on the phenomenon with polarities and reversals, as well as considering universal structures (e.g., time, space, relationship to self or others, cause, or intention) as themes; and (d) synthesis of textural and structural descriptions (Moustakas, 1994; Woodruff Smith, 2007).

"How to:" a model of a phenomenological study

Table 7.4 presents a model of a phenomenological study, which concerns studying abroad. Note how the sociocultural context seemed to interact with attitudes.

7.4.2 Grounded theory

The grounded theory, a "micro-sociological" approach, creates a broad theory or explanation of a process, situation, experience, or interaction. Theoretical sampling is used to obtain varied types of data for different

Table 7.4 "How to:" a model of a phenomenological study

Levine (2008) studied the phenomenology of European Erasmus Programme students' study abroad trips to Germany.

Problem: Many students go on study abroad programmes, but it is often difficult to know what they gain from these programmes and how they relate to others while studying abroad (what strategies they use in these settings).

Procedures:

- The researcher interviewed students in depth, gathered their learning diaries, and gave them individual audio equipment to record everyday interactions with German native speakers, housemates, classmates, and others.
- The researcher analysed the data by carefully examining "intercultural moments."
- He used discourse analysis of data sources in the way portrayed by Gee (2005).

Results:

- Levine discovered how students' multiple identities were enacted in sociocultural settings.
- He found that students placed themselves differently (e.g., in the centre, in the periphery as legitimate peripheral participants, or as "illegitimate participants," expanding on Lave and Wenger, 1991) in various situations.
- In some interactions, a student was able strategically to parlay her minimal German skills so that she seemed to be at the centre of the community of practice. She felt strong and positive.
- A different student, caught up in negative self-judgment, felt other students were making things hard for her because she was late, and soon felt she had the status of an illegitimate participant. She had few strategies to help her in this difficult sociocultural situation.
- It was not just the sociocultural setting, but the learners' attitudes and behaviours, that caused them to experience themselves in particular relationships *vis-à-vis* the learning community.

Source: Based on Levine (2008)

purposes at different stages of the study. The researcher makes multiple site visits to gather data and writes memos (*memoing*) to create ongoing records.

The first analytic phase is *open coding*, which occurs over several iterations of examining the same qualitative data. *Constant comparison*, the analytic tool for open coding, involves constantly comparing the data with the emerging categories (themes) and expanding or altering the categories as needed. Contradictions in the data are seen as useful. Open-coding categories in a hypothetical L2 learning strategy study might be: a learning problem that makes Manuel want to use L2 learning strategies, (b) the specific strategies he uses, (c) his L2 class performance, (d) his learning strategies in other subjects, (e) his general self-perception as a learner, (f) his attitude toward the teacher, and so on. These categories emerge from examining the data repeatedly, are not pre-established, and do not highlight causality.

The second analytic phase is *axial coding*, which employs a pre-established coding paradigm and focuses on causality. Let's say that the main concern is the strategies Manuel uses and their effects. This phase includes (a) causal conditions (influencers, such as Manuel's upcoming test, strategy instruction by the teacher, and informal encouragement to use certain L2 learning strategies); (b) Manuel's strategies; (c) his contexts, including classroom and home; (d) intervening conditions (e.g., time conflicts caused by his part-time job and girlfriend); and (e) consequences (his pattern of strategy use in relation to time and context and the outcome in terms of L2 performance).

The third analytical phase is *selective coding*. It involves relating Manuel's pattern of L2 learning strategy use, to other categories, such as his overall self-perception as a learner. If there is a need to fill in the categories and verify the story line or model, the researcher can keep gathering new data at the same site or at other sites, from the same or additional people, and from additional sources, such as documents (Creswell, 1998; Strauss and Corbin, 2007).

"How to:" a model of a grounded theory study

Table 7.5 offers a model of a grounded theory study of L2 writing strategies. This is a study that needs to be done. Few, if any, L2 learning strategy studies have involved the pure grounded theory methodology, with its theoretical sampling, three types of coding, and repeated data gathering. Many studies use a form of open coding, but that is just one part of grounded theory.

7.4.3   Case study

In a case study, the researcher explores in depth a system or case (i.e., an event, activity, process, person, or several people) "bounded" by relevant criteria, such as time, importance, space, context, group characteristics, role, or function (Miles and Huberman, 1994). The focus can be the case itself (*intrinsic case study*), such as Mme. P's multiple roles as French teacher, department chair, and strategy instructor in an inner-city school. Alternatively, the focus can be an issue illustrated by the case, such as the ways that a school district failed to provide needed resources for developing strategies in Chinese classes (*instrumental case study*) (see Stake, 1995).

A case study can explore a single case (e.g., Nam and Oxford, 1998) or multiple cases (e.g., Oxford *et al.*, 2007). The researcher might study the year-long process of a Luis, who learns to use L2 learning strategies. A different case study might center on a critical incident, such as when a learner, Mona, discovered a very helpful learning strategy website from a Hong Kong university, applied the suggestions, and thus improved her

Table 7.5   "How to:" a model of a grounded theory study

Few if any L2 learning strategy studies employ this highly structured system with its three sequences of coding. However, consider this potential study:

Problem: We need to find out how immigrant children in the primary schools of Frankfurt, Germany use L2 writing strategies to develop their writing in German. Without this information, teachers cannot optimally teach these students to write in German.

Procedure:

- A group of Frankfurt's immigrant primary-school children in three diverse schools is repeatedly visited and interviewed about their writing strategies in German. Their parents are also interviewed in the necessary home languages if the parents do not fully understand or speak German.

- In addition to conducting interviews, the researcher collects documents, such as school German language schoolwork papers, that show how the children in the sample use L2 writing strategies while developing their competence in writing German.

- The *open coding phase* results in emergent categories, such as learners' writing proficiency, writing strategies, motivation, and beliefs; and family attitudes, educational background, linguistic background, and socioeconomic status.

- *Axial coding* results in a logic diagram (theoretical model) highlighting causes of writing strategy use, strategies employed, sociocultural context and intervening conditions (e.g., L1 writing system, number of years in Germany, parental education), and consequences of writing strategy use.

- Further steps of *selective coding* and *gathering new data* in the same sites and other sites are accomplished to produce an expanded "story" of the categories and their interrelationships. This serves to test and refine the model, i.e., the grounded theory that is produced in the study.

- Results bring together the findings of all three coding steps.

Note: This study needs to be conducted. Above is a streamlined outline of the procedures to use.
Source: Based on suggestions by Karen Schramm.

strategy use and L2 performance. Varied data, including qualitative and quantitative, can be included (Yin, 2003), though L2-learning case studies are often qualitative. Yin (2003) called for using as many as six types of data in a case study to "triangulate" information and help develop themes. A qualitative case study often starts with a narrative description, presents a thematic analysis, and closes with assertions about what has been learned in personal or theoretical terms (Stake, 1995).

"How to:" a model of a multiple case study

Table 7.6 is a model of a multiple case study about learner crises and about strategies learners used in those crises. This study indicates how important strategies are for handling serious learning difficulties.

Table 7.6   "How to:" a model of a multiple case study

I conducted this study with my student colleagues (Oxford, Meng, Zhou, Sung, and Jain, 2007).

Problem: L2 learning crises cause some learners to give up and other learners to try harder. The problem was to figure out which factors, including learning strategies, contribute to an individual's transcending an L2 learning crisis in a specific sociocultural situation. This was made more difficult because there has been little or no research directly on the topic of L2 learner crises and resiliency.

Procedures:
- I already had a data bank of several hundred learner history cases, many of which revealed learner crises.
- Some of the co-authors added their own learner history cases to the data bank.
- Together we selected the cases to be included in the study based on the following criteria: (a) importance, (b) representativeness, and (c) interest factor.
- We examined (both via our notes and visuospatially by making graphs and drawings) the "crisis trajectories" of about a dozen cases. We identified stages in the crises, as well as looking at themes, such as learning strategies, beliefs, and sociocultural contexts.
- We continued analyses of these cases over numerous iterations, allowing new themes to emerge and making connections across themes.

Results:
- Variables reflected in one student's lack of ability to handle an L2 learning crisis were lack of "investment" (Norton Pierce, 1995), absence of autonomy, and an ongoing sense of social isolation.
- Other learner crises showed different features.
- Some students were able to transcend L2 learning crises when they consciously used strategies to increase their self-regulation, develop stronger relationships with others, build on their intrinsic motivation, practise the language despite difficulties, lower their anxiety, and make their attitudes as positive as possible. A student who did not transcend the crisis situation did not employ useful strategies and was not highly motivated in the first place.

Conclusions:
- The degree of severity of an L2 learning crisis did not determine the outcome.
- Students often overcame L2 learning crises if they employed a combination of cognitive, affective, and social behaviours and attitudes associated with self-determination (Ryan and Deci, 2000) or self-regulation.
- L2 learning crises offer a fruitful, new area of research. "Such crises, though painful, … [are] testing grounds on which learners can develop or recognize their autonomy, motivation, competence, and sociability" (Oxford *et al.*, 2007, p. 142).

Note: The published version emphasizes the findings more than the procedures.
Source: Based on Oxford, Meng, Zhou, Sung, and Jain (2007).

7.4.4   Ethnography

Ethnography, the study of an intact cultural group in its own setting, is an important L2 research methodology. In an ethnographic study, the *participant researcher* studies an intact cultural group in a natural setting for a long period using extensive fieldwork. The researcher gathers multiple forms of data, such as observations, documents, interviews, pictures, and music, to create a holistic, complex view of the culture-sharing group (Creswell, 1998). The design often evolves during the study. Considering structures (social configurations) and functions (social relations regulating behaviour), ethnographers provide "thick" descriptions of the setting and what happens there. Through multiple rounds of interpretation, ethnographers identify overall patterns, theories, and generalizations (Creswell and Plano Clark, 2006). A common ethnographic data analysis tool is constant comparison, described earlier. Ethnographic research is inductive, with qualitative interpretations – theory – largely arising from the data.

To ensure trustworthiness of the intepretation, the researcher can ask a colleague to interpret some or all of the data separately (peer analysis). Alternatively, an external auditor, who is not a colleague, can check the methodology, results, and interpretations (Creswell, 2008). The researcher can and should ask participants whether interpretations are correct (member check). Ethnography makes no attempt to find simple, linear causality, because situations are very complex. Many ethnographers would agree with the following statement.

Quote 7.3   An argument against linear causality in L2 learning

[L]inear causality can never be more than a minor, relatively uninteresting part of the complex of processes, patterns and structures [in L2 learning].
Leo van Lier (2004, p. 199).

Ethnographers freely admit their own subjectivity. They typically give "positionality statements" describing their particular background, assumptions, and possible biases that might affect interpretations.

"How to:" a model of an ethnographic study

Table 7.7 presents a model of an ethnographic study. This study, mentioned earlier in this book, explores Sri Lankan students' reactions to alien, culturally inappropriate materials and methods used in an English course.

Table 7.7   "How to:" a model of an ethnographic study

In an ethnographic study, Canagarajah (1993) explored students' reactions to the culturally inappropriate materials and methods used in an English course in a school in Sri Lanka.

Problem: Students in the Sri Lankan school were opposed to Western materials and methods used in the English course. The researcher wanted to understand at a deep level the sociocultural dynamics of the situation.

Procedures:

- The researcher noted the students' in-class reactions to the Western materials and teaching methods.
- He carefully examined the graffiti that students wrote and drew in the margins of their English language textbooks.
- He analysed the data based on critical theories about power and opposition in sociocultural settings and in so doing expanded our understanding of "opposition," which is different from outright "resistance."

Results:

- Although the class was taught by the researcher, a Sri Lankan himself, the students felt their own educational culture and values were being threatened by L2 teaching methodologies and cultural values that conflicted with their own. The English textbook presented pictures and stories of materialistic families in a capitalistic society very unlike the society of the Sri Lankan students. Students drew pictures, wrote graffiti, and wrote Sri Lankan song lyrics throughout their English textbook, making sport of the cultural values in textbook's stories.
- Students' classroom behaviour showed opposition to foreign-style cooperative learning and communicative activities.

Note: It seemed to R. Oxford that the learners employed the strategy of Paying Attention in specific ways that were strongly related to their purposes. They paid attention to exactly what they wanted (grammar, because they needed to pass a standardized English test that involved grammar) and turned attention away from anything they did not like (e.g., the materialistic themes in the textbook, the communicative activities.) In their own way, they were very self-directed.

Conclusions:

- The classroom dynamics appeared to reveal a clash of cultural values and an underlying power issue (external culture being imposed over local culture). Students quietly but effectively opposed the foreign materials and methods in their English class. The researcher noted that this was not full-scale resistance but rather opposition.

Note: It would have been very interesting to have gathered participants' reactions to the researcher's interpretation (through a simple member check or some other way). Intensive interviews of some of the students might have also provided additional, relevant data.
Source: Based on Canagarajah (1993).

7.4.5   Narrative research

Narrative (story) is a very broad term. It can refer to an entire type of research on its own. However, depending on one's definition, narratives are sometimes involved in other types of research, such as case study or phenomenology. Narratives are also viewed as a category of data collection techniques useful for assessment of self-regulated L2 learning strategies, but they are more than just this. Narratives can be based on interviews, essays by participants, open-ended discussions, focus groups, or other data collection tools. In any narrative study, it is crucial to open the relationship with the participant by asking inviting questions that encourage participants to share their deepest feelings, thoughts, and experiences (Josselson, 1995). Narrative has two forms of context: pragmatic and mental (see Concept 7.6). Certain types of narratives are especially suited for research on L2 learning strategies, as indicated in Concept 7.7. Examples of narratives in the L2 learning field are given by Nunan and Benson (2005) and Bailey and Nunan (1996).

Distilling the meaning of narratives – "re-narratarizing" or "re-storying" a narrative – requires both art (e.g., intuition, empathy, and imagination) and science (e.g., analysis and reasoning). I have used a range of analytic and interpretive techniques in narrative studies (see Oxford, 1996c; Oxford,

---

Concept 7.6   Two forms of context in narrative studies

- *Pragmatic context* consists of the objectively observed characteristics of the situation and includes factors such as class size, resources, type and level of training of the teachers, decision-making roles, presence of a major examination (and for such an examination, the language on which it rests, the approach to learning and study habits it generates). Such factors powerfully influence students and teachers.

- *Mental context* arises out of:
  - ○ participants' attitudes and beliefs (regarding the L2, the potential relevance of the L2, the community/culture of the L2, the educational setting, L2 learning in general)
  - ○ participants' learning strategies and/or teaching strategies, general approaches [styles], goals, and aspirations
  - ○ the beliefs, values, and educational traditions and practices in the home society.

The interactions between these two contexts are very important. They influence what L2 learning and teaching mean to participants and therefore strongly influence classroom dynamics.

Source: Summarized from Tudor (2002).

Concept 7.7 **Types of narratives useful for uncovering strategies**

- Learner's diaries (journals), dialogue journals, or portfolios – offering openness and support on an ongoing basis; very good for uncovering strategies
- L2 learning histories – usually span an extended period and sometimes include several languages learned; typically reveal cultural issues, beliefs, identity, strategies, motivations, attitudes, and other issues, as well as showing the ups and downs of L2 learning over time; may deal with border-crossings; subject to some forgetting
- Book-length autobiographies – generally include strategies but much more focused on larger-scale issues within the lifespan; often deal with border-crossings; subject to forgetting, but moment-by-moment accuracy is not the purpose

Massey, and Anand, 2005; Oxford *et al.*, 2007). The technique of empathy demands giving up prejudgments and becoming mentally close to the participant (Josselson, 1995). This can produce deeply felt, powerful impressions and understandings. Constant comparison (open coding) is also important for finding rich thematic categories associated with events, quotations, and other details. It helps to set boundaries in a narrative case study, such as roles of the learner and strategic awareness. Another fruitful practice is to ask questions about the narrative, such as: *What is the context? What is the most fundamental need? What is the goal or object at a given time? Who is the key person? Who else is involved? What relationships are involved? What strategies does the subject use? What are the conditions (situation, difficulty, etc.)? How are the strategies modified by the conditions? What is the result of the strategies? What images or metaphors are used to express any part of this process?* It is sometimes valuable to use literary plot analysis by finding the protagonist, the rising action, the climax, and the falling action, although not all narratives have this type of pattern. I have used graphs of "trajectories" of actions that are hidden in the narrative. It is sometimes interesting to consider the story as a piece of music, hitting different types of notes, exhibiting certain rhythms, having a certain melody, revealing harmony, showing discord, and so on.

"How to:" a model of a narrative study

Table 7.8 presents a model of a narrative study. In this particular study, the researcher discovered the opposite of what he expected.

Table 7.8 "How to:" a model of a narrative study

At the start, Schmelter (2004, 2006) believed that in-person tandem learning (German–English and German–French) would contribute to autonomy, personal empowerment (emancipation), and growth for university students.

Problem: The researcher wanted to understand the dynamics of in-person tandem learning and how this type of learning might be related to autonomy, empowerment, and growth.

Procedures:
- The researcher conducted extensive, one-to-one interviews with the university students about their in-person tandem learning to explore the notions of autonomy, self-regulation, and empowerment. This was not life-history narrative research; instead, it focused on a specific segment of the learners' lives: their involvement with this particular learning mode.
- In relation to Holzkamp's approach of *subjective theories*, the researcher reconstructed the students' descriptions of their learning behaviour. He used multiple iterations of analysis and interpretation to discern the students' own experiences.
- He "re-storied" the narratives to provide a deeper and more realistic narrative.

Results:
- Although the researcher expected to find a rich flow of autonomous learning experiences during tandem L2 learning, and perhaps learning strategies reflecting autonomy, he was surprised to discover that the students' learning behaviour reflected only narrow, defensive, non-self-regulated, and non-autonomous work, in which little learning or student responsibility emerged.
- Specifically, the students were using their tandem partners to help them do homework and pass university language classes, but not to learn, grow, or become autonomous.

Conclusions:
- The use of innovative, in-person tandem learning did not result in autonomy, because the students used the tandem learning partnership for purposes other than those for which it was designed. The narrative methodology overturned the researcher's initial assumptions and showed a stark reality.

Source: Based on Schmelter (2004, 2006).

7.4.6 Validity of qualitative studies

In discussing the rigour or quality of a qualitative research study, some researchers apply the term *validity*, while others prefer to employ "trustworthiness" or "credibility." Concept 7.8 on pages 228–229 summarizes the approaches to judging qualitative research.

I now turn to mixed methods, which intentionally link quantitative and qualitative elements.

Concept 7.8 Questions to ask about the validity of qualitative research, with specific applications to a possible ethnographic L2 learning strategy research study

Type of validity	Relevant question	Applications to an ethnographic L2 learning strategy research study (an examination of learning strategy use, attitudes, and beliefs among university-age Japanese learners of English in a test-driven environment)
Descriptive validity (Maxwell, 1992)	Are the reported *facts accurate*?	• Are the methodology and results reported accurately? • Is there a *member check* in which the study participants are asked to verify the accuracy of the setting description, methodology, results, and conclusions? • Is there a *peer debriefing* in which a colleague can challenge, question, or verify any and all aspects of the study?
Credibility (Guba and Lincoln, 1981)	Are all the *complexities and ambiguities* taken into account?	• In this study, does the researcher stay on-site for a long enough period (*researcher participation*) to ask about strategies being used and the often complex attitudes and beliefs related to them? • In the *peer debriefing*, does the colleague/peer point out any areas of complexity or ambiguity? • Is there a *member check* to discern and discuss any complexities or ambiguity in the data? • Is there *triangulation* (use of different data gathering modes) and cross-checking of data to identify and possibly explain any ambiguities? *Example:* Use of strategy interviews with students, comments by teachers, and examination of documents, artifacts, other raw data (e.g., looking at students', in-class essays to infer possible strategy use). • Is there *referential adequacy* (testing of strategy interpretations against documents and other raw data)? • Is there a serious check for *structural coherence or incoherence* (i.e., internal alignment vs. internal conflicts in results of a given data gathering mode)?

Interpretive validity (Maxwell, 1992)	Are the *participants' viewpoints and experiences* accurately interpreted?	• Do we believe we hear the voices and perceptions of the Japanese participants clearly and accurately? • Is there a *member check* in which the study participants verify the accuracy of what is said by them and about them?
Interpretive validity (Schramm, 2008)		• Are problem cases (e.g., the students in the Japanese study whose data seem anomalous) discussed satisfactorily? • Are all alternative interpretations considered? Are these handled well? • Were new insights gained about self-regulated L2 learning strategies from this study?
Theoretical validity (Maxwell, 1992)	Is the researcher's *theory or explanation* relevant to the data?	• If the Japanese ethnographic study offers two theories (about anxiety and threats to learners' sense of competence/identity) to help explain the strategy results, are these theories well suited to the data? Does the theory encompass all the data? • Are there other theories that might explain the data better?
Evaluative validity (Maxwell, 1992), confirmability (Guba and Lincoln, 1981), or objectivity	Does the researcher present the data objectively? [Note: It is impossible to be fully objective, no matter what researchers claim.]	• Does the researcher put aside his or her subjective views and experiences to the extent possible? OR Does the researcher indicate which of his or her statements are more subjective or speculative? • Is the researcher reflexive, i.e., does he or she use a *research journal* to record any assumptions or biases? • Does the researcher make a *positionality statement* that indicates his or her background, assumptions, and biases? • Does the study include *triangulation*, in which multiple data collection types are used for the same phenomenon?
Dependability (Guba and Lincoln, 1981)	Are the results *stable*?	• Does the study use *triangulation*? • Is there an adequate *audit trail* to support the dependability/stability of the data?

Concept 7.8 Questions to ask about the validity of qualitative research, with specific applications to a possible ethnographic L2 learning strategy research study (continued)

Type of validity	Relevant question	Applications to an ethnographic L2 learning strategy research study (an examination of learning strategy use, attitudes, and beliefs among university-age Japanese learners of English in a test-driven environment)
Generalizability or transferability (Guba and Lincoln, 1981; Maxwell, 1992)	Are the results *generalizable* within the studied community? Are the results *generalizable* to other settings?	• In the *member check*, are the study participants asked (a) whether the findings apply to everyone in the study and (b) whether the findings apply to others who were *not* in the study but are studying English at the same level in the same university? • Is there an excellent record (*audit trail*) about each step of planning, data collection, data analysis, and interpretation in this ethnographic study? • Does the strategy researcher keep a *research journal* of perceptions and ideas occurring at different times in the study? • If someone wants to generalize the results to another setting, is that setting very similar in the most salient ways to the setting described in the study?
Validity of use (Schramm, 2008)	Do the results shed further light? Are the data available?	• Without necessarily being generalizable, do the results shed light on any other data from other studies? • Is the researcher willing to allow the data to be inspected, reanalysed, and reinterpreted by another researcher? Are the data supplied in an appendix or a CD?

7.5   Mixed methods, a model of a mixed method L2 study, and validity of mixed method studies

Mixed designs are increasingly important in L2 learning strategy research. These are not opposing poles in a dichotomy but are complementary approaches (Mackey and Gass, 2005). Mixed methods are inspired by the pragmatic worldview of Dewey (1909/2008), Cherryholmes (1999), and Rorty (1990). Pragmatism is flexible, uncommitted to one particular view of reality, because meaning is revealed in practical outcomes and consequences. There is no universal, overarching reality waiting to be discovered (Rorty, 1990). With practicality and common sense as watchwords, researchers have freedom to choose and mix a variety of qualitative and quantitative methods to fulfill particular research purposes and gain a greater under-standing of the phenomenon being studied (Tashakkori and Teddlie, 2003). Concurrent and sequential mixed designs are possible, with different varieties of each (see Creswell and Plano Clark, 2006, and Concept 7.9 on the next page). The *Journal of Mixed Methods Research* has begun publication (*http://mmr.sagepub.com*).

Quote 7.4   About research categories

Most research does not fit clearly into one category – qualitative or quan-titative – or the other. The best often combines features of each. . . . Neither quantitative nor qualitative research is superior to the other; . . . we do not regard quantitative research to be any more scientific than qualitative research.

Gary King, Robert Keohane, and Sidney Verba (1994, pp. 5, 7)

Validity of mixed designs draws upon validity principles from quantita-tive and qualitative research, but it also involves the appropriateness by which the mixed methods study is designed and implemented to answer the particular research questions of interest. For details, see Creswell and Plano Clark (2006) and Tashakkori and Teddlie (2003). Pragmatism rules mixed methods research. It is also a key to action research, the next theme in this chapter.

"How to:" a model of a sequential mixed methods study

Table 7.9 on page 233 is an example of a study employing a sequential mixed methods design. Notice the strong use of triangulation, with three measures of L2 learning strategies used in this study: a quantitative questionnaire in Phase I and a think-aloud protocol and an open interview in Phase II.

Concept 7.9　**Summary of mixed designs**

Type of mixed design	Comments
Concurrent	*Concurrent mixed designs* consist of gathering qualitative and quantitative data at the same time, with an explicit theory being considered. Concurrent mixed designs, as displayed by Creswell (2008), can be of a "triangulation" variety, in which quantitative and qualitative data are collected at the same time but analysed separately and then results are compared; or of a "nested" variety, in which qualitative and quantitative data are analysed together.
Sequential	In the *sequential mixed design* there are (at least) two phases, with qualitative data collection and analysis coming first, followed by quantitative data collection and analysis – or vice versa, with quantitative preceding qualitative. The sequencing depends on the priorities of the study. Interpretive integration of both types of results, qualitative and quantitative, occurs toward the end of the study.
Transformative	For both concurrent and sequential mixed designs, a "transformative" option also exists. In a transformative mixed design, a social advocacy vision or framework is stated from the start and helps to drive the study design.

Source: Adapted from Creswell (2008).

Table 7.9   "How to:" a model of a sequential mixed methods study

Lan's (2008) study involved 1,991 Taiwanese sixth-grade learners of English as a foreign language.

Problem: Lan was very concerned about whether Taiwanese students were employing learning strategies that might help them become communicatively involved in learning English, and she wanted to know which factors related to the use of English-learning strategies by Taiwanese sixth-grade students.

Phase I (quantitative):

Phase I procedures
- The *Taiwanese Children's Strategy Inventory for Language Learners* (strategy questionnaire) was administered to the sixth-graders, along with questions asking for motivational and background information.
- *Independent variables* included gender, liking of English (measured by a Likert-scaled item), self-choice of learning English (voluntary attendance at English language cram schools), parents' educational background, proficiency self-rating, geographic area within Taiwan, prior English learning experience, and English proficiency self-rating.
- *Dependent variable* was frequency of use of various types of English-learning strategies.

Phase I results
- Analysis of variance (ANOVA) showed that all independent variables except geographic area had significant relationships with frequency of use of English-learning strategies.
- Multiple regression showed that liking of English, self-choice, and self-rated proficiency were the strongest predictors of learning strategy use.

Phase II (qualitative):

Phase II procedures
- This phase involved a dozen students, who participated in an actual vocabulary-learning task and then were retrospectively interviewed to find out the strategies they used.

Phase II results
- Some Phase II participants employed a rich array of strategies for the vocabulary learning task, while others used fewer. These students were all capable of discussing their strategies easily.

Conclusions (integration of Phase I and Phase II):
- Overall, the study results emphasized the role of motivational factors and self-perception of English proficiency as predictors of self-reported strategy use for young children. (The importance of motivation coincided with much other strategy research with much older students.) Qualitative, task-oriented think-aloud procedures and open-ended interviews provided significant information about students' strategy use. All these types of data were important in gaining a complete picture.
- The study offered implications for strategy instruction and for the utility of retrospective interviews as accompaniments to general strategy questionnaires.

Source: Based on Lan (2008).

7.6 Action research, a model of an action research L2 study, and validity of action research studies

The main distinction between action research and other research methods is that it focuses on a practical, immediate educational problem, typically in a classroom but not necessarily so. The purpose of action research is generally to create new insights for positive educational change in the specific sociocultural environment. Action research, according to Carr and Kemmis (1986, p. 162), is self-reflective research undertaken to improve one's own practices, understanding of the practices, and situations where the practices occur. However, some people view action research as more of a self-reflective mode aimed at understanding, without necessarily promoting change. Action research can be considered one type of *practitioner research* (Zeichner and Noffke, 2001). Action research is related to pragmatism (Burns, 2008) in two ways: first, qualitative and quantitative designs can be used and coordinated in action research; and second, the very concept of action research reflects an emphasis on what works and what can work better. However, not all research studies founded upon pragmatism are necessarily classified as action research studies.

The current emphasis in action research is not so much on the methods, though action researchers have generally used qualitative techniques in recent years (Burns, 2008). The emphasis is on the attitude of self-reflexivity. Van Lier (1996) argued that action research is likely to go in critical directions, i.e., toward emancipation and transformation, only if teacher researchers take a *problem-posing* approach, looking at the classroom as a sociohistorical entity, instead of taking a merely *problem-solving* approach. Action research can have cyclical stages and can involve collaboration among teacher researchers (Van Lier, 1996). There is also hope that action research will take a strongly ecological perspective, i.e., concerned with contextual analysis, discourse, perceptions, and change (Van Lier, 1997). Anderson, Herr, and Hihlen (1994) provided the following criteria for validity in action research: democratic, outcome, process, catalytic, and dialogic validity (Concept 7.10). In addition, depending on the type of methods used in a given action research study, some of the criteria for validity mentioned previously in this chapter might also be useful.

Quote 7.5 Capability of action research

[Action research can be] a powerful force for changing and improving existing unsatisfactory language teaching situations.

Anne Burns (2008, p. 266)

Concept 7.10 **Questions to ask about the validity of action research, with L2 learning strategy research examples**

Aspects of validity	Questions to ask	L2 learning strategy research examples
Democratic validity	Were the multiple perspectives of all parties in the study accurately represented?	Did the teacher/researcher make sure to gather the perspectives of the instructional aide and the parents who visited the class during the elementary school strategy instruction study?
Outcome validity	Did the action lead to a successful outcome (problem resolution)?	Did the strategy instruction intervention help the poor readers read more effectively?
Process validity	Was the study conducted competently and dependably?	Were the strategy measurement procedures acceptable? Were the intended guidelines for strategy instruction followed well?
Catalytic validity	Did the study findings serve as a catalyst for action?	Did the principal take an interest in the strategy study results and decide that they should be shared with the other teachers in an assembly?
Dialogic validity	Did peers review and discuss the study?	Did the teacher/researcher share the findings with peers on paper or on a blog, and did new understandings emerge thereby?

Note: Also consider criteria for validity of other types of research presented earlier in the chapter as they might apply to action research.
Source: Typology adapted from Anderson (1994, cited by Mills 2000, p. 80), with strategy research examples from R. Oxford.

A model of an action research study

Table 7.10 presents a model of an action research study about L2 learning strategy instruction. This is a simple study that readers might undertake without great difficulty.

So far this chapter has presented information about general worldviews and then about the following broad types of research: quantitative, qualitative, mixed design, and action research. The next part offers general wisdom about research quality.

Table 7.10 "How to:" a model of an action research study

Lessard-Clouston (1996) conducted on an action research case study on L2 learning strategy instruction while teaching a TOEFL preparation course in Canada.

Problem: Students in the TOEFL preparation course needed to develop stronger vocabulary and thus needed vocabulary learning strategies. The problem was that the teacher-researcher did not know whether strategy instruction would help and, if so, what kind to employ, so he chose to do action research in order to find out.

Procedures:
- The researcher first considered his context (part-time teaching of evening college students with a given course textbook).
- He decided to teach vocabulary learning strategies and ask students to reflect on their learning.
- He gave a mini-lecture on vocabulary learning strategies.
- Whenever relevant to class activities, he taught vocabulary learning strategies, tying them into regular class activities. Strategy examples were (a) recording multi-definition words and meanings on cards or in a special notebook and (b) reviewing this vocabulary information regularly.
- He later administered a strategy questionnaire and a week later gave a vocabulary test.
- He shared results with the entire class.

Results:
Strategy instruction made a difference. The researcher's summary of questionnaire results, when shared with the students, sparked class discussions about vocabulary learning strategies and piqued students' interest.

Conclusions:
- Vocabulary learning is highly individualized.
- Success in understanding and using L2 vocabulary requires a variety of learning strategies.
- Strategy instruction creates interest and motivation and should be used.

Source: Based on Lessard-Clouston (1996).

7.7   General thoughts about research quality

Validity is contingent on the processes and goals of particular researchers and methodologies (Winter, 2000). Validity is not a set of permanent criteria, because it arises out of social contexts that are always in flux (Koro-Ljungberg, 2008; Lather, 1993). Most interpretations of validity seem "reductionist," suggesting that meeting a certain set of criteria automatically "grant[s] trust-worthiness, value, and legitimacy to research" (Koro-Ljungberg, 2008, p. 984). Another problem is that validity is not an attribute of the research itself and is beyond the researcher. Even if researchers "document the entire research process in detail, describe the choices [they] have made, and illustrate the values and beliefs associated with research, it remains for the readers and the research community to decide whether the research is actually valid" (Koro-Ljungberg, 2008, p. 984). The best the researcher can do is to provide sound information by which others can decide on the validity of the study in a given sociocultural milieu. The subjective nature of validity or truth is captured by Foucault (1972, 1978), who expressed the belief that the term "truth" is elliptical and the more useful term is "discourse of truth." Foucault contended that statements may be said to be truthful (we might say valid) on three different levels: (a) unisubjective, or personal to the subject; (b) intersubjective, requiring a common positionality of subjects from which all share the same claim to truthfulness or falsity; and (c) transubjective, meaning that truth remains regardless of the positionality of subjects, for instance, a mathematical law. Ultimately, the validity of the research itself depends greatly on the values and beliefs of the researcher and the community.

Concept 7.11 presents questions about research quality and utility regardless of method. These questions are helpful reminders for novice researchers and experienced investigators alike.

Concept 7.11   **Overall questions to ask about the quality and utility of any L2 strategy research study**

- Is there an interesting, engaging **introduction** that presents the research problem, the purpose of the study, and a brief overview?
- Are the **problem statement and purpose** clear and convincing, i.e., do we fully understand why the study is necessary and what the goal is?
- Are the **research questions or hypotheses** clearly stated, and do they relate closely to the problem and purpose?
- If this is a qualitative study, is the researcher's **positionality** (i.e., a statement of professional and personal factors/experiences which could influence research decisions and interpretation) presented early and clearly?

- Does the study have a clear, meaningful, relevant **theoretical framework**, regardless of whether that framework comes at the beginning or as a result of interpretation of the data?

- Does the **literature review** deal with key aspects or variables mentioned in the research questions or hypotheses? Does the literature review (a) give enough information about existing studies to be meaningful and useful; (b) pull studies together by topics or themes, rather than merely summarizing studies; (c) provide a critique if areas are not sufficiently researched or if questionable assumptions/procedures have been employed in studies; and (d) offer a final synthesis of main points?

- Is the **context** of the study (setting, issues) clearly presented? Is there a suitable description of the **participants**? Do you know enough about the participants and their setting to make sense of the study?

- Do the **research method and procedures** fit the purpose of the study? Are the research method and procedures clearly enough stated so that another researcher could replicate them?

- Are the **results** reported in an understandable fashion? Do they clearly and comprehensively address the research questions?

- Is the **discussion/interpretation** of results appropriate? Is it comprehensive enough? Does it present linkages with other existing research studies? Is it clearly expressed, meaningful, and interesting?

- Are the **conclusions** clear and directly linked to the rest of the research? Do they fit the initial problem statement and purpose?

- Are **limitations** stated?

- Is there specific, **convincing evidence of research quality**, e.g., reliability, validity, trustworthiness?

- Are technical terms **defined clearly**? Is the study **free of excessive jargon** and passive voice, which make it seem stilted?

- To what extent is this study **valuable to you** (e.g., to your personal and professional growth and to help you better understand L2 learning and teaching)?

- Is this study **clear and interesting enough** that you could discuss it with your colleagues, friends, and family, who might not know anything about this field of study?

Note: To the extent that quantitative research includes some subjectivity in worldview, choice of methodology, and framing of discussion and conclusions, a positionality statement could also be useful in quantitative studies, though this is not yet a common practice.

7.8   Ethics in L2 learning strategy research

The S²R Model raises ethical issues concerning research on L2 learning strategies. Data collection, analysis, and interpretation are particularly sensitive. Participants must be fully informed about the purpose and nature of the research. They must be made aware of their rights and given opportunities to ask questions and withdraw if desired. In some countries but not others, major institutional processes tend to regulate the process of gaining agreement from participants to be in a given study. Lack of coercion or abuse of power are crucial. Privacy must be respected if any difficult personal material emerges. Anonymity and confidentiality are very important for data collection, analysis, and interpretation. Creswell (2008) outlined other ethical issues, all of which apply to L2 learning strategy research. Avoidance of deception in the problem statement and the purpose statement is crucial. Honesty is the best policy. Writing of results should avoid gender bias and should never involve falsification, suppression, or inventing of findings. Results should not be intentionally written so that they cannot be understood by particular groups or individuals. Researchers should anticipate possible negative repercussions of sensitive findings and have a plan for handling such problems in suitable ways. Investigators should always release the study design at the same time as the results so that readers can understand the study. In addition, in experimental or quasi-experimental studies, all participants, not just the treatment group, should gain something. One way of doing this is to stage the beneficial treatment so that all groups eventually receive it (Creswell, 2008).

7.9   Conclusion

The S²R Model encourages a range of ways to approach research design for self-regulated L2 learning strategy studies, starting with a discussion of worldviews about knowledge and reality and relating those worldviews to research methods and specific procedures for research. Reflection about worldviews can help researchers and those who use research findings to understand the assumptions on which different studies are based.

This chapter's many strategy investigation models show the wide array of possibilities for imaginative researchers. This chapter can help readers plan and conduct strategy research. It can also assist readers in evaluating research through asking targeted questions about research quality. We should realize that research quality criteria are always in flux and are socially constructed, just like the research procedures themselves. Our goal must be to work effectively with the tools at hand and be open to new research tools that might emerge. The books noted below provide many more details pertinent to strategy research.

Further reading

Creswell, J. (1998) *Qualitative Inquiry and Research Design: Choosing among the Five Traditions*. Thousand Oaks, CA: Sage. *Also:* Creswell, J. (2008) *Research Design: Qualitative, Quantitative, and Mixed Methods Approaches*. Third edition. Thousand Oaks, CA: Sage. *Also:* Creswell, J. and Plano Clark, V. (2006) *Designing and conducting mixed methods research*. Thousand Oaks, CA: Sage. These books are among the most readable and useful of all research methods books on the market. They also provide useful information on philosophies underlying different methods.

Josselson, R. and Lieblich, A. (eds) (1995) *Interpreting Experience: The Narrative Study of Lives*. Newbury Park, CA: Sage. This is one of my favourite works on narrative research. A chapter by Josselson provides the basis for using empathy as a research tool. Many other ideas and techniques are found in this lively and profound book.

Mackey, A. and Gass, S. (2005) *Second Language Research: Methodology and Design*. Mahwah, NJ: Erlbaum. This helpful volume addresses key issues in L2 research design, terms and concepts, ethics, validity and reliability, classroom research, data coding and analysis, and writing up research. See also McDonough and McDonough (1997) and Dörnyei (2007).

Mills, G.E. (2000) *Action Research: A Guide for the Teacher Researcher*. Columbus, OH: Merrill. This volume contains important chapters about using action research to plan for change and employing online action research resources. The book's information on validity, reliability, generalizability, and ethics is relevant beyond action research.

Pavlenko, A. (2002) Narrative study: Whose story is it, anyway? *TESOL Quarterly*, 36: 213–218. Pavlenko addresses questions about ownership of the narrative in this challenging article.

Tashakkori, A. and Teddlie, C. (eds) (2003) *Handbook of Mixed Methods in Social and Behavioral Research*. Thousand Oaks, CA: Sage. This edited volume, almost 800 pages long, is a masterwork on mixed methods research.

Yin, R.K. (2003) *Case Study Research: Design and Methods*. Third edition. Thousand Oaks, CA: Sage. The excellent technical chapter on analyzing case studies describes "pattern-matching," explanation-building, time-series analysis, logic models, and cross-case synthesis.

Chapter 8

What we know from L2 learning strategy research

The real voyage of discovery consists not in seeking new landscapes but in having new eyes.

Marcel Proust

Preview questions

1. What does strategy research say about strategies for L2 reading and writing?
2. What findings does strategy research offer for L2 listening and speaking?
3. What do we know from research on strategies for learning L2 vocabulary and grammar?
4. Which of the L2 areas above have had more research, and which areas have had less?
5. What was found in more general studies of L2 learning strategies?

This chapter summarizes research about strategy use in different language areas: reading, writing, listening, and speaking, as well as vocabulary learning and grammar learning. In addition, it encapsulates findings from more general strategy studies. The result is practical guidance useful for further research and teaching. Table 8.1 on page 242 provides an overview of this chapter, which focuses on what we know about strategies in various L2 skill areas and in general. That table also serves as a unified list of concepts and themes for the entire chapter.

Note that the chapter does not follow the S²R Model, because existing research has been done with a variety of different models of L2 learning strategies. Also, while many of these models lead to self-regulated learning, not all of the researchers used that term or concept.

Table 8.1   Overview of this chapter

8.1   L2 reading strategies

    8.1.1   Reading: processing modes
    8.1.2   Reading: an active, nonlinear process
    8.1.3   Reading: metacognitive aspects
    8.1.4   Reading: multiple variables influencing strategy success
    8.1.5   Reading: a phenomenological approach
    8.1.6   Reading: strategy instruction

8.2   L2 writing strategies

    8.2.1   Writing: the role of feedback
    8.2.2   Writing: metacognitive knowledge and the purpose of writing
    8.2.3   Writing: activating background knowledge and sparking ideas
    8.2.4   Writing: planning strategies
    8.2.5   Writing: three instructional approaches and associated learning strategies
    8.2.6   Writing: three directions in research findings

8.3   L2 listening strategies

    8.3.1   Listening: successful and unsuccessful listeners
    8.3.2   Listening: novices versus intermediates
    8.3.3   Listening: individual factors in strategy use
    8.3.4   Listening: strategy instruction

8.4   L2 speaking strategies

    8.4.1   Speaking: communication strategies
    8.4.2   Speaking: speech act strategies

8.5   L2 vocabulary learning strategies

    8.5.1   Vocabulary: factors in instruction
    8.5.2   Vocabulary: learning strategies and strategy instruction

8.6   L2 grammar learning strategies

    8.6.1   Grammar: strategies for noun gender assignment
    8.6.2   Grammar: analysis of four modes of grammar instruction
    8.6.3   Grammar: strategies for implicit learning
    8.6.4   Grammar: strategies for explicit learning

8.7   Comparisons across L2 areas

8.8   Findings across more general strategy studies

    8.8.1   Linear versus curvilinear relationships
    8.8.2   Cause and effect
    8.8.3   Factors in strategy use
    8.8.4   Distance learning strategies
    8.8.5   Effectiveness of strategy instruction

8.9   Conclusion

    Further reading

8.1   L2 reading strategies

The reader must also know how to deploy a strategy successfully and orchestrate its use *vis-à-vis* other strategies according to the tasks at hand. "It is not sufficient to know about strategies; a reader must also be able to apply them strategically" (Anderson, 1991, p. 469). The reading area has enjoyed the most strategy research of any L2 skill area. Early research in L2 reading was considered an extension of L1 reading research trends (Sheorey and Mokhtari, 2001).

8.1.1   Reading: processing modes

Researchers have extensively studied the modes of mental processing in reading. This line of research, based on work by cognitive psychologists (e.g., Stanovich, 1980), was popular among L1 researchers, and then captured the imagination of L2 reading investigators (see Brantmeier, 2001; Grabe and Stoller, 2000).

Top-down and bottom-up processing

Top-down processing refers to a mode in which learners combine their own background knowledge with information they obtain from the text in order to understand the text. Concept 8.1 summarizes ideas about top-down processing.

Concept 8.1   **Top-down processing**

- In top-down processing, learners combine their own background knowledge with the information in a text to comprehend that text (schema theory)
- Two main types of schemata (Carrell, 1983):
  - Content schemata (background knowledge of the world)
  - Formal schemata (background knowledge of the form of the text, i.e., how it is constructed)
- "Every act of [reading] comprehension involves one's knowledge of the world as well" (Carrell and Eisterhold, 1983, p. 73). This means every act of reading comprehension involves one's relevant world knowledge, organized as schemata in long-term memory
- Related theory: Interactionist model, which asserts that readers interact with the text using prior content knowledge and cultural background (Pritchard, 1990)

Hosenfeld (1977), who studied self-reported reading strategies of successful and less successful students of German, Spanish, and French, found that successful learners used "main meaning" strategies (top-down), such as reading or translating in broad phrases, inferring, keeping meaning and context in mind, and only looking up words as a last resort. Less successful readers could not hold onto the main meaning because they were so busy with bottom-up decoding and paying attention to every word.

Block (1986) studied the reading behaviour of less successful college-level learners reading in their L1 or their L2 and compared the better ones with the worse ones within this less successful group. Within this less effective group, the somewhat better readers used strategies that involved background knowledge of text structure (top-down), along with other strategies, while the worse readers focused only on their reaction to the text and did not use strategies involving knowledge of text structure.

Pre-reading tasks are meant to help activate existing background knowledge and, in some instances, provide some relevant knowledge (for top-down processing) if it is missing in the learner. Despite pre-reading tasks, a schema from the learner's native culture can sometimes interfere with the learner's success in understanding what is to be read. For instance, the Day of the Dead is celebrated in Mexico, Halloween is celebrated in the U.S., and Tomb Sweeping Day is a traditional Chinese festival. All of these cultural events honour the dead but in very different ways. A reader from China might not understand a story about Halloween, because a Chinese cultural schema might get in the way. Pre-reading tasks might or might not help in such a situation. Stott (2001) questioned the value of pre-reading tasks, although many teachers find them valuable.

Relevant strategies for top-down processing include, among others, the following: (a) Going Beyond the Immediate Data, which can be enacted through guessing the meaning or predicting what will come next based on background knowledge and context; and (b) Conceptualizing Broadly, one aspect of which is to get the main idea through rapidly reading (skimming), requiring at least some background knowledge. Here is an example of top-down processing. If a learner named Elizaveta is going to read about baseball, she quickly employs the tactic of using imagery (part of the strategy of Activating Knowledge) by mentally envisioning activities on a baseball field. Seeing this image in her mind helps her as she reads and serves as a base for predicting (strategy: Going Beyond the Immediate Data). Schema theorists in the reading area generally contend that using background knowledge (the top-down model of reading) is a sign of a good reader and that decoding all the letters and words signifies a poor reader. Some L2 theorists, such as Gass and Varonis (1994) and Lee and Van Patten (1995), expressed a preference for a top-down model.

However, Eskey (1988), Paran (1997), Stott (2001), and others criticized schema theory for overemphasizing the value of top-down processing, for demeaning bottom-up processing, and for not being consistently validated by research. Research shows that poor readers often use background knowledge for guessing words, thus engaging in top-down processing (Paran, 1997). Top-down processing might sometimes be a compensatory strategy for weak readers, not always a goal to be achieved (Paran, 1997).

A bottom-up approach is concerned with decoding the fine details of letters and words. In contrast to Elizaveta, mentioned above, a learner named Manolo tends to be a bottom-up reader, even when he knows something about the topic. He consistently employs the strategy of Conceptualizing with Details by using tactics such as perceiving and decoding almost every letter in each word in the baseball story, as well as reading every word in the story, so that he can grasp the meaning. Concept 8.2 presents key research findings and concepts about bottom-up processing.

Concept 8.2   **Bottom-up processing**

- Bottom-up processing involves perceiving and decoding almost every letter or word in order to grasp the meaning.
- Some researchers say bottom-up processing is used *only* by less proficient readers, but this is not the case.
  - ○ The grammar-translation method of L2 instruction focuses on details and hence often encourages bottom-up processing for learners, no matter how adept these learners are.
  - ○ Analytic, detail-oriented, left-brain dominant learners sometimes prefer bottom-up tactics, which can be valuable at various stages of learning (Leaver, 2003a, 2003b).
  - ○ Some very rapid readers use bottom-up processing in an almost instantaneous, automatic way (Stanovich, 1980). This would allow them to read more extensively while still decoding.

Additional insights on processing modes in reading

Anderson (1991) compared better readers with less successful readers in the university. He elicited strategies while students read texts and took tests. Resulting strategies were then organized into five categories: supervising, support, paraphrase, coherence, and test-taking. Each category contained some bottom-up (analytic) and top-down (holistic) strategies. Better readers used more but not different strategies in this research, contrary to some other studies; and they orchestrated and monitored them more effectively. In a different study, Abraham and Vann (1987) found that personality type affected preference for "top-down" or "bottom-up'" reading strategies. Finkbeiner (2005) proposed a continuum with different proportions of top-down and bottom-up processing.

8.1.2   Reading: an active, nonlinear process

L2 reading investigations (e.g., Clarke and Silberstein, 1977) have viewed reading as an active, nonlinear process in which readers make and test hypotheses and use world knowledge and linguistic knowledge to determine meaning. This is partially related to the concept that reading comprehension only occurs when the individual actively reflects on what he or she is reading (Scarcella and Oxford, 1992).

8.1.3   Reading: metacognitive aspects

Metacognition in reading "entails knowledge of strategies for processing texts, the ability to monitor comprehension, and the ability to adjust strategies as needed" (Auerbach and Paxton, 1997, pp. 240–241). Better readers are more metacognitive in their approach (Carrell, 1992). Sheorey and Mokhtari's (2001) work is emblematic of the metacognitive approach in L2 reading research. Those researchers created the *Survey of Reading Strategies (SORS)*, a questionnaire containing three types of strategies: metacognitive, cognitive, and support. Their 2001 study explored differences in metacognitive awareness and perceived use of academic reading strategies by ESL students and U.S. college students. ESL students used more support strategies than U.S. students, regardless of proficiency level. Compared with low-ability peers, high-reading-ability students in both groups had higher usage of metacognitive and cognitive strategies.

8.1.4   Reading: multiple variables influencing strategy success

Multiple factors influence the effectiveness of a reading strategy: interactions between the text on the one hand and the reader's background, the setting, the reading level, and the nature of the L1 and the L2 on the other hand. Some strategies that were helpful to certain learners were not helpful to other learners (Sarig, 1987). Sarig (1987) identified four strategy categories: (a) technical aids like skimming and using glossaries; (b) clarification and simplification, e.g., paraphrasing and inferring; (c) coherence detection, e.g., using prior knowledge and recognizing text structure; and (d) monitoring, which can result in changing one's action, such as leaving an unknown phrase and varying reading speed.

8.1.5   Reading: a phenomenological approach

In a phenomenological study, Schramm (2001) used think-aloud protocols of German readers of texts for English for specific purposes to examine their reading strategies and to reconstruct their interactions with authors' written texts. In this in-depth study the researcher discovered new strategy phenomena, such as dissociated translation and compensatory elaboration for conclusion-making. She identified the functions and steps involved and discerned which ones characterized good readers and poor readers.

8.1.6 Reading: strategy instruction

Cultural patterns temporarily influenced strategy instruction success in a Korean EFL quasi-experimental study, but then those patterns fell away as the treatment group students recognized the value of the strategy instruction (Lee, 2007). The treatment group had the advantage of colour-coded, interesting reading strategy instruction. The control group learned and practised reading normally. The strategy instruction was totally new, so the treatment group's midterm score was not good; but by the end of the term, the treatment group statistically surpassed the control group in reading comprehension and had very positive attitudes toward strategy instruction.

Swan (2008) argued that reading strategies can be "transferred" from the L1 to the L2 without any strategy instruction and that therefore L2 learning strategy instruction is useless and unnecessary. Actually, "transfer" does not automatically happen. There is a chance that learners will be able to carry over some strategies from the L1 to the L2, but only under certain conditions: (a) learners' L1 literacy is high, (b) their metalinguistic awareness – ability to notice and understand linguistic details and make connections across languages – is strong, (c) background knowledge is high, and (d) the L1 and the L2 are in the same or a very close language family. Swan's argument is invalid if one of the conditions is absent, which often occurs. For instance, low L1 literacy is common among refugees and immigrants in Europe (Verhoeven, 1987) and elsewhere. Many learners lack metalinguistic awareness. Others lack appropriate background knowledge. Finally, in many cases the L1 and the L2 are very disparate, e.g., for a Chinese student learning English or an Australian student learning Arabic. In such cases, direct strategy instruction is frequently needed if the goal is to increase reading comprehension.

8.2   L2 writing strategies

Some theorists have viewed writing as the written form of the spoken language, while others have depicted the spoken language and the written language as highly distinct. Some extreme views are that writing is (a) a support skill with all errors needing correction, (b) a preparation stage for speaking, (c) an extension of grammar, or (d) purely for conveying meaning.

8.2.1   Writing: the role of feedback

Much research on L2 writing has considered the role of teacher feedback, which is often confusing (Zamel, 1985), inconsistent in nature and effectiveness (Fathman and Walley, 1990), and ignored by students (Semke, 1984). L2 writers often dislike feedback given by one word or a symbol as opposed to a fuller response (Keh, 1990). Teacher feedback affects the use of strategies.

8.2.2   Writing: metacognitive knowledge and the purpose of writing

Research has shown that successful adult L2 writers have metacognitive knowledge about (a) who they are as writers, (b) features of the writing task, and (c) appropriate strategies for achieving their writing purpose (Devine, 1993a, 1993b). Kasper (1997) revealed a positive correlation between metacognitive knowledge and writing proficiency in adult ESL students. In that study, both successful and less successful writers used the strategy of defining the purpose of their writing, but the purpose differed. For successful writers, the expressed purpose was to communicate ideas to readers, while less successful writers said their purpose was to write without grammar mistakes.

8.2.3   Writing: activating background knowledge and sparking ideas

In a study involving adult ESL learners, Weissberg (2006) examined "pre-writing talk" (to activate students' background knowledge and expectations of a writing task) and "invention talk" (to generate ideas and ways to express them). These writing strategies were found to be useful to the learners. Also valuable was oral prompting from teachers while students were composing.

8.2.4   Writing: planning strategies

Sasaki (2002) videotaped L2 learners while they were writing and later asked them to explain their writing-related thinking. This research identified three kinds of planning strategies for L2 writing: (a) global planning, i.e., carefully considering readers' needs and the general organization of a text (an expert-writer strategy); (b) thematic planning, i.e., less detailed planning of the organization of ideas; and (c) local planning, i.e., planning about adding ideas to a text without considering the organization (a novice-writer strategy).

The strategy of planning in the L1 often helps produce better results in L2 writing, but this depends on the nature of the task, the familiarity of the topic, the differences between the L1 and the L2, and other factors. For reviews of research on L2 composing strategies, see Cumming (2001),

Manchón (2001), and Manchón, Roca de Larios, and Murphy (2007). For the teaching of writing, see Grabe and Kaplan (1996).

8.2.5   Writing: three instructional approaches and associated learning strategies

Aside from the conceptions above about the nature of writing, there are three current approaches to writing instruction: (a) the writing process approach, (b) the genre approach, and (c) the functional approach (Gordon, 2008). See Concept 8.3. Gordon (2008) described the good L2 writer as one who reads, pays attention to vocabulary, develops strategies to manage uncertainty, and creates opportunities to write outside the classroom.

Concept 8.3   **Three current approaches to writing instruction**

- **Writing process approach** (since 1980s)
  - ○ Focused largely on cognition.
  - ○ Writer plans, drafts, and revises the material, using problem-solving, goal-oriented recursive strategies (Scardamalia and Bereiter, 1986).
  - ○ Writing process research often asks writers to talk aloud while writing (see, e.g., Flower and Hayes, 1980, 1981). Problems:
    - This captures strategies but not unconscious activity (Dobrin, 1986).
    - It is viewed as an "abnormal" way to write (Berkenkotter, 1983).
    - For identifying L2 writing strategies, the L2 learner often speaks in the L1 while writing in the L2, which increases task difficulty.
    - This approach overemphasizes the writer as an independent text-producer and ignores the sociocultural context in which writing occurs (Swales, 1990).
  - ○ Nonetheless, many L2 writing strategies have been identified through this type of research.
  - ○ In L1 writing process research, Flower and Hayes (1981) developed a model consisting of planning, translating, and reviewing (all of which are strategies or tactics).
    - This model has had much influence in L1 and L2 writing research but lacks a formal way to incorporate feedback and evaluation (McDonough, 1999).
    - McDonough (1999) cited numerous investigations on the L2 writing process indicating that many L2 writers do not plan but instead jump directly into writing.
- **Genre approach** (since mid-1990s)
  - ○ Emphasizes that writing is socioculturally situated communication, not just internal and cognitive (Gordon, 2008; Kent, 1999).
  - ○ Sociocultural settings and purposes influence the writing genre (e.g., personal letter, email, report, article, novel).

- ○ An expert text in a given genre (and for a particular purpose) is analysed, then the teacher models how to write such a text while learners provide input.
- ○ This initial step orients the learner to text analysis and to writing for a purpose in a particular sociocultural situation.
- ○ Students can then construct a text in that genre.
- ○ Writing strategies or tactics keyed to the genre approach can include the following: identifying the purpose, paying attention to the social context, and following a genre model.
- ○ Gordon (2008) recommended that when L2 learners begin to write using the chosen genre, the writing-process mode can be used concurrently, with its recursive stages of planning, composing, and revising.

- • **Functional approach** (2000s)
  - ○ Founded on the idea that certain language forms have particular communicative functions, which students need to learn (Hyland, 2003).
  - ○ Teaches learners to use several strategies: (a) breaking down a chunk of writing, such as a paragraph, into parts; (b) identifying these parts (e.g., topic sentence and supporting sentences); and (c) discussing purposes of these different components.
  - ○ Learners discover the general purpose of a paragraph and then how to achieve coherence and cohesion on a broader scale.
  - ○ This approach focuses on more compositional patterns than on meaning (Hyland, 2003).

Source: Summarized from Gordon (2008).

8.2.6   Writing: three directions in research findings

Manchón, Roca de Larios, and Murphy (2007) provided a general evaluation of research on L2 writing strategies. They mentioned the shift of theoretical frameworks and pointed out three main directions in the research results.

Quote 8.1   Directions in writing strategy research findings

Research findings point in three main directions: (1) L2 writers implement a wide range of general and specific strategic actions in their attempt to learn to write . . . ; (2) given the socio-cognitive dimensions of composing, the L2 writer's strategic behavior is dependent on both learner-internal and learner-external variables; and (3) the writer's strategic behaviour is mediated by the instruction received and can be modified through strategy instruction, although this finding needs further empirical validation. . . .

Rosa M. Manchón, Julio Roca de Larios, and Liz Murphy (2007, pp. 229–250)

8.3   L2 listening strategies

Vandergrift (1997) called listening strategies the "Cinderella of strategies," because other L2 researchers had not given them the same attention as reading, writing, and speaking strategies. There are far fewer L2 listening strategy studies than L2 reading strategy studies. However, by now that situation has shifted, with greater interest in listening research (see Rost, 2010). Themes in the L2 listening field are (a) strategies of successful and unsuccessful listeners, (b) strategies of novice and intermediate listeners, (c) individual factors in listening strategy use, and (d) raising listening strategy awareness and teaching listening strategies.

8.3.1   Listening: successful and unsuccessful listeners

O'Malley, Chamot, and Küpper (1989) studied the strategies of effective and ineffective listeners, classified on the basis of teacher's observations. Effective listeners, compared with ineffective listeners, used four groups of strategies more often: selective attention, self-monitoring, elaboration using background knowledge, and inferring meaning. More specifically, successful learners redirected attention when their concentration lagged. They listened for pause and intonation. They used inferencing from the context. They paid attention to larger chunks of language, like sentences and phrases, centering on individual words only when a comprehension breakdown occurred. Effective listeners used a more top-down approach, which emphasized inference and coherence-detection, while ineffective listeners used a bottom-up, word-by-word approach.

8.3.2   Listening: novices versus intermediates

Vandergrift's Canadian study (in Anderson and Vandergrift, 1996) investigated listening strategies of learners of French in different grades and varied schools. Interestingly, novices relied on background knowledge (top-down processing) but also surface-level strategies such as repetition, transfer, and translation, while intermediates used deeper-processing strategies (comprehension monitoring, elaboration, and inferencing) and dropped surface-level strategies. Style had an effect. For instance, global, concrete style learners used deeper strategies and focused on the main idea, but analytic students focused too much on details and lost the main idea. Vandergrift emphasized that successful listening is interactive, i.e., top-down and bottom-up, and influenced by many external and learner-internal factors. Vandergrift (1997) proposed that the metacognitive strategy of comprehension monitoring was a superordinate strategy for other metacognitive strategies, such as paying attention to important points.

8.3.3   Listening: individual factors in strategy use

Individual factors are highly influential in the use of L2 listening strategies (Bacon, 1992). For example, gender differences in strategy use occurred in Bacon's listening study, with males trying any strategy that seemed to work and females listening for the gist and trying to avoid verbatim translation. Brown (1995) analysed dimensions of difficulty experienced by some learners in listening comprehension. Schramm (2005) studied differences in active listening among schoolchildren listening to stories.

8.3.4   Listening: strategy instruction

Goh's (1997) student diary study revealed listening strategies of Chinese learners of English in Singapore. Goh classified the detailed material in the diaries into three types of metacognitive knowledge: person knowledge, task knowledge, and strategic knowledge (Flavell, 1979; Wenden, 1991). The diary study successfully raised learners' awareness of their own listening strategies.

Robbins taught listening strategies to Japanese university EFL learners (Dadour and Robbins, 1996). One of the key tools was instruction in the Problem-Solving Process Model, consisting of four processes: planning, monitoring (regulating), problem-solving, and evaluation. Another was instruction in the use of vocabulary learning strategies to support listening.

Rost (2010) emphasized a specific set of "teachable strategies" for listening, including: (a) predicting information or ideas before listening, (b) inferring from the context, (c) monitoring comprehension, (d) asking for clarification, and (e) providing a personal response to what is heard. Many other L2 listening strategies are teachable, according to Mendelsohn and Rubin (1995). However, listening strategy instruction is still a confusing field, as argued below.

Quote 8.2   Research on listening strategy instruction

Strategy research has provided fairly conclusive evidence that successful listeners use different strategies and in different combinations to less successful listeners. [Yet] [s]trategy instruction in the skill of listening is very much in its infancy. Very few studies have explicitly tested clear and different models of such instruction....We urgently need more intervention studies that identify more clearly what kind of strategy instruction works with what kinds of learner.

Ernesto Macaro, Suzanne Graham, and Robert Vanderplank (2007, pp. 184–185)

8.4   L2 speaking strategies

The area of L2 speaking strategies has produced important research on (a) communication strategies (Dörnyei and Scott, 1997; Færch and Kasper, 1983) and (b) pragmatics, or performance of speech acts (Olshtain and Cohen, 1989; Cohen and Isihara, 2005). See Hughes (2010) for an in-depth examination of the L2 speaking field.

8.4.1   Speaking: communication strategies

Chapter 4 mentioned communication strategies. As described by Nakatani and Goh (2007), the psycholinguistic view of communication strategies considers communication strategies narrowly, i.e., as only a lexical-compensatory means of overcoming gaps in vocabulary knowledge. For instance, if a learner does not know the word, he or she compensates by using a communication strategy, such as using filler words or substituting a different topic for the original topic, which requires the use of unknown words. Tarone's (1977, 1980, 1981) system of communication strategies included paraphrase, borrowing, and avoidance strategies. Bialystok (1990) studied compensatory communication strategies of young learners of French. Poulisse (1987) used retrospective verbal (think-aloud) techniques for examining repair strategies used to compensate for L2 communication impasse situations.

However, Nakatani and Goh (2007) called for the psycholinguistic perspective to be expanded to involve research on cognitive processes. As these researchers explained, the *interactional* view of communication strategies centers on the interaction process between learners and their interlocutors, often native speakers, especially the way meaning is negotiated (e.g., Ross and Rost, 1991; Williams, Inscoe, and Tasker, 1997). In this view, communication strategies are viewed not just as devices to compensate for communication breakdowns but also as tools for enhancing the message and improving communication effectiveness (see, e.g., Clennel, 1995).

8.4.2   Speaking: speech act strategies

Olshtain and Cohen (1989) studied speech act strategies of learners of Hebrew and delved into the sociolinguistic aspects of speech acts by considering linguistic and cultural standards for acceptable performance. For instance, in Hebrew, five elements must be present for a real apology – apology, explanation, responsibility-taking, repair offer, and promise – and each of these requires a different phrase (Olshtain and Cohen, 1989).

Cohen and Olshtain (1993) applied retrospective think-aloud protocols to ask learners to report strategies they had used during role-plays for apologies, complaints, and requests. Based on results, the researchers labelled participants as different types of learners: metacognizers, avoiders, and pragmatists. Participants used four main strategies: planning (to use specific forms and expressions), thinking in both languages, searching for language forms in different ways, and not paying attention to grammar or pronunciation. To learn correct speech acts, students preferred to receive the teacher's direct explanation of speech act criteria. Cohen and colleagues have continued work on assessing pragmatics (Cohen, 1999; Cohen and Shively, 2003) and on a web-based approach to strategic learning of speech acts (Cohen and Ishihara, 2005).

8.5   L2 vocabulary learning strategies

This area of language learning has received significant attention. Many strategies can be used to activate background knowledge and build schemata, but it is also necessary to teach relevant strategies for L2 vocabulary learning. Concept 8.4 indicates why vocabulary learning strategies are important.

Concept 8.4   Why vocabulary learning strategies are necessary

- Academic achievement rests largely on vocabulary knowledge (Davis and Kelly, 2003; Nation, 1990). Learners need an extensive vocabulary that can be readily accessed (Grabe, 1988).

- Learning how to pronounce, spell and define new vocabulary is important to developing prowess in reading (Davis and Kelly, 2003), but other skills such as listening, speaking, and writing also depend on vocabulary knowledge.

- Native English speakers will acquire 1,000 word families each year of their lives, until they reach the level of 20,000 word families (for a native speaker of English who is a university graduate), and children who are native speakers of English begin school with about 5,000 word families (Nation and Waring, 1997). However, many adult learners of English know much fewer than 5,000 word families after several years of study (Nation and Waring, 1997), partly because they do not use adequate vocabulary learning strategies.

- Beginning language learners must store much vocabulary in their long-term memory within a short amount of time, and vocabulary learning strategies often help (Oxford and Scarcella, 1994).

8.5.1   Vocabulary: factors in instruction

Vocabulary instruction and schemata should be taught side by side (Carrell, 1988). Teaching a word means teaching its form and meaning (Thornbury,

2002). Vocabulary teaching is necessary because inadequate vocabulary causes many difficulties in receptive and productive language (Nation, 1990). When choosing vocabulary to teach or learn, the following factors must be considered: frequency of use in real-life situations or in the curriculum; language needs; availability and familiarity; coverage, or capacity of the word to take the place of another word; and range, or the number of different types of text in which the word will occur. High frequency, wide range words are the most valuable to teach and learn (Nation, 1990). Teachers should take into account that many exposures to a word or phrase in different contexts are necessary before it is learned (Aebersold and Field, 1997). Vocabulary teaching and learning should be systematic, because the mind stores words in an organized, interconnected matter, not as words on a list (Nation, 1990).

8.5.2 Vocabulary: learning strategies and strategy instruction

A range of vocabulary learning strategies was mentioned as positive, either in theoretical or empirical studies. Examples of positive strategies included: (a) using or creating vocabulary clusters or webs (Nation, 1990; Oxford, 1990); (b) total physical response techniques and the use of real objects for vocabulary learning (Oxford, 1990; Thornbury, 2002); (c) dictionary look-up (Gu and Johnson, 1996; McDonough, 1999); (d) the "keyword technique" linking sound and images (Beaton, Gruneberg, and Ellis, 1995; Oxford, 1990); (e) early and self-initiated use of new words (Gu and Johnson, 1996; Oxford, 1990); (f) selective attention, note-taking, and reading for vocabulary learning (Gu and Johnson, 1996); (g) linking new information with existing information and keeping a vocabulary notebook (Oxford, 1990); and (h) mentally linking synonyms, constructing meanings and analogies, using personal experiences to develop vocabulary, and making T-charts (Oxford, 1990).

Two strategies, contextual guessing and rote repetition, had mixed support. Contextual guessing (and checking accuracy of guesses) was praised by Oxford (1990) and was correlated with vocabulary size and overall proficiency in a large Chinese EFL study (Gu and Johnson, 1996). However, in an Australian study of university learners of Italian, Lawson and Hogben (1998) showed that contextual guessing was less efficient than some other strategies, because a rich context reduces the need to focus on the new word itself. The value of the rote repetition was similarly inconsistent. In the Gu and Johnson study, rote oral repetition had a positive relationship with proficiency and size of learned vocabulary, but rote written repetition was negatively related to vocabulary size. Rote oral and written repetition was viewed as very important to Japanese EFL learners (Schmitt, 1997) and Australian learners of Italian (Lawson and Hogben, 1998). Schmitt (1997) found that for Japanese EFL learners, strategies using internal evidence or parallels across languages were not important.

Nyikos and Fan (2007) summarized key pedagogical implications of research concerning vocabulary learning strategies. See below. They also noted the need to pay more attention to the learner's own voice (i.e., his or her perceptions about cognitive processes such as vocabulary learning) and the need to distinguish levels of word knowledge in future research.

Quote 8.3 Lessons from research on vocabulary learning strategies

Pedagogically, the main lessons of research are: (1) that integration of VLS [vocabulary learning strategies] into instruction appears to be more effective than non-integration, (2) that significantly better vocabulary performance is possible with VLS instruction, and (3) that combination of metacognitive and specific VLS seems to work better than either in isolation....In short, VLS instruction should be integrated throughout a course as a crucial pedagogical component in course materials which are sensitive to the learner's needs.

Martha Nyikos and May Fan (2007, p. 273)

8.6   L2 grammar learning strategies

Oxford and Lee (2007) considered L2 grammar strategies the "second Cinderella," because, like listening strategies in their earlier status, grammar strategies have had very little attention. In fact, they have garnered the least interest and concern of any area of L2 learning strategies. What little has been done in grammar strategies has largely been separated from learning strategy research and is not all that well known within grammar instruction research, either. However, this appears to be changing, because Andrew Cohen and his associates are examining grammar strategies used by learners of Spanish as a foreign language and building a masterful website of grammar strategies (Cohen, personal communication, April 5, 2009).

8.6.1   Grammar: strategies for noun gender assignment

One line of L2 grammar strategy research, i.e., investigations resulting in the identification of three general categories of strategies for noun gender assignment (morphological, semantic, and syntactic), occurred in the period 1977 through 1997, with a key publication on this theme every ten years (e.g., Tucker, Lambert, and Rigault 1977; Cain, Weber-Olsen, and Smith 1987; Oliphant 1997). Choice of strategies for assigning noun gender was dependent on age, state of L2 development, nature of the L2 and the L1, and so on. Most learning strategy experts have tended to ignore such sharply focused grammar strategy studies, and investigators studying noun gender assignment and other highly specific grammar-strategy topics have not tended to cite broader areas of learning strategy research.

8.6.2   Grammar: analysis of four modes of grammar instruction

Oxford and Lee (2007) helped to bring grammar strategies into the mainstream, connecting them with the wider world of L2 learning strategy research as well as with research on different modalities of L2 grammar instruction and learning. They offered an overview of four modes for L2 grammar instruction (two implicit modes: focus on meaning and focus on form; and two explicit modes, inductive and deductive), which are allied with different learning strategies. These modes differ according to whether meaning or form is primary, whether a grammatical form is enhanced or otherwise made noticeable, whether a grammar rule is supplied for the learner to apply, and whether the learner is expected to induce a rule or ignore structure entirely. Oxford and Lee stated that adults tend to use cognitive strategies, such as paying attention to target forms and figuring out underlying grammar rules, no matter which instructional mode is employed. Age, gender, ethnic or racial background, linguistic background, educational level, beliefs, goals, values, and degree of consciousness influence both learning style and grammar strategy choice.

8.6.3   Grammar: strategies for implicit learning

Implicit L2 learning means learning grammar patterns without any direction to pay attention to form and without explanations of rules. Theoretically speaking, in implicit learning students develop competence without any awareness of linguistic targets or metalinguistic information, without intention, and without consciousness.

Ellis (1994) asserted that detection of a target structure is needed, while Schmidt (1990, 1995) argued that learners must notice (more than detect) surface elements. Strategies for purely meaning-oriented, implicit learning situations are likely to be nonexistent. However, in implicit learning that focuses on form (i.e., implicit learning that pays attention to form when a temporary roadblock is encountered), grammar strategies might include, based on Schmidt's logic, Going Beyond the Immediate Data, Reasoning, Paying Attention, and Interacting to Learn and Communicate.

8.6.4   Grammar: strategies for explicit learning

Explicit-inductive learning, or rule-discovery, means figuring out rules based on examples (De Keyser, 2003), so relevant grammar strategies might be Obtaining and Using Resources (a grammar notebook) and Reasoning.

Explicit-deductive learning, or rule application, involves grammar strategies such as Paying Attention (to the rule and exceptions), Conceptualizing with Details, and, when grammar colour-coding is used, Using the Senses to Understand and Remember.

8.7   Comparisons across L2 areas

Looking across all the L2 areas reviewed above, it is possible to indicate trends. First, reading has received by far the most research attention, even though reading strategy researchers have not fully agreed on the best strategies. Vocabulary learning has been heavily researched. Researchers have paid far less attention to strategies for grammar learning and for listening. Less focus has been given to integrated combinations of major L2 skills, such as reading and writing together.

8.8   Findings across more general strategy studies

Other strategy studies look at strategies in general rather than associated with a given language area. Here are some findings from these studies.

8.8.1   Linear versus curvilinear relationships

A fairly typical finding outside of the L2 field was that the higher the use of learning strategies, the greater the proficiency or achievement (e.g., Pintrich and De Groot, 1990; Pressley and Woloshyn, 1995; Zimmerman and Martinez-Pons, 1988, 1990), suggesting a linear relationship. However, the situation is not that simple.

In the L2 learning field in the 1990s, linear relationships (the more strategies were used, the better the proficiency) were repeatedly found between reported strategy frequency and scores on standardized L2 tests. Reported strategy use on the *Strategy Inventory for Language Learning* (in Oxford, 1990) significantly predicted proficiency in a number of studies, sometimes with a moderately large percentage of the variance explained by reported strategy use (e.g., Kato, 1996; Ku, 1995; Takeuchi, 1993), but with some other studies showing smaller percentages of explained variance. Some correlational results were striking, with correlations in the .60s and .70s between proficiency and the use of certain types of strategies, though correlations between .30 and .50 were more common (Oxford, 1999b). In the 2000s, similar linear relationships between reported strategy use and L2 proficiency were also revealed (Griffiths, 2003a, 2003b; Wharton, 2000) in different countries.

However, curvilinear relationships were also sometimes found (Green and Oxford, 1995; Phillips, 1990, 1991). In these instances, intermediate-level learners reported higher strategy use than did those with lower or higher proficiency. Perhaps advanced L2 learners had automated many strategies, so that they were no longer conscious and therefore were not reportable as strategies (Oxford, 1999b). In addition, as Alexander (2004) noted, strategies for deeper processing are often used by more expert learners.

8.8.2   Cause and effect

Few researchers have examined relationships between strategies and proficiency using statistical tools that can actually test cause-and-effect relationships (Rees-Miller, 1993). For example, studies using correlation and regression cannot provide evidence of causality. Fortunately, structural equation modelling reveals cause-and-effect relationships. Yin's (2008) large-scale study, which used latent path analysis, a subset of structural equation modeling, revealed that reported use of compensation-vocabulary strategies significantly influenced English proficiency, and this use was influenced by belief in the value of the language and of strategies.

McIntosh and Noels (2004) used path analysis in a study involving need for cognition (NC, viewed as a personality construct), self-determination, and strategy use. The final model showed significant, positive links (a) between NC and self-determination in L2 learning: and (b) between NC and the following types of strategies: cognitive, compensation, metacognitive, and social. Social strategy use was positively related to self-perceptions of L2 proficiency.

Quote 8.4   Need for cognition as a personality aspect influencing strategy use

Specifically, in addition to the widely studied Jungian model (. . .), it appears that other personality constructs can contribute to our understanding of L2 learners' preferences for certain LLS [language learning strategies]. There is likely much rich information to be gained from further integration of the personality literature with the work on LLS.

Cameron N. McIntosh and Kimberly A. Noels (2004)

Many more studies using path analysis and similar techniques should be conducted to elucidate the precise pathways of influence of strategies on proficiency. Causality is important to capture.

8.8.3 Factors in strategy use

Motivation was strongly and repeatedly related to strategy. Other factors in strategy use included gender, age, learning styles, national origin, learner beliefs and attitudes, anxiety, academic major, task, and setting (Oxford and Crookall, 1989; Ehrman, Leaver, and Oxford, 2003; Ma and Research Team, 2006). A recent book on lessons from good language learners (Griffiths, 2008) emphasized the variety of individuals who are successful in L2 learning and the many differences in their characteristics.

8.8.4 Distance learning strategies

The nature of instruction is very important in terms of strategy use. Distance L2 learners have been shown to need more metacognitive and affective strategies than they usually have, because the distance education situation deprives them of immediate guidance and social and affective support (White, 1995, 1997). Jones (1999) found that conceptualizing and personalizing strategies were particularly important for successful computer-assisted L2 vocabulary learning. I explored changes in use of sensory-related L2 learning strategies and strategies related to independent technology-based learning as a result of the "Digital Age" (Oxford, 2008a, 2008b).

8.8.5 Effectiveness of strategy instruction

Well-designed research, e.g., Nakatani's (2005) study of effects of awareness-raising on oral communication strategy use, Lee's (2007) study of reading strategy instruction for Korean university EFL students, and some studies cited by Chamot (2004, 2005), showed that groups that received strategy instruction, compared to control groups, were more successful in L2 learning. Other research (e.g., Rossiter, 2003, in which treatment and control groups both had exposure to the strategy of positive self-talk, thus partially undermining the design) did not show such results. Chamot, Barnhardt, El-Dinary, and Robbins (1996) discovered that systematically planned, learner-relevant strategy instruction was related to an increase of strategy use and self-efficacy among school-age foreign language learners. Chamot and Keatley (2003) found that among low-L1-literacy ESL students, reading strategy instruction had some success. Socioculturally mediated instruction was useful for students with learning disabilities in the L2 (International Center for Enhancement of Learning Potential, 2007; Lavine and Cabal Krastel, 1994; Cabal Krastel, 1999), as well as in the L1 (see, e.g., Ellis, 1993; Strichart and Mangrum, 2001).

Outside of the L2 field, research has revealed that strategy instruction was significantly and rather consistently related to academic achievement in mathematics, L1 writing, L1 reading, and literature, among other subject areas. However, L2 strategy instruction has not been uniformly beneficial; for instance, Ikeda and Takeuchi (2003) found that strategy instruction in a Japanese study of EFL learners was related to increased strategy frequency only for high-proficiency learners. Nevertheless, the following conclusion still stands concerning L2 strategy instruction.

Quote 8.5 **Research conclusion about L2 strategy instruction**

[T]eaching strategies is not universally successful, but the latest research is showing that, in certain modes and circumstances, particularly when incorporated into the teacher's normal classroom behavior, and … [supported by] teacher training as well as learner training, success is demonstrable.

Steven McDonough (1999, p. 15)

8.9   Conclusion

This chapter has revealed that a great amount of research has been done in the area of L2 reading and vocabulary learning, with less in other areas such as listening, writing, speaking, and grammar-learning. The research that exists shows that strategies are important in these areas and strategy instruction has been occurring in these areas, though with varying degrees of intensity. In general, explicit strategy instruction seems to be very useful.

Relationships between strategy use and proficiency are complex. Some research shows linear relationships, while other studies show curvilinearity. It seems important to distinguish between deep learning strategies and surface strategies in studying connections between strategy use and proficiency. Motivation has been a consistent influence on strategy use; if we want students to be strategic, they must be motivated. Other factors are influential as well. Distance L2 learners appear to require significant strategy help because of the difficulties inherent in the instructional mode.

Further reading

Chamot, A.U. (2004) Issues in language learning research and teaching. *Electronic Journal of Foreign Language Teaching*, 1(1): 14–26. This is a brief and insightful look at the complexities of research on L2 learning strategies and on strategy instruction. It also identifies key factors in strategy instruction.

Dreyer, C. and Oxford, R.L. (1996) Prediction of ESL proficiency among Afrikaans-speakers in South Africa. In Oxford, R. (ed.), *Language Learning Strategies around the World: Crosscultural Perspectives*. Manoa: University of Hawai'i Press: 61–74. This is one of the few South African studies of L2 learning strategy use that is widely available. It shows the important influences of strategies and culture.

Griffiths, C. (ed.) (2008) *Lessons from Good Language Learners*. Cambridge, UK: Cambridge University Press. The historical attempt to identify a single type of good language learner has given way to an understanding of many different types of good language learners.

Hurd, S. and Xiao, J. (2006) Open and distance language learning at the Shantou Radio and TV University, China, and the Open University, United Kingdom: a cross-cultural perspective. *Open Learning*, 21 (3): 205–219. This article is a sign of things to come in two different ways: It examines learning strategies in technology-aided distance learning and is a cross-cultural study.

Leaver, B.L. (2003a) *Achieving Native-like Second Language Proficiency: A Catalogue of Critical Factors. Vol. 1: Speaking*. Salinas, CA: MSI Press. This book reports on a study in which very advanced L2 learners were intensively interviewed about their learning strategies and other characteristics. It is in a book series concerning very advanced learners, who have been little studied in L2 learning research.

IV Resources

Chapter 9

Strategic "intellectual geography" and resources for further exploration

My purposes are the geography that marks out my line of travel toward the knowledge I want to have.

Adapted from Alice Koeller

Preview questions

1. What are the key landmarks of the S²R Model?
2. What is the "intellectual geography" of L2 learning strategies, and why is it important?
3. How do L2 learning strategies relate to applied linguistics and educational research?
4. Which professional associations are relevant to learning strategies, autonomy, and self-regulation?
5. Where can I find pertinent handbooks, journals, abstracting journals, and online bibliographies and databases?

This is the final chapter of the book. On the one hand, this chapter is a culmination of one set of explorations, but on the other hand, it leads to new and greater pursuits related to self-regulated L2 learning strategies. The first two sections provide a "geography lesson," laying out the landmarks of the S²R Model and presenting the intellectual terrain of learning strategies. The third section offers a plethora of accessible resources for further explorations, while the last section calls for greater unity between researchers and teachers in those explorations. Table 9.1 outlines this chapter.

9.1 Part I of the geography lesson: review of landmarks of the S²R Model

As a review, Figure 9.1 maps the major landmarks of the S²R Model. The learner is always the central focus. The landmarks of the S²R Model include general aspects (upper left quadrant) that are equally related to all three dimensions of L2 learning. The landmarks also include strategy factors in theory and practice related to each of the three L2 learning dimensions: cognitive, affective, and sociocultural-interactive (the other three quadrants).

General strategy-related factors:	Cognitive dimension:
Consciousness, purposefulness, multidimensionality, flexibility, transferability, chaining, deep processing, strategy-tactic relationship, "meta" level, task-phases, double utility, style link, and modes for strategy assessment, instruction, and research	Cognitive and metacognitive strategies and tactics related to schema development, cognitive information-processing, activity theory, cognitive load, and cognitive neurobiological factors
Learner	
Affective dimension:	Sociocultural-interactive dimension:
Affective and meta-affective strategies and tactics related to emotions, beliefs, attitudes, intrinsic and extrinsic motivation, self-determination, volition, willingness to communicate, goals, and affective neurobiological factors	Sociocultural-interactive (SI) and meta-SI strategies and tactics related to communication and learning, discourse, cultural models, identity, power relations, investment, counterstories, resistance, opposition and accommodation

Figure 9.1   Review of landmarks of the S^{2}R Model

9.2   Part II of the geography lesson: the terrain of self-regulated L2 learning strategies

This section explores the intellectual geography of learning strategies in relationship to three disciplinary areas: applied linguistics, educational psychology, and educational research in general (Figure 9.2).

9.2.1   Learning strategies in applied linguistics

Below I note linkages between learning strategies and applied linguistics. The list of categories in applied linguistics was developed by analysing themes in the *The Handbook of Second Language Teaching and Learning* (Hinkel, 2005), *The Handbook of Second Language Acquisition* (Doughty and Long, 2003), *The Handbook of Applied Linguistics* (Davies and Elder, 2004), *Encyclopedic Dictionary of Applied Linguistics: A Handbook for Language Teaching* (Johnson, 1999), *Critical Applied Linguistics: A Critical Introduction* (Pennycook, 2001), and other resources; examining the interests expressed by major professional associations for language and linguistics; and reviewing research literature (see prior chapters in this book). Results showed linkages between L2 learning strategies and the following:

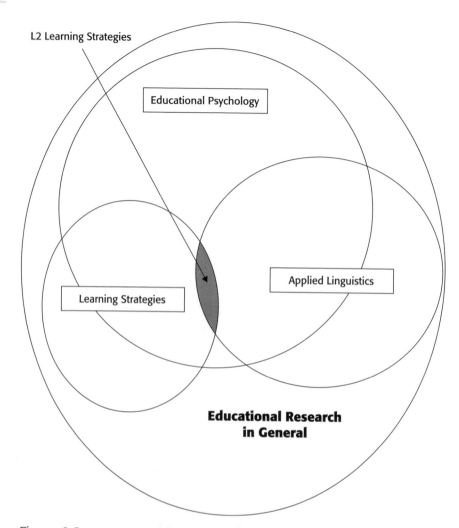

Figure 9.2 Interrelationships among disciplines
Note: Boundaries are permeable.

- Individual differences: age, academic major, gender, ethnicity, socio-economic status, affect (emotions, beliefs, attitudes, and motivation), language disorders, L1 and L2 literacy.
- Sociocultural and critical issues: power, oppression, identity, imagined communities, participation, non-participation, opposition, resistance.
- Teaching and learning: self-regulated learning, education in sociocultural settings, strategy instruction, technology, distance education, teaching and learning language, teaching and learning content through language.

- Assessment, evaluation, and research methods: assessment of strategy frequency, link between strategy instruction/assistance and proficiency, techniques for assessment/evaluation/research, quality issues.
- Memory and neurobiology: brain areas for memory, executive functions, types of memory, memory activation, deep learning, mental foraging.
- Language elements: vocabulary (lexis), meaning (semantics), grammar (syntax), cultural appropriateness (pragmatics); different language areas, e.g., reading, writing, speaking, listening.

In short, L2 learning strategies have been discussed in all of the above arenas within applied linguistics. The nature and degree of relationship naturally varies, depending partly on how much research has been done and the results of the research. See Chapters 1 through 4 and Chapter 8.

9.2.2 Strategies in educational psychology and educational research

Prior chapters have shown a strong, consistent bond between (a) learning strategies and (b) educational psychology and educational research. For instance, many major educational psychology and research handbooks from different world regions (e.g., Alexander and Winne, 2006; Kamil, Mosenthal, Pearson, and Barr, 2000; Keeves and Watanabe, 2003; Richardson, 2001; Wittrock, 1986) discuss learning strategies. The European educational policy report, *Delivering Lifelong Learning for Knowledge, Creativity and Innovation* (Commission of the European Communities, 2007) cites the importance of learning strategies. The *Handbook of Self-Regulation* (Boekaerts, Pintrich, and Zeidner, 2000) emphasizes strategies in most of the self-regulated learning chapters.

9.3 Resources to guide the next part of the journey

With a knowledge of the general geography of learning strategies – a map in hand, so to speak – the reader can pursue the topic much further. The resources presented in this section include: (a) professional associations, (b) journals, (c) an abstracting journal, (d) online bibliographies, and (e) relevant databases.

9.3.1 Professional associations

A detailed investigation of websites from educational research associations in Europe, the Americas, and the Asia-Pacific region revealed special interest groups and divisions that emphasize strategies and self-regulated learning.

Many of the larger professional associations offer regular conferences with outstanding research presentations, as well as teacher development seminars, print resources, and online resources. It is fruitful to examine the association's publications and conference agendas to learn more about its specific concerns at a particular time in history.

Naturally, the greatest learning comes from active involvement with professional associations that provide interesting, challenging, and well designed research addressing relevant questions; exceptional publications that can push us to greater understanding; in-depth professional development opportunities if we desire them; and, if relevant, demonstrations of innovative teaching practice. International, national, and local professional associations bring us varied but useful experiences.

9.3.2 Journals

This section offers information on journals in which readers can find out more about key topics in this book. Table 9.2 lists the key journals that have published articles in the last 10 years on learning strategies (sometimes identified in the articles as reading, writing, speaking, or listening strategies or strategies for pragmatics, grammar learning, or vocabulary learning), metacognition, learner autonomy, learner self-regulation (control, self-determination, etc.), and strategy assessment tools (such as think-alouds and questionnaires) in second language learning, foreign language learning, native language learning, or in special instances, learning in general. This is not an exhaustive list.

9.3.3 An abstracting journal

Cambridge University Press publishes a well-known abstracting journal in the field of language education, *Language Teaching*, published in association with the National Centre for Languages (CILT, *info@cilt.org.uk*) and the British Council (*www.britishcouncil.org*). In a new format, it now offers key survey articles on specific topics, languages, and countries and also invites original articles reporting on replication studies and meta-analyses, which are very necessary for building the scholarly base of knowledge in the L2 teaching and learning field. The journal includes an Annual Review of Research, regional surveys of doctoral dissertations, topic-based "research timelines," in-progress reports, themed book-review articles, articles based on plenary conference addresses, and lists of received publications. See *http://journals.cambridge.org/action/displayJournal?jid=LTA*.

Table 9.2	A selection of journals that have published articles on learning strategies, self-regulation, strategies for various language areas (reading, writing, speaking, listening), or learner autonomy

Annual Review of Applied Linguistics
Applied Language Learning
Applied Linguistics
Australian Review of Applied Linguistics
British Journal of Educational Studies
Canadian Journal of Linguistics / Revue canadienne de linguistique
Canadian Modern Language Review
Cognition and Instruction
Educational Psychologist
Educational Psychology: International Review of Experimental Educational Psychology
English Language Teaching Journal
English Teaching Forum (U.S. State Department)
ERIC Digests (ERIC Clearinghouse on Languages and Linguistics, National Clearinghouse for ESL Literacy Education)
Foreign Language Annals
Hong Kong Journal of Applied Linguistics
International Review of Applied Linguistics in Language Teaching
JACET (Japanese Association of College English Teachers) Bulletin
Language Awareness
Language Learning
Language Teaching
Metacognition and Learning
Modern Language Journal
Reading Research Quarterly
ReCALL Journal
RELC (Regional English Language Centre) Journal
Studies in Second Language Acquisition
System
TESL-EJ
TESOL Quarterly

9.3.4   Online bibliographies

Some online bibliographies might be useful to readers of this book:

- *Language Learning Strategy Bibliography* by Osamu Takeuchi (2005). This bibliography contains some very important historical materials for scholars of L2 learning strategies. See *http://www2.ipcku.kansai-u.ac.jp/~takeuchi/Bib1.html*.

- *Learning Strategies and Metacognition Bibliography* from Neil J. Anderson (n.d.). This extensive bibliography offers many useful materials for scholars. *http://linguistics.byu.edu/faculty/andersonn/learningstrategies/LearningStrategies.html.*

- *Autonomy Bibliography* of 1,700 items, originally compiled by Phil Benson and now maintained by Hayo Reinders (2009), potentially valuable for readers of the present volume. See *http://www.hayo.nl/autonomybibliography.php#.*

9.3.5   Databases

Many major databases and even "databases of databases" are relevant to topics in this book. Some databases are commercial, while others offer open access and are free of charge to individual users. Some offer only abstracts, while some offer full texts of many items. Examples are J-Gate, Scopus, Ovid, Ovid SP, Silver Platter, EBSCO Host, International Bibliography of the Social Sciences, Educational Resources Information Center (ERIC), PsychINFO, Directory of Open Access Journals (DOAJ), Database of English Language Teaching for Adults in Australasia (DELTAA), Linguistics and Language Behavior Abstracts, MLA International Bibliography, JSTOR, and IngentaConnect, and ScienceDirect.

9.4   Strengthening relationships while expanding strategy research and instruction

I will count this book as a success if increasing numbers of teachers and strategy researchers talk with each other more frequently (Quote 9.1), if teachers enrich their curricula with strategy instruction and other self-regulation possibilities (Quote 9.2), if teachers more often conduct their own classroom research on learning strategies, and if learners become more strategic. This chapter and the entire book provide tools for going beyond the pages of this volume and expanding the scope of strategy research and practice.

Quote 9.1 Strengthing relationships
The relationship between researchers and practitioners needs to be strengthened. This is not something new. It has been a leitmotif of many of the more enlightened SLA [second language acquisition] researchers for decades.
Andrew Cohen and Ernesto Macaro (2007, p. 277)

Quote 9.2 Enriching curricula

[T]he affordances [in the classroom] for strategic self-regulated learning...
[can be] enhanced by curricular content rich with self-regulatory possibilities.

Judy Randi and Lyn Corno (2000, p. 652)

Many large gaps still exist in our knowledge of the processes of L2 learning, including strategies. This book encourages readers to help fill some of these gaps and share new findings widely. When L2 learning strategy research and practice advance further, learners will benefit by becoming more strategic, more accurate, more fluent, and more culturally attuned. As learners become more adept at languages beyond their native tongue, they will communicate with greater effectiveness and confidence and will have the opportunity to show increased understanding and compassion across cultural boundaries.

9.5   Conclusion

This chapter opened with the first part of our "geography" lesson, laying out the main tenets of the S²R Model of L2 learning in abbreviated form. After this, it moved to the second part of the lesson, regarding the location of L2 learning strategies in relation to applied linguistics, educational psychology, and educational research, and then presented abundant resources. It also emphasized the need for teachers and researchers to work together and for teachers to conduct their own classroom research. This chapter provides a step forward in the terrain of self-regulated L2 learning strategies and a way to extend the uses of this book.

Throughout this volume readers have gained access to important themes, problems, and people in the strategy landscape; have heard from learners in elementary and secondary schools, universities, government language institutes, corporations, and military units (in the text and the strategy-tactic tables); have explored models of self-regulated learning and strategy instruction; and have pursued intertwining paths of strategy theory, research, and practice. With the help of this chapter, readers can take further steps in excavating, exploring, and shaping the landscape of self-regulated learning strategies. The common goal in these pursuits is not only to enhance L2 learning and communication but also to enrich life opportunities and mutual cooperation of people around the world.

Further reading

Alexander, P. and Winne, P. (2006) *Handbook of Educational Psychology*. Second edition. Mahwah, NJ: Erlbaum. This massive book includes a key strategy on learning strategy and also deals with cognition, motivation, content teaching, individual differences, sociocultural perspectives, instructional design, teacher assessment, and research methodologies.

Davies, A. and Elder, C. (2004) *The Handbook of Applied Linguistics*. Oxford, UK: Wiley-Blackwell. This handbook refers to learning strategies as an important part of language learning and applied linguistics.

Hinkel, E. (ed.) (2005) *Handbook of Research in Second Language Teaching and Learning*. London: Routledge. This handbook contains significant discussion of language learning strategies.

Johnson, H. (1999) *Encyclopedic Dictionary of Applied Linguistics: A Handbook for Language Teaching*. Oxford, UK: Wiley-Blackwell. Numerous references to learning strategies are included in this dictionary.

Nisbett, R. (2004) *The Geography of Thought: How Asians and Westerners Think Differently . . . and Why*. New York: Free Press. This is an example of "intellectual geography" that looks at regions of the world.

Glossary

accommodation – a cultural process that involves adjusting attitudes or behaviour to those expected in the dominant culture, even if one disagrees. Accommodation can also refer to a cognitive process in which an existing schema accommodates or adjusts to incoming information (different from the cognitive process of assimilation).

action research – research that is focused on a practical problem and that involves gathering data on perspectives of all stakeholders, as well as perhaps conducting an intervention. Further action is based on results of the research.

Activating Knowledge – a cognitive learning strategy that enables the learner to tap into existing knowledge already in his or her mind when needed for a language task.

Activating Supportive Emotions, Beliefs, and Attitudes – an affective strategy that helps the learner express feelings, create or maintain positive emotions and attitudes, gain supportive beliefs, and reduce anxiety.

activity – "the who, what, when, where, and why, the small recurrent dramas of everyday life, played on the stage of home, school, community, and workplace" (Donato and McCormick, 1994, p. 455). An activity satisfies a human *need*, is thus based on a *motive*, and exists as action and action chains (Leontiev, 1974). See below.

activity theory – Leontiev's (1978) theory, applied to language learning by Donato and McCormick (1994) and in the present book. In activity theory, an activity contains the following elements (Leontiev, 1978): (a) *subject* or person; (b) an *object* or goal; (c) the *actions*, i.e., strategies employed to move toward the goal (Donato and McCormick, 1994); (d) *the conditions* of the situation, task, person, and sociocultural context; and (e) *operations*, or specific ways (equivalent to tactics) by which the actions are carried out, manifested, or implemented, depending on the conditions in given situations.

275

actual-task strategy assessment – a form of strategy assessment that involves asking the learner to identify strategies used in a specific, actual language task in which the learner participates during the strategy assessment.

affect – attitudes, beliefs, emotions, and motivation.

affective – referring to attitudes, beliefs, emotions, and motivation.

affective dimension – a learning dimension that involves attitudes, beliefs, emotions, and motivation. The affective dimension is fundamental to living (Rogers, 1983), to all learning, and particularly to language learning (Horwitz, 2007).

affective strategy – a strategy that helps the learner deal effectively with attitudes, beliefs, emotions, and motivation and optimize them for learning (O'Neil and Spielberger, 1979; Oxford, 1990). The S^{2}R Model contains two affective strategies: Activating Supportive Emotions, Beliefs and Attitudes; and Generating and Maintaining Motivation.

affordance – a property of a sociocultural setting that either encourages or constrains learning (Van Lier, 1997).

agent – one who is capable of having an effect (on one's own learning or in some other area of life).

agency – the capability of having an effect (on one's own learning or in some other area of life.)

amygdala – an almond-shaped organ deep in the temporal lobes of the brain; part of the limbic system; produces and responds to nonverbal signs of anger, avoidance, defensiveness, and fear, as well as being the centre of the appraisal system mentioned by Schumann (2001a, 2001b). Plays an important role in motivation and emotional behaviour.

anxiety – fear or apprehension. See social anxiety, language anxiety, communication apprehension.

apprentice – a newcomer in a community of practice.

apprenticeship – see cognitive apprenticeship.

appropriate strategy – a strategy that (a) addresses the learner's goal or need, (b) fits the learning circumstances and the sociocultural context, (c) works well with the student's learning styles, i.e., general learning preferences, or in some cases helps bring greater flexibility to those preferences; and (d) positively influences learning. No strategy is appropriate under all circumstances and for all purposes. Less effective language learners often do not select appropriate strategies (Reiss, 1981, 1983; Vann and Abraham, 1989, 1990).

assimilation – a cognitive process by which incoming information is taken into (assimilated into) an existing schema without the existing schemata being significantly adjusted. Different from the cognitive process of accommodation.

attitude – positive or negative perspective toward a phenomenon or person.

attribution – the process of identifying the source or cause of one's success or failure of performance; or the result of that process.

autonomy – the quality or state of being self-governing; related to self-regulation, self-direction, and self-determination (Oxford, 2010).

avoidance – a set of communication strategies that involves substituting an easier or more familiar topic for a more difficult or less familiar one.

behavioural self-regulation – self-regulation of behaviours or performance (Zimmerman, 2000); different from covert self-regulation.

belief – the psychological state in which a person holds a premise to be true; cognitive in nature but often included in the affective dimension because beliefs are highly related to emotions, attitudes, and motivation.

blocking – the blocking or suppressing of negative thoughts or feelings that undermine motivation.

borrowing – a set of communication strategies that includes translating literally, switching languages temporarily (code switching), asking for assistance, and miming/gesturing.

bottom-up processing – text processing that involves perceiving and decoding almost every letter or word in order to grasp the meaning.

bounded case – the unit of analysis in a case study bounded by criteria such as priority, timing, geography, etc.

case – the unit of analysis in a case study. It might be an individual, group, event, institution, process, etc.

case study – a type of research that explores an individual, group, event, institution, or process in depth, sometimes over a long period of time.

central participation – a process by which experts or old-timers participate in a community of practice (Lave and Wenger, 1991).

cerebral hemispheres – the two symmetrical halves of the cerebrum of the brain.

cerebrum – the large, rounded brain structure occupying most of the cerebral cavity; the largest part of the brain in humans.

chunking – a technique involving putting similar things together in memory and reducing cognitive load (Paas, Renkl, and Sweller, 2004), thus freeing working memory for other uses.

cognitive – refers to construction, transformation, and application of knowledge.

Cognitive Academic Language Learning Approach (CALLA) – a model that combines learning strategies, content (mathematics, social studies, science), and language learning (Chamot, 2009). This model has proven useful in K-12 settings in many locations in the world.

cognitive apprenticeship – a strategic, practical learning-based relationship with a more capable other (Collins, 1988). Cognitive apprenticeship helps students to acquire, develop, and use learning strategies in authentic activities via interaction, social construction of knowledge, scaffolding, modelling, goal-setting, peer sharing, and learner reflection (Brown, Collins, and Duguid, 1989).

cognitive dimension – a learning dimension that involves construction, transformation, and application of knowledge.

cognitive information-processing – a mental process by which declarative information is transformed through practice to procedural knowledge; a process of gaining automaticity in learning a language or another subject.

cognitive information-processing theory – a theory by Anderson (1985, 1990, 1993) adapted for language learning by O'Malley and Chamot (1990), that explains the way cognitive information is transformed into automatic habits (procedures).

cognitive load – pressure experienced in the mind of an individual based on a number of factors. Can be either positive or negative. Consists of intrinsic cognitive load and non-intrinsic cognitive load, the latter of which can be either germane or extraneous.

cognitive load theory – theory of how cognitive pressure is created and how it affects the learner (Clark, Nguyen, and Sweller, 2005; Chandler and Sweller, 1992; Sweller, 2005). Learning strategies can help the learner manage cognitive load, as the present book shows.

Cognitive-Metacognitive Performance Framework – a generic learning model or strategy chain that involves the following strategies: Orient, Organize, Execute, and Verify (DeCorte, Verschaffel, and Op 'T Eynde, 2000).

cognitive strategy – a learning strategy that helps the learner construct, transform, or apply language knowledge. Example: Activating Knowledge (when needed for a language task).

colour-coding – a form of task-related strategy assessment that employs indicating the use of a given strategy by means of a particular colour; first used in research by K.R. Lee (2007).

communication – the heart of the communicative approach to language learning; includes exchanges of ideas and information among people, words or silences that have influential message value, and an overall system of relationships (see Johnson-Laird, 1990); can be verbal or nonverbal.

communication apprehension – anxiety about using language (L1 or L2) to communicate with others.

communication strategies – strategies that are used to allow continued communication despite gaps in knowledge. These include paraphrasing, borrowing, and avoidance. In actuality, these strategies can also be used to keep the learner in the conversation for long enough to learn more.

commitment control – a tactic involving reminding oneself of the value of the goals and remembering positive incentives.

community of practice – an authentic, meaningful group centred on specific practices, goals, beliefs, and areas of learning within an environment, which can be local or electronically networked (Fine, 1987; Lave and Wenger, 1991, Wenger, McDermott, and Snyder, 2002). Newcomers or apprentices at first "participate peripherally" in the community and observe strategies used by those who have been in the group longer, especially central people known as "old-timers" or experts (Lave and Wenger, 1991; Levine, Reves, and Leaver, 1996). Gradually newcomers move closer to the centre of the community of practice if the circumstances are welcoming.

Conceptualizing Broadly – a cognitive strategy that involves pulling information together, such as through summarizing or synthesizing.

Conceptualizing with Details – a cognitive strategy that involves breaking information down into parts, such as through analysing, highlighting important aspects, prioritizing, and so on.

concurrent validity (of a quantitative instrument) – the extent to which the measurement instrument correlates with other instruments that measure the same construct; a form of criterion validity.

conditional knowledge – a form of metaknowledge that involves knowing which strategies are most useful for which purposes and when to employ them. Goes beyond strategy knowledge.

constructivism – a worldview that assumes that instead of a single, universal truth/reality, multiple realities exist; people construct their own subjective realities to a great extent. Meaning is an active social construction. In Constructivism, subjective realities are discovered through induction, i.e., letting meaning evolve from the data. Knowledge is complex and individual, so reductionism is dangerous; better to maintain the contradictions, ambiguities, and richness of the data. Significant focus on qualitative research.

content validity (of a quantitative instrument) – the extent to which the measurement instrument has valid content, which relates to how well the items were selected to represent the domain of all possible items in the topic.

convergent validity (of a quantitative instrument) – the extent to which the measurement instrument correlates with other instruments measuring theoretically similar constructs/concepts; a form of construct validity.

context (in narrative studies) – two forms: pragmatic context and mental context (Tudor, 2002).

contexts – "complex and overlapping communities in which variously positioned participants learn specific, local, historically constructed, and changing practices" (Norton and Toohey, 2001, p. 312); the social identity of the speaker or writer in a given historical moment and sociocultural setting, the social activity he or she is trying to accomplish, or the setting where this is being done (Gee, 2005); prior communication; shared assumptions; and the social, cultural, cognitive, material, and political effects of all these (Gee, 2005). Contexts "repeat" and "accumulate" across time and space, creating the relative enduring shapes of history, institutions, and society (Gee, 2005).

contextualization cues – features of language that cue what the speaker or writer means (the situated meaning) in a given context and in a particular cultural model (Gumperz, 1982).

control – regarding a task, the decision as to whether to continue doing the task (using a given strategy) the way it is now going, stop entirely, or make changes; can also mean the decision as to whether to transfer a strategy to a new task.

controlling attributions – purposefully selecting causal attributions to maintain or increase motivations. Example: blaming failures on external factors and attributing success to one's own effort or strategy use.

cortex – the extensive outer layer of gray matter of the cerebral hemispheres of the brain, largely responsible for higher brain functions.

counter-story – a narrative used to counter others' negative beliefs about oneself or one's group.

cover strategies – language use strategies employed by learners to create the false impression they have control over the language material, in the hope of not appearing unprepared, foolish, and so on (Cohen, 1996, 2010).

covert self-regulation – regulation of one's own cognitive and affective states that are not observable by others (Zimmerman, 2000); different from behavioural self-regulation.

credibility of a qualitative study – the extent to which all the complexities and ambiguities have been taken into account (Guba and Lincoln, 1981).

critical – the political aspect of sociocultural theory, focusing on power dynamics, social inequality, injustice, and imperialism (cultural, linguistic, and political) in society.

cross-measure/same-construct agreement for qualitative measures – the extent to which the instrument's results appear to cohere well with results of other instruments that claim to measure the same construct.

cross-measure/similar-construct agreement for qualitative measures – the extent to which the instrument's results appear to cohere well with results of other instruments measuring theoretically similar constructs.

cultural appropriateness – a characteristic of strategy assessment or strategy assistance that fits the *modus operandi* and belief systems of a given culture.

cultural model – an unexamined, taken-for-granted theory or storyline about how things are, as believed by a socioculturally defined group of people (Gee, 2007). A given cultural model is not stored in just one person's mind but is distributed across different kinds of expertise and varied view-points in the group. Cultural models organize knowledge, thought, and situated meanings in various groups. Cultural models indicate what or who counts as normal, valuable, desirable, and hence powerful in particular sociocultural settings and what or who is understood to be deviant, less valuable, less desirable, and less powerful.

cultural tools – in Vygotsky's (1978) theory, tools from the culture that mediate learning. Examples: books, media, technology, and language itself.

Dealing with Sociocultural Contexts and Identities – a sociocultural-interactive (SI) strategy that involves imitating cultural behaviours; exploring the meaning of social roles, identity, and power; considering criteria for entering "imagined communities;" and creating counter-stories as needed in problematic situations.

declarative knowledge – in cognitive information-processing, "declarable" (speakable, identifiable) knowledge that is *not* automatic or outside of consciousness. Consists of *semantic knowledge* (facts, concepts, names, dates, rules) and *episodic knowledge* (based on memory of an event). A learning strategy can be a form of declarative knowledge if the learner can readily talk about it. Learners mentally organize and represent declarative knowledge as schemata. Such knowledge is easily lost if not practised and used.

declarative memory – memory of facts or events, not yet automated or habitualized.

defensive pessimism – a tactic of highlighting unpreparedness or inability in order to pressure oneself to try harder.

dependability of a qualitative study – the extent of stability in the results (Guba and Lincoln, 1981).

descriptive statistics – statistics that describe a sample (e.g., mean, median, standard deviation).

descriptive validity of a qualitative study – the extent to which all reported facts are accurate (Maxwell, 1992).

deep processing – processing of information during learning such that the information is made long-lasting in memory; involves elaboration of schemata.

delayed verbal self-report – a verbal self-report that occurs after the language task is over, sometimes aided by a videotape of the learner doing the task.

dialogue – verbal interaction between two people; in sociocultural theory, interaction in which a more capable other helps the learner by providing scaffolding.

dimension – one of three major aspects of learning: cognitive, affective, and sociocultural-interactive (SI). These dimensions interact significantly with each other in language learning.

direct strategy instruction – strategy instruction that is conducted by a teacher, is generally didactic in nature, and has the goal of improving learners' use of strategies. Different from other forms of strategy assistance.

discourse – language in action. It has linguistic aspects (oral or written language in use) and sociocultural/sociopolitical aspects (language as situated in a given place and time and critically attuned to the world). Discourses that both reflect and shape repeated, accumulated social contexts (history, institutions, society) are called "Discourses" ("big D Discourses") (Gee, 2005).

discourse analysis – analysis of discourse to identify not just main themes, but also biases, prejudices, hidden arguments, metaphors and their entailments, and many other features (Rogers, 2004); sometimes useful to identify learning strategies (Schramm, 2001).

discriminant validity (of a quantitative instrument) – the extent to which the measurement instrument has a low correlation with other instruments designed to measure theoretically different constructs/concepts; a form of construct validity.

distinguished language learners – those language learners who have attained a very high proficiency level and are therefore able to use the foreign or second language for complex, demanding professional and social purposes with significant accuracy and fluency.

distributed cognition – the concept that learning, knowledge, and even intelligence are distributed across people and across social practices and cultural tools (symbols, technologies, artifacts, and language) used by communities (Gee, 2007; Vygotsky, 1978).

double utility – a feature of learning strategies, which can be employed for ordinary learning purposes and for dealing with severe learning problems.

during-task verbal self-report – a think aloud.

dynamic assessment – a "test-teach-test" mode involving a dialogue between the learner and a more competent person, who first tests the learner's performance, then teaches operations or strategies for improving performance, and finally retests the strategy-enhanced performance (Feuerstein, Rand, and Hoffman, 1979; Kozulin and Garb, 2001).

efficacy self-talk – positive self-talk about one's ability to meet the goal or complete the task.

emotion – a mental state that arises spontaneously rather than by conscious effort and is often accompanied by physiological changes.

ethnography – the study and systematic recording of human cultures or of people within the cultural context; an approach to research often involving narrative style, extensive detail, sensory description, participant observation, and long-term involvement in the setting.

environmental self-regulation – self-regulation of the learning environment (Zimmerman, 2000).

Evaluating – a metastrategy that involves assessing the success of (a) task performance, (b) whole-process performance, and/or (c) a strategy chain or strategy. In the different dimensions, this metastrategy is known as Evaluating Cognition, Evaluating Affect, and Evaluating for Contexts, Communication, and Culture.

evaluative validity of a qualitative study – the extent of objectivity in presentation of the data (Maxwell, 1992) or confirmability (Guba and Lincoln, 1981); use of triangulation.

expert-judgment validity – the extent to which a group of expert judges agrees that the measurement instrument measures the theoretical construct; a form of construct validity for quantitative and qualitative measures.

external validity of an experiment or quasi-experiment – the extent to which the study is free from threats (e.g., threat to generalizability to the population, treatment replicability threat, threat from multiple treatment interference, novelty-effect threat, Hawthorne effect threat, treatment × group interaction threat, time effect threat, pretest or posttest sensitization threat, dependent measure threat) that limit generalizability from the sample to the population.

extraneous cognitive load – a deleterious form of cognitive load that is imposed by tasks or materials that do not help with the learner's schema development and automation. A key element of extraneous cognitive load is split attention, which occurs when the tasks or materials are poorly designed, forcing learners to pay attention to irrelevant information.

extrinsic motivation – the desire to do something based on external rewards, such as money, praise, prestige, or grades.

experimental research – a type of research in which one or more independent variables is manipulated in order to discern the presence or absence of an effect, within a certain probability of error; an attempt is made to control all possible variability that might harm the validity of the study.

face validity – the degree to which a measurement instrument intuitively appears, on the face of it, to measure what it seems to measure in the eyes of a non-expert.

features of self-regulated language learning strategies – (a) are employed consciously, involving four elements of consciousness (awareness, attention, intention, and effort, Schmidt, 1995); (b) make learning easier, faster, more enjoyable, and more effective; (c) are manifested through specific tactics in different contexts and for different purposes; (d) reflect the whole, multidimensional learner, not just the learner's cognitive or metacognitive aspects; (e) are often combined into strategy chains; and (f) are applied in a given situation but can be transferred to other situations when relevant.

flow – the state of being ultimately contented; an ultimate state of intrinsic motivation in which the individual is completely engaged, feels fulfilled, and simultaneously experiences both challenge and competence (Csíkszentmihályi, 1990, 1996, 1998).

foreign language – a language learned in a setting in which the language is not the main vehicle of everyday communication for the majority of people. Example: German as a foreign language in Korea. Note: Due to the complexities of globalization, the terms *foreign language* and *second language* are becoming more problematic.

frontal cortex – frontal part of the cerebral cortex.

functional approach – a writing instruction approach based on the idea that writing is best learned by focusing on the different functions that writing performs.

future time perspective – interest in and concern for what will happen in the future (Husman, McCann, and Crowson, 2000; Simons, Vansteenkiste, Lens, and Lacante, 2004). Learners with this perspective are often particularly concerned with setting long-term goals.

general strategy assessment – a form of strategy assessment that involves asking the learner to identify strategies typically used now or in the past; the learner does not participate in a language task as part of the strategy assessment.

generalizing – the process of attributing results from a sample to an entire population from which the sample is carefully drawn.

generalizability – the degree to which generalizing is warranted and justified.

Generating and Maintaining Motivation – an affective strategy that helps learners gain motivation and stay motivated by using a range of possible tactics.

genre approach – a sociocultural writing instruction approach that emphasizes purpose and setting. Can be used concurrently with the writing process approach.

germane cognitive load – positive load imposed by tasks or materials that help with the learner's schema development and automation; can be increased by combining the senses to process the information.

goal-setting – part of the metacognitive strategy of Planning. Setting goals can improve motivation, evaluation of progress, beliefs in one's capabilities, mobilization of learning strategies, and ability to alter strategies if needed (Schunk, 2002).

Going Beyond the Immediate Data – a cognitive strategy that involves moving beyond existing information through prediction or guessing.

group/culture knowledge – a form of metaknowledge that involves understanding cultural or group norms and expectations, including those concerning learning strategies.

grounded theory research approach – a research approach in which the theory arises from the data through multiple rounds of coding and interpretation. Opposite of any approach in which the theory is given in advance and tested via the research.

habit – a former strategy that has become proceduralized (has been made automatic) and is hence out of conscious control or awareness.

hippocampus – a ridge in the floor of each lateral ventricle of the brain that consists largely of gray matter and has a major role in memory functions. Also appears to be involved in "downregulation" of difficult or negative emotions (Kuhl, 2000), such as anxiety, frustration, and anger.

hybrid strategy assessment – a form of strategy assessment that describes, in scenario form, a specific language task and asks the learner to identify the strategies he or she would use if doing this task; the learner is not asked to do the task.

hypothalamus – an organ in the limbic system of the brain that organizes basic nonverbal responses associated with emotions, coordinates survival behaviour, and helps control the autonomic nervous system and the endocrine system.

identity – self-perception or other-perception of the sociocultural group with which the person is affiliated; often a site of struggle for language learners.

imagined community – a desirable sociocultural community which the individual would like to enter.

Implementing Plans – a metastrategy that helps learners to take plans already made and put them into action. In the different dimensions, this metastrategy is known as Implementing Plans for Cognition, Implementing Plans for Affect, and Implementing Plans for Contexts, Communication, and Culture.

inferential statistics – statistics that infer the characteristics of a population based on sample characteristics with a certain probability of error.

instrument – see measurement instrument.

Instrumental Enrichment (IE) Program – a program designed by Reuven Feuerstein to help modify mental structures (schemata) and teach operations (i.e., strategies) through mediation by a skilled teacher (Feuerstein, Falik, Rand, and Feuerstein, 2006; Feuerstein, Rand, Hoffman, and Miller, 1997). The IE Program's mediated learning experiences help learners draw out general rules and principles (the "abstraction" process) from tasks and then bridge to other tasks and applications. IE uses dynamic assessment.

instrumental motivation (more precisely, **instrumental motivational orientation**) – the desire to use language learning for a practical reason, such as career advancement (Gardner, 2001).

integrative motivation (more accurately **integrative motivational orientation**) – desire to come closer psychologically or socially to the other language community and identify with that community (Gardner, 2001).

Interacting to Learn and Communicate – a sociocultural-interactive (SI) strategy that involves working and learning with someone else and/or asking for certain forms of information from the other person.

interactive – referring to interaction between two or more individuals; can also refer to interaction between a person and a computer.

Interactive Model of Learner Self-Management – a generic language learning model or strategy chain that involves the following strategies: Planning, Monitoring, Evaluating, Problem-Identification/Problem-Solution, and Implementation of Problem-Solution (Rubin, 2001). This model integrates expert learners' knowledge base with strategies needed to manage and control learning.

inter-coder/intra-interpreter reliability (of a qualitative instrument) – the extent to which the instrument obtains similar interpretations from different researchers.

internal consistency reliability (of a quantitative instrument) – consistency of measurement within a single instrument administered one time. Examples: Average inter-item correlation; average item-total correlation; split-half reliability; Cronbach alpha (α).

internal validity of an experimental or quasi-experimental study – the extent to which the study is free of extraneous threats (e.g., history, maturation, reactivity, instrumentation, selection, attrition, researcher bias, design implementation, procedures, comprehensiveness threats) that could cloud the interpretation of results.

interpretive validity of a qualitative study – the extent to which participants' viewpoints and experiences are accurately represented, anomalous cases are discussed satisfactorily, alternative interpretations are considered, and insights are explained effectively (Maxwell, 1992; Schramm, 2008).

inter-rater reliability (of a quantitative instrument) – consistency of measurement across two or more raters.

intra-coder/intra-interpreter reliability (of a qualitative instrument) – the extent to which the instrument obtains similar interpretations from the same researcher at different times. Example: Same researcher looks several times at same videotape of a think-aloud measure and attains the same interpretations.

intrinsic cognitive load (complexity, difficulty) – the number of information elements to be learned and their interconnectedness; related to the innate complexity of the information to be learned. Load imposed by the number of information elements and their interactivity (interconnectedness).

intrinsic motivation – the desire to do something "as an end in itself, for its own self-sustaining pleasurable rewards of enjoyment, interest, challenge, or skill and knowledge development" (Ushioda, 2008, p. 21); is often accompanied by higher levels of involvement, more creative thinking, a wider range of strategies, and greater retention of information (Ushioda, 2008).

investment – the "socially and historically constructed relationship of learners to the target language, and their often ambivalent desire to learn and practise it" (Norton, 2000, p. 10). Investment depends largely on learners' response to relations of power. Investment is mediated by the desire for symbolic and material resources, the expectation of whether those resources will be received, and other factors, such as fear of being marginalized or resistance when one's professional status or cultural background is not valued (Ushioda, 2008).

L1 – first or native language; mother tongue.

L2 – a language learned after the first or native language; a foreign or second language.

language anxiety – fear of social performance in a second or foreign language.

language learning – process of developing ability in a second or foreign language; can be done through informal or formal means. Note: This book does not make a firm distinction between language acquisition and language learning.

language learning purposes – general purposes for learning a language, such as constructing, internalizing, storing, retrieving, and using information; completing short-term tasks; and/or developing language proficiency and self-efficacy in the long term. See also motivational orientation.

language learning strategy – see self-regulated language learning strategy.

language use strategies – several sets of oral-language strategies including communication strategies, retrieval strategies, rehearsal strategies, and cover strategies (Cohen, 1996, 2010, based on Selinker, 1972). Cohen distinguishes these from language learning strategies, though at least some language use strategies can keep the learner engaged in the conversation so that learning, not just communication, can continue.

learned helplessness – an attitude of lack of agency and lack of self-efficacy based on a belief that one is helpless in a situation.

learner guidebook – a printed or online resource that gives guidance about how to learn a second or foreign language.

learner self-determination – see self-determination theory.

learner self-direction – the learner's desire or attempt to direct his or her own learning; similar to learner self-management.

learner self-management – the learner's desire or attempt to manage his or her own learning; similar to learner self-direction; focus of a theory by Rubin (2001).

learner self-regulation – same as self-regulated learning.

learner strategy – a strategy used by a learner for learning or other purposes. This is not the term of choice in the S²R Model.

learning strategy – a deliberate attempt to manage and control efforts toward a learning goal.

learning style – a general learning preference influenced by heredity and socialization. Example: extroversion/introversion.

legitimate peripheral participation – a process by which newcomers to a community of practice participate by observing the strategies of others who have been in the group longer, especially the old-timers or experts (Lave and Wenger, 1991).

mastery goals – achievement goals oriented to developing competence.

measurement instrument – an instrument that is used to measure a certain feature or characteristic, such as learning strategy use, motivation, or attitude.

mediation – technical term in the sociocultural learning field meaning assistance.

mediated learning – learning that occurs with the assistance of a more competent person or with a book, tool, or technology that provides aid.

mental context (in narrative studies) – participants' attitudes and beliefs (regarding the language, the potential relevance of the language, the community/culture of the language, the educational setting, language learning in general) and out of participants' learning or teaching strategies, learning styles, and aspirations; beliefs, values, and educational traditions and practices in the society (Tudor, 2002).

mental foraging system – a stimulus appraisal system uniting affect and cognition (Schumann, 2001a, 2001b) and influencing sustained, deep learning. This system involves multiple neurobiological structures. The appraisal system learns to recognize environmental cues predicting learner rewards, evaluated through five criteria: relevance (significance) to needs/goals, coping potential, pleasantness, novelty, and compatibility. The appraisal creates bodily sensations/feelings on which the learner makes learning decisions, and the present book suggests these include strategy use decisions.

mentalistic – occurring in the mind, not observable.

meta-affective – means "beyond affect;" refers to the learner's control or guidance of affect.

meta-affective knowledge – any of the six forms of metaknowledge, applied in the affective dimension.

meta-affective strategy – a strategy in the affective dimension that helps the learner control (through Planning, Organizing, Evaluating, etc.) his or her affective strategy use.

metacognition – "often considered to be the highest level of mental activity, involving knowledge, awareness, and control of one's lower level cognitive skills, operations and strategies . . ." (Kozulin, 2005, p. 2). Metacognition is considered to include (a) metacognitive knowledge and (b) metacognitive regulation.

metacognitive – means "beyond cognition;" refers to the learner's control or guidance of cognition.

metacognitive knowledge – any of the six forms of metaknowledge, applied in the cognitive dimension of learning.

metacognitive regulation – use of one or more metacognitive strategies.

metacognitive strategy – a strategy in the cognitive dimension that helps the learner control (through Planning, Organizing, Evaluating, etc.) his or her cognitive strategy use. Metacognitive strategies are the best known type of metastrategies.

metaknowledge – knowledge underlying the use of metastrategies that enables a learner to learn more effectively. In the S^2R Model, six types of metaknowledge exist: (a) person knowledge, (b) group/culture knowledge, (c) task knowledge, (d) whole-process knowledge, (e) strategy knowledge, and (f) conditional knowledge. Wenden (1991), building on Flavell (1978, 1979), mentioned only three types of metaknowledge (person, task, and strategy knowledge) and called all three metacognitive knowledge.

metastrategy – a strategy, such as Planning, Organizing, Monitoring, and Evaluating, that guides and controls the use of cognitive, affective, or sociocultural-interactive (SI) strategies at either the task level or the whole-process level; provides executive control and management in each of the learning dimensions.

metascript – a technique for strategy instruction created by Lavine and Cabal Krastel (1994) based partly on the work of Harris and Graham (1992) and Oxford (1990); a step-by-step plan, developed by the teacher, by an individual learner, or by collaborating learners, to explain how to employ language learning strategies related to a given language task.

meta-sociocultural-interactive (meta-SI) – means "beyond sociocultural interaction;" refers to the learner's control or guidance of his or her role in contexts, culture, and communication.

meta-sociocultural-interactive (meta-SI) strategy – a strategy in the sociocultural-interactive (SI) dimension that helps the learner control (through Planning, Organizing, Evaluating, etc.) his or her SI strategy use.

mixed design research (mixed methods research) – research that involves both quantitative and qualitative methods. Can use qualitative and quantitative sequentially or concurrently. Can involve social advocacy.

Monitoring – a metastrategy that helps learners paying attention to their mistakes, errors, emotional/mental states, and interactions. In the different dimensions, this metastrategy is known as Monitoring Cognition, Monitoring Affect, and Monitoring for Contexts, Communication, and Culture.

more capable/competent other – in Vygotsky's (1978) theory, a teacher, more advanced peer, or another person who helps the learner by modelling "higher mental functions" (e.g., analysis, synthesis) or who provides scaffolding until the learner no longer needs it.

motivation – the desire to do something; the spark that initiates action; the motivating force.

motivational intensity – the degree or strength of motivation for language learning.

motivational orientation – the reason for learning a particular language or learning languages in general. Examples of motivational orientations are: instrumental orientation (desire to learn the language for practical reasons), integrative orientation (desire to come closer psychologically or socially to the other language community and identify with that community (Gardner, 2001); curiosity about the language structures and interest in the culture or the language community (Oxford, Park-Oh, Ito, and Sumrall, 1993a, 1993b); intellectual stimulation, self-identity, guilt, and personal development (McIntosh and Noels 2004).

motivational strategy – an affective strategy to increase motivation.

narrative – a story; a genre of research.

narrative research – story-based qualitative research, which can involve interviews, essays, biography, autobiography, and other modes.

negative incentive – negative consequences of failure; anticipating these consequences can stimulate motivation to avoid them.

neurobiology – a field of study focusing on the brain and associated systems.

newcomer (apprentice) – a person who has newly arrived in a community of practice and wishes to participate or who might be participating through legitimate peripheral participation (Lave and Wenger, 1991).

non-intrinsic cognitive load – cognitive load that is not connected to the innate complexity of the information to be learned. Can be germane or extraneous.

Obtaining and Using Resources – a metastrategy that helps learners gain and apply the resources needed for language learning tasks or for the whole process of language learning. In the different dimensions, this metastrategy is known as Obtaining and Using Resources for Cognition, Obtaining and Using Resources for Affect, and Obtaining and Using Resources for Contexts, Communication, and Culture.

old-timer – an expert, one who has been in a community of practice for a long while and whom others emulate (Lave and Wenger, 1991).

open-ended – description of an assessment mode that allows and encourages respondents to answer freely, without structured item types.

opposition – an ambivalent identity-management route that involves objection to the dominant culture but, unlike resistance, occasionally allows some accommodation to the dominant culture when deemed useful. The choice of opposition instead of resistance reflects the learner's recognition of a "domination [that] reaches into the structure of personality itself" (Giroux, 1983, p. 106).

Orchestrating Strategy Use – a metastrategy that helps learners coordinate strategy use in a systematic way, often through strategy chains. In the different dimensions, this metastrategy is known as Orchestrating Cognitive Strategy Use, Orchestrating Affective Strategy Use, and Orchestrating Strategies for Contexts, Communication, and Culture.

Organizing – a metastrategy that helps learners organize themselves and their environment for optimal language learning. In the different dimensions, this metastrategy is known as Organizing for Cognition, Organizing for Affect, and Organizing for Contexts, Communication, and Culture.

other-report – a report on the characteristics of the learner, such as learning strategy use, feelings, and attitudes, by someone other than the learner. Opposite of self-report.

Overcoming Knowledge Gaps in Communicating – a sociocultural-interactive (SI) strategy that involves compensation for missing knowledge (e.g., through making up new words or switching back to the home language briefly). This is not only a communication strategy but can also be a language learning strategy.

paradoxical intention – a means of lowering anxiety by preemptively making a mistake or making a joke about a mistake.

parallel forms reliability – consistency of measurement across two parallel (alternate, "equivalent") forms of the measurement instrument.

paraphrasing – a set of communication strategies that includes approximating the message, coining a new word, or "talking around" the word.

Paying Attention – a metastrategy that helps learners manage their attention, either generally (global attention) or specifically (focal attention). In the different dimensions, this metastrategy is known as Paying Attention to Cognition, Paying Attention to Affect, and Paying Attention to Contexts, Communication, and Culture.

performance goals – achievement goals aimed at demonstrating competence in comparison to other people (social comparison) and avoiding the relative appearance of incompetence.

person knowledge – a form of metaknowledge that involves the learner's understanding of his or her learning styles, goals, strengths, and weaknesses or of the same features in someone else.

phenomenology – a form of research that seeks to identify the "essence" of the phenomenon for the participant(s), with essence meaning what participants experienced and how they experienced it; requires bracketing of the researcher's own experiences; uses intuition, imagination, universal structures, and highly detailed data from participants. In this method, finding the essence is not meant to oversimplify the person's experience.

Planning – a metastrategy that helps learners plan for strategy use. In the different dimensions, this metastrategy is known as Planning for Cognition, Planning for Affect, and Planning for Contexts, Communication, and Culture.

portfolio – as a tool for strategy assessment and strategy assistance, can raise the learner's consciousness or awareness of strategies he or she is using and can help the learner consider additional strategies.

positionality statement – a statement of professional and personal factors/experiences which could influence research decisions and interpretation; generally included in an ethnographic study; sometimes included in other qualitative research studies.

positive incentives – positive consequences of success; anticipating positive incentives can stimulate motivation.

positivism – the worldview that a single, universal truth/reality exists outside of the mind of the researcher and can be positively, i.e., with certainty, identified through the "scientific method."

postpositivism – the worldview that a single, universal truth/reality exists outside of the mind of the researcher but that the scientific method cannot positively identify that truth/reality; statistical methods are therefore needed to show the probability of error. Post-positivism is the basis of almost all quantitative language learning research at this time.

poststructuralism – a worldview that holds many of the beliefs of constructivism but also focuses on structural violence, inequity, power struggles, multiple identities and roles, and agency, all within specific sociocultural contexts. Goal of poststructuralist research is empowerment and social/cultural/educational transformation. Asserts that all knowledge is political, founded on human interests in particular sociocultural-historical settings. Asserts that there is no such thing as a stable, free, coherent, autonomous, rationally aware person who is not influenced by the surrounding context. Poststructuralism often decentres and destabilizes assumptions about meaning (Peters and Burbules, 2003). Significant focus on qualitative research.

post-task verbal self-report – a verbal self-report in which the learner reveals strategies that were used during the language task. Two types of post-task verbal self-report: (a) initial reporting of strategies (with no during-task report) and (b) "think-after" (Branch, 2000), i.e., a retrospective follow-up in which learners evaluate the utility of strategies they reported during the task.

pragmatic context (in narrative studies) – objectively observed characteristics of the situation within a narrative study; includes factors such as class size, resources, type and level of training of the teachers, decision-making roles, major examinations, etc. (Tudor, 2002).

pragmatism – a worldview that is open to multiple ways of looking at reality. Asserts that the meaning of concepts is revealed in practical outcomes and consequences; no universal overarching truth/reality; not necessary to pledge allegiance to a given way of doing research. Asserts that qualitative, quantitative, and mixed research designs are all helpful for various purposes.

predictive validity (of a quantitative instrument) – degree to which the measurement instrument successfully predicts results on some other instrument that is theoretically related to the first instrument; a form of criterion validity.

prefrontal cortex – the anterior part of the frontal cortex, lying in front of the motor and premotor areas; is implicated in executive functions (e.g., orchestrating thoughts and actions, planning complex cognitive behaviours, making decisions, expressing personality, and mediating social behaviours).

pre-task verbal self-report (prospective verbal self-report) – a self-report that the learner gives before the language task, stating the strategies he or she plans to use in doing the task.

Problem-Solving Process – a generic problem-solving model or strategy chain that involves the following strategies: Analyze, Explore (i.e., consider equivalent problems and break the problem into subgoals), and Verify (Schoenfield, 1985).

Problem-Solving Process Model – a generic learning strategy model or strategy chain used in language learning and involving the following strategies: (a) Planning, (b) Monitoring, (c) Solving Problems (i.e., finding solutions to problems just identified), and (d) Evaluating (Chamot *et al.*, 1996).

procedural knowledge – in cognitive information-processing, habitual or automatic knowledge that is outside of consciousness.

procedural memory – memory of "how to" (how to accomplish something) without conscious declarative knowledge.

qualitative research – research that does not involve quantification of data and whose purpose is to deeply describe and analyse a particular phenomenon, rather than to generalize to a larger population.

quantitative research – research that involves quantification or the use of numbers; ordinarily involves descriptive statistics (describing the features of a sample) and inferential statistics (inferring the features of a population from a sample, thus generalizing).

quasi-experimental research – Research in which one or more independent variables is manipulated but without being able to control for all important variability.

Reasoning – a cognitive strategy that involves using logic or reason to deal with a language task.

rehearsal strategies – language use strategies, such as form-focused practice, for rehearsing language structures to be used in communication (Cohen, 1996, 2010).

Reciprocal Teaching Approach – an approach to reading in which the teacher first models and scaffolds expert, self-regulated reading strategies and then "fades" the scaffolding gradually, allowing learners to share the results of their own strategy use with each other and receive feedback from other learners (Palincsar and Brown, 1984); known as an example of cognitive apprenticeship.

recollective study (recollective research) – a form of narrative research in which learners look back at their prior learning and recollect facets of that learning (e.g., the situation, the challenges, the emotions and attitudes, the strategies used, the other people involved).

reliability – precision, accuracy, or consistency of measurement.

resistance – an identity-management route that involves rejection of the dominant culture's values (Canagarajah, 1993; Giroux, 1983). Resistance is more consistent than opposition.

retrieval strategies – language use strategies, such as mnemonics and visual images, for retrieving information when needed for communication (Cohen, 1996, 2010).

satiation control – a tactic for eliminating boredom by adding humour or a new twist.

scaffolding – a more capable person's assistance, which is gradually withdrawn when no longer needed by the learner, much like scaffolding on a house that is being constructed.

schema (pl. schemata) – a mental framework that can be expanded or modified

schema theory – theory of the development of a schema or a set of schemata.

second language – a language learned in an environment in which that language is the main vehicle of everyday communication for the majority of people. Note: Due to the complexities of globalization, the terms *second language* and *foreign language* are becoming more problematic.

self-consequating – heightening motivation through planning for self-reward or self-punishment, depending on the outcome.

self-determination theory – Deci and Ryan's (1985) theory of self-determination, which deals with extrinsic motivation and with intrinsic motivation, the latter connected to autonomy, competence, and relatedness. Strategies have been part of the research on self-determination.

self-direction – the learner's desire and attempt to direct his or her own learning; similar to self-management

self-efficacy – a belief that one is capable of achieving that which is attempted or desired, such as task completion.

self-efficacy tactic – a tactic, such as positive self-talk, intended to heighten the belief that one is capable of achieving that which is intended or desired.

self-handicapping – a tactic of making the task more difficult than it needs to be, either to provide additional motivation or an excuse if failure occurs.

self-management – the learner's desire and attempt to manage his or her own learning; similar to self-direction

self-regulated language learning strategy – a deliberate, goal-directed attempt to manage and control efforts to learn the foreign or second language (based on Afflerbach, Pearson, and Paris, 2008). Such a strategy is a broad, teachable action that learners choose from among alternatives and employ for language learning purposes. See features of self-regulated language learning strategies. Some self-regulated language learning strategies, such as Planning or Monitoring, are deployed for learning many subjects and for problem-solving in general throughout one's life. Other strategies, such as Overcoming Knowledge Gaps in Communicating (e.g., through making up new words or switching back to the home language briefly), are often tied to language learning.

self-regulation – a phenomenon comprised of such processes as "setting goals for learning, attending to and concentrating on instruction, using effective strategies to organize, code, and rehearse information to be remembered, establishing a productive work environment, using resources effectively, monitoring performance, managing time effectively, seeking assistance when needed, holding positive beliefs about one's capabilities, the value of learning, the factors influencing learning, and the anticipated outcomes of actions, and experiencing pride and satisfaction with one's efforts" (Schunk and Ertmer, 2000, p. 631).

self-regulated learning strategy – a general, goal-directed action that a self-regulated learner employs to achieve a goal.

self-regulated learning tactic – a highly specific, goal-directed action that a self-regulated learner employs in a particular sociocultural setting for particular learning-related purposes and needs. Tactics are the way or ways the learner applies the strategy at a specific level in a given situation, under particular conditions, to meet immediate requirements. Same as an operation in activity theory.

Self-Regulation Strategy Development (SRSD) – an approach to teaching self-regulated writing strategies that involves both group and individual writing strategies (Harris and Graham, 2005).

self-report – a report of one's own characteristics, such as learning strategy use, feelings, and attitudes. Opposite of other-report.

situated learning (situated cognition) – the embeddedness of learning in particular sociocultural settings in given times in history (Brown, Collins, and Duguid, 1989; Greeno, 1998); the concept that all learning is embedded or situated and is thus influenced by sociocultural and historical factors. This concept implies that learners are active agents, whose choice of strategies is influenced but not determined by the context (Oxford, 2003).

skills – actions that are automatic and out of awareness. Can be contrasted with strategies, which are intentional and deliberate. Note that it is impossible to tell whether an action is a strategy or a skill without finding out whether it is under the learner's automatic or deliberate control.

social anxiety (social performance anxiety) – fear or apprehension about communicating in a social situation.

sociocultural – an area that includes both the social and the cultural; a perspective on learning that deals with learning with others and interacting with others in the larger context of society and culture. The term *sociocultural* is often applied to Vygotsky's (1978) theory of mediated learning, which he called sociohistorical and psychological, and other theories, such as communities of practice, cognitive apprenticeship, situated cognition, distributed cognition. The political aspect of the sociocultural area is often called *critical*.

sociocultural context – learning context that includes the social identities of communicators; shared assumptions based on the past; future-oriented imaginings, hopes, and dreams; the communication setting; the communication activity; and the social, cultural, cognitive, material, and political effects of all of these (based on Gee, 2005; Kramsch, 1998).

sociocultural-interactive (SI) dimension – a learning dimension that involves communication, sociocultural contexts, and identity.

sociocultural-interactive (SI) strategy – a strategy that helps the learner with communication, sociocultural contexts, and identity. The three SI strategies are: Interacting to Learn and Communicate, Learning Despite Knowledge Gaps in Communication, and Dealing with Sociocultural Contexts and Identities.

split attention – the result of learning tasks or materials being poorly designed, forcing learners to pay attention to competing, sometimes irrelevant information.

strategic – referring to "the way in which . . . [self-regulated] learners approach challenging tasks and problems by choosing from a repertoire of tactics those they believe best suited to the situation, and applying those tactics appropriately" (Winne and Perry, 2000, 533–534).

strategic awareness – awareness of one's own strategies and of strategies that could be used for various purposes.

strategic forethought – typically the first task-phase, during which the learner pays attention to the demands of the task, sets goals, plans how to address them, and activates existing knowledge.

strategic implementation, monitoring, and control – same as strategic performance.

strategic performance – typically the second task-phase, during which the learner (a) implements the plan, (b) monitors how well the plan is working, and (c) decides whether to continue the task as it is going, stop entirely, or make changes in the approach to the task. The aspect labelled (c) is the "control" or "regulation" part of this task-phase.

strategic reflection and evaluation – typically the third task-phase, which includes making judgments of value about outcomes, effectiveness of strategies, and self (e.g., self-efficacy, which is the learner's belief he or she can meet a given goal).

strategically self-regulated learners – learners who (a) actively participate in their own learning (Griffiths, 2008; Malpass, O'Neil, and Hocevar, 1999); (b) achieve learning goals by controlling various aspects of their learning (Malpass, O'Neil, and Hocevar, 1999; Oxford, 1990); (c) regulate their cognitive and affective states, their observable performance or behaviours, and the environmental conditions for learning (Zimmerman, 2000); (d) use strategies to control their own beliefs about learning and themselves (Schunk and Zimmerman, 1998); (e) cognitively move from declarative (conscious) knowledge to procedural (automatic) knowledge with the use of strategies (Anderson, 1976, 1985; O'Malley and Chamot, 1990); (f) choose appropriate strategies for different conditions, purposes, situations, and settings (Ehrman, Leaver, and Oxford, 2003); (g) understand that no strategy is necessarily appropriate under every circumstance or for every purpose (Hsiao and Oxford, 2002; Cohen and Macaro, 2007); and (h) show awareness of the relationship between strategy use and learning outcomes; i.e., these learners consider whether a given strategy is associated with successful performance (Malpass, O'Neil, and Hocevar, 1999).

strategic, self-regulated learning – "ways of tackling the learning task at hand and managing the self in overseeing the learning process . . . under the constraints of the learning situation and learning context for the purpose of learning success" (Gu, 2010, p. 2).

Strategic Self-Regulation (S²R) Model – Oxford's model of strategic, self-regulated language learning. This model encompasses three dimensions: cognitive, affective, and sociocultural-interactive (SI). Within each dimension, the model includes strategies and metastrategies: cognitive strategies and metacognitive strategies; affective strategies and meta-affective strategies; SI strategies and meta-SI strategies. The model also includes tactics.

strategy – a deliberate, conscious attempt to manage and control efforts toward a goal; same as actions in activity theory.

strategy assessment – the gathering of data regarding strategy use; can involve different types of tools, such as questionnaires, interviews, observations, colour-coding, narratives, and others.

strategy assistance – the giving of aid to learners to help them improve their strategy use; can include but is not limited to direct strategy instruction by the teacher; can involve a range of other tools: strategy guidebooks, strategies incorporated into language textbooks, metascripts, learner consultations, and others.

strategy chain – a group or sequence of strategies (sometimes called a strategy cluster) working together in a systematic, coordinated way (Oxford, 1990). Effective language learners generally create their own strategy chains as needed, but formalized strategy chains also exist. See, e.g., the Interactive Model of Learner Self-Management (Rubin, 2001); the Problem-Solving Process Model (Chamot *et al.*, 1996); the Problem-Solving Process (Schoenfield, 1985); and the Cognitive-Metacognitive Performance Framework (DeCorte, Verschaffel, and Op'T Eynde, 2000). Less competent language learners often do not use strategy chains or appropriate strategies (Reiss, 1981, 1983; Vann and Abraham, 1989, 1990).

strategy chart – a strategy instruction device involving a chart or table.

strategy instruction – the teaching of strategies to learners in order to improve their learning. Generally refers to direct strategy instruction by the teacher.

strategy interview – an oral mode of gathering strategy data; can be semi-structured, structured, or open; can be conducted with an individual or a group.

Strategy Inventory for Language Learning – a structured learning strategy questionnaire; has one form for learning English as a second or foreign language and another form for English learners learning other languages; the most widely used strategy questionnaire.

strategy knowledge (sometimes **strategic knowledge**) – a form of meta-knowledge that involves knowing available strategies and metastrategies, how they work, and their benefits and limitations.

strategy questionnaire – a written mode of gathering strategy data; can be structured, semi-structured, or open; can be general, task-oriented, or hybrid.

strategy wheel – a circular device created by Pamela Gunning by which young children can develop improved language learning strategies.

stress management – managing one's stress through tactics such as listening to music, exercising, and relaxing.

structural coherence (of a qualitative instrument) – the extent to which the instrument coheres well internally, e.g., an interview's questions are all in the same register (e.g., personal, friendly, and welcoming for an interview in a narrative study), rather than shifting registers midway.

subcortical – located or operating below the cerebral cortex.

subjectivity – "the conscious and unconscious thoughts and emotions of the individual, her sense of herself and her ways of understanding her relation to the world" (Weedon, 1987, p. 32).

surface processing – processing of information such that the information is remains at a superficial level and is easily forgotten.

survey research – research involving questionnaires or interviews; can be quantitative, qualitative, or mixed.

tactic – a specific, "ground-level" application of a strategy or metastrategy by a particular learner in a given setting for a certain, real-life purpose to meet particular, immediate needs; same as operations in activity theory. Example: "I understand better when I look at the visible structure of the Spanish story," reflecting the strategy of Using the Senses to Understand and Remember. In comparison to tactics, strategies are broad and general, and many possible tactics can relate to a given strategy (Winne and Perry, 2000).

task knowledge – a type of metaknowledge that involves understanding the characteristics and requirements of the language learning task.

task-phase – one of three phases of a language task; phases include (a) strategic forethought; (b) strategic performance (strategic implementation, monitoring, and control), and (c) strategic reflection and evaluation. Other names are sometimes used for the task-phases (see Bandura, 1997; Eisenberg and Berkowitz, 1988; Winne and Hadwin, 1998).

task cycle – a cycle of learner activity phases related to a specific language task. See task-phase; also strategic forethought, strategic performance (strategic implementation, monitoring, and control), and strategic reflection and evaluation.

task-related strategy assessment – see actual-task strategy assessment.

temporal lobe – a region of the cerebral cortex located beneath the Sylvian fissure; is involved in auditory processing, is important to the semantics of speech, and (because it houses the hippocampus) is significant in memory. Also involved in visual recognition of faces and scenes.

test-retest reliability – consistency of measurement across two or more administrations of the instrument.

theoretical validity of a qualitative study – the degree of relevance of the researcher's theory or explanation to the data (Maxwell, 1992).

think-after – a retrospective verbal self-report conducted soon after the language task in which the learner evaluates the utility of strategies reported during the task (Branch, 2000).

think aloud – a verbal self-report of learning strategies (or reading or listening strategies) that occurs as the learner does a language task, with or without prompts to verbalize.

top-down processing – text processing in which learners combine their own background knowledge with the information in a text to comprehend that text (schema theory).

trace measure – a computer trace that can signify the learning strategy a student uses while doing a language task on the computer.

transferability of results of a qualitative study – degree to which results are generalizable within the studied community or to other relevant settings (Guba and Lincoln, 1981; Maxwell, 1992).

Using the Senses to Understand and Remember – a cognitive strategy that involves using vision, hearing, touch, or movement to facilitate comprehension and memory.

validity (of a measurement instrument) – the extent to which an instrument measures what it purports to measure.

validity (of an action research study) – the extent to which the study involves perspectives of all relevant stakeholders (democratic validity), leads to a successful outcome (outcome validity), is conducted competently (process validity), serves as a catalyst for action (catalytic validity), and is reviewed and discussed (dialogic validity) (adapted from Anderson, Herr, and Nihlen, 1994; Mills, 2000).

validity (of an experimental or quasi-experimental study) – the extent to which the study has evidence of internal validity and external validity.

validity of a qualitative study – the extent to which the study has one of the following kinds of validity: descriptive validity, credibility, interpretive validity, theoretical validity, evaluative validity, dependability, transferability, or validity of use.

validity (of a quantitative study that is neither experimental nor quasi-experimental) – the extent to which the study is free from threats such as: instrumentation, maturation, history, regression to the mean, attrition, mortality, explanatory reactivity, selection, researcher bias, and so on.

validity of use of a qualitative study – the extent to which the results, even without being generalizable, shed light on other data from other studies or can be accessed and reinterpreted by another researcher (Schramm, 2008).

verbal self-report (verbal report) – a self-report in which the learner mentions learning strategies that he or she is using during a task (think-aloud, or during-task self-report), that he or she plans to use during a task (pre-task verbal self-report), or that he or she used during a task (post-task verbal self-report).

volition – sometimes means persistence after initial motivation is over (Deimann and Keller, 2006; DeWitte and Lens, 1999). However, some theorists claim that volition is a form of self-regulation that governs all stages of learning (Corno, 2001, 2004; Elstad, 2008). To William James (1910/1987), volition is the "hot" merger of personal desire, excitement, will, and tension to create a higher level of energy. Inversely related to learned helplessness (Kuhl, 1984).

volitional strategy – any affective strategy that increases volition. The range of these strategies depends on the definition of volition (Pintrich, 1999).

whole-process knowledge – a type of metaknowledge that involves understanding, in general or specific terms, what the process of language learning is likely to entail as a whole. Transcends knowledge of a specific task, although can include such knowledge. Very often found among learners seeking to develop a high level of proficiency and among those who have a future time perspective (see Simons, Vansteenkiste, Lens, and Lacante, 2004).

willingness to communicate (WTC) – the probability that an individual will choose to initiate communication, more specifically talk, when free to do so (MacIntyre, 2003). WTC in the L1 and the L2 was found to be positively correlated with self-perceived oral communication competence and negatively correlated with anxiety about communication (communication apprehension).

worldview – one of a number of broad belief systems reflected in various research approaches. Example: post-positivism.

writing process approach – a cognitively based approach to teaching writing, using problem-solving, goal-oriented recursive strategies.

zone of proximal development (ZPD) – the area of learning that a particular student can optimally traverse with assistance (in Vygotsky's sociocultural theory).

References

Abraham, R. and Vann, R. (1987) Strategies of two language learners: a case study. In Wenden, A. and Rubin, J. (eds) *Learner Strategies: Implications for the Second Language Teacher and Researcher*. Englewood Cliffs, NJ: Prentice Hall: 85–102.

Adcock, R. and Collier, D. (2001) Measurement validity: a shared standard for qualitative and quantitative research. *American Political Science Review*, 95: 529–546.

Aebersold, J.A. and Field, M.L. (1997) *From Reader to Reading Teacher*. Cambridge: Cambridge University Press.

Afflerbach, P. (1990) The influence of prior knowledge on expert readers' main idea construction strategies. *Reading Research Quarterly*, 25(1): 31–46.

Afflerbach, P. (2000) Verbal reports and protocol analysis. In Kamil, M.L., Mosenthal, P.B., Pearson, P.D., and Barr, R. (eds), *Handbook of Reading Research*, Vol. 3. Mahwah, NJ: Erlbaum: 163–179.

Afflerbach, P., Pearson, P., and Paris, S. (2008) Clarifying differences between reading skills and reading strategies. *The Reading Teacher*, 61(5), 364–373.

Alexander, P.A. (1997) Mapping the multidimensional nature of domain learning: the interplay of cognitive, motivational, and strategic forces. In Maehr, M.L. and Pintrich, P.R. (eds), *Advances in Motivation and Achievement*. Vol. 10. Greenwich, CT: JAI Press: 213–250.

Alexander, P.A. (2003a, Aug.) Expertise and academic development: a new perspective on a classic theme. Keynote address presented at the Tenth Biennial Conference of the European Association for Research on Learning and Instruction, Padua, Italy. *http:www.education/umd.edu/EDHD/faculty2/Alexander/ARL/projects.html*

Alexander, P.A. (2003b) The development of expertise: The journey from acclimation to proficiency. In Alexander, P.A. (ed.), Special issue: *Reconceptualizing Expertise: New Models, Alternative Perspectives, Promising Results. Educational Researcher*, 32(8): 10–14.

Alexander, P.A. (2004) A model of domain learning: Reinterpreting expertise as a multidimensional, multistage process. In Dai, D.Y. and R.J. Sternberg, R.J. (eds), *Interactive Models*. Mahwah, NJ: Erlbaum: 271–298.

Alexander, P.A. (2006a) Evolution of a learning theory: a case study. *Educational Psychologist*, 41(4): 257–264.

Alexander, P.A., Graham, S., and Harris, K. (1998) A perspective on strategy research: Progress and prospects. *Educational Psychology Review*, 10: 129–154.

Alexander, P.A. and Winne, P.H. (2006) *Handbook of Educational Psychology*. London: Routledge.

Alpert, R. and Haber, R.N. (1960) Anxiety in academic achievement situations. *Journal of Abnormal and Social Psychology*, 10: 207–215.

Anderson, G.L., Herr, K., and Nihlen, A.S. (1994) *Studying Your Own School: An Educator's Guide to Practitioner Action Research*. Thousand Oaks, CA: Corwin.

Anderson, J. (1976) *Language, Memory, and Thought*. Hillsdale, NJ: Erlbaum.

Anderson, J. (1985) *Cognitive psychology and its implications*. Second edition. New York: Freeman.

Anderson, J. (1990) *The Adaptive Character of Thought*. Hillsdale, NJ: Erlbaum Associates.

Anderson, J. (1993) *Rules of the Mind*. Hillsdale, NJ: Erlbaum.

Anderson, J.R., Bothell, D., Byrne, M.D., Douglass, S., Lebiere, C., and Qin, Y. (2004) An integrated theory of the mind. *Psychological Review*, 111(4): 1036–1060.

Anderson, N.J. (1991) Individual differences in strategy use in second language reading and testing. *Modern Language Journal*, 75(4): 460–472.

Anderson, N.J. (n.d.) *Learning Strategies and Metacognition Bibliography*. http://linguistics.byu.edu/faculty/andersonn/learningstrategies/LearningStrategies.html

Anderson, N.J. (2008) Metacognition and good language learners. In Griffiths, C. (ed.), *Lessons from Good Language Learners*. Cambridge, UK: Cambridge University Press.

Anderson, N.J. and Vandergrift, L. (1996) Increasing metacognitive awareness in the L2 classroom by using think-aloud protocols and other verbal report formats. In Oxford, R.L. (ed.), *Language Learning Strategies around the World: Crosscultural Perspectives*. Manoa: University of Hawai'i Press.

Antón, M. and DiCamilla, F.J. (1999) Socio-cognitive functions of L1 collaborative interaction in the L2 classroom. *Modern Language Journal*, 83(2): 233–247.

Arnold, J. (ed.) (1999) *Affect in Language Learning*. Cambridge, UK: Cambridge University Press.

Auerbach, E.R. and Paxton, D. (1997) "It's not the English thing": bringing reading research into the ESL classroom. *TESOL Quarterly*, 31(2): 237–255.

Bacon, S. (1992) The relationship between gender, comprehension, processing strategies, and cognitive and affective response in foreign language listening. *Modern Language Journal*, 76: 160–176.

Bailey, K.M. (1983) Competitiveness and anxiety in adult second language learning: Looking at and through the diary studies. In H.W. Seliger and M.H. Long (eds), *Classroom-oriented Research in Second Language Acquisition*. Rowley, MA: Newbury House: 67–103.

Bailey, K.M. and Nunan, D. (1996) *Voices from the Language Classroom*. Cambridge, UK: Cambridge University Press.

Baily, C. (1996) Unobtrusive computerized observation of compensation strategies for writing to determine the effectiveness of strategy instruction. In Oxford, R.L. (ed.), *Language Learning Strategies around the World: Crosscultural Perspectives*. Manoa: University of Hawai'i Press: 141–150.

Bakhtin, M. (1998) Discourse in the novel. In Rivkin, J. and Ryan, M. (eds), *Literary Theory: An Anthology*. Oxford, UK: Blackwell: 32–44.

Bandura, A. (1997) *Self-Efficacy: The Exercise of Control*. New York: Freeman.

Bandura, A. (2002) Social cognitive theory in cultural context. *Applied Psychology*, 51(2): 269–290.

Barcelos, A.M.F. (2000) *Understanding Teachers' and Students' Language Learning Beliefs in Experience: A Deweyan Perspective.* Unpublished dissertation, University of Alabama, Tuscaloosa, AL.

Barraclough, R.A., Christophel, D.M., and McCroskey, J.C. (1988) Willingness to communicate: a cross-cultural investigation. *Communication Research Reports*, 5(2): 187–192.

Barron, K.E. and Harackiewicz, J.M. (2001) Achievement goals and optimal motivation: testing multiple goal models. *Journal of Personality and Social Psychology*, 80(5): 706–722.

Beaton, A., Gruneberg, M., and Ellis, N.C. (1995) Retention of foreign vocabulary learned using the Keyword method: a ten year follow-up. *Second Language Research*, 11: 112–120.

Bedell, D. and Oxford, R.L. (1996) Crosscultural comparisons of language learning. In Oxford, R.L. (ed.), *Language Learning Strategies around the World: Crosscultural Perspectives.* Manoa: University of Hawai'i Press: 47–60.

Begley, S., Springen, K., Katz, S., Hager, M., and Jones, E. (1986). Memory: science achieves important new insights into the mother of the Muses. *Newsweek*, Sept. 29, pp. 48–54.

Berkenkotter, C. (1983) Student writers and their audiences: case studies of the revising decisions of three college freshmen. Paper presented at the 16th Annual Meeting of the Canadian Council of Teachers of English.

Bialystok, E. (1978) Language skills and the learner: the classroom perspective. In C.H. Blatchford and Schachter (eds), *On TESOL '78: EFL Policies, Programs, Practices.* Washington, DC: Teachers of English to Speakers of Other Languages.

Bialystok, E. (1990) *Communication Strategies.* Oxford, UK: Blackwell.

Bialystok, E. and Sharwood Smith, M. (1985) Interlanguage is not a state of mind: an evaluation of the construct for second-language acquisition. *Applied Linguistics*, 6(2): 101–117.

Block, E.L. (1986) The comprehension strategies of second language learners. *TESOL Quarterly*, 20(3): 463–494.

Boekaerts, M., Pintrich, P.R., and Zeidner, M. (eds) (2000) *Handbook of Self-Regulation.* San Diego: Academic Press.

Bourdieu, P. (1977) *Outline of a Theory of Practice.* Cambridge, UK: Cambridge University Press.

Bourdieu, P. (1999) *Language and Symbolic Power.* Cambridge, MA: Harvard University Press.

Bourdieu, P. and Passeron, J.-C. (1977/1990) *Reproduction in Education, Society and Culture.* London: Sage.

Branch, J.L. (2000) Investigating the information-seeking processes of adolescents: the value of using think alouds and think afters. *Library and Information Science Research*, 22(4): 71–392.

Brantmeier, C. (2001) Second language reading research on passage content and gender: challenges for the intermediate level curriculum. *Foreign Language Annals*, 34: 325–333.

Briand, L., El Emam, K., and Morasca, S. (1996) On the application of measurement theory in software engineering. *Empirical Software Engineering*, 1(1): 61–88.

Brodscholl, J.C., Kober, H., and Higgins, E.T. (2006). Strategies for self-regulation in goal attainment and goal maintenance. *European Journal of Social Psychology*, 37(4): 628–648.

Bronowski, J. (1973) *The Ascent of Man*. New York: Little Brown.

Brooks, F.B. and Donato, R. (1994) Vygotskyan approaches to understanding foreign language learner discourse during communicative tasks. *Hispania*, 77(2): 262–274.

Brown, G. (1995) Dimensions of difficulty in listening comprehension. In Mendelsohn, D. and Rubin, J. (eds), *A Guide for the Teaching of Second Language Listening*. San Diego: Dominie Press: 113–131.

Brown, H.D. (1989) *A Practical Guide for Language Learning: A Fifteen-week Program of Strategies for Success*. New York: McGraw-Hill.

Brown, H.D. (1991) *Breaking the Language Barrier*. Yarmouth, ME: Intercultural Press.

Brown, H.D. (2001) *Strategies for Success: A Practical Guide to Learning English*. Upper Saddle River, NJ: Pearson ESL.

Brown, J.S., Collins, A., and Duguid, P. (1989) Situated cognition and the culture of learning. *Educational Researcher*, 18(1): 32–43.

Burden, R. and Williams, M. (eds) (1998) *Thinking through the Curriculum*. London: Routledge.

Burns, A. (2008) Action research. *Essays in honor of Dr. Hyo Woong Lee*. Pusan: Korea Maritime University: 250–278.

Cabal Krastel, T. (1999) *Accommodating the Needs of Students with Learning Difficulties in the Foreign Language Classroom*. Unpublished dissertation, University of Massachusetts at Amherst.

Cain, J., Weber-Olsen, M., and Smith, R. (1987) Acquisition strategies in a first and second language: are they the same? *Journal of Child Language*, 14: 333–352.

Campbell, C., Shaw, V., Plageman, M., and Allen, T. (1993) Exploring student beliefs about language learning. In W.N. Hatfield (ed.)., *Visions and Realities in Foreign Language Teaching: Where We Are, Where We Are Going*. Lincolnwood, IL: National Textbook: 29–39.

Canagarajah, A.S. (1993) Critical ethnography of a Sri Lankan classroom: ambiguities in opposition to reproduction through ESOL. *TESOL Quarterly*, 27(4): 601–626.

Canagarajah, A.S. (1997) Safe houses in the contact zone: coping strategies of African-American students in the academy. *College Composition and Communication*, 48(2): 173–196.

Candlin, C. (1983). Preface. In C. Faerch and G. Kasper (eds), *Strategies in Inter-language Communication* (pp. ix–xiv). London: Longman.

Carr, W. and Kemmis, S. (1986) *Becoming Critical: Knowing through Action Research*. London: Falmer.

Carrell, P.L. (1983) Some issues in studying the role of schemata, or background knowledge, in second language comprehension. *Reading in a Foreign Language*, 1: 81–92.

Carrell, P.L. (1988) Some causes of text-boundedness and schema interference in ESL reading. In Carrell, P.L., Devine, J., and Eskey, D.E. (eds), *Interactive Approaches to Second Language Reading*. Cambridge: Cambridge University Press.

Carrell, P. (1992) Awareness of text structure: effects on recall. *Language Learning*, 42: 1–20.

Carrell, P.L. and Eisterhold, J.C. (1983) Schema theory and ESL reading pedagogy. In Carrell, P.L., Devine, J., and Eskey, D.E. (eds), *Interactive Approaches to Second Language Reading*. Cambridge: Cambridge University Press.

Carrell, P.L., Prince, M.S., and Astika, G.G. (1996) Personality types and language learning in an EFL context. *Language Learning*, 46(1): 75–99.

Carver, C.S. and Scheier, M.F. (2000) On the structure of behavioral self-regulation. In Boekaerts, M., Pintrich, P.R., and Zeidner, M. (eds), *Handbook of Self-Regulation*: 41–84.

Carson, J.G. and Longhini, A. (2002) Focusing on learning styles and strategies: a diary study in and immersion setting. *Language Learning*, 52: 401–438.

Chaloub-Deville, M., Chapelle, C.A., and Duff, P. (eds) (2006) *Inference and Generalizability in Applied Linguistics: Multiple Perspectives*. Amsterdam: Benjamins.

Chamot, A.U. (2004) Issues in language learning research and teaching. *Electronic Journal of Foreign Language Teaching*, 1(1): 14–26.

Chamot, A.U. (2005) Language learning strategy instruction: current issues and research. *Annual Review of Applied Linguistics*, 25: 112–130.

Chamot, A.U. (2007) Accelerating academic achievement of English language learners: a synthesis of five evaluations of the CALLA Model. In Cummins, J. and Davison, C. (eds), *The International Handbook of English Language Learning, Part I*. Norwell, MA: Springer: 317–331.

Chamot, A.U. (2008) Learning strategies in my life. Unpublished manuscript.

Chamot, A.U. (2009) *The CALLA Handbook: Implementing the Cognitive Academic Language Learning Approach*. Second edition. White Plains, NY: Pearson Education/Longman.

Chamot, A.U., Barnhardt, S., El-Dinary, P., and Robbins, J. (1996) Methods for teaching learning strategies in the foreign language classroom. In Oxford, R.L. (ed.), *Language Learning Strategies around the World: Cross-cultural Perspectives*. Manoa: University of Hawai'i Press: 175–188.

Chamot, A.U., Barnhardt, S., El-Dinary, P., and Robbins, J. (1999) *Learning Strategies Handbook*. White Plains, NY: Addison Wesley Longman.

Chamot, A.U. and El-Dinary, P.B. (1999) Children's learning strategies in immersion classrooms. *Modern Language Journal*, 83(3): 319–341.

Chamot, A.U. and Küpper, L. (1989) Learning strategies in foreign language instruction. *Foreign Language Annals*, 22: 13–24.

Chamot, A.U. and Keatley, C. (2003) *Learning Strategies of Adolescent Low-Literacy Hispanic ESL Students*. Paper presented at the 2003 Annual Meeting of the American Educational Research Association, Chicago, IL.

Chamot, A.U. and O'Malley, J.M. (1987) The Cognitive Academic Language Learning Approach: a bridge to the mainstream. *TESOL Quarterly*, 21(2): 227–249.

Chandler, P. and Sweller, J. (1992) The split-attention effect as a factor in the design of instruction. *British Journal of Educational Psychology*, 62: 233–246.

Cherryholmes, C.H. (1999) *Reading Pragmatism*. New York: Teachers College Press.

Chi, M.T.H., Glaser, R., and Rees, E. (1982) Expertise in problem solving. In Sternberg, R.S. (ed.), *Advances in the Psychology of Human Intelligence*. Vol. 1. Hillsdale, NJ: Erlbaum: 1–75.

Clark, R.C., Nguyen, F., and Sweller, J. (2005) *Efficiency in Learning: Evidence-Based Guidelines to Manage Cognitive Load*. New York: Wiley/Pheiffer.

Clarke, M. and Silberstein, S. (1977) Towards a realization of psycholinguistic principles in the ESL reading class. *Language Learning*, 27(1): 135–154.

Clément, R.C., Baker, S.C., and MacIntyre, P.D. (2003) Willingness to communicate in a second language: the effects of context, norms, and vitality. *Journal of Language and Social Psychology*, 22(2): 190–209.

Clennel, C. (1995) Communication strategies of adult. ESL learners: a discourse perspective. *Prospect*, 10: 4–20.

Cohen, A.D. (1996) Second language learning and use strategies: clarifying the issues. Working paper. Center for Advanced Research on Language Acquisition, University of Minnesota, Minneapolis, MN.

Cohen, A.D. (1999) Assessing language pragmatics: The case of speech acts. In Bouton, L.F. (ed.), *Pragmatics and Language Learning*. Monograph Series Vol. 10. Urbana, IL: Division of English as an International Language Intensive.

Cohen, A.D. (2007) Coming to terms with language learner strategies: surveying the experts. In Cohen, A.D. and Macaro, E. (eds), *Language Learner Strategies: Thirty Years of Research and Practice*. Oxford, UK: Oxford University Press: 29–45.

Cohen, A.D. (2010) *Strategies in Learning and Using a Second Language*. London: Longman. (First edition 1998).

Cohen, A.D. and Ishihara, N. (2005) *A Web-based Approach to Strategic Learning of Speech Acts: Research Report*. Center for Advanced Research on Language Acquisition, University of Minnesota, Minneapolis, MN.

Cohen, A.D. and Macaro, E. (eds) (2007) *Language Learner Strategies: Thirty Years of Research and Practice*. Oxford, UK: Oxford University Press.

Cohen, A.D. and Olshtain, E. (1993) The production of speech acts by EFL learners. *TESOL Quarterly*, 27(1): 33–56.

Cohen, A.D. and Oxford, R.L. (2002) *Young Learners' Language Strategy Use Survey*. Minneapolis, MN: University of Minnesota Center for Advanced Research on Language Acquisition.

Cohen, A.D., Oxford, R.L., and Chi, J. (2003). *Learning Strategies Survey*. Minneapolis, MN: University of Minnesota Center for Advanced Research on Language Acquisition.

Cohen, A.D., Oxford, R.L., and Chi, J. (2005). *Language Strategy Use Survey*. Minneapolis, MN: University of Minnesota Center for Advanced Research on Language Acquisition. *http://www.carla.umn.edu/maxsa/documents/langstratuse_inventory.pdf*

Cohen, A.D. and Scott, K. (1996) A synthesis of approaches to assessing language learning strategies. In Oxford, R.L. (ed.), *Language Learning Strategies Around the World: Crosscultural Perspectives*. Manoa: University of Hawai'i Press: 89–106.

Cohen, A.D. and Shively, R. (2003) Measuring speech acts with multiple rejoinder DCTs. *Language Testing Update*, 32: 39–42.

Cohen, A.D. and Weaver, S. (1998) Strategies-based instruction for second language learners. In Renandya, W.A., and Jacobs, G.M. (eds), *Learners and Language Learning* (Anthology Series 39) Singapore: SEAMEO Regional Language Centre: 1–25.

Cohen, A.D. and Weaver, S. (2006) *Styles and Strategies-Based Instruction: A Teachers' Guide*. Minneapolis, MN: National Language Resource Center, University of Minnesota.

Cole, K. (2003, May 2) Research fails to support link between high self-esteem, positive behavior. *George Street Journal of Brown University*. *http://www.brown.edu/Administration/George_Street_Journal/vol27/27GSJ26e.html*

Collins, A. (1988) *Cognitive Apprenticeship and Instructional Technology*. Technical Report No. 6899. Cambridge, MA: BBN Labs.

Commission of the European Communities (2007) *Delivering Lifelong Learning for Knowledge, Creativity, and Innovation: Draft 2008 Joint Progress Report of the Council and the Commission on the Implementation of the "Education and Training 2010 Work Programme."* Brussels: Commission of the European Communities.

Corno, L. (2001) Volitional aspects of self-regulated learning. In Zimmerman, B.J. and Schunk, D.H. (eds), *Self-Regulated Learning and Academic Achievement: Theoretical Perspectives*. Second edition. Mahwah, NJ: Erlbaum: 191–255.

Corno, L. (2004) Introduction to the special issue: work habits and work styles: volition in education. *Teachers College Record*, 106(9): 1669–1694.

Cotterall, S. (1999) Key variables in language learning: what do learners believe about them? *System*, 27: 493–513.

Council of Europe (2001) *Common European Framework of Reference for Languages: Learning, Teaching, Assessment*. Cambridge: Cambridge University Press. http://www.coe.int/t/dg4/Linguistic/

Creswell, J. (1998) *Qualitative Inquiry and Research Design: Choosing among the Five Traditions*. Thousand Oaks, CA: Sage.

Creswell, J. (2008) *Research Design: Qualitative, Quantitative, and Mixed Methods Approaches*. Third edition. Thousand Oaks, CA: Sage.

Creswell, J. and Plano Clark, V. (2006) *Designing and Conducting Mixed Methods Research*. Thousand Oaks, CA: Sage.

Crookall, D. and Oxford, R.L. (eds) (1990) *Simulation, Gaming, and Language Learning*. New York: HarperCollins/Newbury House.

Csíkszentmihályi, M. (1990) *Flow: The Psychology of Optimal Experience*. New York: Harper & Row.

Csíkszentmihályi, M. (1996) *Creativity: Flow and the Psychology of Discovery and Invention*. New York: Harper Perennial.

Csíkszentmihályi, M. (1998) *Finding Flow: The Psychology of Engagement with Everyday Life*. New York: Basic Books.

Cumming, A. (2001) Learning to write in a second language: two decades of research. *International Journal of English Studies*, 1(2): 1–23.

Dadour, E.S. and Robbins, J. (1996) University-level studies using strategy instruction to improve speaking ability in Egypt and Japan. In Oxford, R.L. (ed.), *Language Learning Strategies around the World: Crosscultural Perspectives*. Manoa: University of Hawai'i Press: 157–166.

Damasio, A. (1994) *Descartes' Error: Emotion, Reason and the Human Brain*. New York: Avon.

Damon, C., Harackiewicz, J.M., Butera, F., Mugny, G., and Quiamzade, A. (2007) Performance-approach and performance avoidance goals: when uncertainty makes a difference. *Personality and Social Psychology Bulletin*, 33(6): 813–827.

Davies, A. and Elder, C. (2004) *The Handbook of Applied Linguistics*. Oxford, UK: Wiley-Blackwell.

Davis, S.M. and Kelly, R.R. (2003) Comparing deaf and hearing college students' mental arithmetic calculations under two interference conditions. *American Annals of the Deaf*, 148: 213–221.

Deci, E.L. and Ryan, R.M. (1985) *Intrinsic Motivation and Self-Determination in Human Behavior*. New York: Plenum.

DeCorte, E., Verschaffen, L., and Op'T Eynde, P. (2000) Self-regulation: a characteristic and a goal of mathematics education. In Boekaerts, M., Pintrich, P., and Zeidner, M. (eds), *Handbook of Self-Regulation*. San Diego: Academic Press: 687–727.

Deimann, M. and Keller, J. (2006) Volitional aspects of multimedia learning. *Journal of Educational Multimedia and Hypermedia*, 15(2): 137–158.

De Keyser, R. (2003) Implicit and explicit learning. In Doughty, C. and Long, M. (eds), *The Handbook of Second Language Acquisition*. Oxford, UK: Blackwell: 313–348.

Devine, J. (1993a) ESL readers' internalized models of the reading process. In Handscombe, J., Orem, R., and Taylor, B. (eds), *On TESOL '83*. Washington, DC: 95–108.

Devine, J. (1993b) The role of metacognition in second language reading and writing. In Carson, J., and Leki, I. (eds), *Reading in the Composition Classroom: Second Language Perspectives*. Boston MA: Heinle and Heinle: 105–121.

Dewey, J. (1909/2008) *Moral Principles in Education*. Rockville, MD: Wildside Press.

Dewey, J. (1956/1990) *The Child and the Curriculum. The School and Society*. (Combined edition.) Chicago: University of Chicago Press.

DeWitte, S. and Lens, W. (1999) Volition: use with measure. *Learning and Individual Differences*, 11(3): 321–333.

Dickinson, L. (1987) *Self-Instruction in Language Learning*. Cambridge, U.K.: Cambridge University Press.

Dobrin, D. (1986) Protocols once more. *College English*, 48: 713–726.

Donato, R. and McCormick, D.E. (1994) A socio-cultural perspective on language learning strategies: the role of mediation. *Modern Language Journal*, 78: 453–64.

Dörnyei, Z. (2003a) Attitudes, orientations, and motivations in language learning: advances in theory, research, and applications. In Dörnyei, Z. (ed.), *Attitudes, Orientations and Motivations in Language Learning*. Oxford, UK: Blackwell: 3–32.

Dörnyei, Z. (2003b) *Questionnaires in Second Language Research: Construction, Administration, and Processing*. Mahwah, NJ: Erlbaum.

Dörnyei, Z. (2005) *The Psychology of the Language Learner: Individual Differences in Second Language Acquisition*. Mahwah, NJ: Erlbaum.

Dörnyei, Z. (2007) *Research Methods in Applied Linguistics*. Oxford, UK: Oxford University Press.

Dörnyei, Z. and Ushioda, E. (2010) *Teaching and Researching Motivation*. Second edition. London: Longman/Pearson Education.

Dörnyei, Z. and Scott, M.L. (1997) Communication strategies in a second language: Definitions and taxonomies. *Language Learning*, 47: 173–210.

Dörnyei, Z. and Skehan, P. (2003) Individual differences in second language learning. In Doughty, C. and Long, M.H. (eds), *Handbook of Second Language Acquisition*. Oxford, UK: Blackwell: 589–630.

Doughty, C. and Long, M.H. (eds) (2003) *Handbook of Second Language Acquisition*. Oxford, UK: Blackwell.

Dreyer, C. and Oxford, R.L. (1996) Prediction of ESL proficiency among Afrikaans-speakers in South Africa. In Oxford, R.L. (ed.), *Language Learning Strategies around the World: Crosscultural Perspectives*. Manoa: University of Hawai'i Press: 61–74.

Ehrman, Madeline E. (1994). The type differentiation indicator and adult language learning success. *Journal of Psychological Type*, 30: 10–29.

Ehrman, M. (1999) Bringing learning strategies to the student: The FSI language learning consultation service. Paper presented at the Georgetown University Round Table, Georgetown University, Washington, DC. *http://digital.georgetown.edu/gurt/1999/gurt_1999_05.pdf*

Ehrman, M.E., Leaver, B.L., and Oxford, R.L. (2003) A brief overview of individual differences in language learning. *System*, 31(3): 313–330.

Ehrman, M.E. and Oxford, R.L. (1990) Adult language learning styles and strategies in an intensive training setting. *Modern Language Journal*, 74: 311–327.

Ehrman, M.E. and Oxford, R.L. (1995). Cognition plus: correlates of language learning success. *Modern Language Journal*, 79(1): 67–89.

Ehrman, M., Romanova, N., Braun, I., and Wei, M. (2004) Paths to native-like proficiency: personalized experiences in English. In Leaver, B.L. and Shektman, B. (eds), *Teaching and Learning to Near-Native Levels of Proficiency: Proceedings of the Spring and Fall 2003 Conferences of the Coalition of Distinguished Language Centers*. Salinas, CA: MSI Press: 43–55.

Eisenberg, M. and Berkowitz, R. (1988) *Information Problem-Solving: The Big Six Skills Approach to Library and Information Skills Instruction*. Norwood, NJ: Ablex.

Ellis, E.S. (1993) Integrative strategy instruction: a potential model for teaching content area subjects to adolescents with learning disabilities. *Journal of Learning Disabilities*, 26: 358–383.

Ellis, G. and Sinclair, B. (1989) *Learning to Learn English: A Course in Learner Training*. Cambridge: Cambridge University Press.

Ellis, R. (1994) *The Study of Second Language Acquisition*. Oxford, UK: Oxford University Press.

Ellis, R. (ed.) (1999) *Learning a Second Language through Interaction*. Amsterdam: John Benjamins.

Ellis, R. (2005) Principles of instructed language learning. *System*, 33(2): 209–224.

Elstad, E. (2008) Building self-discipline to promote learning: students' volitional strategies to navigate the demands of schooling. *Learning Inquiry*, 2(1): 53–71.

Ericsson, K.A. and Simon, H.A. (1993) *Protocol Analysis: Verbal Report as Data*. Cambridge, MA: MIT Press.

Eskey, D.E. (1988) Holding in the bottom: an interactive approach to the language problems of second language readers. In Carrell, P.L., Devine, J., and Eskey, D.E. (eds), *Interactive Approaches to Second Language Reading*. Cambridge: Cambridge University Press: 93–100.

Færch, C. and Kasper, G. (eds) (1983) *Strategies in Interlanguage Communication*. New York: Longman.

Fan, M.Y. (2003) Frequency of use, perceived usefulness, and actual usefulness of second language vocabulary strategies: a study of Hong Kong learners. *Modern Language Journal*, 87: 222–241.

Fathman, A.K. and Walley, E. (1990) Teacher response to student writing: focus on form versus content. In Kroll, B. (ed.), *Second Language Writing*. Cambridge, UK: Cambridge University Press: 178–190.

Fellag, L.R. (2004) *Tapestry Reading, Level 3, Middle East Edition*. Boston: Heinle and Heinle/Cengage.

Ferguson, G.A. and Takane, Y. (2005) *Statistical Analysis in Psychology and Education*. Sixth edition. Montréal, Quebec: McGraw-Hill Ryerson.

Festinger, L. (1954) A theory of social comparison processes. *Human Relations*, 7(2): 117–140.

Feuerstein, R., Falik, L., Rand, Y., and Feuerstein, R.S. (2006) *The Feuerstein Instrumental Enrichment Program: Creating and Enhancing Cognitive Modifiability*. Jerusalem: ICELP Press.

Feuerstein, R., Rand, Y., and Hoffman, M. (1979) *Dynamic Assessment of the Retarded Performer*. Baltimore, MD: University Park Press.

Feuerstein, R., Rand, Y., Hoffman, M., and Milller, R. (1997) Cognitive modifiability of retarded adolescents: Effects of instrumental enrichment. *Pediatric Rehabilitation*, 7: 20–29.

Feyton, C.M., Flaitz, J.J., and LaRocca, M.A. (1999) Consciousness raising and strategy use. *Applied Language Learning*, 10(1/2): 15–38.

Fine, G.A. (1987) *With the Boys*. Chicago: University of Chicago.

Finkbeiner, C. (2005) *Interessen und Strategien beim fremdsprachlichen Lesen: Wie Schülerinnen und Schüler englische Texte lesen und verstehen. [Interests and Strategies in Foreign Language Reading: How Students Read and Understand English Texts.]* Tübingen: Narr.

Flaitz, J. and Feyton, C. (1996) A two-phase study involving consciousness raising and strategy use for foreign language learners. In Oxford, R.L. (ed.), *Language Learning Strategies around the World: Crosscultural Perspectives*. Manoa: University of Hawai'i Press: 211–226.

Flavell, J.H. (1978) Metacognitive development. In Scandura, J.M. and Brainerd, C.J. (eds), *Structural/process Theories of Complex Human Behavior*. Alphen a.d. Rijn, Netherlands: Sijthoff and Noordhoff: 213–245.

Flavell, J.H. (1979) Metacognition and cognitive monitoring: a new area of cognitive developmental inquiry. *American Psychologist*, 34: 906–911.

Flippo, R.F. and Caverly, D.C. (eds) (2008) *Handbook of College Reading and Study Strategy Research*. London: Routledge.

Flores-Gonzáles, N. (2002) *School Kids, Street Kids*. New York: Teachers College Press.

Flower, L. and Hayes, J. (1980) The cognition of discovery: defining a rhetorical problem. *College Composition and Communication*, 31: 21–32.

Flower, L. and Hayes, J.R. (1981) A cognitive process theory of writing. *College Composition and Communication*, 32: 365–387.

Forgas, J.P., Williams, K.D., and Laham, S.M. (eds) (2004) *Social Motivation: Conscious and Unconscious Processes*. NY: Cambridge University Press: 1–20.

Foucault, M. (1972) *The Archeology of Knowledge*. London: Tavistock.

Foucault, M. (1978) Politics and the study of discourse. *Ideology and Consciousness*, 3: 7–26.

Fragiadakis, H. and Maurer, V. (2000) *Tapestry Listening and Speaking, Level 4*. Boston: Heinle and Heinle/Cengage.

Frankl, V. (1997) *Man's Search for Meaning: An Introduction to Logotherapy*. Boston: Beacon.

Friend, M. and Cook, L. (2007) *Interactions: Collaboration Skills for School Professionals*. Fifth edition. White Plains, NY: Longman.

Fuller, G.E. (1987) *How to Learn a Foreign Language*. Washington, DC: Storm King Press.

Gahala, E., Carlin, P.H., Hening-Boynton, A.L., Otheguy, R., and Rupert, B.J. (2007) *¡Avancemos!* Boston: McDougal Littell.

Garb, E. and Kozulin, A. (1998) "I think, therefore . . . I read." *Cognitive Approach to English Teaching (Student's Workbook and Teacher's Guide)*. Jerusalem: Academon.

Garcia, G.E. (2000) Bilingual children's reading. In Kamil, M.L., Mosenthal, P.B., Pearson, P.D., and Barr, R. (eds), *Handbook of Reading Research*. Mahwah, NJ: Erlbaum: 813–834.

Gardner, R.C. (1985) *Social Psychology and Second Language Learning: The Role of Attitudes and Motivation*. London, Ontario: Edward Arnold.

Gardner, R.C. (1988) The socio-educational model of second language learning: assumptions, findings, and issues. *Language Learning*, 38: 101–126.

Gardner, R.C. (2001) Language learning motivation: the student, the teacher, and the researcher. *Texas Papers in Foreign Language Education*, 6: 1–18.

Gardner, R.C. and Lambert, W. (1972) *Attitudes and Motivation in Second Language Learning.* Rowley, MA: Newbury House.

Gardner, R.C., Tremblay, P., and Masgoret, A.-M. (1997) Towards a full model of second language learning: an empirical investigation. *Modern Language Journal*, 81(3): 344–362.

Gass, S.M. (1997) *Input, Interaction, and the Second Language Learner.* Mahwah, NJ: Erlbaum.

Gass, S.M. and Mackey, A. (2007) *Data Elicitation for Second and Foreign Language Research.* Mahwah, NJ: Erlbaum.

Gass, S. and Varonis, E. (1994) Input, interaction, and second language production. *Studies in Second Language Acquisition*, 16(3): 283–302.

Gee, J.P. (2005) *An Introduction to Discourse Analysis: Theory and Method.* Second edition. London: Routledge.

Gee, J.P. (2007) *Social Linguistics and Literacies: Ideology in Action.* London: Taylor and Francis.

Giroux, H.A. (1983) *Theory and Resistance in Education: A Pedagogy for the Opposition.* London: Heinemann.

Goh, C. (1997) Metacognitive awareness and second language listeners. *ELT Journal*, 51(4): 361–369.

Gordon, L. (2008) Writing and good language learners. In Griffiths, C. (ed.), *Lessons from Good Language Learners.* Cambridge, UK: Cambridge University Press: 244–254.

Grabe, W. (1988) Reassessing the term "interactive." In Carrell, P.L., Devine, J. and Eskey, D.E. (eds), *Interactive Approaches to Second Language Reading.* Cambridge: Cambridge University Press: 56–70.

Grabe, W. and Kaplan, R.B. (1996) *Theory and Practice of Writing: An Applied Linguistic Perspective.* New York: Longman.

Grabe, W. and Stoller, F. (2000) *Teaching and Researching Reading.* London: Longman.

Graham, S. and Harris, K. (1996) Self-regulation and strategy instruction for students who find writing and learning challenging. In Levy, C.M. and Ransdell, S. (eds), *The Science of Writing: Theories, Methods, Individual Differences, and Applications.* Mahwah, NJ: Erlbaum: 347–360.

Graham, S. and Harris, K. (2000) Writing development: the role of cognitive, motivational, and social/contextual factors. *Educational Psychologist*, 35(1): 3–12.

Green, J. and Oxford, R. (1995) A closer look at learning strategies, L2 proficiency and sex differences. *TESOL Quarterly*, 29(2): 261–297.

Greeno, J.G. (1998) The situativity of knowing, learning, and research. *American Psychologist*, 53(1): 5–26.

Grenfell, M. and Harris, V. (1999) *Modern Languages and Learning Strategies in Theory and Practice.* London: Routledge.

Grenfell, M. and Harris, V. (2004) Language-learning strategies: a case for cross-curricular collaboration. *Language Awareness*, 13(2): 116–130.

Grenfell, M. and Macaro, E. (2007) Claims and critiques. In Cohen, A. and Macaro, E. (eds), *Thirty Years of Research and Practice.* Oxford, UK: Oxford University Press: 9–28.

Griffiths, C. (2003a) Patterns of language learning strategy use. *System*, 31: 367–383.

Griffiths, C. (2003b) *Language Learning Strategy Use and Proficiency. http://hdl.handle.net/ 2292/9*

Griffiths, C. (ed.) (2008) *Lessons from Good Language Learners*. Cambridge, UK: Cambridge University Press.

Grotjahn, R. (1987) On the methodological basis of introspective methods. In Faerch, C. and Kasper, G. (eds), *Introspection in Second Language Research*. Clevedon, UK: Multilingual Matters: 54–81.

Gu, P. (1996) Robin Hood in SLA: What has the learning strategy researcher taught us? *Asian Journal of English Language Teaching*, 6: 1–29.

Gu, P. (2008) *Listening Strategies of Primary School Pupils in Singapore*. Paper presented at the conference of the International Association for Applied Linguistics, Essen, Germany

Gu, P.Y. and Johnson, R.K. (1996) Vocabulary learning strategies and language learning outcomes. *Language Learning*, 46: 643–679.

Gu, Y. (2010) Advance review: A new book on *Teaching and Researching Language Learning Strategies*. Unpublished review, Wellington University, N.Z.

Guba, E. and Lincoln, Y. (1981) *Effective Evaluation*. San Francisco: Jossey-Bass.

Guiora, A.Z. (1983) The dialectic of language acquisition. *Language Learning*, 33: 3–12.

Gumperz, J. (ed.) (1982) *Language and Social Identity*. Cambridge: Cambridge University Press.

Gunning, P. (1997) *The Learning Strategies of Beginning ESL Learners at the Primary Level*. Unpublished master's thesis, Montréal: Concordia University.

Gunning, P. (2002) *A New Twist to English*, Cycle 3, Book 1. Montreal: Lidec.

Gunning, P. (2003) *A New Twist to English*, Cycle 3, Book 2. Montreal: Lidec.

Gunning, P. (2008) *Task-Based Children's SILL*. Unpublished manuscript, Montréal: Concordia University.

Gunning, P. and Lalonde, R. (1997) *The Spinning Series*, Level 2. Montreal: Lidec.

Gunning, P., Lalonde, R., Schinck, M., and Watts, W. (2001) *A New Twist to English*, Cycle 2, Book I. Montreal: Lidec.

Gunning, P., Lalonde, R., Schinck, M., and Watts, W. (2001) *A New Twist to English*, Cycle 2, Book 2. Montreal: Lidec.

Gunning, P., Lalonde, R., and Watts, W. (2007) *A Tiny Twist to English*, Cycle 1, Book 2. Montreal: Lidec.

Gunning, P., Oxford, R., and Gatbonton, E. (2006) The ESL learning strategies of Québecois Francophone children. Unpublished manuscript, Montréal: Concordia University.

Haberlandt, K. (1998) *Human Memory: Exploration and Application*. Boston: Allyn & Bacon.

Hajer, M., Meestringa, T., Park, Y., and Oxford, R.L. (1996) How print materials provide strategy instruction in various countries. In Oxford, R.L. (ed.), *Language Learning Strategies around the World: Crosscultural Perspectives*. Manoa: University of Hawai'i Press: 119–140.

Hall, J.K. (2010) *Teaching and Researching Language and Culture*. Second edition. Harlow, Essex, UK: Pearson Longman/Beijing: Foreign Language Teaching and Research Press. (First edition 2003/2005.)

Harris, K. and Graham, S. (1992) *Helping Young Writers Master the Craft*. Cambridge: MA: Brookline Books.

Harris, K. and Graham, S. (2005) *Writing Better: Effective Strategies for Teaching Students with Learning Disabilities*. Baltimore, MD: Brookes.

Harris, V. (2003) Adapting classroom-based strategy instruction to a distance learning context. *TESL-EJ*, 7(2): 1–19. *http://www-writing.berkeley.edu/TESL-EJ/ej26/a1.html*

Harris, A., Yuill, N., and Luckin, R. (2008) The influence of context-specific and dispositional achievement goals on children's paired collaborative interaction. *British Journal of Educational Psychology*, 78(3): 355–374.

Hauck, M. and Hurd, S. (2005) Exploring the link between language anxiety and learner self-management in open language learning contexts. *European Journal of Open, Distance, and E-learning. http://www.eurodl.org/materials/contrib/2005/Mirjam_Hauck.htm#Language%20Anxiety*

Hinkel, E. (ed.) (2005) *Handbook of Research in Second Language Teaching and Learning.* London: Routledge.

Holliday, A. (2003) Social autonomy: addressing the dangers of culturism in TESOL. In Palfreyman, D. and Smith, R.C. (eds), *Learner Autonomy across Cultures: Language Education Perspectives.* London: Palgrave Macmillan: 110–128.

Holschuh, J.P. and Aultman, L.P. (2008) Comprehension development. In Flippo, R.F. and Caverly, D.C. (eds), *Handbook of College Reading and Study Strategy Research.* London: Routledge: 121–144.

Homiak, M. (2007) Moral character. *Stanford Encyclopedia of Philosophy.* Palo Alto, CA: Stanford University. *http://plato.stanford.edu/entries/moral-character/*

Horwitz, E.K. (1987) Surveying student beliefs about language learning. In Wenden, A. and Rubin, J. (eds), *Learner Strategies in Language Learning.* Englewood Cliffs, NJ: Prentice Hall: 119–129.

Horwitz, E.K. (1999) Cultural and situational influences on foreign language learners' beliefs about language learning: a review of BALLI studies. *System*, 27(4): 557–576.

Horwitz, E. (2007) Words fail me: foreign language anxiety crippling for some students. E. Horwitz interviewed by K. Randall. *University of Texas at Austin Feature Story. http://www.utexas.edu/features/2007/language/*

Horwitz, E. and Young, D.J. (eds) (1991) *Language Anxiety: From Theory and Research to Classroom Implications.* Englewood Cliffs, NJ: Prentice Hall.

Hosenfeld, C. (1977) A preliminary investigation of the reading strategies of successful and nonsuccessful second language learners. *System*, 5(2): 110–123.

Howatt, A.P.R. (1984) *A History of English Language Teaching.* Oxford: Oxford University Press.

Hsiao, T. and Oxford, R.L. (2002) Comparing theories of language learning strategies: a confirmatory factor analysis. *Modern Language Journal*, 86(3): 368–383.

Hughes, R. (2010). *Teaching and Researching Speaking.* Second edition. London: Pearson/Longman.

Hurd, S., Beaven, T., and Ortega, A. (2001) Developing autonomy in a distance language learning context: issues and dilemmas for course writers. *System*, 29: 341–355.

Hurd, S. and Xiao, J. (2006) Open and distance language learning at the Shantou Radio and TV University, China, and the Open University, United Kingdom: a cross-cultural perspective. *Open Learning*, 21(3): 205–219.

Husman, J., McCann, E.J., and Crowson, H.M. (2000) Volitional strategies and future time perspective: embracing the complexity of dynamic interactions. *International Journal of Educational Research*, 33: 777–799.

Hyland, K. (2003) *Second Language Writing.* Cambridge: Cambridge University Press.

Ikeda, M. and Takeuchi, O. (2003) Can strategy instruction help EFL learners to improve their reading ability?: An empirical study. *JACET Bulletin*, 37: 49–60.

International Center for Enhancement of Learning Potential (2007) Feuerstein Partnership: Evaluation Report – Executive Summary. *http://www.icelp.org/asp/News_data.asp?id=71*

Jaccard, J. and Wan, C.K. (1996) *LISREL Approaches to Interaction Effects in Multiple Regression*. Thousand Oaks, CA: Sage.

Jacobsen, M.J., Maouri, C., Mishra, P., and Kolar, C. (1995) Learning with hypertext learning environments: theory, design, and research. *Journal of Educational Multimedia and Hypermedia*, 4(4): 321–364.

Jacobson, R. and Faltis, C. (1990) *Language Distribution Issues in Bilingual Schooling*. Clevedon, UK: Multilingual Matters.

James, W. (1910/1987) *Writings 1902–1910*. Second edition. New York: Library of America.

Johnson, B. (2001) Toward a new classification of nonexperimental quantitative research. *Educational Researcher*, 30(2): 3–13.

Johnson, H. (1999) *Encyclopedic Dictionary of Applied Linguistics: A Handbook for Language Teaching*. Oxford, UK: Wiley-Blackwell.

Johnson, R.B. and Christensen, L.B. (2000) *Educational Research: Quantitative and Qualitative Approaches*. Boston: Allyn and Bacon.

Johnson-Laird, P. (1990) What is communication? In Mellor, D. (ed.), *Ways of Communicating*. Cambridge: Cambridge University Press.

Jones, C. (1999) Contextualise and personalize: key strategies for vocabulary acquisition. *ReCALL*, 11(3): 34–40.

Josselson, R. (1995) Imagining the real: empathy, narrative, and the dialogic self. In R. Josselson and A. Lieblich (eds), *Interpreting Experience: The Narrative Study of Lives*. Thousand Oaks, CA: Sage: 27–44.

Josselson, R. and Lieblich, A. (eds) (1995) *Interpreting Experience: The Narrative Study of Lives*. Newbury Park, CA: Sage.

Kajala, P. and Barcelos, A.M.F. (2003) *Beliefs about SLA: New Research Approaches*. Dordrecht: Kluwer.

Kamil, M.L., Mosenthal, P.B., Pearson, P.D., and Barr, B. (eds) (2000) *Handbook of Reading Research*, Vol. III. Mahwah, NJ: Erlbaum.

Kanno, Y. and Norton, B. (2003) Imagined communities and educational possibilities: an introduction. *Journal of Language, Identity, and Education*, 2(4): 241–249.

Kant, I. (1788/1997) *Critique of Practical Reason*. M.J. McGregor (ed.) Cambridge, UK: Cambridge University Press.

Kasper, L.F. (1997) Assessing the metacognitive growth of ESL student writers. *TESL-EJ*, 3(1). *http://tesl-ej.org/ej09/a1abs.html*

Kato, F. (1996) Results of an Australian study of strategy use in learning Japanese Kanji characters. Unpublished manuscript, University of Sydney, Australia.

Kauffman, D. and Husman, J. (2004) Effects of time perspective on student motivation: Introduction to a special issue. *Educational Psychology Review*, 16: 1–7.

Keatley, C.W., Anstrom, K.A., and Chamot, A.U. (2004) *Keys to Learning: Skills and Strategies for Newcomers*. New York: Pearson EFL.

Keeves, J.P. and Watanabe, R. (eds) (2003) *The International Handbook of Educational Research in the Asia-Pacific Region*. New York: Springer.

Keh, C.L. (1990) Feedback in the writing process: a model and methods for implementation. *EFL Journal*, 44(4): 294–304.

Kent, T. (ed.) (1999) *Post-Process Theory: Beyond the Writing-Process Paradigm*. Carbondale, IL: Southern Illinois University Press.

King, G., Keohane, R.O., and Verba, S. (1994) *Designing Social Inquiry: Scientific Inference in Qualitative Research*. Princeton, NJ: Princeton University Press.

Kojic-Sabo, I. and Lightbown, P.M. (1999) Students' approaches to vocabulary learning and their relationship to success. *Modern Language Journal*, 83(2): 522–533.

Koriat, A. (2002) Metacognition research: An interim report. In Perfect, T.J. and Schwartz, B.L. (eds), *Applied Metacognition*. Cambridge, UK: Cambridge University Press: 261–286.

Koro-Ljungberg, M. (2008) Validity and validation in the making in the context of qualitative research. *Qualitative Health Research*, 18: 983–989.

Kowal, M. and Swain, M. (1994) Using collaborative language production tasks to promote students' language awareness. *Language Awareness*, 3(2): 73–93.

Kozulin, A. (2005, Apr.) Who needs metacognition more: students or teachers? Paper presented at the Annual Meeting of American Educational Research Association, Montréal, Canada.

Kozulin, A. and Garb, E. (2001, Aug.) Dynamic assessment of EFL text comprehension of at-risk students. Paper presented at the Ninth Conference of the European Association for Research on Learning and Instruction, Fribourg, Switzerland. *http://www.icelp.org/files/research/DynamicAssessOfESL.pdf*

Kozulin, A., Gindis, B., Ageyev, V.S., and Miller, S.M. (2003) *Vygotsky's Educational Theory in Cultural Context.* Cambridge, UK: Cambridge University Press.

Kramsch, C. (1998) *Language and Culture*. Oxford: Oxford University Press.

Ku, P.N. (1995) *Strategies Associated with Proficiency and Predictors of Strategy Choice: A Study of Language Learning Strategies of EFL Students at Three Educational Levels in Taiwan*. Unpublished doctoral dissertation, Indiana University, Bloomington, IN.

Kuhl, J. (1984) Volitional aspects of achievement motivation and learned helplessness: toward a comprehensive theory of action control. In Maher, B.A. and Maher, W.B. (eds), *Progress in Experimental Personality Research*. Orlando: Academic Press: 101–171.

Kuhl, J. (2000) A functional-design approach to motivation and self-regulation: the dynamics of personality systems interactions. In Boekaerts, M., Pintrich, P.R., and Zeidner, M. (eds), *Self-Regulation: Directions and Challenges for Future Research*. New York: Academic Press: 111–169.

Kumaravadivelu, B. (1993) Maximizing learning potential in the communicative classroom. *ELT Journal*, 47(5): 12–21.

Kuusela, H. and Paul, P. (2000) A comparison of concurrent and retrospective verbal protocol analysis. *American Journal of Psychology*, 113(3): 387–404.

Lan, R. (2008) *Language Learning Strategies of Young Taiwanese Learners*. Paper presented at the conference of the International Association for Applied Linguistics, Essen, Germany.

Lan, R.L. and Oxford, R.L. (2003) Language learning strategy profiles of elementary school students in Taiwan. *International Review of Applied Linguistics and Language Teaching*, 41(4): 339–379.

Language Teaching Journal. *http://journals.cambridge.org/action/displayJournal?jid=LTA*

Lather, P. (1993) Fertile obsession: validity after poststructuralism. *Sociological Quarterly*, 34(4): 673–693.

Lave, J. and Wenger, E. (1991) *Situated Learning: Legitimate Peripheral Participation*. Cambridge: Cambridge University Press.

Lavine, R. (2008) Strategy Metascripts. Unpublished manuscript, University of Maryland, College Park, MD.

Lavine, R. and Cabal Krastel, T. (1994) ¡Sí, Puedo! Maximizing Textbooks and Materials for Students with Learning Disabilities. Paper presented at the Annual Meeting of the American Council on the Teaching of Foreign Languages, Chicago, IL.

Law, Y-K., Chan, C.K.K., and Sachs, J. (2008) Beliefs about learning, self-regulated strategies, and text comprehension among Chinese children. *British Journal of Educational Psychology*, 78(1): 51–73.

Lawrence, N.S., Ross, T.J., Hoffman, R., Garavan, H., and Stein, E.A. (2003) *Multiple Neuronal Networks Mediate Sustained Attention*. Cambridge, MA: MIT Press.

Lawson, M.J. and Hogben, D. (1998) Learning and recall of foreign language vocabulary: effects of a keyword strategy for immediate and delayed recall. *Learning and Instruction*, 8: 179–194.

Leaver, B.L. (1990) *Navigating the DSL Czech Course: A Guide for Students*. Monterey, CA: Defense Language Institute.

Leaver, B.L. (2003a) *Achieving Native-like Second Language Proficiency: A Catalogue of Critical Factors. Vol. 1: Speaking*. Salinas, CA: MSI Press.

Leaver, B.L. (2003b) *Individualized Study Plans for Very Advanced Students of Foreign Languages*. Salinas, CA: MSI Press.

Leaver, B.L. (2008) Keynote address. In D.B. Butler and Y. Zhou (eds), *Teaching and Learning to Near-Native Levels of Language Proficiency IV: Proceedings of the Spring and Fall 2006 Conferences of the Consortium of Distinguished Language Centers*. San Juan Bautista, CA: MSI Press: 9–14.

Leaver, B.L., Ehrman, M., and Shekhtman, B. (2005) *Achieving Success in Second Language Acquisition*. Cambridge, UK: Cambridge University Press.

Leaver, B.L. and Shekhtman, B. (2004) *Teaching and Learning to Near-native Levels of Language Proficiency: Proceedings of the Spring and Fall 2003 Conferences of the Coalition of Distinguished Language Centers*. Salinas, CA: MSI Press.

LeDoux, J. (1996) *The Emotional Brain*. New York: Simon & Schuster.

Lee, J. and Van Patten, B. (1995) *Making Communicative Language Teaching Happen*. New York: McGraw-Hill.

Lee, K.R. (2007) *Strategy Awareness-Raising for Success: Reading Strategy Instruction in the EFL Context*. Unpublished doctoral dissertation, University of Maryland, College Park, MD, USA.

Lee, K.R. and Oxford, R.L. (2008) Understanding EFL learners' strategy use and strategy awareness. *Asian EFL Journal*, 10(1): 7–32.

Leontiev (Leont'ev), A.N. (1974/1984) Der allgemeine Tätigkeitsbegriff [The general activity concept]. In Viehweger, D. (ed.), *Grundfragen einer Theorie der sprachlichen Tätigkeit*. Stuttgart: Kohlhammer: 13–30.

Leontiev (Leont'ev), A.N. (1978) *Activity, Consciousness, and Personality*. Englewood Cliffs, NJ: Prentice Hall.

Leontiev (Leont'ev), A.N. (1981) The concept of activity in Soviet Psychology, an introduction. In Wertsch, J. (ed.), *The Concept of Activity in Soviet Psychology*. Armonk, NY: Sharpe.

Lessard-Clouston, M. (1996) ESL vocabulary learning in a TOEFL preparation class: a case study. *Canadian Modern Language Review*, 53(1): 97–119.

Levine, A., Reves, T., and Leaver, B.L. (1996) Relationship between language learning strategies and Israeli versus Russian cultural-educational factors. In Oxford, R.L. (ed.), *Language Learning Strategies around the World: Crosscultural Perspectives*. Manoa: University of Hawai'i Press: 35–45.

Levine, G. (2008) Exploring intercultural communicative competence through L2 learners' intercultural moments. In Schulz, R. and Tschirner, E. (eds), *Crossing Borders: Developing Intercultural Competence in German as a Foreign Language*. Munich: Iudicium.

Lewis, M. (1999) *How to Study a Foreign Language*. Houndsmills, Basingstoke: Palgrave Macmillan.

Li, J. and Qin, X. (2006) Language learning styles and learning strategies of tertiary learners in China. *RELC Journal: A Journal of Language Teaching and Research*, 37(1): 67–90.

Linnenbrink, E.A. (2005) The dilemma of performance-approach goals: the use of multiple goal contexts to promote students' motivation and learning. *Journal of Educational Psychology*, 97: 197–213.

Little, D. (2003, 16 Jan.) Learner autonomy and second/foreign language learning. *The Higher Education Academy Guide to Good Practice. http://www.llas.ac.uk/resources/gpg/1409*

Little, D. (2006) The Common European Framework of Reference for Languages: content, purpose, origin, reception and impact. *Language Teaching*, 39: 167–190.

LoCastro, V. (1994) Learning strategies and learning environments. *TESOL Quarterly*, 28(2): 409–414.

Locke, E.A. (1996) Motivation through conscious goal setting. *Applied and Preventive Psychology*, 5: 117–124.

Ma, X. and Research Team. (2006) *Personalized English Learning System: Diagnosis and Advice*. Xi'an Jiaotong University, Xi'an, China. *http://220.200.164.6:8086/*

Macaro, E. (2001a) *Learning Strategies in Foreign and Second Language Classrooms*. London: Continuum.

Macaro, E. (2001b) *Strategies in Foreign and Second Language Classrooms: Learning to Learn*. London: Cassell.

Macaro, E. (2006) Strategies for language learning and for language use: revising the theoretical framework. *Modern Language Journal*, 90(3): 320–337.

Macaro, E. (2007) My experience with strategies. Unpublished manuscript, Oxford University, Oxford, UK.

Macaro, E., Graham, S., and Vanderplank, R. (2007) A review of listening strategies: focus on sources of knowledge and on success. In Cohen, A.D. and Macaro, E. (eds), *Language Learner Strategies*. Oxford, UK: Oxford University Press: 165–185.

MacIntyre, P.D. (2002) Motivation, anxiety, and emotion in second language acquisition. In Robinson, P. (ed.), *Individual Differences and Instructed Language Learning*. Amsterdam: John Benjamins: 45–68.

MacIntyre, P.D. (2003, June 1) Willingness to Communicate in the Second Language: Proximal and Distal Influences. Paper presented at the annual conference of the Canadian Association of Applied Linguistics, Halifax, NS, Canada.

MacIntyre, P.D., Baker, S., Clément, R., and Donovan, L.A. (2003) Talking in order to learn: willingness to communicate and intensive language programs. *Canadian Modern Language Review*, 59: 589–607.

MacIntyre, P.D., Clément, R., Dörnyei, Z., and Noels, K.A. (1998) Conceptualising willingness to communicate in a L2: a situational model of L2 confidence and affiliation. *Modern Language Journal*, 82, 545–562.

Mackey, A. and Gass, S.M. (2005) *Second Language Research: Methodology and Design*. Mahwah, NJ: Erlbaum.

Malpass, J.R., O'Neil, H.F., and Hocevar, D. (1999) Self-regulation, goal orientation, self-efficacy, worry, and high-stakes math achievement for mathematically gifted high school students. *Roeper Review*, 21(4): 281–288.

Manchón, R.M. (2001) Trends in the conceptualizations of second language composing strategies: a critical analysis. *International Journal of English Studies* 1(2): 47–70.

Manchón, R.M., Roca de Larios, J., and Murphy, L. (2007) A review of writing strategies: focus on conceptualizations and impact of first language. In Cohen, A. and Macaro, E. (eds), *Language Learner Strategies: Thirty Years of Research and Practice*. Oxford, UK: Oxford University Press: 229–250.

Mandler, G. (2001) Remembering. In Underwood, G. (ed.), *Oxford Guide to the Mind*. Oxford, UK: Oxford University Press: 30–32.

Mariani, L. (2004) Learning to learn with the CEF. In Morrow, K. (ed.), *Insights from the Common European Framework*. Oxford: Oxford University Press: 32–42.

Marsh, H.W. (1984) Self-concept, social comparison, and ability grouping: A reply to Kulik and Kulik. *American Educational Research Journal*, 21(4): 799–806.

Martella, R.C., Nelson, J.R., and Marchand-Martella, N.E. (1999) *Research Methods: Learning to Become a Critical Research Consumer*. Boston, MA: Allyn and Bacon.

Matsumoto, K. (1994) Introspection, verbal reports and second language learning strategy research. *The Canadian Modern Language Review*, 50(2): 363–386.

Maxwell, J.A. (1992) Understanding and validity in qualitative research. *Harvard Educational Review*, 62(3): 279–300.

McCaslin, M. and Hickey, D.T. (2001) Self-regulated learning and academic achievement: A Vygotskian view. In Zimmerman, B.J. and Schunk, D. (eds), *Self-regulated Learning and Academic Achievement*. Second edition. Mahwah, NJ: Erlbaum: 227–252.

McClelland, J.L., McNaughton, B.L., and O'Reilly, R.C. (1995) Why there are complementary learning systems in the hippocampus and the neocortex. *Psychological Review*, 102: 419–457.

McDonough, S.H. (1999) Learner strategies: State of the art article. *Language Teaching*, 32: 1–18.

McIntosh, C.N. and Noels, K.A. (2004) Self-determined motivation for language learning: The role of need for cognition and language learning strategies. *Zeitschrift für Interkulturellen Fremdsprachenunterricht*, 9(2). *http://zif.spz.tu-darmstadt.de/jg-09-2/beitrag/Mcintosh2.htm*

Mendelsohn, D.J. and Rubin, J. (eds) (1995) *A Guide for the Teaching of Second Language Listening*. San Diego, CA: Dominie Press.

Meskill, C. (1991) Language learning strategy advice: a study on the effects of on-line messaging. *System*, 19(3): 277–287.

Miles, M.B. and Huberman, A.M. (1994) *Qualitative Data Analysis*. Second edition. Thousand Oaks, CA: Sage.

Mills, G.E. (2000) *Action Research: A Guide for the Teacher Researcher*. Columbus, OH: Merrill.

Mokhtari, K. (1998–2000) *Metacognitive Awareness of Reading Strategies Inventory (MARSI)*. Unpublished instrument, Oklahoma State University, Stillwater, OK.

Mokhtari, K. and Reichard, C.A. (2002) Assessing students' metacognitive awareness of reading strategies. *Journal of Educational Psychology*, 94(2): 249–259.

Moustakas, C. (1994) *Phenomenological Research Methods*. Thousand Oaks, CA: Sage.

Nakatani, Y. (2005) The effects of awareness-raising training on oral communication strategy use. *Modern Language Journal*, 89: 76–91.

Nakatani, Y. and Goh, C. (2007) A review of oral communication strategies: focus on interactionist and psycholinguistic perspectives. In Cohen, A. and Macaro, E. (eds), *Language Learner Strategies: Thirty Years of Research and Practice*. Oxford, UK: Oxford University Press.

Nam, C. and Oxford, R.L. (1998) Portrait of a future teacher: Case study of learning styles, strategies, and language disabilities. *System* 26(1): 51–63.

Nation, I.S.P. (1990) *Teaching and Learning Vocabulary*. New York: Newbury House.

Nation, I.S.P. and Waring, R. (1997) Vocabulary size, text coverage, and word lists. *http://www1.harenet.ne.jp/~waring/papers/cup.html*

National Capital Language Resource Center (NCLRC) (2000a) *Elementary Immersion Students' Perceptions of Language Learning Strategies Use and Self-Efficacy*. ERIC Document Reproduction Service ED 445 521; FL 026 392.

National Capital Language Resource Center (NCLRC) (2000b) *High School Foreign Language Students' Perceptions of Language Learning Strategies Use and Self-Efficacy*. ERIC Document Reproduction Service ED 445 517; FL 026 388.

National Capital Language Resource Center (NCLRC) (2003) *Elementary Immersion Learning Strategies Resource Guide*. Washington, DC: National Capital Language Resource Center.

National Capital Language Resource Center (NCLRC) (2004a) *Secondary Education Strategies Resource Guide*. Washington, DC: National Capital Language Resource Center.

National Capital Language Resource Center (NCLRC) (2004b) *Higher Education Strategies Resource Guide*. Washington, DC: National Capital Language Resource Center. *http://www.nclrc.org/guides/HED/*

Nelson, T.O. and Narens, L. (1994) Why investigate metacognition? In Metcalf, J. and Shimamura, A.P. (eds), *Metacognition: Knowing about Knowing*. Cambridge, MA: MIT Press: 1–26.

Newell, A. and Simon, H.A. (1972) *Human Problem Solving*. Englewood Cliffs, N.J.: Prentice Hall.

Niness, C., Rumph, R., Vasquez, E., Bradfield, A., and Niness, S. (2002) Multivariate randomization tests for small-N behavioral research: A web-based application. *Behavior and Social Issues*, 12: 64–74.

Nisbett, R. (2004) *The Geography of Thought: How Asians and Westerners Think Differently . . . and Why*. New York: Free Press.

Noels, K.A. (2001) New orientations in language learning motivation: Towards a model of intrinsic, extrinsic, and integrative orientations. In Dörnyei, Z. and Schmidt, R.W. (eds), *Motivation and Second Language Acquisition*. Honolulu, HI: University of Hawai'i Second Language Teaching and Curriculum Center: 43–68.

Noels, K.A., Pelletier, L., Clément, R., and Vallerand, R.J. (2000) Why are you learning a second language? Motivational orientations and self-determination theory. *Language Learning*, 50(1): 57–856.

Norquest. (2007) Nine quick learning strategies for success: Strategy 10: Smart goal setting. *http://student.norquest.ca/onlinelearning/ninequick/strategies/goals.htm#strategy*

Norton, B. (2010) *Identity and Language Learning: Gender, Ethnicity and Educational Change*. Second edition. London: Longman/Pearson Education. (First edition 2000.)

Norton, B. (2001) Non-participation, imagined communities, and the language classroom. In Breen, M. (ed.), *Learner Contributions to Language Learning: New Directions in Research*. London: Longman: 159–171.

Norton, B. and Toohey, K. (2001) Changing perspectives on good language learners. *TESOL Quarterly*, 35(2): 307–322.

Norton Pierce, B. (1995) Social identity, investment and language learning, *TESOL Quarterly*, 29(1): 9–31.

Nunan, D. and Benson, P. (2005) *Learners' Stories: Difference and Diversity in Language Learning*. Cambridge, UK: Cambridge University Press.

Nyikos, M. and Fan, M. (2007) A review of vocabulary learning strategies: focus on language proficiency and learner voice. In Cohen, A.D. and Macaro, E. (eds), *Language Learner Strategies*. Oxford, UK: Oxford University Press: 251–273.

Nyikos, M. and Oxford, R. (1993) A factor analytic study of language learning strategy use: Interpretations from information processing theory and social psychology. *Modern Language Journal*, 77(1): 11–22.

Oliphant, K. (1997) Acquisition of grammatical gender in Italian as a foreign language. Second Language Teaching and Curriculum Center, University of Hawai'i, Manoa. *http://www.nflrc.hawaii.edu/NetWorks/NW07/default.html*

Olshtain, E. and Cohen, A. (1989) Speech act behaviour across languages. In Dechert, H. and Manfred, R. (eds), *Transfer in Language Production*. Norwood, NJ: Ablex, 53–67.

O'Malley, J.M. and Chamot, A.U. (1990) *Learning Strategies in Second Language Acquisition*. Cambridge: Cambridge University Press.

O'Malley, J.M., Chamot, A.U., and Küpper, L. (1989) Listening comprehension strategies in second language acquisition. *Applied Linguistics*, 10(4): 418–437.

O'Malley, J.M., Chamot, A.U., Stewner-Manzanares, G., Küpper, L., and Russo, R.P. (1985) Learning strategy applications with students of English as a second language. *TESOL Quarterly*, 19(3): 285–296.

O'Malley, J.M., Chamot, A.U., and Walker, C. (1987) Some applications of cognitive theory in second language acquisition. *Studies in Second Language Acquisition*, 9(3): 287–306.

O'Neil, H.F. (ed.) (1978) *Learning Strategies*. New York: Academic Press.

O'Neil, H.F. (ed.) (2005) *What Works in Distance Learning Guidelines*. Los Angeles: University of Southern California/CRESST.

O'Neil, H.F. (ed.) (2008) *What Works in Distance Learning: Sample Lessons Based on Guidelines*. Los Angeles: University of Southern California: CRESST.

O'Neil, H.F. and Spielberger, C. (ed.) (1979) *Cognitive and Affective Learning Strategies*. New York: Academic Press.

Oxford, R.L. (1986) *Development and Psychometric Testing of the Strategy Inventory for Language Learning (SILL)*. ARI Technical Report 728. Alexandria, VA: Training Research Laboratory, US Army Research Institute for the Behavioral and Social Sciences.

Oxford, R.L. (1989) "The Best and the Worst": An exercise to tap perceptions of language-learning experiences and strategies. *Foreign Language Annals*, 22(5): 447–454.

Oxford, R.L. (1990) *Language Learning Strategies: What Every Teacher Should Know*. Boston: Heinle and Heinle/Cengage.

Oxford, R.L. (1996a) Employing a questionnaire to assess the use of language learning strategies. *Applied Language Learning*, 7: 25–45.

Oxford, R.L. (ed.) (1996b) *Language Learning Strategies around the World: Cross-cultural Perspectives*. Manoa: University of Hawai'i Press.

Oxford, R.L. (1996c) When emotion meets (meta)cognition in language learning histories. *The teaching of culture and language in the second language classroom: Focus on the learner*. Special issue. Moeller, A. (ed.), *International Journal of Educational Research* 23(7): 581–594.

Oxford, R.L. (1998) Anxiety and the language learner: New insights. In Arnold, J. (ed.), *Affective Language Learning*. Cambridge, UK: Cambridge University Press.

Oxford, R. (1999a) Relationships between second language learning strategies and language proficiency in the context of learner autonomy and self-regulation. *Revista Canaria de Estudios Ingleses*, 38: 108–126.

Oxford, R. (1999b) *The Strategy Inventory for Language Learning*. Theoretical Context, Research, and Concerns. Paper presented at the meeting of the International Association for Applied Linguistics, Tokyo, Japan.

Oxford, R.L. (2001) Language learning styles and strategies. In Celce-Murcia, M. (ed.), *Teaching English as a second language*. Boston: Heinle/Thomson Learning: 359–366.

Oxford, R.L. (2003) Toward a more systematic model of second language learner autonomy. In Palfreyman, D. and Smith, R. (eds), *Learner Autonomy across Cultures*. London: Palgrave Macmillan.

Oxford, R.L. (2007) Co-teaching English. Keynote presentation at the Second Annual Conference on Co-Teaching, Hinschu City, Taiwan.

Oxford, R.L. (2008a) Learning strategies and autonomy in second or foreign language (L2) learning. In Lewis, T. and Hurd, S. (eds), *Language Learning Strategies in Independent Settings*. Clevedon, UK: Multilingual Matters: 41–66.

Oxford, R.L. (2008b) White water: Sensory learning styles in the Digital Age. *Essays in Honor of Dr. Hyo Woong Lee*. Pusan: Korea Maritime University: 191–200.

Oxford, R.L. (2010) Learner autonomy in the crucible. In A.M.F. Barcelos (ed.), *Applied linguistics: Reflections on learning and teaching native language and foreign language. [Lingüística aplicada: Reflexões sobre ensino e aprendizagem de lingua materna e lingua estrangeira]*. Campinas, Brazil: Pontes Publishers.

Oxford, R.L. and Burry-Stock, J.A. (1995) Assessing the use of language learning strategies worldwide with the ESL/EFL version of the *Strategy Inventory for Language Learning (SILL)*. *System*, 23(1): 1–23.

Oxford, R.L., Cho, Y., Leung, S., and Kim, H. (2004) Effect of the presence and difficulty of task on strategy use: An exploratory study. *International Review of Applied Linguistics and Language Teaching*, 42: 1–47.

Oxford, R.L. and Cohen, A.D. (1992) Language learning strategies: Crucial issues in concept and classification. *Applied Language Learning*, 3(1–2): 1–35.

Oxford, R.L. and Crookall, D. (1989) Research on language learning strategies: methods, findings, and instructional issues. *Modern Language Journal*, 73(4): 403–419.

Oxford, R.L. and Ehrman, M.E. (1995) Adults' language learning strategies in an intensive foreign language program in the United States. *System*, 23(3): 359–386.

Oxford, R.L., Lavine, R.Z., Felkins, G., Hollaway, M.E., and Saleh, A. (1996) Telling their stories: language students use diaries and recollection. In Oxford, R.L. (ed.), *Language Learning Strategies around the World: Cross-Cultural Perspectives*. Honolulu: University of Hawa'i Press: 19–34.

Oxford, R.L. and Leaver, B.L. (1996) A synthesis of strategy instruction for language learners. In Oxford, R.L. (ed.), *Language Learning Strategies around the World: Cross-cultural Perspectives*. Manoa: University of Hawai'i Press: 227–246.

Oxford, R.L. and Lee, K.R. (2007) L2 grammar strategies: the second Cinderella and beyond. In Cohen, A. and Macaro, E. (eds), *Language Learner Strategies: Thirty Years of Research and Practice*. Oxford, UK: Oxford University Press: 117–139.

Oxford, R.L., Massey, K.R., and Anand, S. (2005) Transforming teacher-student style relationships: toward a more welcoming and diverse classroom discourse. In Holten, C. and Frodesen, J. (eds), *The Power of Discourse in Language Learning and Teaching*. Boston: Heinle and Heinle: 249–266.

Oxford, R.L., Meng, Y., Zhou, Y., Sung, J., and Jain, R. (2007) Uses of adversity: moving beyond L2 learning crises. In Barfield, A. and Brown, S. (eds), *Reconstructing Autonomy in Language Education: Inquiry and Innovation.* London: Palgrave Macmillan: 131–142.

Oxford, R.L. and Nyikos, M. (1989) Variables affecting choice of language learning strategies by university students. *Modern Language Journal*, 73(3): 291–300.

Oxford, R.L., Park-Oh, Y., Ito, S., and Sumrall, M. (1993a). Japanese by satellite: Effects of motivation, language learning styles and strategies, gender, course level, and previous language learning experiences on Japanese language achievement. *Foreign Language Annals*, 26: 359–371.

Oxford, R.L., Park-Oh, Y., Ito, S., and Sumrall, M. (1993b). Learning a language by satellite: What influences achievement? *System*, 21: 31–48.

Oxford, R.L. and Scarcella, R.C. (1994) Second language vocabulary learning among adults: state of the art in vocabulary instruction. *System*, 22(2): 231–43.

Oxford, R.L. and Schramm, K. (2007) Bridging the gap between psychological and sociocultural perspectives on L2 learner strategies. In Cohen, A.D. and Macaro, E. (eds), *Thirty Years of Research on Language Learner Strategies.* Oxford, UK: Oxford University Press: 47–68.

Oxford, R.L. and Shearin, J. (1994) Language learning motivation: expanding the theoretical framework. *Modern Language Journal*, 78: 12–28.

Oxford, R.L. and Shearin, J. (1996) Language learning motivation in a new key. In Oxford, R.L. (ed.), *Language Learning Motivation: Pathways to the New Century.* Honolulu: University of Hawai'i Press: 121–144.

Ozeki, N. (2000) *Listening Strategy Instruction for Female EFL College Students in Japan.* Unpublished doctoral dissertation, Indiana University of Pennsylvania.

Paige, M., Cohen, A.D., Kappler, B., Chi, J., and Lassegard, J. (2006) *Maximizing Study Abroad: A Student's Guide to Strategies for Language and Culture Learning and Use.* Minneapolis, MN.

Paige, R.M., Cohen, A.D., and Shively, R. (2004) Assessing the impact of a strategies-based curriculum on language and culture learning abroad. *Frontiers: The Interdisciplinary Journal of Study Abroad* 10: 253–276.

Palincsar, A.S. and Brown, A.L. (1984) Reciprocal teaching of comprehension-fostering and comprehension-monitoring activities. *Cognition and Instruction*, 2(2): 117–175.

Paran, A. (1997) Bottom-up and top-down processing. *English Teaching Professional*, 3. http://www.rdg.ac.uk/app_ling/buptdown.htm

Paas, F., Renkl, A., and Sweller, J. (2003) Cognitive load theory and instructional design: Recent developments. *Educational Psychologist* 38(1): 1–4.

Paas, F., Renkl, A., and Sweller, J. (2004) Cognitive load theory: Instructional implications of the interaction between information structures and cognitive architecture. *Instructional Science*, 32: 1–8.

Pavlenko, A. (2002) Narrative study: whose story is it, anyway? *TESOL Quarterly*, 36: 213–218.

Pedhazur, E. and Schmelkin, L. (1991) *Measurement, Design and Analysis.* Hillsdale, NJ: Erlbaum.

Pennycook, A. (2001) *Critical Applied Linguistics: A Critical Introduction.* Mahwah, NJ: Erlbaum.

Pereira-Laird, J. and Deane, F.P. (1997) Development and validation of a self-report measure of reading strategy use. *Reading Psychology: An International Quarterly*, 18: 185–235.

Peters, M. and Burbules, N.C. (2003) *Poststructuralism and Educational Research*, Lanham, MD: Rowman and Littlefield.

Phillips, V. (1990) *English as a Second Language Learner Strategies of Adult Asian Students Using the Strategy Inventory for Language Learning.* Unpublished doctoral dissertation, University of San Francisco, San Francisco, CA.

Phillips, V. (1991, Nov.) A look at learner strategy use and ESL proficiency. *CATESOL Journal*: 57–67.

Piaget, J. (1981) *Intelligence and Affectivity: Their Relationship during Child Development.* Palo Alto, CA: Annual Reviews.

Pinter, A. (2006) Verbal evidence of task-related strategies: child versus adult interactions *System*, 34: 615–630.

Pintrich, P.R. (1999) Taking control of research on volitional control: challenges for future theory and research. *Learning and Individual Differences*, 11(3): 335–355.

Pintrich, P.R. (2000) Educational psychology at the millennium: a look back and a look forward. *Educational Psychologist*, 35(4): 221–226.

Pintrich, P.R. (2002, Autumn) The role of metacognitive knowledge in learning, teaching, and assessing. *Theory into Practice*, 41(4): 219–225.

Pintrich, P.R. and De Groot, E. (1992) An Integrated Model of Motivation and Self-Regulated Learning. Paper presented at the annual meeting of the American Educational Research Association, San Francisco, CA.

Pintrich, P.R., Marx, R.W., and Boyle, R.A. (1993) Beyond cold conceptual change: the role of motivational beliefs and contextual factors in the process of contextual change. *Review of Educational Research*, 63(2): 167–199.

Pintrich, P.R., Smith, D.A., Garcia, T., and McKeachie, W.J. (1991) *A Manual for the Use of the Motivated Strategies for Learning Questionnaire (MSLQ).* Ann Arbor, MI: National Center for Research to Improve Post Secondary Teaching and Learning (NCRIPTAL).

Politzer, R. and McGroarty, M. (1985) An exploratory study of learning behaviours and their relationships to gains in linguistic and communicative competence. *TESOL Quarterly* 19: 103–124.

Poulisse, N. (1987) Problems and solutions in the classification of compensatory strategies. *Second Language Research*, 3: 131–153.

Pressley, M. and Afflerbach, P. (1995) *Verbal Protocols of Reading: The Nature of Constructively Responsive Reading.* Hillsdale, NJ: Erlbaum.

Pressley, M. and Woloshyn, V.E. (1995) *Cognitive Strategy Instruction that Really Improves Children's Academic Performance.* Cambridge, MA: Brookline Books.

Pritchard, R. (1990) The effects of cultural schemata on reading processing strategies. *Reading Research Quarterly*, 25(4): 273–293.

Randi, J. and Corno, L. (2000) Teacher innovations in self-regulated learning. In Boekaerts, M., Pintrich, P., and Zeidner, M. (eds), *Handbook of Self-Regulation.* San Diego: Academic Press: 651–685.

Rheinberg, F., Vollmeyer, R., and Rollett, W. (2000) Motivation and action in self-regulated learning. In Boekaerts, M., Pintrich, P.R., and Zeidner, M. (eds), *Handbook of Self-Regulation.* San Diego: Academic Press: 503–529.

Reinders, H. (2009) Autonomy bibliography. *Innovation in Teaching.* http://www.hayo.nl/autonomybibliography.php#

Rees-Miller, J. (1993) A critical appraisal of learner training: theoretical bases and teaching implications. *TESOL Quarterly*, 27: 679–689.

Reiss, M-A. (1981) Helping the unsuccessful language learner. *Modern Language Journal*, 65(2): 121–128.

Reiss, M-A. (1983) Helping the unsuccessful language learner. *Forum*, 21: 2–24.

Richardson, V. (2001) *Handbook of Research on Teaching*. Second edition. Washington, DC: American Educational Research Association.

Robbins, J. (n.d.) Cuddly learning strategies: animal mascots. National Capital Language Resource Center. *www.nclrc.org/profdev/nclrc_inst_pres/summer_inst.h*

Rogers, C. (1983) *Freedom to learn for the 80s*. Columbus, OH: Charles Merrill.

Rogers, R. (2004) *Introduction to Critical Discourse Analysis*. Mahwah, NJ: Erlbaum.

Rorty, R. (1990) *Objectivity, Relativism, and Truth: Philosophical Papers*. Cambridge, UK: Cambridge University Press.

Ross, S. and Rost, M. (1991) Learner use of strategies in interaction: typology and teachability. *Language Learning*, 41(2): 236–273.

Rossiter, M. (2003) The effects of affective strategy training in the ESL classroom. *TESL-EJ*, 7(2): 20–40.

Rost, M. (2010). *Teaching and Researching Listening*. Second edition. London: Longman.

Rubin, J. (1996) Using multimedia for learner strategy instruction. In Oxford, R.L. (ed.), *Language Learning Strategies Around the World: Crosscultural Perspectives*. Manoa: University of Hawai'i Press: 151–156.

Rubin, J. (1981) Study of cognitive processes in second language learning. *Applied Linguistics* 11: 117–131.

Rubin, J. (2001) Language learner self-management. *Journal of Asian Pacific Communications*, 11: 25–37.

Rubin, J. (ed.) (2007, Mar.) *Learner Counseling*. Special issue. *System: An International Journal of Educational Technology and Applied Linguistics*, 35(1).

Rubin, J. and Thompson, I. (1994) *How to Be a More Successful Language Learner*. Boston: Heinle and Heinle.

Ryan, R.M. and Deci, E.L. (2000) Self-determination theory and the facilitation of intrinsic motivation, social development, and well-being. *American Psychologist*, 55(1): 68–78.

Sarig, G. (1987) High-level reading in the first and in the foreign language: some comparative process data. In Devine, J., Carrell, P.L., and Eskey, D.E. (eds), *Research in Reading in English as a Second Language*. Washington, D.C.: TESOL: 107–120.

Sasaki, M. (2002) Building an empirically-based model of EFL learners' writing processes. In Ransdell, S. and Barbier, M. (eds), *New Directions for Research in L2 Writing*. Boston: Kluwer: 49–80.

Scarcella, R.C. and Oxford, R.L. (1992) *The Tapestry of Language Learning: The Individual in the Communicative Classroom*. Boston: Heinle/Thomson Learning.

Scardamalia, M. and Bereiter, C. (1986) Educational relevance of the study of expertise. *Interchange*, 17(2): 10–24.

Schiffrin, D., Tannen, D., and Hamilton, H. (2003) *Handbook of Discourse Analysis*. Oxford, UK: Blackwell.

Schmeck, R. (1988) *Learning Strategies and Learning Styles*. New York: Plenum.

Schmelter, L. (2004) *Selbstgesteuertes oder potenziell expansives Fremdsprachenlernen im Tandem*. [*Self-Directed or Potentially Expansive Foreign Language Learning in Tandem*]. Tübigen: Narr.

Schmelter, L. (2006) Prekäre Verhältnisse: Bildung, Erziehung oder Emanzipation? – Was will, was soll, was kann die Beratung von Fremdsprachenlernen leisten? [Precarious conditions: education, training, or emancipation? What will, what should, what can the advice be about foreign language learning?] ZIF 11(2). *http://zif.spz.tu-darmstadt.de/jg-11-2/beitrag/Schmelter1.htm*

Schmidt, R. (1990) The role of consciousness in second language learning. *Applied Linguistics*, 11: 129–155.

Schmidt, R. (1995) *Attention and Awareness in Foreign Language Learning.* Manoa, HI: University of Hawai'i, Second Language Teaching and Curriculum Center.

Schmitt, N. (1997) Vocabulary learning strategies. In Schmitt, N. and McCarthy, M. (eds), *Vocabulary: Description, Acquisition and Pedagogy.* Cambridge: Cambridge University Press: 199–228.

Schoenfeld, A.H. (1985) *Mathematical Problem Solving.* London: Academic.

Schramm, K. (2001) *L2-Leser in Aktion. Der fremdsprachliche Leseprozeß als mentales Handeln [L2-readers in action. The foreign language reading process as mental action].* Münster, Germany/New York: Waxmann.

Schramm, K. (2005) Aktives Zuhören beim Geschichtenerzählen [Active listening during story-telling]. *Grundschule Deutsch*: 20–22.

Schramm, K. (2008, Aug. 25) Personal communication.

Schumann, J.H. (2001a) Appraisal psychology, neurobiology, and language. *Annual Review of Applied Linguistics*, 31: 23–42.

Schumann, J.H. (2001b) Learning as foraging. In Dörnyei, Z. and Schmidt, R. (eds), *Motivation and Second Language Acquisition.* Manoa: University of Hawai'i Press: 21–28.

Schumann, J.H. (2004) *The Neurobiology of Learning: Perspectives from Second Language Acquisition.* London: Routledge.

Schunk, D.H. (2002) Self-regulation through goal-setting. ERIC Digest. *http://www.ericdigests.org/2002-4/goal.html*

Schunk, D.H. and Ertmer, P.A. (2000) Self-regulation and academic learning: self-efficacy enhancing interventions. In Boekaerts, M., Pintrich, P.R., and Zeidner, M. (eds), *Handbook of Self-Regulation.* San Diego: Academic Press: 631–650.

Schunk, D.H. and Zimmerman, R. (1998) *Self-Regulated Learning: From Teaching to Self-Reflective Practice.* New York: Guilford.

Selinker, L. (1972) Interlanguage. *International Review of Applied Linguistics*, 10(2): 209–231.

Semke, H.D. (1984) Effects of the red pen. *Foreign Language Annals*, 17: 195–202.

Seng, G.H., and Hashim, F. (2006) Use of L1 in L2 reading comprehension among tertiary ESL learners. *Reading in a Foreign Language*, 18(1): 29–54.

Shakespeare, W. (1604/2005) *Measure for Measure.* New York: Washington Square Press.

Shekhtman, B. (2003a) *How to Improve Your Foreign Language Immediately: Foreign Language Communication Tools.* Salinas, CA: MSI Press.

Sheorey, R. and Mokhtari, K. (2001) Differences in the metacognitive awareness of reading strategies among native and non-native readers. *System*, 29: 431–449.

Shepherd, R. (2006, Fall) Volitional strategies and social anxiety among college students. *College Quarterly*, 9(4). *http://www.senecac.on.ca/quarterly/2006-vol09-num04-fall/shepherd.html*

Simons, J., Vansteenkiste, M., Lens, W., and Lacante, M. (2004) Placing motivation and future time perspective theory in a temporal perspective. *Educational Psychology Review*, 16: 121–139.

Sinclair. B. (2000) *Learner Autonomy and its Development in the Teaching of English to Speakers of Other Languages (TESOL).* Unpublished Ph.D Thesis, University of Nottingham.

Sinclair, B. (n.d.) *Learner Training (Part II)*. Online newsletter of the Learner Autonomy Special Interest Group, International Association of Teachers of English as a Foreign Language. *http://www.learnerautonomy.org/learnertrainingarticle1.html*

Sinclair, B. and Ellis, G. (1992) Survey: learner training in EFL course books. *ELT Journal*, 46(2): 209–225.

Sobotka, S.S., Davidson, R.J., and Senulis, J.A. (1992) Anterior brain electrical asymmetries in response to reward and punishment. *Electroencephalography and Clinical Neurophysiology*, 83: 236–247.

Stake, R.E. (1995) *The Art of Case Study Research*. Thousand Oaks, CA: Sage.

Stanovich, K.E. (1980) Toward an interactive-compensatory model of individual differences in the development of reading fluency. *Reading Research Quarterly*, 16(1): 32–71.

Stern, H.H. (1983) *Fundamental Concepts of Language Teaching*, Oxford: Oxford University Press.

Stevick, E. (1989) *Success with Foreign Languages: Seven Who Achieved It and What Worked for Them*. Englewood Cliffs, NJ: Prentice Hall International.

Stott, N. (2001) Helping ESL students become better readers: schema theory applications and limitations. *Internet TESL-Journal*, 7(11). *http://iteslj.org/*

Strauss, A. and Corbin, J. (2007) *Basics of Qualitative Research: Techniques and Procedures for Developing Grounded Theory*. Third edition. London: Sage.

Strichart, S.S. and Mangrum, C.T. (2001) *Teaching Learning Strategies and Study Skills to Students with Learning Disabilities, Attention Deficit Disorders, and Special Needs*. Third edition. Boston: Allyn & Bacon.

Sullivan, R. (1989) *Immanuel Kant's Moral Theory*. Cambridge: Cambridge University Press.

Swales, J.M. (1990) *Genre Analysis*. Cambridge: Cambridge University Press.

Swan, M. (2008) Talking sense about learning strategies. *RELC Journal*, 39: 262–273.

Swartz, D. (1998) *Culture and Power: The Sociology of Pierre Bourdieu*. Chicago: University of Chicago Press.

Sweller, J. (2005) Implications of cognitive load theory for multimedia learning. In Mayer, R.E. (ed.), *The Cambridge Handbook of Multimedia Learning*. Cambridge: Cambridge University Press: 19–30.

Takeuchi, O. (1993) Language learning strategies and their relationship to achievement in English as a foreign language. *Language Laboratory*, 30: 17–34.

Takeuchi, O. (2005) *Language Learning Strategy Bibliography*. *http://www2.ipcku.kansai-u.ac.jp/~takeuchi/Bib1.html*

Tarone, E. (1977) Conscious communication strategies in interlanguage: a progress report. *On TESOL 1977*. Washington, DC: TESOL, Inc.

Tarone, E. (1980) Communication strategies, foreigner talk, and repair in interlanguage. *Language Learning*, 30(2): 417–431.

Tarone, E. (1981) Decoding a Primary Language: The Crucial Role of Strategic Competence. Paper presented at the Conference of Interpretive Strategies in Language Learning, University of Lancaster, UK.

Tarone, E. (1983) On the variability of interlanguage systems. *Applied Linguistics*, 4: 143–163.

Tashakkori, A. and Teddlie, C. (eds) (2003) *Handbook of Mixed Methods in Social and Behavioral Research*. Thousand Oaks, CA: Sage.

Taylor, C. (1994) *Multiculturalism: Examining the Politics of Recognition*. Princeton: Princeton University Press.

Thornbury, S. (2002) *How to Teach Vocabulary*. London: Longman.

Tsai, C., Kim, J-H., and Kim, H. (2000) When Is "Rote" Not Really Rote? Paper presented at the annual meeting of the American Association for Applied Linguistics.

Tucker, G.R., Lambert, W.E., and Rigault, A.A. (1977) *The French Speaker's Skill with Grammatical Gender: An Example of Rule-governed Behavior*. The Hague: Mouton.

Tudor, I. (2002, Mar.) Exploring context: Localness and the role of ethnography. *Humanistic Language Teaching Magazine. www.hltmag.co.uk/martmar021.rtf*

Upton, T.A. (1997) First and second language use in reading comprehension strategies of Japanese ESL students. *Teaching English as a Second or Foreign Language*, 3(1): 35–61.

Ushioda, E. (2008) Motivation and good language learners. In C. Griffiths (ed.), *Lessons from good language learners*. Cambridge, UK: Cambridge University Press: 19–34.

Valdes, G. (2001) *Learning and Not Learning English: Latino Students in American Schools*. New York: Teachers College Press.

Vance, S.J. (1999) *Language Learning Strategies: Is There a Best Way to Teach Them?* ERIC Document Reproduction Service ED 438 716; FL 026 146.

Vandergrift, L. (1997) The comprehension strategies of second language (French) listeners: a descriptive study. *Foreign Language Annals*, (30): 387–409.

Vandergrift, L., Goh, C., Mareschal, C., and Tafaghodatari, M.H. (2006) *The Metacognitive Awareness Listening Questionnaire (MALQ)*: Development and validation. *Language Learning*, 56: 431–462.

Van Lier, L. (1996) *Interaction in Language Curriculum: Awareness, Autonomy, and Authenticity*. London: Longman.

Van Lier, L. (1997) Observation from an ecological perspective. *TESOL Quarterly*, 31(4): 783–786.

Van Lier, L. (2004) *The Ecology and Semiotics of Language Learning: A Sociocultural Perspective*. New York: Springer.

Vialpando, J., Linse, C., and Yedlin, J. (2005) *Educating English Language Learners: Understanding and Using Assessment*. Washington, DC: National Council of La Raza. *http://www.nclr.org/files/32971_file_Eng_Lang_Learners_Assessment_Guide.pdf*

Vann, R. and Abraham, R. (1989, Apr.) Strategies of Unsuccessful Language Learners. Paper presented at the Annual Meeting of Teachers of English to Speakers of Other Languages, San Francisco, CA.

Vann, R. and Abraham, R. (1990) Strategies of unsuccessful language learners. *TESOL Quarterly*, 24(2): 177–198.

Vansteenkiste, M., Simons, J., Lens, W., Sheldon, K.M., and Deci, E.L. (2004) Motivating learning, performance, and persistence: the synergistic effects of intrinsic goal contexts and autonomy-supportive contexts. *Journal of Personality and Social Psychology*, 87(2): 246–260.

Verhoeven, L.T. (1987) *Ethnic Minority Children Acquiring Literacy*. Berlin: De Gruyter.

Vygotsky, L.S. (1978) *Mind in Society: The Development of Higher Psychological Processes*. Cambridge, MA: Harvard University Press.

Vygotsky, L.S. (1979) Consciousness as a problem of psychology of behavior. *Soviet Psychology*, 17: 29–30.

Vygotsky, L. (1981) The genesis of the higher mental functions. In Wertsch, J.V. (ed.), *The Concept of Activity in Soviet Psychology*. Armonk, NY: Sharpe.

Wade, S.E., Trathen, W., and Schraw, G. (1990) An analysis of spontaneous study strategies. *Reading Research Quarterly*, 25: 147–166.

Weaver, S. and Cohen, A. (1997) *Strategies-Based Instruction: A Teacher-Training Manual.* Minneapolis: Center for Advanced Research on Language Acquisition, University of Minnesota.

Weber, R. (2004) Editor's comments: the rhetoric of positivism versus interpretivism – a personal view. *MIS Quarterly*, 28(1): iii–xii.

Weedon, C. (1987) *Feminist Practice and Poststructuralist Theory.* Oxford: Blackwell.

Weinstein, C., Goetz, E.T., and Alexander, P.A. (eds) (1988) *Learning and Study Strategies: Issues in Assessment, Instruction, and Evaluation.* San Diego: Academic Press.

Weinstein, C.E. and Mayer, R.E. (1986) The teaching of learning strategies. In Wittrock, M.C. (ed.), *Handbook of Research on Teaching.* Third edition. New York, NY: Macmillan: 315–327.

Weinstein, C.E., Schulte, A.C., and Palmer, D.R. (1987) *Learning and Study Strategies Inventory (LASSI).* Clearwater, FL: H & H Publishing.

Weissberg, R. (2006) Scaffolded feedback: tutorial conversations with advanced L2 writers. In Hyland, K. and Hyland, F. (eds), *Feedback in Second Language Writing: Contexts and Issues.* New York: Cambridge University Press: 246–265.

Wen, Q. (1996) *On English Learning Strategies.* Shanghai: Shanghai Foreign Language Education Press.

Wen, Q. (2003) *The Road to Successful English Learning.* Shanghai: Shanghai Foreign Language Education Press.

Wenden, A.L. (1986) Helping language learners think about learning. *ELT Journal*, 7(2): 186–205.

Wenden, A.L. (1987) Incorporating learner training in the classroom. In Wenden, A. and Rubin, J. (eds), *Learner Strategies in Language Learning.* Englewood Cliffs, NJ: Prentice-Hall: 159–168.

Wenden, A.L. (1991) *Learner Strategies for Learner Autonomy: Planning and Implementing Learner Training for Language Learners.* Englewood Cliffs, NJ: Prentice Hall.

Wenden, A.L. (1998) Metacognitive knowledge and language learning. *Applied Linguistics*, 19(4): 515–537.

Wenden, A.L. and Rubin, J. (eds) (1987) *Learner Strategies in Language Learning.* Englewood Cliffs, NJ: Prentice Hall.

Wenger, E., McDermott, R., and Snyder, W.M. (2002) *Cultivating Communities of Practice.* Cambridge, MA: Harvard Business School Press.

Wharton, G. (2000) Language learning strategy use of bilingual foreign language learners in Singapore. *Language Learning*, 50(2): 203–243.

White, C.J. (1995) Autonomy and strategy use in distance foreign language learning. *System*, 23(2): 207–221.

White, C.J. (1997) Effects of mode of study on foreign language learning. *Distance Education*, 18(1): 178–196.

White, C., Schramm, K., and Chamot, A.U. (2007) Research methodology. In Cohen, A.D. and Macaro, E. (eds), *Language Learner Strategies: Thirty Years of Research and Practice.* Oxford, UK: Oxford University Press: 93–116.

Williams, J., Inscoe, R., and Tasker, T. (1997) Communication strategies in an interactional context: the mutual achievement of comprehension. In Kasper, G. and Kellerman, E. (eds), *Communication Strategies: Psycholinguistic and Sociolinguistic Perspectives.* Longman: London.

Winne, P.H. and Hadwin, A.F. (1998) Studying as self-regulated learning. In Hacker, D.J., Dunlosky, J., and Graesser, A.C. (eds), *Metacognition in Educational Theory and Practice*. Mahwah, NJ: Erlbaum: 277–304.

Winne, P.H. and Perry, N.E. (2000) Measuring self-regulated learning. In Boekaerts, M., Pintrich, P.R., and Zeidner, M. (eds), *Handbook of Self-Regulation*. San Diego: Academic Press: 531–556.

Winter, G. (2000) A comparative discussion of the notion of "validity" in qualitative and quantitative research. *The Qualitative Report*, 4(3–4). *www.nova.edu/ssss/QR/QR4-3/winter.html*

Wittrock, M.C. (ed.) (1986) *Handbook of Research on Teaching*. Third edition. New York, NY: Macmillan.

Wolters, C.A. (2003) Regulation of motivation: evaluating an underemphasized aspect of self-regulated learning. *Educational Psychologist*, 38: 189–205.

Wolters, C.A., Pintrich, P., and Karabenick, S.A. (2003, Mar.) Assessing academic self-regulated learning. Paper presented at the conference on Indicators of Positive Development: Definitions, Measures, and Prospective Validity, Washington, DC.

Woodruff Smith, D. (2007) *Husserl*. London: Routledge.

Yamamori, K., Isoda, T., Hiromori, T., and Oxford, R.L. (2003) Using cluster analysis to uncover L2 learner differences in strategy use, will to learn, and achievement over time. *International Review of Applied Linguistics and Language Teaching*, 41(4): 381–409.

Yang, N.-D. (1992) *Second Language Learners' Beliefs about Language Learning and Their Use of Learning Strategies: A Study of College Students of English in Taiwan*. Unpublished doctoral dissertation, University of Texas at Austin.

Yang, N.-D. (1996) Effective awareness-raising in language learning strategy instruction. In Oxford, R.L. (ed.), *Language learning strategies around the world: Cross-cultural perspectives*. Manoa: University of Hawai'i Press: 205–210.

Yang, N.-D. (1998) An interviewing study of college students' English learning strategy use. *Studies in English Language and Literature*, 4: 1–11.

Yang, N.-D. (1999) The relationship between EFL learners' beliefs and learning strategy use. *System*, 27: 515–535.

Yang, N.-D. (2003) Integrating portfolios into learning-strategy-based instruction for EFL college students. *International Review of Applied Linguistics in Language Teaching*, 41: 293–317.

Yang, N.D. (2005) Developing a Web-Based Learning Portfolio System. Paper presented at the 2005 Congress of the International Association for Applied Linguistics, Madison, WI.

Yang, N.D. (2006) Enhance English Learning with a Web-Based Learning Portfolio System. Paper presented at the Annual Conference of Applied Linguistics Association of Australia, Brisbane, Australia.

Yashima, T. and Zenuk-Nishide, L. (2008) The impact of learning contexts on proficiency, attitudes, and L2 communication: creating an imagined international community. *System*, 36(4): 566–585.

Yin, C. (2008) *Language Learning Strategies in Relation to Attitudes, Motivations, and Learner Beliefs: Investigating Learner Variables in the Context of English as a Foreign Language in China*. Unpublished doctoral dissertation, University of Maryland, College Park, MD.

Yin, R.K. (2003) *Case Study Research: Design and Methods*. Third edition. Thousand Oaks, CA: Sage.

Young, D.J. (1993) Processing strategies of foreign language readers: Authentic and edited input. *Foreign Language Annals*, 26(4): 451–468.

Zamel, V. (1985) Responding to student writing. *TESOL Quarterly*, 19: 79–102.

Zeichner, K. and Noffke, S. (2001) Practitioner research. In Richardson, V. (ed.), *Handbook of Research on Teaching*. Fourth edition. New York: Macmillan: 298–330.

Zimmerman, B.J. (1989) A social cognitive view of self-regulated academic learning. *Journal of Educational Psychology*, 81(3): 329–339.

Zimmerman, B.J. (1990) Self-regulated learning and academic achievement: an overview. *Educational Psychologist*, 25(1): 3–17.

Zimmerman, B.J. (2000) Attaining self-regulation: a social cognitive perspective. In Boekaerts, M., Pintrich, P.R., and Zeidner, M. (eds), *Handbook of Self-Regulation*. San Diego: Academic Press: 13–39.

Zimmerman, B.J. (2008) Investigating self-regulation and motivation: historical background, methodological developments, and future prospects. *American Educational Research Journal*, 45(1): 166–183.

Zimmerman, B.J., Bonner, S., and Kovach, R. (1996) *Developing Self-Regulated Learners: Beyond Achievement to Self-Efficacy*. Washington, DC: American Psychological Association.

Zimmerman, B.J. and Martinez-Pons, M. (1986) Development of a structured interview for assessing student use of self-regulated learning strategies. *American Educational Research Journal*, 23(4): 614–628.

Zimmerman, B.J. and Martinez-Pons, M. (1988) Construct validation of a strategy model of self-regulated learning. *Journal of Educational Psychology*, 80: 284–290.

Zimmerman, B.J. and Martinez-Pons, M. (1990) Student differences in self-regulated learning: relating grade, sex, and giftedness to self-efficacy and strategy use. *Journal of Educational Psychology*, 82: 51–59.

Zimmerman, B.J. and Schunk, D. (eds) (2001) *Self-Regulated Learning and Academic Achievement*. Second edition. Mahwah, NJ: Erlbaum.

Index